Incarcerating Criminals

READINGS IN CRIME AND PUNISHMENT
Michael Tonry, *General Editor*

What Works in Policing
David H. Bayley

Criminology at the Crossroads:
Feminist Readings in Crime and Justice
Kathleen Daly and Lisa Maher

Incarcerating Criminals:
Prisons and Jails in Social and Organizational Context
Timothy J. Flanagan, James W. Marquart, and Kenneth G. Adams

Community Corrections:
Probation, Parole, and Intermediate Sanctions
Joan Petersilia

Incarcerating Criminals

Prisons and Jails in Social and
Organizational Context

Edited by
Timothy J. Flanagan
James W. Marquart
Kenneth G. Adams

New York   Oxford
OXFORD UNIVERSITY PRESS
1998

Oxford University Press

Oxford   New York
Athens   Auckland   Bangkok   Bogota   Bombay   Buenos Aires
Calcutta   Cape Town   Dar es Salaam   Delhi   Florence   Hong Kong
Istanbul   Karachi   Kuala Lumpur   Madras   Madrid   Melbourne
Mexico City   Nairobi   Paris   Singapore   Taipei   Tokyo   Toronto   Warsaw

and associated companies in
Berlin   Ibadan

Copyright © 1998 by Oxford University Press, Inc.

Published by Oxford University Press, Inc.
198 Madison Avenue, New York, NY 10016

Library of Congress Cataloging-in-Publication Data
Incarcerating criminals : prisons and jails in social and
organizational context / edited by Timothy J. Flanagan, James W.
Marquart, Kenneth G. Adams.
p.   cm — (Readings in criminology and criminal justice)
ISBN 0-19-510540-0. — ISBN 0-19-510541-9 (alk. paper)
1. Correctional institutions—United States.   2. Imprisonment—
United States.   3. Prison administration—United States.
I. Flanagan, Timothy J.   II. Marquart, James W. (James Walter),
1954– .   III. Adams, Kenneth, 1953– .   IV. Series.
HV9471.I53   1998
365'.973—dc21   97-18088
                                                                CIP

2 4 6 8 9 7 5 3 1

Printed in the United States of America
on acid-free paper

Contents

Preface

In late twentieth-century America, prisons and jails have become the imposing physical embodiment of the nation's crime control policy. The annual increase in the prison population and the incarceration rate, announced with great fanfare by the media, is intended to convey that Americans are dedicated to a "tough-on-crime" approach. Should anyone doubt the diligence of our efforts toward this end, each legislative season brings a new crop of laws designed to send more lawbreakers to prison and jail and keep them confined for ever longer periods of time. Should anyone doubt the efficacy of this approach, numerous policy makers and pundits are available to assert that declining crime rates in the 1990s are evidence that increasing punishment reduces crime. To guard against growth in crime in the future, more punishment, more prisons, more jails are required. The singular policy dilemma facing American criminal justice as we approach the twenty-first century is that we would like to incarcerate more offenders at earlier ages and for longer periods of time, but incarceration is very expensive. Because criminal justice competes with other legitimate and necessary public services for public funds, the only meaningful damper on the growth of incarceration is the price tag. The "solution" to the dilemma is to devise ways to incarcerate more cheaply, so that the marginal costs of additional imprisonment can be reduced.

The premise of *Incarcerating Criminals* is that prisons and jails are best understood within the social, economic, political, ideological, and organizational contexts or environments in which they exist. It is not accidental that America in the last years of the twentieth century imprisons a larger percentage of its citizens than at any time in its history, and more than any other developed nation. The country's millions of inmates did not fall out of the sky, and the prison populations that the next generation will support through its tax dollars are being created in legislative halls today. We choose to incarcerate as our fundamental response to crime, because we are convinced that this is a practical, just, cost-effective response to crime victimization. We believe that most criminals make willful, volitional decisions to commit crime and that the best way to influence the prospective criminal's decision process is to maintain the possibility of incarceration as a consequence. Once we have reached that conclusion, considerations about what should happen to the offender in confinement become secondary, because the hope of deterrence has failed and the thirst for retribution must be satisfied.

Very few Americans today voice the inspiring, enriching motivations behind incarceration that our predecessors held. We approach prisons today with expectations that are minimal—we demand that these institutions keep them away from us, for as long as possible and as inexpensively as possible. Time in prison has become the metric through which effective response to crime is measured, and we demand more time for more offenders. We are impatient with the numerous community-based alternatives to prison that were pursued in previous decades, because anything that is an alternative to or in lieu of the "real" penalty of incarceration represents a "slap on the risk" and an evasion of legitimate punishment.

The readings that comprise this book were selected to illustrate the dimensions of the social and organizational contexts of American prisons and jails. We hope that these readings will assist students in understanding the reasons underlying the development of prisons and jails, the premises underlying contemporary correctional operations, and the rationales behind contemporary crime control proposals. Prisons and jails exist within the context of society's sanctioning policy as created by political authority and administered by the criminal justice system. Understanding why prisons are built when they are, where they are, and administered as they are requires that students appreciate the inextricable linkages between these institutions, the rest of the criminal justice system, and the social and political atmosphere that supports them.

This book is divided into six chapters. Chapter One discusses its historical context. The selections trace the development of punishment from physical torture to loss of liberty and describe the philosophical and societal developments that promoted these changes. Chapter Two explores the legal environment in which all correctional institutions exist. These selections examine the struggle for effective oversight of prison and jail operations, and debate whether judicial intervention in prison administration is the best way to assure safe, orderly, and constitutionally acceptable institutions for punishment.

Chapter Three structures an analysis of prisons and jails as institutions that are primarily "people-processing" entities. The selections examine how changes in the composition of the prison population—including changes within the keepers and the kept—alter the social structure and interactions within the organization. For example, the development of prison gangs has fundamentally altered the relationship between the keepers and the kept, and reduced the dependence of inmates on staff for support, protection, and goods and services. This shifting of the balance of power and influence within the closed world of the prison has important consequences for inmates and staff. The introduction of female correctional officers and leaders into the previously all-male bastion has also wrought changes in social interaction within prisons and jails. Viewing these institutions as people-processing organizations encourages us to look at governance structures, sanctioning systems, and patterns of influence and communication within prisons.

Chapter Four focuses on the process of corrections, the portfolio of programs, services, and management strategies designed to run prisons that are safe, orderly, and effective. The selections in this chapter deal with the challenge of providing disease prevention and health care services, appropriate separation of inmates according to security and treatment needs, employment opportunities, educational services of numerous kinds, and fair and effective social control within the prison environment.

Chapter Five looks at jails, the high-volume, transient facilities that process many millions of defendants and prisoners each year. Jails have been described as the "cloacal region " of corrections, and critics contend that the abominable conditions in local jails are designed to encourage a high rate of guilty pleas among pretrial detainees. Not surprisingly, as an institution the jail presents Herculean challenges for a democratic society that prides itself on the presumption of innocence.

Chapter Six samples contemporary issues in sanctioning policy and correctional administration. These selections examine the recent meteoric increase in prison populations in the United States, the widening disproportion of imprisonment rates by race, and the growth of privately financed, built, and operated prisons in several nations. The other selections in Chapter Six offer perspectives on judging the performance of prisons, the appropriate role of incarceration in a comprehensive national crime control strategy, and likely developments in prisons and jails in the next century.

If *Incarcerating Criminals* is successful, students, professors, and interested citizens will use it as a means of broadening their perspective on prisons and jails and as a medium to better appreciate the social, political, ideological, and organizational contexts within which these institutions function. We hope that students find the book to be relevant and readable, but most of all that they find it thought provoking and challenging.

We have been assisted by several individuals in the preparation of this book, and we would be inexcusably remiss if we didn't express our thanks. First, we appreciate the opportunity that the series editors Michael Tonry and Jeffrey Fagan provided for us to collaborate on this project, and to the staff of Oxford University Press for creating this Readers series. Within the Criminal Justice Center at Sam Houston State University, Julia May, Kay Billingsley, and Karen Jeffries prepared materials for the manuscript with great care, and we deeply appreciate their time and talent. Finally, we greatly appreciate the cooperation of the authors and publishers who permitted us to excerpt and reprint their work in this volume. We trust that they will judge their work to be in good company, and we hope that they are pleased with the compendium.

Huntsville, Texas   T. J. F.
October 1997   J. W. M.
                                                         K. G. A.

Incarcerating Criminals

CHAPTER 1

The Role of Punishment and the Development of Incarceration

What to do about crime and criminals has plagued humankind since the dawn of civilization. At one time or another penal codes have specified that criminals be executed, humiliated by being publicly whipped, branded, or shamed by being put on display in the stocks in the town square. Even in the Garden of Eden all was not utopia as Cain killed Abel and was banished from paradise. Until the late eighteenth century, most of the accused, especially those that committed serious crimes, were executed or banished from society. Elimination was thought to serve as the most powerful deterrent. Prior to the execution of sentence, though, criminals were often confined in prisons.

The idea of prison as a punishment was not discovered or made a part of social policy until after the American Revolution. The late 1700s was a time of social and political unrest. It was also a time of new thinking about what to do about crime and criminals. The utility of old methods of torture and the savagery of public executions were questioned. Hangings, beheadings, burnings at the stake, and banishment to distant penal colonies where many died enroute or from hard labor failed to deter people from committing crime. Something new was sought that stressed treatment and self-reflection rather than elimination.

The philosophy of treatment evolved in Pennsylvania with the Quakers' concern for the horrible jail conditions in Philadelphia. Males were confined with females, children with adults, and the violent with the nonviolent. Wardens often allowed their prisoners to imbibe in alcohol and gambling in overcrowded living areas. After the American Revolution a group of Philadelphians formed the Pennsylvania Prison Society. The group stressed that individual rehabilitation, not brutality, was the objective of punishment and that confinement in isolation was the vehicle for treatment. In 1790 the Walnut Street Jail opened as the first prison in the world to rehabilitate crimi-

1

nals. However, in a few short years it suffered from overcrowded conditions and idleness.

The readings that follow have been arranged to give the reader an appreciation for the emergence of the penitentiary as a place for the reformation of criminal offenders. The idea of the penitentiary was novel and must be regarded as one of the most important social inventions and experiments in history. Why did the prison emerge in the 1790s? Who helped propel the idea of confinement and isolation as the new tools of punishment? What were the goals, both intended and unintended, of the new institutions? How were the prisoners to live in these institutions? In this section, the student will obtain answers to these questions and come to better understand the competing theories of the origins of prisons in our society. The reader will also see that there were vast differences in prisons for men and women.

The Disappearance of Public Executions

PIETER SPIERENBURG

After the mid-eighteenth century confidence in public punishment began to crumble. In the Netherlands the earliest signs of a fundamental change of attitudes can be traced back to at least the 1770s, although the completion of the transformation of repression was a long way off. The actual abolition of public executions took another hundred years. A similar chronology characterized most European countries. The transformation of repression was a far from sudden transition, which began in the middle of the eighteenth century and ended towards the close of the nineteenth century. It compromised changes which took place both on the ideological and on the institutional level. At least three phases can be distinguished: first, there is the quest for legal and penal reform which began during the Enlightenment. It is relatively well known and has been analyzed in several studies of the period. Second, there is imprisonment: not the "birth of the prison," as is sometimes stated, but the rise of confinement to a more prominent position within the penal system and the emergence of the penitentiary. Several recent works document this phase. Finally, and only after the rise of the penitentiary, there is the abolition of public punishment. This phase and the political struggle involved have only been made a subject of systematic research in the case of England. None of these three phases forms the main subject of this chapter. What is of concern here is the change of mentality implicit in them.

Source: Excerpted from Spierenburg, Pieter. The Disappearance of Public Executions. Adapted from *The Spectacle of Suffering* (Chapter 6, pp. 183–89). London: Cambridge University Press, 1984.

The aim is to present the following argument: first, the transformation of repression, before and after 1800, was not a matter of political and legal changes alone, but primarily a consequence of a fundamental change in sensibilities, and, second, this change in sensibilities preceded the actual abolition of public executions. This abolition constituted the "political conclusion," only drawn in the end.

The term "sensibility" should not be misunderstood. It refers to verifiable expressions of anxiety or repugnance and the question of whether these reflect a genuine concern for the well-being of delinquents or for that matter of anyone at all is left aside. Traditional historiography attributed the Enlightenment's opposition to *ancien régime* justice or the early nineteenth-century advocacy of imprisonment simply to humanitarianism. This is actually no explanation at all. Words like "humanitarian" are recurrent in the rhetoric of reformers in several countries, but the historian cannot use humanitarianism as a neutral, descriptive category, as he does "industrialization" or "nation-state." Paradoxically, the criticism of this traditional approach by Foucault and others has confirmed humanitarianism in its status of historical category. Instead of striving for a more adequate conceptualization of changes in mentality, Foucault essentially argues that the reformers were not humanitarian. He stresses that their motives were basically utilitarian and that their concern was with the prevention of crime. Control was the guiding principle, instead of a respect for the humanity of delinquents. This contrast, however, is a false contrast. An increased sensitivity toward executions is not at all incompatible with the wish to establish more control over lawbreakers. In fact, the desire to control was always there; also in the sixteenth century. But the ways sought to achieve this control change and these changes reflect an underlying shift in mentalities. As I will demonstrate in this chapter, the gradual transformation of attitudes leading to the privatization of repression set in earlier and took longer than the penal forms of the late eighteenth and early nineteenth centuries. Therefore I think that the former was more fundamental.

Without elaborating on it, Foucault himself indicated the real nature of the shift in sensibilities. The suffering, he says, which the mitigation of punishment was supposed to prevent, was primarily that of the judges and the spectators. The convicts might still be seen as traitors or monsters. Both remarks are crucial. The privatization of repression meant first and foremost the removal from public view of a spectacle that was becoming intolerable. The convict's fate within prison walls was of less concern. Second, the fact that the criminals were still seen as wicked underlines the change in sensibilities which is involved. It means that the spectacle of punishment, even though it was inflicted upon the guilty, was still becoming unbearable. By the end of the eighteenth century some of the audience could feel the pain of delinquents on the scaffold. The implication, paradoxically, is that interhuman identification had increased. The aspect of identification in connection with the execution of rioters was examined. The lower-class audience identified with these specific convicts and hence could feel their pain. This is a static analysis but it can be transformed into a dynamic one. Increased inter-human identification is an element of the changes in mentality. The death and suffering of fellow human beings were increasingly experienced as painful, just because other people were increasingly perceived as fellow human beings.

This process of identification proceeds along two lines. More categories of persons are considered as "just like me" and more ways of making people suffer are viewed as distasteful. Even in the Middle Ages spectators sometimes experienced sadness at the sight of an execution. When the audience in Paris wept in the early fifteenth century, it was because the person on the scaffold was a nobleman and an Armagnac leader. Not many other people would have been the object of pity. When an intended execution in Seville around 1600 "provoked the compassion of all" it was because the condemned was seventeen years old and believed to be innocent. Around the same time a few Amsterdam magistrates stated that the house of correction should serve to spare juvenile delinquents who were not real rogues a scaffold punishment. They identified with them enough to want to avoid a physical punishment. But it was only after the mid-eighteenth century that the pain of delinquents who had committed serious crimes and whose guilt was not in doubt, produced feelings of anxiety in some of the spectators. This implies that a new threshold was reached in the amount of mutual identification human beings were capable of.

The second element has also been noted before. The disappearance of most forms of mutilation in the early seventeenth century has been discussed. Commentators from the later eighteenth century already took their absence for granted and often considered it as a sign of the greater civilization of their own times. Writers who commented on the esoteric, physical punishment still in use on ships felt obliged to excuse themselves for confronting the reader with a tale of "cruelty and inhumanity." Again it is only around 1800 that certain groups among the elites considered all forms of public, physical punishment as "uncivilized."

Thus, the process certainly covered many centuries. Around 1800, however, it accelerated. Before that date human identification was only extended to the few or, to put it differently, a large amount of suffering was considered acceptable. Yet another way of putting it is to say that the system of public repression met with no significant opposition. Rejection increased from the 1770s onwards. If delinquents were made to suffer, it should at least be done privately. Towards 1870 continued opposition indeed resulted in the privatization of repression.

In the Dutch Republic a few "precocious" spurts towards sensitivity antedated the main transformation of repression: a shift from stone to wooden scaffolds and an early wave of opposition to torture. The first has not yet been clearly verified and can only be reconstructed tentatively. In chapter four it was noted that some members of the elites felt a little uneasiness about public executions in the late seventeenth century. It looks as though this feeling extended to the sight of the scaffold. They agreed that public execution was necessary, but they disliked to be reminded of it every day. Hence the outward signs at the place of execution should not be there permanently. In the sixteenth century most Dutch towns had a permanent scaffold with a gallows on it. It was often made of stone. A characteristic shape of the execution place was that of a so-called *groen zoodje*: a square surrounded by a low fence and grass verges. In the middle the floor was elevated or a small scaffold built. These execution places seem to have disappeared in the course of the seventeenth century.

We saw that Amsterdam had a removable scaffold. According to Wagenaar, the wooden poles and planks were ready-made, so that the scaffold could be erected and dismantled "in a very short time." The city had permanent places of execution in the sixteenth century. The shift must have occurred in the early seventeenth century. It occurred in other towns as well. The city of Leiden had been executing its delinquents on a *groen zoodje* for centuries. This was pulled down in 1671–2 and from then on a wooden scaffold was erected in front of the Papestraat before each execution. In Maastricht the stone scaffold on the Vrijthof, which had stood there from about 1300, was removed in the middle of the seventeenth century. In Haarlem, however, the reverse happened. As part of a project to rebuild the town hall in the 1630s the old wooden—but permanent—scaffold was replaced by one made of stone. This stone scaffold on the east wall remained there until 1855. Although this is clearly a counter-example, it should be noted that the new scaffold had the appearance of a classical balcony and that the equipment of justice was normally kept inside the building.

The case of Haarlem calls for caution. Nevertheless, the shift from permanent to removable scaffolds must have been common in the seventeenth century. The Court of Holland made such a decision rather late, but in this case it can be clearly observed that the shift was an expression of changing sensibilities. Constantin Huygens had already lobbied for the destruction of the stone scaffold in the 1670s. It stood along the Vijverberg close to the meeting place of the Estates and in that part of The Hague where most patricians and foreign ambassadors lived. It was precisely in that area which fell under the immediate jurisdiction of the Court of Holland; the rest of the agglomeration was judged by the court of The Hague which had recently replaced its stone scaffold with one of painted wood. Juygens wished that the Court of Holland would follow this example. Incidentally, since 1672 the scaffold conjured up the memory of the grand pensionary John de Witt and his brother who had fallen victim to population justice on that very spot. There is no indication, however, that Huygens was motivated by a desire to eradicate the memory of the event.

In 1674 he wrote to William III about the matter: his pleas to several magistrates had been to no avail, although they had at least decided not to do repairs. Huygens considered the Vijverberg as the most beautiful place in the world; the scaffold, on the other hand, was "the most villainous of all possible constructions." The Vijverberg was 'a too noble and glorious place to be perpetually embarrassed by the sight of wheels and gibbets, to the great chagrin of so many residents of quality'. Huygens proposed to replace the stone scaffold by a statue of *Justitia* with sword and balance. Beneath it a fountain should be constructed, against which a wooden scaffold could be erected when necessary. Apparently the *stadholder* could not help him either. Seven years later he wrote a poem in which he regretted the failure of his efforts: "A foreign gentlemen saw this stinking thing in The Hague" ... "and wondered why Holland's rulers were so gross as to let it stand there." Huygens did not live to see its demolition. A wooden scaffold was finally introduced in 1720.

Huygens' poem suggested that revulsion against the sight of the scaffold—which in any case is clearly different from the popular fear of touching it—was international. This would be in line with the remark about the unpleasantness of executions by the English gentlemen visiting Holland in 1695. An event in Danzig in 1708 also tunes in to it. Because the Queen of Poland was in the city and lived right opposite the regular place of execution, a decapitation was performed elsewhere. In this case the reason might simply be that the queen did not wish to see a multitude of people gathered in front of her door. But on the whole the conclusion seems warranted that a slight increase in sensitivity toward executions was already visible among the elites in the later seventeenth century. They felt some uneasiness about public justice and did not want to be confronted with its physical apparatus all the time. But they did not oppose the prevailing system of repression. It was a mere prefiguration of the transformation which set in after the middle of the eighteenth century.

The second "precocious" spurt was a prefiguration as well, but probably confined to the Netherlands. A few seventeenth-century writers pleaded for the abolition of torture. The movement became widespread and international in the second half of the eighteenth century. The actual abolition of torture was the first visible expression of the transformation of repression. Although we are not dealing with a public feature, torture is still typical of *ancien régime* repression because infliction of pain is the essence of it. Its abolition in some states was the only reform of criminal law which was carried through under *ancien régime*.

Torture was practiced privately because secrecy during the trial itself was a guiding principle of criminal procedure. The sentences recited during an execution often began with the standard formula that the prisoner had confessed "outside of pain and chains." Apart from this, they occasionally contained references to concrete acts of torture. Thus the sentence of a burglar in 1661 adds to the account of his crime: "and the court did not take the other accusations into consideration, which he, prisoner, impertinently denied even during torture at the post." Similar passages, with only one erasure, slipped into other sentences, also in the early eighteenth century.

Historians often assumed that the abolition of torture during the Enlightenment was a logical consequence of the rationalism of the age. This is simply not true. Throughout history authorities have been aware of the uncertainties inherent to the procedure and of the possibility of convicting an innocent person. The fabric of rules which has been woven around the practice of torture, was meant precisely to combat uncertainties. Still, various prominent persons, including Augustine, Pope Nicholas I and several humanists, condemned torture. But, despite the uncertainties, the authorities thought it a necessary custom. In a recent study Langbein rejected the "rationalist explanation": "The eighteenth-century abolitionist literature is the produce of its age in tone, but not in substance. The works of Thomasius, Beccaria, Voltaire, and the others do little more than restate the arguments that have been advanced against torture for centuries." According to Langbein, abolition was an overdue reaction to the fact that the old law of proof lost its force from the seventeenth century onwards. I find his argument unconvincing. I think that the first of the two quoted sentences is more important than Langbein himself seems to realize. The rationalist critique, which had never been successful before, could acquire a new effectiveness because of a change in sensibilities.

This argument forms the reason why I called the opinion of a minority in the Dutch Republic in the first half of the seventeenth century a prefiguration of the abolition movement. Its representatives, besides repeating the rationalist critique, also put forward emotional arguments. Johannes Grevius, an exiled Remonstrant preacher, wrote the first book devoted entirely to the abolition of torture. It was written in Latin and published in Hamburg in 1624. Hence its influence was restricted. A less-radical view was espoused by Johan van Heemskerk, a member of the High Council. He advocated a moderate use of the rack and expressed his compassion for the delinquents subjected to it. The most influential work was published by Daniel Jonctijs in 1650. He was *schepen* in Rotterdam. His is actually a Dutch adaptation of Grevius' book. Jonctijs condemns the "fieriness" of the judges who find torture necessary. They have become immune to the "sighs and moanings of the miserable."

This emotional appeal was not successful at the time, because the majority of the elites did not harbor such feelings of repugnance toward the physical treatment of suspected delinquents. In the seventeenth century the common feeling was probably only a little uneasiness with regard to torture, just as in the case of executions. This was also expressed in France. During the preparation of the criminal ordinance of 1670 two counselors, Lamoignon and Pussort, discussed the articles on torture. The first proposed to prescribe a uniform method, because the practice was "too rude" in certain places. The other, however, argued that this was simply impossible: it would necessitate a description of torture, "which would be indecent in an Ordonnance." The solemnity of an official legal document could not stand the blunt description of physical suffering.

A major change in sensibilities occurred in the second half of the eighteenth century. It is most clearly expressed in the fact that the defenders of torture felt obliged to display feelings of repugnance as well. Characteristically a writer would open with the announcement that he too found it an unpleasant method. Thus the Amsterdam lawyer Calkoen acknowledged a "humanitarianism" towards delinquents but wished to bestow his compassion in the first place on "the body of respectable citizens." He advocated "humanitarianism without cowardice and severity without cruelty." The opening remarks of the Viennese professor Josef von Sonnenfels' "On the abolition of torture" are the exact opposite of Calkoen's argument and therefore reflect the general sensitivity of the age just as well. 'Many people', he said, 'reproach the opponents of torture because they only appeal to their readers' feelings, while they fall short of convincing them rationally. Therefore I renounce all the advantages which such an appeal to emotion and pity for the suffering could provide me with. I am treating the topic with the cool indifference of the lawyer, who turns his face away from the twitchings of the tortured; who closes his ears to their cries and sees nothing but a scholarly debate before him. Thus Sonnenfels took feelings of repugnance for granted. He wishes to attain a new detachment from these feelings, if not his opening represents a covert emotional appeal after all.

Torture was abolished in Prussia in 1754; in Saxony in 1770; in Austria and Bohemia in 1776; in France in 1780–8, in the Southern Netherlands in 1787–94; in the Dutch Republic in 1795–8. The rise of sensitivity with regard to torture had prepared the way for other elements of the transformation of repression. The next step was the abolition of exposure of corpses.

The display of the dead bodies of capitally punished delinquents was discontinued in Western Europe around 1800. It antedated the abolition of public executions by at least half a century. There can be no doubt that increased sensitivity moved the authorities to act. Abandonment of the custom was usually motivated by calling it a relic of the 'barbarity of former times'.

Before the second half of the eighteenth century people were occasionally bothered by the exposure of corpses. The reason was usually that the standing gallows was situated too close to inhabited areas. The growth of a city meant that the site of exposure, originally well outside the walls, came to be nearer and nearer the outskirts. When a storm had blown down Utrecht's standing gallows in 1674, the owners of the nearby sawmill and brick-fields took the opportunity to petition for a change of location. They noted that gallows fields were normally situated 'outside the common frequency of people'. Their arguments are a little ambiguous. The request calls the smell of the dead horrible, but also the sight. Another consideration may have been more important: the value of buildings and premises was lower when situated close to the gallows. Thus, to live and work permanently in the proximity of corpses was considered objectionable in the seventeenth century. Nevertheless, the magistrates in Utrecht turned down the request.

In the second half of the eighteeth century exposure of corpses became objectionable *tout court*. For example, when the bodies of condemned mutineers were to be exposed in 1764, a protest was leveled. A court martial had sentenced, among others, ten persons to hanging and three to breaking on the wheel. They had led a mutiny the year before on a ship owned by the East India Company. Their bodies were to be exposed on a gallows erected on the first row of dunes along the sea close to the village of Huisduinen. The scene was to be a warning to all sailors on the company's ships, which left the coast of Holland from that very spot. The gallows could be observed from a distance of three hours at sea. The court martial wished to secure permanence for the gallows for at least fifty years. The regional administrative council protested against this, though in vain. They argued, among other things, that the villagers and fishermen of Huisduinen disliked the idea. The council referred to the gallows as an 'offensive and horrible spectacle'; the more so since it was not meant for the inhabitants at all.

Another indication comes from events in the town of Amersfoort in 1770. There the council decided indeed to move the standing gallows, which the magistrates of Utrecht had refused to do a century earlier. The old gallows was pulled down because of its bad state of repair and a provisional wooden one was erected some twenty meters to the north. The original site was situated quite close to the Utrecht road. The magistrates stated that the sight of the corpses 'cannot be but horrible for traveling persons'. In this case there is no talk of people living close by. Traveling persons were precisely the ones for whom exposure of corpses had been instituted in an earlier age.

In many countries the abolition of exposure of delinquents' bodies coincided with the end of the *ancient régime*. In the Netherlands it was the only major alteration in the system of public punishment brought about by the Batavian Revolution. In Bavaria it took place at the beginning of the nineteenth century. The structures on the gallows mountains there were often made of excellent oak. Following an order by the royal administration, all gallows and *Rabensteine* were sold between 1805 and 1814 to the highest bidders.

Why should exposure of capitally punished delinquents have disappeared earlier than public executions? There are two reasons for it. The first is that the change was not primarily related to a shift in attitudes towards the infliction of pain and suffering. It was rather related to changing attitudes toward death. Obviously, developments in both realms are interconnected in their turn. In the long run familiarity with death and with the infliction of pain decreased. In both cases actions directly related to the human body were hidden behind the scenes of social life; in both cases the encompassing process of privatization is the force behind it. But the realm of attitudes toward death is the one to which exposure of corpses is most directly related.

The Historical Origins of the Sanction of Imprisonment for Serious Crime

JOHN H. LANGBEIN

The abolition movement that we associate with Beccaria and Voltaire was a second-stage affair. Indeed, it had to be. For abolition presupposes the existence of a workable alternative for the punishment of serious crime. By the time of the American Revolution, the sanction of imprisonment for serious crime was in use throughout Europe, and England had developed a near equivalent. Although it is commonly said that "[t]he history of imprisonment has often been told," Americans have not listened with much care. The claim is incessantly made that "[p]risons ... are a pervasive American export, like tobacco in their international acceptance and perhaps also in their adverse consequences." There were indeed some novelties to the nineteenth-century American prisons, but the essentials were long established in Europe. This article draws upon the rich but scattered Continental scholarship in order to describe the origins of imprisonment in Europe and to relate it to the parallel developments that had taken place in the common law by the eve of American independence.

THE BLOOD SANCTIONS

At about the time that the medieval sanctions were entering their long decline, they were codified in the German Empire in the Constitutio Criminalis Carolina of 1532. The statute provides a typical assortment of modes of capital punishment. An ordinary murderer or burglar merits hanging in chains or beheading with the sword. A woman who murders her infant is buried alive and impaled, a traitor is drawn and quartered. Other grave offenders may be burned to death, or drowned, or set out to die in agony upon the wheel with their limbs smashed. If the court thinks that the circumstances of the crime merit severer punishment, it may order that the criminal be dragged to the place of execution, and that his flesh be torn with red-hot tongs before he is killed. For less grave offenses the Carolina prescribes afflictive punishments—flogging, pillorying, cutting off the ears, chopping off the fingers, cutting out the tongue—usually accompanied by a sentence of banishment. The Carolina's catalog of sanctions for serious crime exemplifies not only German but general European practice of the age.

Source: Excerpted from Langbein, John H. The Historical Origins of the Sanction of Imprisonment for Serious Crime. *Journal of Legal Studies* 5:35–60, 1976.

The substitution of various forms of imprisonment for the sanctions of the medieval law began in the sixteenth and seventeenth centuries both on the Continent and in England. By the middle of the eighteenth century, when the first demands for total abolition of capital punishment were made, the death penalty had everywhere ceased to be the exclusive punishment for serious crime. The abolition movement is much celebrated. The article examines the development that made it possible.

MEDIEVAL IMPRISONMENT

Imprisonment had an important place in European criminal procedure in the Middle Ages, but not as a sanction. The rule of the ius commune, constantly repeated by the jurists and codified in statutes like the Carolina, was that prisons were meant to detain and not to punish. In cases of serious crime the only function that the jurists conceded to imprisonment was pretrial detention, keeping custody of the accused while the court decided whether to acquit him or to convict and punish him with a blood sanction. This "custodial" "preventive" imprisonment is distinguished from the other common medieval usage that the jurists approved: "coercive" imprisonment designed to compel someone to take some other procedural step, characteristically the payment of a crown debt or a civil judgment debt.

Penal imprisonment did enter the secular legal systems in the late Middle Ages, but not in place of the blood sanctions for serious crimes. Rather, it was imposed as a sanction for petty crime: often as a "surrogate penalty" for a petty offender who was unable to pay a fine, sometimes as a "collateral penalty" in addition to a fine. In Italy, France, Germany, and England the sources evidence growing use of short-term imprisonment as a sanction for economic and moral regulation from the fourteenth century onward. When the Belgian jurist Damhouder summarized the practice of the mid-sixteenth century, it was still true that of the "several sorts of prisons" only those of the church were being used to punish serious crime. The secular prisons existed to guard serious offenders until their trials. Only for petty crime were the secular courts sentencing culprits to brief prison terms, occasionally on a diet of bread and water.

THE GALLEY SENTENCE

The galley sentence arose not from the needs of criminal justice, rather its origin is most closely connected with the development of the medieval fleets of the naval powers of southern Europe. Although sailing ships were coming into use by the end of the Middle Ages, galleys rowed by oarsmen continued to be important military vessels in the Mediterranean into the eighteenth century. Because galleys were highly maneuverable, they were more suitable for Mediterranean coastal waters than were the ocean-ships of the Atlantic. Unlike wind-powered craft, they could not be becalmed. Not until the eighteenth century did the superior size, speed and firepower of the sailing ships fully overcome the military advantages of the galleys and render them obsolete.

THE WORKHOUSE

In the second half of the sixteenth century the institution of the workhouse was developed. Like the galley sentence, "the great novelty" in criminal sanctions of the first half of the sixteenth century, the workhouse also arose to serve social purposes somewhat removed from the ordinary criminal law. It was a response to "the problem of poverty and vagrancy [that] had reached an acuteness probably never before encountered." Nevertheless, the workhouse like the galleys helped bring about a lasting alteration in the system of punishment of serious crime. The modern sanction of imprisonment for serious crime traces back to the workhouse for the poor more than to any other source.

The total social response to the problem of pauperism and vagabondage ranged far beyond the development of the workhouse. There were efforts to induce almsgiving and other charity, to generate tax revenue for poor relief, to restrict movement off the land, to control the price of food, and so forth. In England "the practice of London and certain other towns was in advance of the regulations of the statutes; the main feature of the period is the municipal organization of poor relief." Bridewell, the former royal palace in London whose name became a generic term for later English houses of correction, appears to have been converted to the purpose by the 1550s. The Bridewell in Norwich was operating in 1565. Both cities instituted relatively benign schemes of public relief for the resident poor who could not work or who were in temporary distress, and both were alert to rid themselves of those recent immigrant poor whose place of settlement was identifiable. To the Bridewells were sent the "sturdy beggars" and "disordered" persons, especially the young, and they were compelled to work for their sustenance. In Norwich the order of 1571 read: "The men to grind malt and other works, and the woman to use their hándedede [*sic*] and, expect they work, not to eat."

The workhouse offered two significant advantages over prior sanctions for petty crime. Because it was reformative, it meant to correct as well as to punish. The reformed man would emerge skilled for and reconciled to work. Second, because the workhouse was in fact a small manufactory, it might recover its costs from the labor of its inmates. This form of imprisonment would not burden the perpetually inadequate public revenues of the time. In Norwich the men were "to grind malt;" in London some "twenty-five occupations were practised in Bridewell. Amongst these were such trades as the making of gloves, silk lace, pins, bays, felts and tennis balls. . . ." The Amsterdam workhouses began with spinning and weaving. When the Dutch weaving industry declined, the women's house turned to the sewing of linen goods and the knitting of nets while the men's house was put to grinding logs into chips from which pigment could be extracted. "The system of labor used would in modern terminology be called a contract system. The users of the rasped [i.e., ground] wood purchased it from the [workhouse] under contracts approved by the burgomasters." It is a significant indication of the economic potential of the workhouse that inmates were paid in money for production above the minimum required of them in return for their daily keep. "This money constituted a small fund given to the prisoner on his discharge."

IMPRISONMENT

From the middle of the seventeenth century there is evidence that the workhouses for the poor were receiving some inmates who had been convicted of serious crime. By the end of the century specialized institutions were in operation in which serious offenders who would formerly have been subjected to the blood sanctions were confined for long terms at hard labor. The workhouse suggested the prison. This development recorded itself upon the German language. The Dutch *tuchthuis* became in German the *Zuchthaus*, a word which lost the meaning of "workhouse" for vagabonds and petty offenders and acquired the modern sense of "prison" or "penitentiary" for serious offenders.

In Bremen in 1648 a young man whose thieving merited death by hanging was, on account of his age and other mitigating factors, sentenced to perpetual imprisonment in irons, then put in the Bremen Zuchthaus to labor for his keep. He was released in 1652. In Amsterdam one writer reported in 1663 that capital offenders were sometimes not executed, but sent to the tuchthuis for terms from two to twenty years. Another observer in 1696 reported "sentences of the same class of prisoners" from three years to life. An ordinance of 1639 provided for 10 and 15 year terms in the Danzig Zuchthaus. In the second half of the century Hamburg was replacing death sentences with long terms of confinement at hard labor. The Prussian sentence to Festungsarbeit, forced labor on construction projects on the military fortresses and roads, was in use before 1685. Sentences to forced labor on the highways were used in Nuremberg and Wurtemberg in the seventeenth century, while at the same time Austria was employing convict labor in the mines and fortresses.

The rationale for the determinate sentences—that is, for terms less than life—was more complex. In Wurtemberg an executive rescript of 1627 instructed the courts to replace the blood sanctions with sentenced to forced labor (except for criminals whose crime merited the most extreme death penalties), especially for skilled craftsmen for whose reform there was some hope. The rescript was obeyed, and offenders who would previously have been banished or maimed or killed were instead put to terms of years or months at forced labor. In Prussia, Frederick William established the prisons at Spandau and Magdeburg in order to develop a domestic woolen industry with convict labor. We see, therefore, motives as diverse as for the workhouse: to reform offenders, to save the lives of skilled workers who could contribute to the mercantilist state, to render criminal sanctions more humane, and to exploit forced labor.

By the middle of the eighteenth century, the combination of the galleys and the prisons had produced a drastic diminution in the use of the blood sanctions. The maiming sanctions largely disappeared, and the death penalty declined. Although careful statistical study is thus far lacking, we have enough snippets of evidence to see the pattern. For example, the Nuremberg executioner Franz Schmidt inflicted an average of more than eight capital sentences per year in that city alone from 1573 to 1617. By contrast, in the 1770s executions averaged less than 12 per year for the whole of Prussia, and just over 31 per year for Austria-Bohemia.

English law was notorious for prescribing the death penalty for a vast range of offenses as slight as the theft of goods valued at twelve pence. Transportation was by no means the only mechanism for avoiding the imposition of the death penalty. Benefit of clergy permitted many first offenders to escape with their lives after being whipped and branded. Sympathetic juries might acquit the guilty or undervalue stolen goods in order to convict culprits of noncapital petty larceny. Royal pardons were surprisingly frequent. However, it was transportation that gave England a *via media* between the blood sanctions and the petty sanctions, comparable to the French galley sentence or the Austrian and Prussian *Festungsstrafe.*

The transportation system seems to have declined at the end of the seventeenth century. In Maryland and Virginia, the two principal importers, the colonial legislatures passed hostile laws that "cramped the trade," while "the demand for white servants had lessened in the West Indies. . . ." During the period 1704–1715 Smith found "negligible" evidence of transportation and some suggestion that men were instead being pardoned for service in the army. (Marlborough's major campaigns in the War of the Spanish Succession ran from 1702 to 1709; the Treaty of Utrecht of 1713 ended the war.) Transportation revived somewhat thereafter: in 1715 and 1716 upwards of 100 convicts were pardoned for transportation.

EUROPE AND ENGLAND

The transportation system was England's analogue to the Continental galley and prison sanctions, and contemporaries knew it. For example, in a tract written in 1725 Bernard Mandeville criticized various aspects of the transportation system. Convicts escaped before shipment, he complained, or re-

turned to England prematurely. In the New World they were les
than a liability, corrupting the Negro slaves. By contrast, Mandevi
out, the French and Spanish "make use of Malefactors in their Galleys, ...
"the great Cities of [Holland] have all Work-houses for Criminals. At *Amsterdam* there is one, where Felons are kept constantly employed in rasping
of *Brasil* Wood." Hence the author's modest proposal, to send English felons
into galley service with the Moroccans in exchange for the captive British
sailors now there.

The parallels between the European galley and prison schemes and the
English transportation system are numerous and striking:

(1) Both sanctions were introduced in the exercise of executive clemency
for convicts who would otherwise have been subjected to the blood sanctions. In time, both were incorporated into the ordinary criminal process as
sanctions imposed by the courts.

(2) Both represent an administrative feat, in organizing and refining relatively complex schemes to extract convict labor.

(3) Both were used as sanctions for serious crimes, but not the most serious. Transportation was overwhelmingly limited to property crimes, and
we have seen that the worst offenders continued to be executed on the Continent. Nevertheless, the new sanctions achieved a drastic diminution of capital punishment on both sides of the English Channel.

(4) Both served a similar combination of purposes—to moderate the
blood sanctions, to eliminate criminals from the society, to exploit convict
labor, to reform offenders. Human life became more valuable in the mid-sev-
enteenth century. The Europeans had suffered the catastrophic population
losses of the Thirty Years War, and the English were trying to populate an
empire while fending off the French.

(5) Both paved the way to the present systems of penal servitude. In
the eighteenth century French galley convicts and English transportees
found themselves confined to hulks in domestic ports, from which they were
led forth to daily labor on public works—like their counterparts in the
fortresses, mines, and prisons of Austria, Prussia, and the Netherlands.

The Invention of the Penitentiary

DAVID J. ROTHMAN

In the 1820's New York and Pennsylvania began a movement that soon
spread through the Northeast, and then over the next decades to many mid-

Source: Rothman, David J. The Invention of the Penitentiary. Adapted from *The Discovery of
the Asylum: Social Order and Disorder in the New Republic*. (Chapter 5, pp. 78–107). Boston:
Little, Brown and Co., 1971.

western states. New York devised the Auburn or congregate system of penitentiary organization, establishing it first at the Auburn State Prison between 1819 and 1923, and then in 1825 at the Ossining institution, familiarly known as Sing-Sing. Pennsylvania officials worked out the details of a rival plan, the separate system, applying it to the penitentiary at Pittsburgh in 1826 and to the prison at Philadelphia in 1829. In short order, the Connecticut legislature stopped using an abandoned copper mine to incarcerate offenders, and in 1827 built a new structure at Wethersfield. Massachusetts reorganized its state prison at Charlestown in 1829; that same year, Maryland erected a penitentiary, and one year later New Jersey followed suit. Ohio and Michigan built penitentiaries in the 1830's, and so did Indiana, Wisconsin, and Minnesota in the 1840's.

The results of all this activity deeply concerned Americans, so that annual reports to state legislators and popular journals as well contained long and detailed discussions and arguments on the merits of various enterprises. Europeans came to evaluate the experiment and the major powers appointed official investigators. France in 1831 dispatched the most famous pair, Alexis de Tocqueville and Gustave Auguste de Beaumont; in 1832 England sent William Crawford, and in 1834, Prussia dispatched Nicholas Julius. Tourists with no special interest in penology made sure to visit the institutions. Harriet Martineau, Frederick Marryat, and Basil Hall would no more have omitted this stop from their itinerary than they would have a southern plantation, a Lowell textile mill, or a frontier town. By the 1830's, the American penitentiary had become world famous.

The focus of attention was not simply on whether the penitentiary accomplished its goals, but on the merits of the two competing modes of organization. The debate raged with an incredible intensity during these decades, and the fact that most prisons in the United States were modeled after the Auburn system did not diminish it. Even more startling, neither did the basic similarity of the two programs. In retrospect they seem very much alike, but nevertheless an extraordinary amount of intellectual and emotional energy entered the argument. The fervor brought many of the leading reformers of the period to frequently bitter recriminations, and often set one benevolent society against another. Periodicals regularly polled foreign visitors for their judgment or printed a vigorous defense by one school and then a critical rejoinder by the other. Every report from the New York and Pennsylvania penitentiaries was an explicit apology for its procedures and an implicit attack on its opponents. And as soon as a state committed its prison organization to one side or the other then it too entered the controversy with the zeal of a recent convert.

The content of the debate between the Auburn and Pennsylvania camps points to the significance of the ideas on the causes of crime to the creation of the penitentiary, and the zeal reflects the expectations held about the innovation. To understand why men became so passionate about internal questions of design is to begin to comprehend the origins and popularity of in-

stitutionalization in this era. Under the Auburn scheme, prisoners were
sleep alone in a cell at night and labor together in a workshop during the
day for the course of their fixed sentences in the penitentiary. They were
forbidden to converse with fellow inmates or even exchange glances while
on the job, at meals, or in their cells. The Pennsylvania system, on the other
hand, isolated each prisoner for the entire period of his confinement. According to its blueprint, convicts were to eat, work, and sleep in individual
cells, seeing and talking with only a handful of responsible guards and selected visitors. They were to leave the institution as ignorant of the identity of other convicts as on the day they entered. As both schemes placed
maximum emphasis on preventing the prisoners from communicating with
anyone else, the point of dispute was whether convicts should work silently
in large groups or individually within solitary cells.

To both the advocates of the congregate and the separate systems, the
promise of institutionalization depended upon the isolation of the prisoner
and the establishment of a disciplined routine. Convinced that deviancy was
primarily the result of the corruptions pervading the community, and that
organizations like the family and the church were not counterbalancing them,
they believed that a setting which removed the offender from all temptations and substituted a steady and regular regimen would reform him. Since
the convict was not inherently depraved, but the victim of an upbringing
that had failed to provide protection against the vices at loose in society, a
well-ordered institution could successfully re-educate and rehabilitate him.
The penitentiary, free of corruptions and dedicated to the proper training
of the inmate, would inculate the discipline that negligent parents, evil com-
panions, taverns, houses of prostitution, theaters, and gambling halls had
destroyed. Just as the criminal's environment had led him into crime, the institutional environment would lead him out of it.

The duty of the penitentiary was to separate the offender from *all*
contact with corruption, both within and without its walls. There was obviously no sense to removing a criminal from the depravity of his sur-
roundings only to have him mix freely with other convicts within the
prison. Or, as Samuel Gridley Howe put it when composing a prisoner
prayer: "In the name of justice, do not surround me with bad associates
and with evil influences, do not subject me to unnecessary temptation, do
not expose me to further degradation. . . . Remove me from my old com-
panions, and surround me with virtuous associates." Sharing this perspective, officials in the 1830's argued that the great mistake of the prisons of the 1790's had been their failure to separate inmates. Lacking an
understanding of the forces of the environment and still caught up with
the idea that humane and certain punishment would eradicate deviancy,
they had neglected to organize or supervise the prisoners' immediate sur-
roundings. Consequently their institutions became seminaries of vice.
Now, however, reformers understood the need to guard the criminal
against corruption and teach him the habits of order and regularity. Iso-

lation and steady habits, the right organization and routine, would yield unprecedented benefits.

As a result of this thinking, prison architecture and arrangements became the central concern of reformers of the period. Unlike their predecessors, they turned all their attention inward, to the divisions of time and space within the institution. The layout of cells, the methods of labor, and the manner of eating and sleeping within the penitentiary were the crucial issues. The most influential benevolent organization devoted to criminal reform, the Boston Prison Discipline Society, appropriately considered architecture one of the most important of the *moral* sciences. "There are," the society announced, "principles in architecture, by the observance of which great moral changes can be more easily produced among the most abandoned of our race. . . . There is such a thing as architecture adapted to morals; that other things being equal, the prospect of improvement, in morals, depends, in some degree, upon the construction of buildings." Those who would rehabilitate the deviant had better cultivate this science.

The Pennsylvania camp had no doubt of its superiority, defining in countless pamphlets, articles, and reports its conception of the model institution. It aggressively insisted that the separate design carried the doctrine of isolation to a logical and appropriate conclusion. The arrangements at the Philadelphia prison, as partisans described them, guaranteed that convicts would avoid all contamination and follow a path to reform. Inmates remained in solitary cells for eating, sleeping, and working, and entered private yards for exercise; they saw and spoke with only carefully selected visitors, and read only morally uplifting literature—the Bible. No precaution against contamination was excessive. Officials placed hoods over the head of a new prisoner when marching him to his cell so he would not see or be seen by other inmates.

Once isolated, the prisoner began the process of reform. "Each individual," explained Pennsylvania's supporters, "will necessarily be made the instrument of his own punishment; his conscience will be the avenger of society." Left in total solitude, separated from "evil society . . . the progress of corruption is arrested; no additional contamination can be received or communicated." At the same time the convict "will be compelled to reflect on the error of his ways, to listen to the reproaches of conscience, to the expostulations of religion." Thrown upon his own innate sentiments, with no evil example to lead him astray, and with kindness and proper instruction at hand to bolster his resolutions, the criminal would start his rehabilitation.

For its part, the Auburn school vigorously defended the principle of separation and the reformatory promise of the penitentiary, fully sharing the axioms and optimism of its rival. But in reply to criticism, Auburn was necessarily on the defensive, for its arrangements did not so totally isolate the inmates or so studiously aim to prevent all chance of contamination. Auburn's supporters, therefore, spent more time picking fault with their opponents than advancing the superiority of their own procedures. Wherever possible they moved the debate from the ideal to the real, insisting that New York had the more practical scheme, a balanced combination of commitment and flexibility. They argued that Pennsylvania did not carry out its program perfectly, and then went on to contend that the very consistency of the separate design was itself a grave fault. Auburn's partisans answered complaints of frequent inmate communication in congregate prisons by contending that the walls of the Philadelphia prison were not thick enough and its sewer pipes not arranged well enough to prevent convict conversations. Charge, of course, prompted countercharge and before long intricate measurements of institutional walls and elaborate diagrams of the layout of pipes filled much of the penitentiary pamphlet literature.

One main thrust, however, of the congregate school came on the issue of the effects of constant and relieved isolation of prisoners. It was unnatural, the New York camp insisted, to leave men in solitary, day after day, year after year; indeed, it was so unnatural that it bred insanity. The organization of the Philadelphia institution, argued Francis Wayland, was "at variance with the human constitution," and his supporters tried to marshall appropriate statistics. The comparative mental health of prisoners under the two arrangements, the causes and rates of death, the physical health of the convicts entered the debate. No accurate data allowed precise calculations of these phenomena and partisans did little more than set down subjective judgments in the guise of absolute numbers. But the Auburn attack did manage to cast some doubt on the wisdom of Pennsylvania's routine.

After asserting that the separate system was no more effective or perfect than the congregate one, the New York school presented what proved to be its most persuasive point: the added expenses of establishing the Pennsylvania program were unnecessary. Auburn-type institutions, their defenders flatly, and accurately, declared, cost less to construct and brought in greater returns from convict labor. Since the two systems were more or less equal, with faults and advantages fairly evenly distributed, states ought not to incur the greater costs of the separate plan. By having prisoners work together in shops, Auburn's cells did not have to be as large as those at Philadelphia; also, a greater variety of goods could be efficiently manufactured in congregate prisons. The New York program provided the best of both worlds, economy and reform.

The problem of [rule] enforcement in the congregate system raised the dilemma of whether obedience was worth any price. Did the end of discipline justify every means of punishment? Was the cure more dangerous than the disease? The question had obvious relevance to an institution like Sing-Sing, which on the whole managed to curtail communication between convicts but with a type and frequency of correction that public investigators found cruel and sadistic. The issue, however, was not confined to one penitentiary or notorious warden. Prisons everywhere had to decide what punishments were proper for enforcing the system. Were the regular use of the whip, the yoke, the ball and chain, cold showers, or curtailed rations appropriate weapons in the battle to preserve order? Were offenders against prison law without rights, without protection from their keepers?

The whip was commonplace in Auburn and in Charlestown, in Columbus and in Wethersfield. Pennsylvania had recourse to the iron gag, Maine to the ball and chain, Connecticut to the cold shower. And officials wholeheartedly defended these punishments. Auburn's chaplain insisted that it would be "most unfortunate . . . if the public mind were to settle down into repugnance to the use of such coercive means." To isolate and rehabilitate convicts, corporal punishment was unquestionably proper and legitimate. "Only relax the reins of discipline . . . and a chaplain's labors would be of no more use here than in a drunken mob." A Pennsylvania investigatory body justified using an iron gag on refractory prisoners. Convicts were "men of idle habits, vicious propensities, and depraved passions," who had to be taught obedience as the first step to reformation. Ohio's warden also considered the whip vital to a prison system. "For whenever the Penitentiary becomes a pleasant place of residence," he declared, "whenever a relaxation of discipline . . . converts it into something like an *Asylum* for the wicked, then it loses all its influence for good upon the minds of men disposed to do evil."

Penal institutions' widespread and unembarrassed reliance on harsh disciplinary measures was due in part to the newness of the experiment. It reflected too a nagging concern that convicts might possibly join together to overpower their keepers—no one was yet altogether confident that forty men could control eight hundred. Yet even more fundamental was the close fit between the punitive measures and the reform perspective. The prevailing concepts of deviance put a premium on rigorous discipline. The premises underlying the penitentiary movement placed an extraordinary emphasis on an orderly routine. Confident that the deviant would learn the lessons of discipline in a properly arranged environment, everyone agreed that prison life had to be strict and unrelenting. And with regularity a prerequisite for success, practically any method that enforced discipline became appropriate.

Reformers and prison officials agreed on the need for inmates to obey authority. Criminals, in their view, had never learned to respect limits. To correct this, the penitentiary had to secure absolute obedience, bending the convicts' behavior to fit its own rigid rules. Should wayward inmates resist, their obstinacy would have to be "broken," and as the word itself implied, the means were not nearly so important as the ends. Perhaps the most striking testimony to the influence of these ideas in legitimating disciplinary procedures came from Tocqueville and Beaumont. The visitors were under no illusions as to the nature or the extent of penitentiary punishments. "We have no doubt," they concluded, "but that the habits of order to which the prisoner is subjected for several years . . . the obedience of every moment to inflexible rules, the regularity of a uniform life, in a word, all the circumstances belonging to this severe system, are calculated to produce a deep impression upon his mind. Perhaps, leaving the prison he is not an honest man, but he has contracted honest habits . . . and if he is not more virtuous, he has become at least more judicious." Sing-Sing officials quoted these findings at length, and with obvious satisfaction.

State legislators and wardens found these notions attractive and were eager to implement them. Secure in the knowledge that they were acting in the best interests of taxpayers and inmates alike, that they were simultaneously furthering financial and reformist goals, they had no objection to making some contracts with private manufacturers to lease convict labor or to establishing a prison routine of long hours with little relief. Hoping in this way to make the penitentiary a self-supporting, even profitable venture while rehabilitating the offender, they favored a schedule that maximized work. The results in New York were not unusual: convicts were up at five o'clock for two hours of work before breakfast, then back to it for three hours and forty-five minutes; lunch was at noon for one hour and fifteen minutes, then a return to the shop for another four hours and forty-five minutes. The weekly workday averaged ten hours, from sunup to sunset six days a week. A Christian Sunday and the lack of artificial lighting prevented a lengthening of the schedule.

The doctrines of separation, obedience, and the labor became the trinity around which officials organized the penitentiary. They carefully instructed inmates that their duties could be "comprised in a few words"; they were *to labor diligently, to obey all orders, and preserve an unbroken silence.* Yet to achieve these goals, officers had to establish a total routine, to administer every aspect of the institution in accord with the three guidelines, from inmates' dress to their walk, from the cells' furnishings to the guards' deportment. The common solution was to follow primarily a quasi-military model. The regulations based on this model promised to preserve isolation, to make labor efficient, and to teach men lacking discipline to abide by rules; this regimented style of life would inculcate strict discipline, precision, and instantaneous adherence to commands. Furthermore, a military model in a correctional institution seemed especially suitable for demonstrating to the society at large the right principles of organization. Here was an appropriate example for a community suffering a crisis of order.

Regimentation became the standard mode of prison life. Convicts did not walk from place to place; rather, they went in close order and single file, each looking over the shoulder of the man in front, faces included to the right, feet moving in unison, in lockstep. The lockstep became the trademark of American prisons in these years, a curious combination of march and shuffle that remained standard procedure well into the 1930's. Its invention and adoption exemplified the problems and responses of the first penitentiary officials. How were they to move inmates about? Prison officials with fixed ideas on convict communication and obedience had to reject informal movement. Searching for greater discipline, they turned to the military march, crossed it with a shuffle to lessen its dignity, and pointed heads to the right, rather than facing straight ahead, to prevent conversation. The result, the lockstep, was an immediate success and became the common practice.

Wardens organized the convicts' daily schedule in military style. At the sound of a horn or bell, keepers opened the cells, prisoners stepped onto the deck, and then in lockstep marched into the yard. In formation they emptied their night pails, moved on and washed them, took a few more steps, and placed them on a rack to dry. Still in line they marched to the shops. There they worked at their tasks in rows on long benches until the bell rang for breakfast. They grouped again in single file, passed into the kitchen, picked up their rations (regulations admonished them not to break step), and continued on to their cells, or in some institutions, to a common messroom where they ate their meal. (Regulations again instructed them to sit erect with backs straight.) At the bell they stood, reentered formation, and marched back to the shops. They repeated this routine at noon, and again at six o'clock; then they returned to their cells for the night and at nine o'clock lights went out, as at a barracks. Although some institutions were more exacting than others in enforcing these procedures, almost all of them tried to impose a degree of military routine on their prisoners.

The furnishings of convicts' cells also indicates the relevance of the military model. A cot and pail and tin utensils were the basic objects. Prisoners now wore uniforms of a simple, course, striped fabric, and all had their hair cut short to increase uniformity. The military example affected keepers as well as convicts. Several wardens came to their positions directly from an army or navy career, legislators obviously eager to have them apply their former training to this setting. Guards wore uniforms, mustered at specific hours, and kept watch like sentries. Regulations ordered them to behave in a "gentlemanly manner," like officers, without laughter, ribaldry, or unnecessary conversation while on duty. As Sing-Sing's rules put it, in only a slight overstatement of a general sentiment: "They were to require from the convicts the greatest deference, and never suffer them to approach but in respectful manner; they are not to allow them the least degree of familiarity, nor exercise any towards them; they should be extremely careful to *command* as well as to compel their respect."

The military style also influenced the construction and appearance of the institutions. Some were modeled after medieval fortresses. An adaptation of a structure from the Middle Ages was necessarily monumental, appropriate in size to a noble experiment like the penitentiary, capable of stimulating a citizen's pride and a visitor's respect. It also had functional qualities, for thick walls promised security against prison breaks, and turrets became posts for guarding an enclosed space. Another popular alternative was to construct the prison along factory lines—a long and low building, symmetrically arranged with closely spaced windows, all very regular and methodical. Whatever it lacked in grandeur it tried to make up in fixity and order.

The functioning of the penitentiary—convicts passing their sentences in physically imposing and highly regimented settings, moving in lockstep from bare and solitary cells to workshops, clothed in common dress, and forced into standard routines—was designed to carry a message to the community. The prison would train the most notable victims of social disorder to discipline, teaching them to resist corruption. And success in this particular task should inspire a general reformation of manners and habits. The institution would become a laboratory for social improvement. By demonstrating how regularity and discipline transformed the most corrupt persons, it would reawaken the public to these virtues. The penitentiary would promote a new respect for order and authority.

Complete and Austere Institutions

Michel Foucault

I. COMPLETE AND AUSTERE INSTITUTIONS

Baltard called them "complete and austere institutions" (Baltard, 1829). In several respects, the prison must be an exhaustive disciplinary apparatus: it must assume responsibility for all aspects of the individual, his physical training, his aptitude to work, his state of mind; the prison, much more than the school, the workshop or the army, which always involved a certain specialization, is "omni-disciplinary." Moreover, the prison has neither exterior nor gap; it cannot be interrupted, except when its task is totally completed, its action on the individual must be uninterrupted: an unceasing discipline. Lastly, it gives almost total power over the prisoners; it has its internal mechanisms of repression and punishment: a despotic discipline. It carries to their greatest intensity all the procedures to be found in the other disciplinary mechanisms. It must be the most powerful machinery for imposing a new form on the perverted individual; its mode of action is the constraint of a total education: "In prison the government may dispose of the liberty of the person and of the time of the prisoner; from then on, one can imagine the power of the education which, not only a day, but in the succession of days and even years, may regulate for man the time of waking and sleeping, of activity and rest, the number and duration of meals, the quality and ration of food, the nature and product of labour, the time of prayer, the use of speech and even, so to speak, that of thought, that education which, in the short, simple journeys from refectory to workshop, from workshop to the cell, regulates the movements of the body, and even in moments of rest, de-

Source: Excerpted from: Foucault, Michel. Complete and Austere Institutions. Adapted from *Discipline and Punish* (Chapter 6, pp. 235–48). New York: Vintage, 1979.

termines the use of time, the time-table, this education, which, in short, takes possession of man as a whole, of all the physical and moral faculties that are in him and of the time in which he is himself" (Lucas, 1836, 123–4). This complete "reformatory" lays down a recoding of existence very different from the mere juridical deprivation of liberty and very different, too, from the simple mechanism of exempla imagined by the reformers at the time of the *idéologues*.

1. The first principle was isolation. The isolation of the convict from the external world, from everything that motivated the offence, from the complicities that facilitated it. The isolation of the prisoners from one another. Not only must the penalty be individual, but it must also be individualizing—in two ways. First, the prison must be designed in such a way as to efface of itself the harmful consequences to which it gives rise in gathering together very different convicts in the same place: to stile plots and revolts, to prevent the formation of future complicities that may give rise to blackmail (when the convicts are once again at liberty), to form an obstacle to the immorality of so many "mysterious associations." In short, the prison should form from the malefactors that it gathers together a homogeneous and interdependent population: "There exists at this moment among us an organized society of criminals. . . . They form a small nation within the greater. Almost all these men met or meet again in prison. We must now disperse the members of this society." Moreover, through the reflection that it gives rise to and the remorse that cannot fail to follow, solitude must be a positive instrument of reform: "Thrown into solitude, the convict reflects. Placed alone in the presence of his crime, he learns to hate it, and, if his soul is not yet blunted by evil, it is in isolation that remorse will come to assail him" (Beaumont and Tocqueville, 1831, 109). Through the fact, too, that solitude assures a sort of self-regulation of the penalty and makes possible a spontaneous individualization of the punishment: the more the convict is capable of reflecting, the more capable he was of committing his crime; but, also, the more lively his remorse, the more painful his solitude; on the other hand, when he has profoundly repented and made amends without the least dissimulation, solitude will no longer weigh upon him: "Thus, according to this admirable discipline, each intelligence and each morality bears within itself the principle and measure of a punishment whose error and human fallibility cannot alter the certainty and invariable equity. . . . It is not in truth like the seal of a divine and providential justice" (Aylies, 1837, 132–3). Lastly, and perhaps above all, the isolation of the convicts guarantees that it is possible to exercise over them, with maximum intensity, a power that will not be overthrown by any other influence; solitude is the primary condition of total submission.

It is at this point that the debate on the two American systems of imprisonment, that of Auburn and that of Philadelphia, was situated. In fact, this debate, which was so wide-ranging and long drawn out, concerned only the way in which isolation should be used, it being accepted by all.

The Auburn model prescribed the individual cell during the night, work and meals in common, but under the rule of absolute silence, the convicts being allowed to speak only to the warders, with their permission and in a low voice. It was a clear reference to the monastic model; a reference, too, to the discipline of the workshop. The prison must be the microcosm of a perfect society in which individuals are isolated in their moral existence, but in which they come together in a strict hierarchical framework, with no lateral relation, communication being possible only in a vertical direction. The advantage of the Auburnian system, according to its advocates, was that it formed a duplication of society itself. Constraint was assured by material means, but above all by a rule that one had to learn to respect and which was guaranteed by surveillance and punishment. Rather than keep the convicts "under lock and key like wild beasts in their cages," they must be brought together, "made to join together in useful exercises, forced together to adopt good habits, preventing moral contagion by active surveillance, maintaining reflection by the rule of silence"; this rule accustoms the convict "to regard the law as a sacred precept whose violation brings just and legitimate harm" (Mittermaier, 1836). Thus this operation of isolation, assembly without communication and law guaranteed by uninterrupted supervision, must rehabilitate the criminal as a social individual: it trains him to a "useful and resigned activity" (Gasparin); it restores for him "habits of sociability" (Beaumont and Tocqueville, 112).

In absolute isolation—as at Philadelphia—the rehabilitation of the criminal is expected not of the application of a common law, but of the relation of the individual to his own conscience and to what may enlighten him from within. "Alone in his cell, the convict is handed over to himself; in the silence of his passions and of the world that surrounds him, he descends into his conscience, he questions it and feels awakening within him the moral feeling that never entirely perishes in the heart of man." It is not, therefore, an external respect for the law or fear of punishment alone that will act upon the convict but the workings of the conscience itself. A profound submission, rather than a superficial training; a change of "morality," rather than of attitude. In the Pennsylvanian prison, the only operations of correction were the conscience and the silent architecture that confronted it. At Cherry Hill, "the walls are the punishment of the crime; the cell confronts the convict with himself; he is forced to listen to his conscience." Hence work there is more in the nature of a consolation than an obligation; supervisors do not have to exert force—this is assured by the materiality of things—and consequently, their authority may be accepted: "At each visit, a few benevolent words flow from his honest mouth and bring to the heart of the inmate gratitude, hope and consolation; he loves his warder; and he loves him because he is gentle and sympathetic. Walls are terrible, but man is good" (Blouet, 1834). In this closed cell, this temporary sepulchre, the myths of resurrection arise easily enough. After night and silence, the regenerated life. Auburn was society itself reduced to its bare essentials. Cherry Hill was life annihilated and begun again. Catholicism soon absorbed this Quaker technique into its discourses. "I see your cell as no more than a frightful sepulchre where, instead of worms, remorse and despair come to gnaw at you and turn your existence into a hell in anticipation. But . . . what is for an irreligious prisoner merely a tomb, a repulsive ossuary, becomes, for the sincerely Christian convict, the very cradle of blessed immortality."

2. "Work alternating with meals accompanies the convict to evening prayer; then a new sleep gives him an agreeable rest that is not disturbed by the phantoms of an unregulated imagination. Thus the six weekdays pass by. They are followed by a day devoted exclusively to prayer, instruction and salutary meditations. Thus the weeks, the months, the years follow one another; thus the prisoner who, on entering the establishment, was an inconstant man, or one who was single-minded only in his irregularity, seeking to destroy his existence by the variety of his vices, gradually becomes by dint of a habit that is at first purely external, but is soon transformed in a second nature, so familiar with work and the pleasures that derive from it, that, provided wise instruction has opened up his soul to repentance, he may be exposed with more confidence to temptations, when he finally recovers his liberty" (Julius, 1831, 417–18). Work is defined, with isolation, as an agent of carceral transformation. This is to be found as early as the code of 1808: "Although the penalty inflicted by the law has as its aim the reparation of a crime, it is also intended to reform the convict, and this double aim will be fulfilled if the malefactor is snatched from that fatal idleness which, having brought him to prison, meets him again within its walls and, seizing hold of him, brings him to the ultimate degree of depravity." Work is neither an addition nor a corrective to the régime of detention: whether it is a question of forced labour, reclusion or imprisonment, it is conceived, by the legislator himself, as necessarily accompanying it. But the necessity involved is precisely not the necessity of which the eighteenth-century reformers spoke, when they wished to make imprisonment either an example for the public or a useful reparation for society. In the carceral régime, the link between work and punishment is of another type.

The perfect image of prison labour was the women's workshop at Clairvaux; the silent precision of the human machinery is reminiscent of the regulated rigour of the convent: "On a throne, above which is a crucifix, a sister is sitting; before her, arranged in two rows, the prisoners are carrying out the task imposed on them, and, as needlework accounts for almost all the work, the strictest silence is constantly maintained. . . . It seems that, in these halls, the very air breathes penitence and expiation. One is carried back, as by a spontaneous movement, to the time of the venerable habits of this ancient place, one remembers those voluntary penitents who shut themselves up here in order to say farewell to the world." Compare this with the following: "Go into a cotton-mill; listen to the conversations of the workers and the whistling of the machines. Is there any contrast in the world more afflicting than the regularity and predictability of these mechanical movements, compared with the disorder of ideas and morals, produced by the contact of so many men, women and children" (Faucher, 1838, 20).

3. But prison goes beyond the mere privation of liberty in a more important way. It becomes increasingly an instrument for the modulation of

the penalty; an apparatus which, through the execution of the sentence with which it is entrusted, seems to have the right, in part at least, to assume its principle. Of course, the prison institution was not given this "right" in the nineteenth century or even in the twentieth, except in a fragmentary form (through the oblique way of release on license, semi-release, the organization of reformatories). But it should be noted that it was claimed very early on by those responsible for prison administration, as the very condition of the good functioning or a prison, and of its efficiency in the task of reformation that the law itself had given it.

The same goes for the duration of the punishment; it makes it possible to quantify the penalties exactly, to graduate them according to circumstances and to give to legal punishment the more or less explicit form of wages; but it also runs the risk of having no corrective value, if it is fixed once and for all in the sentence. The length of the penalty must not be a measurement of the "exchange value" of the offence; it must be adjusted to the "useful" transformation of the inmate during his term of imprisonment. It is not a time-measure, but a time finalized. The form of the operation, rather than the form of the wages. "Just as the prudent physician ends his medication or continues it according to whether the patient has or has not arrived at a perfect cure, so, in the first of these two hypotheses, expiation ought to end with the complete reform of the prisoner; for, in this case, all detention has become useless, and from then on as inhuman to the reformed individual as it is vainly burdensome for the State" (Bonneville, 1846, 6). The correct duration of the penalty must be calculated, therefore, not only according to the particular crime and its circumstances, but also according to the penalty itself as it takes place in actual fact. This amounts to saying that, although the penalty must be individualized, it is so not on the basis of the individual-offender, the juridical subject of his act, the responsible author of the offence, but on the basis of the individual punished, the object of a supervised transformation, the individual in detention inserted in the prison apparatus, modified by it or reacting to it. "It is a question only of reforming the evil-doer. Once this reform has come about, the criminal must return to society" (Lucas, 1837).

The quality and content of detention should no longer be determined by the nature of the offence alone. The juridical gravity of a crime does not at all have the value of a univocal sign for the character of the convict, whether or not he is capable of reform. In particular the crime—offence distinction, which the penal code recognized in drawing the corresponding distinction between mere imprisonment and imprisonment with hard labour, is not operational in terms of reform. This was the almost universal opinion expressed by the directors of the *maisons centrales*, during an inquiry carried out by the ministry in 1836: "The minor offenders are generally the most vicious. . . . Among the criminals, one meets many men who have given in to the violence of their passions and to the needs of a large family." "The behaviour of criminals is much better than that of the minor offenders; the former are more submissive, harder-working than the latter, who, in general are pick-pockets, debauchees and idlers." Hence the idea that punitive rigour must not be in direct proportion to the penal importance of the offence—nor determined once and for all.

As an operation of correction, imprisonment has its own requirements and dangers. It is its effects that must determine its stages, its temporary increases, its successive reductions, in severity; what Charles Lucas called the "mobile classification of moralities." The progressive system applied at Geneva since 1825 was often advocated in France. It took the form, for example, of three areas: a trial area for prisoners in general, a punishment area and a reward area for those who had embarked on the way of reform. Or it took the form of four phases: a period of intimidation (deprivation of work and of any internal or external relations); a period of work (isolation, but work which, after the phase of forced idleness, would be welcomed as a benefit); a régime of moralization (more or less "lectures" from the directors and official visitors); a period of work in common. Although the principle of the penalty was certainly a legal decision, its administration, its quality and its rigours must belong to an autonomous mechanism that supervises the effects of punishment within the very apparatus that produces them. A whole régime of punishments and rewards that is a way not simply of gaining respect for the prison regulations, but of making the action of the prison on the inmates effective. The legal authority itself came to accept this: "One should not be surprised, said the supreme court of appeal, when consulted on the subject of a bill concerning the prisons, at the idea of granting rewards, which might consist either for the most part in money, or in a better diet, or even in a reduction of the duration of the penalty. If anything can awaken in the minds of convicts the notions of good and evil, bring them to moral reflections and raise them to some extent in their own eyes, it is the possibility of obtaining some reward" (Lucas, 441–42).

And it must be admitted that the legal authorities can have no immediate control over all these procedures that rectify the penalty as it proceeds. It is a question, in effect, of measures that by definition can intervene only after the sentence and can bear only on something other than the offences. Those who administer detention must therefore have an indispensable autonomy, when it comes to the question of individualizing and varying the application of the penalty: supervisors, a prison governor, a chaplain or an instructor are more capable of exercising this correction function than those who hold the penal power. It is their judgment (understood as observation, diagnosis, characterization, information, differential classification) and not a verdict in the form of an attribution of guilty, that must serve as a support for this internal modulation of the penalty—for its mitigation or even its interruption. When in 1846, Bonneville presented his project of release on license, he defined it as "the right of the administration, with the previous approval of the legal authority, to place in temporary liberty, after a sufficient period of expiation, the completely reformed convict, on condition that he will be brought back into prison on the slightest well-founded complaint" (Bonneville, 5). All this "arbitrariness" which, in the old penal system, enabled the judges to modulate the penalty and the princes to ignore it if they so wished, all this arbitrariness, which the modern codes have withdrawn from the judicial power, has been gradually reconstituted on the side of the power that administers and supervises punishment. It is the sovereignty of knowledge possessed by the warder: "He is a veritable magistrate called upon to reign as sovereign in the prison ... who, in order not to fall short in his mission, must combine the most eminent virtue with a profound knowledge of mankind."

And so we arrive at a principle, clearly formulated by Charles Lucas, which, although it marks the virtual beginning of modern penal functioning, very few jurists would dare to accept today without some hesitation; let us call it the Declaration of Carceral Independence—in it is claimed the right to be a power that not only possesses administrative autonomy, but is also a part of punitive sovereignty. This affirmation of the rights of the prison posits as a principle: that criminal judgment is an arbitrary unity; that it must be broken down; that the writers of the penal codes were correct in distinguishing the legislative level (which classifies the acts and attributes penalties to them) and the judicial level (which passes the sentences); that the task today is to analyse in turn this later judicial level; that one should distinguish in it what is properly judicial (assess not so much acts as agents, measure "the intentionalities that give human acts so many different moralities," and therefore rectify if it can the assessments of the legislator); and to give autonomy to "penitentiary judgment," which is perhaps the most important; in relation to it the assessment of the court is merely a "way of prejudging," for the morality of the agent can be assessed "only when put to the test. The judge, therefore, requires in turn a compulsory and rectifying supervision of his assessments; and this supervision is that provided by the penitentiary prison."

One may speak, therefore, of an excess or a series of excesses on the part of imprisonment in terms of legal detention—of the "carceral" in relation to the "judicial." Now this excess was observed very early on, from the very birth of the prison, either in the form of real practices, or in the form of projects. It did not come later, as a secondary effect. The great carceral machinery was bound up with the very functioning of the prison. The sign of this autonomy is very apparent in the "useless" acts of violence perpetrated by warders or in the despotism of an administration that has all the privileges of an enclosed community. Its roots lie elsewhere: precisely in the fact that the prison is required to be "useful," that the deprivation of liberty—that juridical levying on an ideal property—must, from the outset, have exercised a positive technical role, operating transformations on individuals. And, for this operation, the carceral apparatus has recourse to three great schemata: the politico-moral schema of individual isolation and hierarchy; the economic model of force applied to compulsory work; the technico-medical model of cure and normalization. The cell, the workshop, the hospital. The margin by which the prison exceeds detention is filled in fact by techniques of a disciplinary type. And this disciplinary addition to the juridical is what, in short, is called the "penitentiary."

REFERENCES

Aylies, S. 1837. *Du système pénitentiaire.*

Baltard, L. 1829. *Architectonographie des prisons.*

Beaumont, E. de and Tocqueville, A. de. 1831. *Note sur le système pénitentiaire. Le Système pénitentiaire aux États-Unis,* ed. 1845.

Blouet, A. 1843. *Projet de prisons cellulaires.*

Farge, A. 1974. *Le Vol d'aliments à Paris au XVIIIe siècle.*

Julius, N. H. 1831. *Leçons sur les prisons,* I, (Fr. trans.).

Lucas, C. 1836. *De la réforme des prisons.*

Mittermaier, K. J. 1848. *Traité de la preuve* (Fr. trans.).

Prisons for Women, 1790–1980

Nicole Hahn Rafter

ORIGINS OF THE CUSTODIAL MODEL: FROM 1790 TO 1870

The period from 1790 to 1870 was characterized by the gradual establishment, within primarily male prisons, of separate quarters for female convicts. During this period, moreover, the first independent prison for women was founded—New York's Mount Pleasant Female Prison, an institution with its own enabling legislation and staff. And during this stage there developed the custodial model of women's prison unit that continues to affect the nature of women's prisons today.

THE FIRST STEP: PHYSICAL ISOLATION OF FEMALE PRISONERS

In the late eighteenth century, city lockups made little or no effort to separate prisoners by sex or according to the other criteria (such as age, race, and offense seriousness) by which prisoners have been classified and seg-

Source: Excerpted from: Hahn Rafter, Nicole. Prisons for Women, 1790–1980. Adapted from *Crime and Justice: An Annual Review of Research.* Volume 5. (pp. 129–67). Michael Tonry and Norval Morris, editors. Chicago: University of Chicago Press.

regated in more recent times. For instance, the jail operated by Philadelphia at the corner of High and Third streets in the 1780s was reputed to have been an "abode of guilt and wretchedness" that held "in one common herd . . . , by day and by night, prisoners of all ages, colours, and sexes!.." Discipline was poor to nonexistent in these Revolutionary War era city jails, a situation which led those who founded the first state prisons in the late eighteenth and early nineteenth centuries to insist on segregation of the sexes.

Eventually, women too came to be locked into individual cells, and as this happened the incarceration of women changed considerably in character. By the late 1830s a number of states, including New York, Ohio, and Pennsylvania, had abandoned the old, large-room plan and removed their female convicts to cells. With the change, care of women came once again to resemble that of men, especially in its physical aspects. From the point of view of the women who experienced the change, it probably had both advantages and disadvantages. Crowding was reduced (at least initially), and in their single cells the women now had somewhat more privacy. On the other hand, the shift to cellular housing in this period ordinarily brought higher security, greater isolation, more intense regimentation, and stricter discipline. The care of women was now more equitable, corresponding as it did more closely to that of men. However, in many respects it remained inferior.

MOUNT PLEASANT FEMALE PRISON:
THE FIRST PRISON FOR WOMEN

The initial step toward the establishment of a system of separate prisons for women was taken in 1835, when New York founded the Mount Pleasant Female Prison. This was the first and only penal institution for women established before the great era of prison construction that commenced in the late nineteenth century.

Situated on the hill behind Sing-Sing, overlooking the Hudson River, Mount Pleasant opened in 1839. According to a description of the late 1860s, it was "a handsome building, two stories high. . . . It has a front of fifty feet, with a Doric portico of imposing proportions, and a depth of one hundred and fifty feet" (Wines and Dwight 1867, p. 107). Its interior contained three tiers of cells with twenty-four cells in each tier. At the western end of the building, which had the best view, quarters for the matron were located. At the eastern end, within the inmates' area, was an elevated platform used for chapel services and lectures. Below it was a nursery. In addition to the main building, the plant included a workshop and two separate punishment cells, each with its own yard. The women's complex was surrounded by a high wall. Mount Pleasant's cellblock plan and high level of security became typical of women's units of the custodial type.

Punishments for disobedient convicts at Mount Pleasant, as at other women's units of the custodial type, were often severe, including strait-jacketing, solitary confinement, extended bread-and-water diets, and the "shower bath" that bombarded prisoners with water until they were close to drowning. Dorothea Dix was appalled by the punishment of gagging, "which seems to me shocking and extremely objectionable." One of Sing-Sing's inspectors informed her that " 'the gag has been sometimes applied, but it has been only among the females that it has been rendered absolutely necessary!' " On the other hand, she learned that " 'in the women's prison, the lash is never used. There the punishments are confinement to their own cells in the main dormitory, or in separate cells, with reduction of food' " and, of course, gagging.

THE CUSTODIAL MODEL

To this point I have been describing both the incarceration of women in the pre-1870 period and the emergence of a particular type of penal unit for women. In what follows I analyze the custodial model in more detail, identifying key traits along five dimensions: (1) physical aspects and operation costs; (2) inmate characteristics; (3) administration; (4) discipline; and (5) programs.

1. *Physical Aspects and Operating Costs.* Custodial prisons for women originated as units within the walls of state prisons for men. But in several respects, women's units departed from the architectural and custody practices of men's prisons. Little if any extra room was allotted for exercise or work: women were thought to have less need for recreation and less capacity for industrial labor; and their quarters, usually crammed into corners of men's institutions, could not be expanded. The burden of separation of the sexes, moreover, fell on the female departments.

To cost-conscious officials, female convicts appeared to be a greater drain on resources than the men. Because they were few in number, their per capita costs were higher, especially when matrons were hired for their supervision. Chaplains, physicians, and other officials considered it bothersome to visit female departments after making their usual rounds. And because women were assigned to less productive labor (often to making and washing clothing for the men), their work was less profitable than that of male convicts.

2. *Inmate Characteristics.* Custodial institution for women received mainly felons. Women sentenced to New York's Newgate prison between 1797 and 1801 had been convicted of property offenses such as arson, burglary, forgery, and larceny. Most held at the Mount Pleasant State Prison in the 1840s and 1850s had been convicted of property offenses, and a few crimes of violence. Of the thirty-two women sentenced to the Tennessee State Penitentiary between 1840 and 1865, eighteen had been convicted of property offenses, nine of crimes of violence, and the rest of other felonies such as bigamy and perjury.

3. *Administration.* From about 1850 onward, daily operations at

women's custodial institutions were supervised by matrons, women who lived within the walls and worked long hours for low wages. The main responsibility for and authority over such institutions, however, lay with officials of the neighboring prisons for men. The warden of the nearby men's prison hired the head matron and often her assistants as well. The women's unit rarely had a support staff of its own but rather was dependent for services on the chaplain, head teacher, and physician of the men's branch. Ultimate administrative authority over women's custodial institutions, moreover, fell to the states' boards of prisons; in the pre-1870 period these were exclusively male in membership and hence less attuned to the problems of female than of male convicts. The matrons of custodial prisons were seldom positioned to challenge the status quo: often they were older women, widowed and poorly educated, forced by necessity to accept unpleasant and poorly paid positions.

4. *Discipline*. Women's custodial institutions approached discipline—rules, punishments, and routines—in a manner similar to that of the men's prisons with which they were associated. In general, the same standards were applied to women as to men, though with less consistency. Whether women were compelled to conform to the same rules was a function of one or more of three factors: the degree of overcrowding; the extent to which officials at the main penitentiary bothered to monitor activities in the women's unit; and the state's willingness to hire a matron.

Without supervision by a matron, female convicts could lead a riotous and even dangerous existence in their separate quarters. According to a report of the mid-1840s on the women's annex at the Ohio penitentiary, for example, its nine women gave more trouble than the institution's five hundred males: "The women fight, scratch, pull hair, curse, swear and yell, and to bring them to order a keeper has frequently to go among them with a horsewhip." Similarly, Dorothea Dix observed of the Ohio penitentiary, "There was no matron in the women's wing at the time I was there, . . . and they were not slow to exercise their good and evil gifts on each other."

5. *Programs*. Custodial women's institutions seldom took much interest in any program other than work. Insofar as they offered educational training at all, they provided it in the evening. Classes were taught, not by trained teachers, but by educated inmates. Recreational programs tended to be even more impoverished. Because custodial women's institutions allocated space for little other than cells, their inmates often had no yard for exercise and no room other than the mess hall for attending religious services, meeting with visitors, or (when permitted) socializing with one another.

Work programs, in contrast, were often well developed. An industry organized along factory lines was operated by many units of the custodial type. In some, inmates produced clothing for the rest of the state's prisons; in others they caned chairs or otherwise finished off products manufactured in the neighboring prison for men. Although the tasks to which female convicts were assigned did not produce the profits of men's industries, they were expected to reduce operating costs. Women frequently labored eight or more hours a day, and they were sometimes paid a pittance for their work, money they could collect on release.

EMERGENCE AND DIFFUSION OF THE REFORMATORY MODEL, 1870–1935

The Reformatory Model

In what follows, I describe the reformatory model in more detail, identifying its traits along the five dimensions used earlier to define the custodial model.

1. *Physical Aspects and Operating Costs.* Reformatories were usually located on large tracts of their own, sometimes several hundred acres of farmland. Most were constructed on the cottage plan, with a central administrative building. Around the administration building were grouped separate cottages, each with beds for twenty to fifty inmates. As one reformatory advocate explained in a passage applying to both adult and juvenile reformatories for females: "The idea of having small houses with little groups . . . was that each cottage should be a real home, with an intelligent, sympathetic woman at the head to act as mother. . . . It was believed that if small groups could be placed in cottages enough motherly women could be found to give them the sort of affections which would most surely help to redeem them."

In addition to creating the context for familial treatment, the cottage plan had other advantages which appealed to reformatory founders. It facilitated classification ("honor" inmates, for example, could be grouped together in one cottage, babies in another). Because each had its own kitchen and dining room, the cottage provided opportunities to hone inmates' domestic skills. Furthermore, the cottage symbolized the rural values held dear by the reformers, who associated the countryside and fresh air with betterment, the city with crime and corruption.

2. *Inmate Characteristics.* Whereas inmates of custodial institutions were mainly felons, those of reformatories were usually misdemeanants or even less serious offenders. Developers of the reformatory plan aimed at rehabilitating women who, as Katherine Bement Davis put it, "led immoral lives or 'acted on impulse'." Reformatory populations included women convicted of petty larceny, prostitution, and vagrancy and of even less serious offenses like "being in danger of falling into vice," "lewd and lascivious carriage," and "waywardness."

Not surprisingly, women committed to the reformatories tended to be young. During their early years, some reformatories had populations in which the majority of inmates were between sixteen and twenty-five years old. A few states went so far as to prohibit their reformatories from receiving women over thirty on the theory that older women were unlikely to reform.

Racially, too, reformatories differed in their populations from custodial institutions for women. Whereas disproportionate numbers of blacks were incarcerated in the latter, the former held mainly whites, particularly during the institutions' early years. Evidently judges were ready to save white women by committing them to reformatories but were reluctant to similarly save women of color, deeming the latter less worthy of rehabilitative efforts. Another factor which worked to exclude blacks was racial prejudice on the part of the institutions themselves. Two southern reformatories openly refused to receive black women during their first years of operation, and there are indications in admission ledgers of at least one northern reformatory that its early administrators did not even consider the possibility of non-white commitments.

3. *Administration.* In contrast to custodial institutions, the reformatories were run entirely by women, and these women enjoyed high degrees of administrative independence. Most states required by law that their reformatory be superintended by a woman, and some specified that she should hire mainly female staff. Thus not only the guards but also the physician and head farmer were women in some reformatories. This emphasis on female staff was in part a result of the conviction (expressed most strongly by female reformers themselves) that only other women could understand and deal with the problems of female offenders.

4. *Approaches to Discipline.* Women's institutions of the custodial type approached discipline in a manner similar to that of the men's prisons with which they were associated, albeit less consistently. Women's reformatories, in contrast, "feminized" prison discipline, stressing individualization of treatment, mildness in punishments, and a noninstitutional, homelike atmosphere. Discipline in women's reformatories was further congruent with the female gender role in its emphasis on sexual purity and its tendency to infantilize inmates. This translation of rehabilitation into feminine terms was very much influenced by the social feminist and social purity movements that themselves helped precipitate the reformatory movement.

5. *Programs.* Work programs in reformatories consisted mainly of training in cleaning, cooking, sewing and waiting on tables. Although inmates of custodial institutions were also assigned to maintenance chores, the reformatories glorified such activities, even to the point of offering courses in them. One, for instance, set up a Cooking Department with worktables, sinks, and stoves so that inmates could be instructed in food preparation. Many provided instruction in different types of knitting and sewing, courses which might culminate with production of one's "parole outfit." The reformatories developed such vocational programs because they aimed at producing proper women who would, on release, assume positions as domestic servants or marry and become good wives. A New York report of 1927 on the Western House of Refuge explained that "no industries are maintained, but every inmate is taught to cook and care for a home."

Diffusion, Decline, and Eventual Demise of the Reformatory Model

The movement to establish reformatories for women did not affect all regions of the country equally. It was strongest in the Northeast, where the social feminist and social purity movements also took strongest hold. Nearly every state in the Northeast established a reformatory, and New York founded three. Eight of the twelve states in the north central area also established reformatories. However, although the reformatory model had originated in the north central region (in the Detroit House of Shelter, the Indiana Reformatory Institution, and the 1870 Cincinnati prison convention), by the late 1870s leadership of the movement had passed to the northeastern states. Moreover, the north central institutions were seldom as successful as their eastern counterparts in achieving reformatory ideals: they tended to provide weaker programs; few made consistent use of the indeterminate sentence; only one placed an upper limit on the age of women who might be received; and several (such as the crowded, unambitious institution at Marysville, Ohio) made little effort to achieve reformatory aims.

The South was not entirely unaffected by the reformatory movement, for three institutions of this type were established in the region (in Arkansas, North Carolina, and Virginia). But in the southern reformatory movement, indigenous women's groups were less involved. The reformatory in Arkansas, for example, was established largely through the work of Martha P. Falconer, a visitor from the Northeast. Southern reformatories were less likely than those of the North to be entirely separate from institutions for men; only one of the three adopted the cottage plan; none placed an upper limit on the age of women who might be received; and only one, in North Carolina, excluded felons. Thus the women's reformatory movement was less extensive in the South and produced relatively weak institutions.

The West was even less affected than the South by the reformatory movement. Only California established a women's prison designed along reformatory lines, and that in 1929, when the movement had nearly run out of steam. The California Institution for Women took felons from the start, and after its first few years of operation it entirely excluded misdemeanants, the traditional reformatory population. Moreover, this institution at Techachapi was so remote that in time it was abandoned as a reformatory for women, its population being relocated to Frontera in 1952.

Women's prisons that had begun as reformatories now changed character, perforce incorporating elements of the custodial model. This debasement of the reformatory plan caused little dismay among members of the women's groups that traditionally had backed women's reformatories, however. By 1935, the women's reformatory movement had run its course, having largely achieved its objective (establishment of separate prisons run by women) in those regions of the country most involved with Progressive reforms in general. Moreover, by the 1930s alarm over prostitution and venereal disease had abated and the attention of penologists had begun to shift from rehabilitation of individuals to efficient management of the statewide prison systems (see, e.g., New York State Prison Survey Committee 1920). Thus, around 1935, states stopped building institutions according to the reformatory model, and the reformatory movement drew to a close.

THE THIRD STAGE, 1935–80: A BRIEF OVERVIEW OF RECENT DEVELOPMENTS

The third stage in the development of the women's prison system is less clear-cut in character than the previous two, in part because no distinctive model or type emerged during this period, in part because regional patterns differed greatly. In what follows, I combine the chronological with a regional approach, looking at developments in the women's prison system in, first, the northeastern and north central states, then those of the South, and finally those of the West.

By 1935, most northeastern and north central states were sending female felons to the institutions that had originated as reformatories, and the idealistic reformatory movement had died of exhaustion. The former reformatories naturally began to incorporate aspects of the custodial model, including its tradition of less adequate care for female than for male prisoners. Outsiders took little interest in the plight of female felons, and prison officials devoted the bulk of attention and resources to problems in men's institutions; thus inadequacies of women's prisons took low priority, just as they had in women's custodial institutions from the early nineteenth century.

To understand the nature of developments in the South in the post-1935 period, it is necessary to step back a moment to get a longer-term view of the evolution of women's prison in the region. After the Civil War, many southern states established or rebuilt some sort of penal institution for men in or near which female prisoners were also held. In some states, this was a penitentiary to which a custodial unit for women was appended and maintained until overcrowding forced establishment of a separate prison for women. The latter event, with few exceptions, occurred in 1930–80. This route of maintaining women's institutions as adjuncts to men's penitentiaries was taken, for example, by North Carolina, which held felons of both sexes together at the state prison at Raleigh until lack of beds forced removal in 1933 of the women to old prison buildings on the outskirts of town; over the years new buildings were added to the plant, and the North Carolina women's prison remains at the Raleigh location only today.

Despite the many variations, the women's prisons established and operated in the South since the 1930s have shared two traits. First, as in the previous period, their populations were overwhelmingly black. Second, nearly all of these institutions conformed to the custodial model—often with a vengeance. They were usually more crowded than the women's institutions of other regions, in some cases appallingly so; and their programs were even weaker. Often crammed into unsanitary dormitories without the slightest opportunity for privacy, at times brutalized sexually, either abandoned to idleness or assigned to hard and at times crippling labor, women incarcerated in southern prisons in 1935–80 generally had poorer care than women prisoners in other regions during that time (see, e.g., Murton 1969).

Until the 1960s, provision for female prisoners in the West remained at a stage out of which eastern states had begun to move about a century earlier. Only California had established a separate institution for women, and that only after a titanic struggle between women's groups and the state prison bureaucracy (Monahan 1941). Other western states, having few female prisoners, continued to hold them in a central penal institution. Sometimes locked in a second-story room of the administration building, sometimes tucked away in a small annex of their own, these prisoners experienced the same disadvantages as had women held in the mid-nineteenth century in institutions like Auburn and the Ohio Penitentiary. Occasionally they were supervised by the warden's wife or a hired matron, but often they were left alone, vulnerable to each other and male staff. Because they were few in number, they did not seem to warrant the expense of special programs and equipment; yet they were isolated from the resources of the male population. As late as 1979, Montana and Utah were apparently still relying on the old solution of holding female state prisoners in small appendages to their central prisons for men.

During the 1960s and 1970s, however, nearly all of the other western states created a women's prison system where none had been before by establishing seven separate institutions for women. This sudden expansion was caused mainly by over-crowding and, frequently, decrepitude of the older units for women. Six of the seven new institutions (in Arizona, Colorado, Nevada, New Mexico, Oregon, and Wyoming) basically continued in the custodial tradition.

The seventh of these recently established western prisons, Washington's Purdy Treatment Center, has been hailed as "the best women's prison in the country." When it opened in 1971, Purdy consisted of "low brick and concrete buildings [that] face a landscaped and paved inner courtyard"; its architects were said to have "captured more of a community college atmosphere than that of a prison."

In the design and operation of Purdy, we can perhaps detect the emergence (albeit tentative) of a third model of women's prison, one which rejects the traditions of both custodialism and the reformatory and might be called a *campus model*. During its first years, Purdy attempted to provide rehabilitative programs and to be sensitive to the special needs of women (thus rejecting the custodial tradition) and at the same time to avoid treating its inmates as children (thus turning its back on the reformatory model). Yet it is debatable whether Purdy achieved a radical break with the women's prison system's legacy of differential treatment.

Women's prison history has implications for policy as well as theory, indicating alternatives to current practices. Today, for example, there is growing concern to preserve the ties between incarcerated women and their children (Haley 1977). Lessons can be learned from the reformatories, many of which allowed prisoners to keep their infants. The past can also instruct when it comes to so-called coed prisons. Within the last several decades, a number of states and the federal system have returned to the nineteenth-century practice of holding women and men together (Anderson 1978). These experiments have increased the range of opportunities available to women, but due to women's own hesitancy or unwitting discouragement by staff, they may not use these opportunities to full advantage. As in the outside world, moreover, women tend to get in more trouble when there is illicit contact between the sexes (SchWeber 1980). History suggests that the potential benefits of coed prisons cannot be realized unless there are equal numbers of men and women and an administrative sensitivity to forces which push women toward the end of the line.

This leads to a third policy area, the current pressure for equal treatment of male and female prisoners. Differential treatment, over time, has been a product of unequal numbers as well as of gender-role assumptions. As Beaumont and de Toqueville pointed out in the early nineteenth century, "It is because they [female prisoners] occupy little space ... that they have been neglected" (1833/1964, p. 72). If equal treatment is to be achieved or even attempted, the implications of the "numbers" problems will have to be faced. Equal treatment will necessarily involve much greater expenditure on female prisoners since it is more costly to operate institutions for relatively few. The current economic situation and crisis of overcrowding within prisons—not to mention nearly two hundred years of differential care—suggest that equal treatment of female prisoners will not be achieved in the foreseeable future.

REFERENCES

Alpert, Geoffrey P., and John J. Wiorkowski. 1977. "Female Prisoners and Legal Services." *Quarterly Journal of Corrections* 1 (4): 28–33.

American Correctional Association. 1980. *Directory 1980*. College Park, Md.: American Correctional Association.

Anderson, David C. 1978. "Co-Corrections." *Corrections Magazine* 4 (3): 33–42.

Arditi, Ralph R., Fredrick Goldberg, Jr., M. Martha Hartle, John H. Peters, and William R. Phelps. 1973. "The Sexual Segregation of American Prisons." *Yale Law Journal* 82:1229–73.

Arkansas Penitentiary Study Commission. 1968. *Report of the Arkansas Penitentiary Study Commission*. Little Rock: Arkansas Department of Corrections.

Banner, Lois. 1974. *Women in Modern America: A Brief History*. New York: Harcourt Brace Jovanovich.

Barnes, Harry Elmer. 1972. *The Story of Punishment*. 2d ed., rev. Montclair, N.J.: Patterson Smith. Originally published 1930.

Barrows, Isabel C. 1910. "The Reformatory Treatment of Women in the United States." In *Penal and Reformatory Institutions*, edited by Charles Richmond Henderson. New York: Charities Publication Committee.

Beaumont, Gustave de, and Alexis de Tocqueville. 1964. *On the Penitentiary System in the United States, and Its Application in France*. Carbondale: Southern Illinois University Press. Originally published 1833.

Bird, Maryann. 1979. "The Women in Prison: No Escape From Stereotyping." *New York Times* (June 23).

Brenzel, Barbara. 1980. "Domestication as Reform: A Study of the Socialization of Wayward Girls, 1856–1905." *Harvard Educational Review* 50:196–213.

Brockway, Zebulon Reed. 1969. *Fifty Years of Prison Service: An Autobiography*. Montclair, N.J.: Patterson Smith. Originally published 1912.

Burkhart, Kathryn W. 1973. *Women in Prison*. Garden City, N.Y.: Doubleday & Co.

Butler, June Rainsford. 1934. "A Study of Some Reformatory Systems for Women Offenders in the United States, with Particular Reference to the Industrial Farm Colony at Kinston, North Carolina." M.A. thesis, University of North Carolina at Chapel Hill.

Carpenter, Mary. 1969. *Our Convicts*. Vol. 1. Montclair, N.J.: Patterson Smith. Originally published 1864.

Coffin, Mrs. C. F. [Rhoda]. 1886. "Women's Prisons." In National Prison Association, *Proceedings for 1885*. Boston: Geo. E. Crosby & Co.

Connelly, Mark Thomas. 1980. *The Response to Prostitution in the Progressive Era*. Chapel Hill: University of North Carolina Press.

Conway, Jill. 1976. "Women Reformers and American Culture, 1870–1930." In *Our American Sisters: Women in American Life and Thought*, edited by Jean E. Friedman and William G. Shade. 2d ed. Boston: Allyn & Bacon.

Crawford, William. 1969. *Report on the Penitentiaries of the United States*. Montclair, N.J.: Patterson Smith. Originally published 1835.

Crofton, Sir Walter. 1871. "The Irish System of Prison Discipline." In *Transactions of the National Congress on Penitentiary and Reformatory Discipline*, edited by E. C. Wines. Albany, N.Y.: Weed, Parsons.

Currie, Elliott Park. 1973. "Managing the Minds of Men: The Reformatory Movement, 1865–1920." Ph.D. dissertation, University of California, Berkeley.

Davis, Katherine Bement. 1911. "A Reformatory for Women." *Ohio Bulletin of Charities and Correction* 2:43–48.

Detroit House of Correction. 1869. *Seventh Annual Report of the Officers of the Detroit House of Correction . . . 1868*. Detroit: Free Press Book and Job Printing House.

Dix, Dorothea Lynde. 1967. *Remarks on Prisons and Prison Discipline in the United States*. 2d ed. Montclair, N.J.: Patterson Smith. Originally published 1845.

Farnham, E. W. 1846. Notes and illustrations to M. B. Sampson, *Rationale of Crime and Its Appropriate Treatment: Being a Treatise on Criminal Jurisprudence Considered in Relation to Cerebral Organization*. From the 2d ed. New York: D. Appleton.

Feldman, Egal. 1967. "Prostitution, the Alien Woman and the Progressive Imagination, 1910–1915." *American Quarterly* 19:192–206.

Fernald, Mabel Ruth, Mary H. S. Hayes, and Almena Dawley. 1920. *A Study of Women Delinquents in New York State*. New York: Century.

Flynn, Edith Elisabeth. 1971. "The Special Problems of Female Offenders." In National Conference of Corrections, *Proceedings, December 5–8, 1971*, pp. 113–17.

Foucault, Michel. 1977. *Discipline and Punish: The Birth of the Prison*. New York: Pantheon Books.

Freedman, Estelle B. 1974. "Their Sisters' Keepers: An Historical Perspective on Female Correctional Institutions in the United States: 1870–1900." *Feminist Studies* 2:77–95.

———. 1976. "Their Sisters' Keepers: The Origins of Female Corrections in America." Ph.D. dissertation, Columbia University.

———. 1981. *Their Sisters' Keepers: Women's Prison Reform in America, 1830–1930*. Ann Arbor: University of Michigan Press.

Fry, Elizabeth. 1847. *Memoir of the Life of Elizabeth Fry with Extracts from her Journal and Letters*, edited by two of her daughters, in 2 vols. Philadelphia: J. W. Moore.

Giallombardo, Rose, 1966. *Society of Women: A Study of a Women's Prison*. New York: John Wiley & Sons.

Gibson, Helen E. 1973. "Women's Prisons: Laboratories for Penal Reform." *Wisconsin Law Review* 1973, pp. 210–33.

Glick, Ruth M. and Virginia V. Neto. 1977. *National Study of Women's Correctional Programs*. Washington, D.C.: Government Printing Office.

Glueck, Sheldon, and Eleanor T. Glueck. 1934. *Five Hundred Delinquent Women*. New York: Alfred A. Knopf.

Hahn, Nicolas Fischer [Nicole H. Rafter]. 1980a. "Female State Prisoners in Tennessee: 1831–1979." *Tennessee Historical Quartery* 39:485–97.

———. [Nicole H. Rafter]. 1980b. "Too Dumb to Know Better: Cacogenic Family Studies and the Criminology of Women." *Criminology* 18:3–25.

Haley, Kathleen. 1977. "Mothers behind Bars: A Look at the Parental Rights of Incarcerated Women." *New England Journal of Prison Law* 4:141–55.

Hindelang, Michael J. 1979. "Sex Differences in Criminal Activity." *Social Problems* 27:143–56.

Hindelang, Michael J., Michael R. Gottfredson, and Timothy J. Flanagan, eds. 1981. *Sourcebook of Criminal Justice Statistics—1980*. Washington, D.C.: Government Printing Office.

Horne, Jim, Hazel Robinson, Lora Stonefeld, and Martha Wandel. N.d. "Female Recidivism in Washington from 1966–1976." Unpublished manuscript. Seattle: University of Washington.

Ignatieff, Michael. 1981. "State, Civil Society, and Total Institutions: A Critique of Recent Social Histories of Punishment." In *Crime and Justice: An Annual Review of Research*, vol. 3, edited by Michael Tonry and Norval Morris. Chicago: University of Chicago Press.

Indiana Reformatory Institution for Women and Girls. 1874, 1876, 1877. *Report of the Indiana Reformatory Institution for Women and Girls*. Indianapolis: Sentinel Co.

Indiana Senate. 1869. *Indiana Senate Journal*, March 3, 1869. Indianapolis: Alexander H. Conner, State Printer.

Indiana State Prison South. 1869. *Annual Report of the Officers and Directors of the Indiana State Prison, South.* Indianapolis: Alexander H. Conner, State Printer.

――――. 1874. *Annual Report of the Directors and Officers of the Indiana State Prison, South. December 15, 1873.* Indianapolis: Sentinel Co.

Johnson, Ellan C. 1891. "Discipline in Female Prisons." In National Prison Association, *Proceedings for 1891*, pp. 137–43.

Kansas Women's Industrial Farm. 1920. *Second Biennial Report of the Women's Industrial Farm . . . for the Two Years Ending June 30, 1920.* Topeka: State Prison.

Kennedy, John S. 1921. "Report to the Governor relative to the Investigation and Inquiry into Allegations of Cruelty to Prisoners in the New York State Reformatory for Women, Bedford Hills." In New York State Commission of Prisons, *Annual Report for 1920*, Ossining, N.Y.: Sing Sing Prison.

Laub, John. 1980. "Criminal Behavior and the Urban-Rural Dimension." Ph.D. Dissertation, State University of New York at Albany.

Lekkerkerker, Eugenia Cornelia. 1931. *Reformatories for Women in the United States.* Batavia, Holland: Biij J. B. Wolters' Uitgevers-Maatschappij.

Lewis, Orlando F. 1967. *The Development of American Prisons and Prison Customs, 1776–1845.* Montclair, N.J.: Patterson Smith. Originally published 1922.

Lewis, W. David. 1961. "The Female Criminal and the Prisons of New York, 1825–1845." *New York History* 42:215–36.

――――. 1965. *From Newgate to Dannemora: The Rise of the Penitentiary in New York, 1796–1848.* Ithaca, N.Y.: Cornell University Press.

――――. 1971. "Eliza Wood Burhans Farnham." In *Notable American Women 1607–1950*, vol. 1, edited by Edward T. James, Janet Wilson James, and Paul S. Boyer. Cambridge, Mass.: Harvard University Press, Belknap Press.

Lieber, Francis. 1964. "Translator's Preface." In G. de Beaumont and A. de Tocqueville, *On the Penitentiary System in the United States, and Its Application in France.* Carbondale: Southern Illinois University Press. Originally published 1833.

McKelvey, Blake. 1972. *American Prisons: A Study in American Social History Prior to 1915.* Montclair, N.J.: Patterson Smith. Originally published 1936.

Martineau, Harriet. 1838. *Retrospect of Western Travel.* Vol. 1. London: Saunders & Otley.

Mennel, Robert M. 1973. *Thorns and Thistles: Juvenile Delinquents in the United States, 1825–1940.* Hanover, N.H.: University Press of New England.

Monahan, Florence. 1941. *Women in Crime.* New York: Ives Washburn.

Murton, Tom. 1969. *Accomplices to the Crime.* New York: Grove Press.

Nagel, William G. 1973. *The New Red Barn: A Critical Look at the Modern American Prison.* New York: Walker & Co.

New York Auburn State Prison. 1833. *Annual Report of the Auburn State Prison* [for 1832]. N.Y. Sen. Doc. no. 20.

New York Bedford State Reformatory. 1911. *Tenth Annual Report of the Board of Managers . . . for the year ending September 30, 1910.* N.Y. Sen. Doc no. 23.

New York Committee on State Prisons. 1832. *Report of the Commitee on State Prisons.* N.Y. Sen. Doc. no. 74.

New York Hudson House of Refuge. 1890. *Annual Report of the Board of Managers . . . for Year Ending September 30, 1889.* Albany: James B. Lyon (Ass. Doc. no. 50).

New York Inspectors of State Prisons. 1801. *An Account of the State Prison or Penitentiary House, in the City of New-York.* New York: Isaac Colling & Son.

————. 1852. *Fourth Annual Report of the Inspectors of State Prisons of the State of New York.* N.Y. Sen. Doc. no. 35.

New York Mount Pleasant State Prison. Various years. *Report of the Inspectors of the Mount Pleasant State Prison.* N.Y. Sen. Docs., 1831 (no. 3), 1836 (no. 23), 1844 (no. 20), 1845 (no. 9), 1847 (no. 5).

————. 1848. *Report of the Minority of the Late Board of Inspectors of the Mount Pleasant State Prison.* N.Y. Sen. Doc. No. 17.

New York Western House of Refuge for Women. 1899, 1918. *Annual Report.* N.Y. Ass. Doc. no. 25, (1899), 20 (1918).

New York State Commission of Correction. 1927. *Annual Report for 1927.*

New York State Prison Survey Committee. 1920. *Report.* Albany: J. B. Lyon.

Ohio Penitentiary. 1880. *Annual Report of the Directors and Warden for the Year 1880.* Columbus: G. J. Brand & Co.

O'Neill, William L. 1969. *Everyone Was Brave: The Rise and Fall of Feminism in America.* Chicago: Quadrangle Books.

Oregon Advisory Committee to the U.S. Commission on Civil Rights. January 1976. *Civil and Human Rights in Oregon State Prisons.*

Pivar, David J. 1973. *Purity Crusade: Sexual Morality and Social Control, 1868–1900.* Westport, Conn.: Greenwood Press.

Platt, Anthony M. 1977. *The Child Savers: The Invention of Delinquency.* 2d ed., enlarged. Chicago: University of Chicago Press.

Potter, Joan. 1978. "In Prison, Women Are Different." *Corrections Magazine* (December), pp. 14–24.

Quarles, Mary Ann Stillman. 1966. "Organizational Analysis of the New Jersey Reformatory for Women in Relation to Stated Principles of Corrections, 1913–1963." Ph.D. dissertation, Boston University.

Rafter, Nicole Hahn. 1982. "Hard Times: Custodial Prisons for Women and the Example of the New York State Prison for Women at Auburn, 1893–1933." In *Judge, Lawyer, Victim, Thief: Women, Gender Roles, and Criminal Justice*, edited by Nicole H. Rafter and Elizabeth A. Stanko. Boston: Northeastern University Press.

————. Forthcoming. "Chastising the Unchaste: Social Control Functions of a Women's Reformatory, 1894–1931." In *Social Control and the State: Comparative and Historical Essays*, edited by A. Scull and S. Cohen. Oxford: Martin Robertson.

Reeves, Margaret. 1929. *Training Schools for Delinquent Girls.* New York: Russell Sage Foundation.

Resch, John P. 1972. "Ohio Adult Penal System, 1850–1900: A Study in the Failure of Institutional Reform." *Ohio History* 81:236–62.

Resnik, Judith, and Nancy Shaw. 1980. "Prisoners of their Sex: Health Problems of Incarcerated Women." In *Prisoner's Rights Source Book: Theory, Litigation, and Practice*, vol. 2, edited by Ira P. Robbins. New York: Clark Boardman.

Robert, Jeanne. 1917. "The Care of Women in State Prisons." In *Prison Reform*, edited by Corrine Bacon. New York: H. W. Wilson.

Robinson, Louis N. 1921. *Penology in the United States*. Philadelphia: John C. Winston.

Rogers, Helen Worthington. 1929. "A History of the Movement to Establish a State Reformatory for Women in Connecticut." *Journal of Criminal Law and Criminology* 19:518–41.

Rothman, David J. 1971. *The Discovery of the Asylum: Social Order and Disorder in the New Republic*. Boston: Little, Brown.

Schlossman, Steven. 1977. *Love and the American Delinquent: The Theory and Practice of "Progressive" Juvenile Justice, 1825–1920*. Chicago: University of Chicago Press.

Schlossman, Steven, and Stephanie Wallach. 1978. "The Crime of Precocious Sexuality: Female Juvenile Delinquency in the Progressive Era." *Harvard Educational Review* 48:65–94.

SchWeber Claudine. 1980. "Beauty Marks and Blemishes: The Co-ed Prison as a Microcosm of Integrated Society." Paper read at 1980 meeting of the Academy of Criminal Justice Sciences, Oklahoma.

———. 1982. " 'The Government's Unique Experiment in Salvaging Women Criminals': Cooperation and Conflict in the Administration of a Women's Prison." In *Judge, Lawyer, Victim, Thief: Women, Gender Roles and Criminal Justice*. Edited by Nicole H. Rafter and Elizabeth A. Stanko, Boston: Northeastern University Press.

Scott, Joseph F. 1910. "American Reformatories for Male Adults." In *Penal and Reformatory Institutions*, edited by Charles Richmond Henderson. New York: Russell Sage Foundation, Charities Publication Committee.

Singer, Linda R. 1973. "Women and the Correctional Process." *American Criminal Law Review* 11:295–308.

Thomas, David Y. 1930. *Arkansas and Its People: A History, 1541–1930*. Vol. 2. New York: American Historical Society.

U.S. Comptroller General. 1980. *Women in Prison: Inequitable Treatment Requires Action*. Washington, D.C.: Government Printing Office.

U.S. Department of Justice, Bureau of Justice Statistics. October–November 1982. "Prisoners at Midyear 1982," Bulletin NCJ-84875. Washington, D.C.: Department of Justice.

U.S. General Accounting Office. 1979. *Female Offenders: Who Are They and What Are the Problems Confronting Them?* Washington, D.C.: Government Printing Office.

U.S. House of Representatives, Committee on the Judiciary. 1979. *Hearings Before the Subcommittee on Courts* . . . , 96th Cong. 1st sess., pts. 1 and 2 (October 10 and 11).

Van Wyck, Mrs. Katherine. 1913. "Reformatory for Women—Wisconsin's Outstanding Need." In Wisconsin Conference on Charities and Corrections, *Proceedings, October 5–8, 1912*. Madison: Democrat Printing Co.

Vaux, Roberts. 1826. *Notices of the Original, and Successive Efforts, To Improve the Discipline of the Prison at Philadelphia and To Reform the Criminal Code of Pennsylvania: With a Few Observations on the Penitentiary System*. Philadelphia: Kimber & Sharpless.

Victor, Mrs. Sarah Maria. 1887. *The Life Story of Sarah M. Victor*. . . . Cleveland: Williams Publishing Co.

Voight, Lloyd L. 1949. *History of California Correctional Administration from 1930 to 1948*. San Francisco: n.p.

Ward, David A., and Gene G. Kassebaum. 1965. *Women's Prison: Sex and Social Structure*. Chicago: Aldine Publishing Co.

Welter, Barbara. 1966. "The Cult of True Womanhood." *American Quarterly* 18:151–74.

Wheaton, Liz. 1979. "Rewarding Neglect: A New Women's Prison." *ACLU Women's Rights Report* 1 (3): 5–6.

Wines, E. C., ed. 1871. *Transactions of the National Congress on Penitentiary and Reformatory Discipline*. Albany, N.Y.: Weed, Parsons.

Wines, E. C., and Theodore W. Dwight. 1867. *Report on the Prisons and Reformatories of the United States and Canada*. Albany, N.Y.: Van Benthuysen & Sons.

Wisconsin State Prison. 1926. *Twenty-second Biennial Report of the Wisconsin State Prison for the* . . . *Period ending June 30, 1926*.

Young, Clifford M. 1932. *Women's Prisons Past and Present and Other New York State Prison History*. Elmira Reformatory: Summary Press.

Zaretsky, Eli. 1976. *Capitalism, the Family, and Personal Life*. New York: Harper Colophon.

CHAPTER 2

The Legal Environment of Incarceration

One of the most fundamental propositions about prisons is that they are part of the larger social, political, and economic environments. Shifts in the age structure of society can have major consequences for prison managers. A precipitous increase in the number of 12- to 13-year-olds in the general population can lead to more prison admissions in five to six years. Declines in the economy can leave a prison organization with less operating capital than in times when the tax base was wider and stronger. Conservative crime control policies can lead to increases in the number of offenders sent to prison as well as affect the amount of time a felon can expect to serve in prison. The current fad of long determinate sentences (e.g., three strikes laws, habitual offender laws) can lead to more prisoners staying in prison for longer periods of time. Prison managers will therefore have to provide programming to these long-term populations for many years at great expense.

Prisons do not exist in a vacuum. They are impacted by developments, trends, and changes that occur with regularity in the larger society. The same can be said of legal changes as well. In general, the offenders flowing into prison today originate from the same segments of society as in times past. However, the way in which we manage prisons today is a far cry from management principles in effect three, or even two, decades ago. Until around 1960, prisons were isolated from the rest of society. Inmate complaints about mistreatment fell on deaf ears. For the most part policy makers were indifferent to the needs and concerns of prisoners. The judiciary deferred to the expertise of prison wardens when it came to the internal affairs of prisons. Judges abided by a "hands-off doctrine" in which they left the control and order of prisons to the custody staff. Inmates were regarded and treated as slaves of the state.

The hands-off doctrine ended or died in the late 1960s as a result of federal judges who intervened in the internal operations of prisons. Yet the hands-off doctrine began to erode in 1954 when the Supreme Court, as a result of *Brown v. Board of Education,* ushered in a new era of democratization in which many disadvantaged persons were extended the same rights and protections as other citizens. This historic ruling set the context in which all persons have a right to be heard and that no one will be denied access to the legal system.

This chapter considers the evolution of the hands-off doctrine and how it affected the operation of prisons. The reader will also gain insights into how and why the iron curtain between prisons and judiciary was brought down by inmate lawsuits and judicial intervention that began in the early 1960s. The student will also come to understand that with litigation comes change and prison organizations have changed dramatically in the last two to three decades. Perhaps most important, the reader will come to realize that while prison walls may be made of concrete and wire, they cannot restrain or deflect the forces of change that occur in the broader human community.

The Legacy and Future of Corrections Litigation

SUSAN STURM

There is little doubt that litigation has profoundly changed the conditions and practices in correctional institutions. The most far-reaching and significant effects of litigation have been on the structure, organization, and relationship of corrections to the larger community. These changes in turn affect the capacity of correctional leadership to manage and improve the quality of life in correctional institutions. The following are examples of such changes.

LITIGATION HAS CONTRIBUTED TO A GREATER UNDERSTANDING AND ACCEPTANCE OF CONSTITUTIONAL STANDARDS GOVERNING CORRECTIONAL INSTITUTIONS

There is strong evidence that litigation has fostered the development of norms and standards of minimally adequate treatment of inmates within correctional systems. Virtually every case study of judicial intervention in cor-

Source: Excerpted from Sturm, Susan. The Legacy and Future of Corrections Litigation, *University of Pennsylvania Law Review* 142: 639–738, 1993.

rectional institutions recounts the internal development of correctional standards to govern future practices and conduct within the institution, following major litigation invalidating the conditions and practices in those institutions. The court in *Holt v. Hutto* summarized the shift in Arkansas from official resistance to official adoption of judicially imposed norms and standards as the policy of the institution.

Of course, litigation is not solely responsible for the growing internalization of professional norms. Independent efforts within the corrections field, such as the emergence of a network of professional organizations that promulgate standards and the incorporation of these standards in state statutes and administrative regulations, have also contributed to this development. However, litigation and professionalization have not occurred in isolation. Litigators and courts rely on professional standards and experts to evaluate the adequacy of conditions and practices and to apply those standards in a particular institutional context. The corrections field has, in turn, developed standards, rules, and regulations with an eye toward avoiding further judicial intervention. Litigation has thus played a major role in the development and further refinement of professional standards and oversight.

LITIGATION HAS CONTRIBUTED TO THE PROFESSIONALIZATION OF CORRECTIONS LEADERSHIP AND PROGRAMMATIC STAFF

Corrections litigation has prompted the professionalization of correctional leadership, both in many individual cases and in the corrections field more generally. Twenty years ago, many correctional administrators had little training or expertise in management. Often, the corrections commissioners or directors were purely political appointments. As long as administrators maintained a low profile and avoided major scandals or disturbances, their performance remained insulated from public scrutiny. The corrections field lacked any effective political or institutional incentives to develop performance standards and mechanisms for holding administrators accountable.

LITIGATION HAS CONTRIBUTED TO THE BUREAUCRATIZATION OF CORRECTIONAL INSTITUTIONS

Court intervention has fostered the centralization of correctional management and the formalization of decision-making within correctional institutions. Litigation requires corrections officials to account for a wide range of activities and conditions in their institutions. This requirement has prompted the development of improved information systems, extensive documentation, and rational, visible decision-making. Partly in response to litigation, officials have developed regularized procedures governed by written rules and regulations such that "every prison and jail in the United States . . .

must work within the structure of modern bureaucratic organization. Litigation's transformative impact occurred most dramatically in southern prisons, which moved from prebureaucratic plantation-style systems to modern bureaucracies. The case studies document that governance by personal dominance and official sanctioned brutality is a thing of the past. Many scholars argue that the move toward bureaucracy has led to safer, less arbitrary, and more human institutions.

LITIGATION IS ASSOCIATED WITH SHORT-TERM DEMORALIZATION OF STAFF AND DISRUPTION OF INSTITUTIONAL ORDER

A number of commentators have observed that litigation contributes, at least in the short run, to inmate violence and staff demoralization by raising inmates' expectations, undermining prison officials' authority, widening the gap between administration and staff, and by limiting the discretion of prison officials *vis-à-vis* inmates. The most frequent cited studies, however, fail to establish a causal chain between violence and litigation. Others have attributed violence following litigation to abdication by prison administrators and staff of responsibility for developing legitimate forms of inmate control to replace the traditional, repressive control mechanisms invalidated by the courts. Similar short-term reactions have been observed in connection with purely administrative attempts to reform programs and organization, suggesting that any attempt at prison reform will initially trigger destabilization and resistance. Case studies analyzing the impact of litigation suggest with virtual unanimity that even when violence and turmoil occur, they may well be short-lived and may give way to effective and legal methods of control over inmate behavior.

LITIGATION HAS INCREASED THE VISIBILITY AND ACCOUNTABILITY OF CORRECTIONS

Litigation has opened corrections institutions to scrutiny by lawyers, judges, state and local agencies, and the media. Institutions previously insulated from rigorous scrutiny by their remote locations, the lack of public concern over their inadequacies, and their careful control over public access face regular evaluation by lawyers, state agencies, and the courts. The sustained presence of outsiders, particularly inmates' lawyers, has reduced some of the more egregious practices and has led to greater adherence to rules and regulations. In some cases, litigation has led to the institution of regular inspections by state agencies charged with overseeing compliance with state health and safety regulations. Litigation has also generated considerable media coverage of prison conditions. Virtually every case study reports extensive media coverage of the litigation and the conditions and practices in the targeted institutions. This media coverage exposed serious abuses and inhumane conditions in correctional institutions, and is widely credited with increasing public awareness of the inadequacies in correctional institutions and acceptance of the need for reform.

In sum, litigation has had a considerable effect on the organization, leadership, and structure of corrections institutions. It has fostered the acceptance of norms and standards governing correctional institutions, contributed to the professionalization of corrections leadership, prompted the rationalization and formalization of correctional institutions, and increased their visibility and accountability. Litigation has also been associated with short-term demoralization of staff and disruption of institutional order.

LITIGATION'S IMPACT ON CONDITIONS AND PRACTICES

The case studies also show that court intervention generally has improved the living conditions and practices in the facilities at issue. In some cases, the improvements linked to court-ordered change have been quite dramatic and have concerned virtually every aspect of inmate life. Yet, in many systems improvements have been limited to raising living conditions to minimal standards, and have failed to provide a systemic response to the overcrowding problem plaguing most correctional institutions.

The most blatant abuses, such as Arkansas's Tucker telephone, Alabama's "doghouses," and widespread use of officially sanctioned violence, have been virtually eliminated, often in direct response to litigation. The case studies also show that in many instances, previous legislative and administrative efforts to eliminate these abuses had been unsuccessful, and that litigation was a crucial factor in exposing and correcting these abuses.

The case studies suggest that litigation may be particularly successful in improving the quality of medical care and physical conditions in targeted institutions. Even in cases where compliance has otherwise been uneven, litigation has led to the development and maintenance of a vastly improved system of medical care.

Litigation has virtually eliminated the use of inmates as trusties or building tenders. This system of governance, which relied on inmates to manage other inmates and maintain order, prevailed in many Southern institutions and contributed strongly to the arbitrary and violent environment that characterized prison life. Its elimination dramatically transformed the structure of governance in Southern prisons and eliminated some of the worst abuses in those systems. In many jurisdictions, staffing ratios improved dramatically in response to court orders. In Alabama, once court-ordered reforms took hold, the rate of violence plummeted, and inmates reported that they felt safe in dormitories that were described as a "jungle atmosphere" prior to the litigation. Crouch and Marquart report that the Texas Department of

Corrections is a safer place as a result of the bureaucratic order instituted in response to court intervention.

In most of the cases studied involving adult institutions, litigation has not resulted in the development of progressive, state-of-the-art facilities or deinstitutionalization of offenders. For example, there is a wide consensus within the corrections field that corrections should move in the direction of small, decentralized living units governed by unit management, rather than large, centrally managed institutions. Indeed, experience suggests that a move to unit management eliminates many of the problems prompting judicial intervention. Yet, litigation does not mandate or necessarily increase the use of unit management. Courts have not interpreted the Eighth Amendment to invalidate outdated institutions that warehouse inmates, even if levels of violence are predictably higher in those institutions, as long as inmates receive the basic necessities of life. Methods of incarceration that are generally acknowledged to be ineffectual or undesirable, such as housing inmates in large, rural institutions with dormitory-style housing and little opportunity for work or education, persist in systems that achieved compliance with court orders concerning prison conditions.

The case studies reveal considerable variation in litigation's long-term impact on conditions in correctional institutions. In some cases, particularly where systematic reforms have been achieved and effective local monitoring mechanisms have been institutionalized, changes appear to have endured over time. In other cases, the studies reveal substantial backsliding in institutions that have previously made considerable progress toward achieving constitutional conditions.

The impact of judicial intervention on incarceration rates and construction of new facilities is mixed. In many overcrowding cases, courts have used caps to limit the population in facilities. The direct impact of caps on institutions is obvious; if the court enforces its order the population of the targeted facilities falls.

The more difficult issue concerns the impact of court intervention on the system's overall approach to the overcrowding problem. The case studies do not answer this question definitively. Several patterns of response emerge from the case studies. In some cases, court intervention simply failed to have any significant effect on the overcrowding problem. In a significant number of cases, administrators responded in a short run to population caps by transferring inmates to other facilities. Population limits in state correctional institutions have in some cases caused delays in the transfer of sentenced prisoners to state custody, thereby dramatically increasing overcrowding in local jails.

A second type of response to overcrowding by state and local officials or the courts involves the use of emergency or stopgap measures, such as emergency releases of inmates. In many instances, this approach has not been sufficient to alleviate overcrowding even in the short run. This type of response has sometimes triggered a strong political backlash that has limited its future availability as a population control mechanism.

A third type of response observed in most of the case studies is the expansion of the capacity of the targeted system through prison construction and increased use of temporary housing. In some of these cases, plans were already in the works for construction of new facilities, but litigation was credited by some for pushing through previously unsuccessful bond issues or expediting construction. In almost every case studied involving adult institutions, responsible officials responded to overcrowding orders at least initially by seeking to build new facilities. In some cases, "the promise of a new jail slowed down effective action" toward dealing with the overcrowding problem. Invariably, the hope that construction of new facilities alone would solve the overcrowding problem proved illusory; within a short time, the new facilities were full and population pressures continued.

ACCOUNTING FOR LITIGATION'S MIXED SUCCESS

A careful analysis of case studies of court intervention in correctional institutions suggests that the impact of litigation on conditions and practices varies considerably. In some cases litigation has prompted dramatic, systemic change that has endured for years after a court ceased active involvement. In other cases court intervention has had a more superficial impact, and positive reforms appear to be short-lived. Before attempting to explain these varying results, it is important to understand how litigation ever has a significant impact on conditions, practices, and organizational capacity in correctional institutions.

Given the view articulated by some commentators that courts lack the capacity to implement their orders, one might ask why litigation has been at all successful in promoting reform. Analysis of the case studies suggests several factors that prompt government officials to change in response to court intervention. First, discovery mechanisms and monitoring devices serve to uncover the existence of gross inadequacies in prison conditions that are otherwise insulated from sustained public scrutiny. Extensive and sustained media attention paid to corrections litigation creates pressure to address these inadequacies. Second, the case studies suggest that corrections officials are motivated to achieve compliance with court orders by an overwhelming desire to get rid of judicial involvement and oversight. "The decision makers don't like to be sued, hate going to court, and fear personal liability." Corrections officials are accustomed to considerable autonomy, resent the outside intrusion into their domain, and are extremely anxious to eliminate it. This response appears to be particularly pronounced where judicial oversight has been active and where courts have used judicial sanctions to respond to noncompliance. Third, major corrections litigation is frequently accompanied by an influx of expertise and resources that expands the capacity of government officials to manage the process of reform and to maintain constitutional facilities.

Finally, prisoners' rights litigators have developed a considerable presence in the corrections world and have been able to pursue litigation on a wide scale. In systems that have a centralized administration, administrators are likely to be aware of litigation against a major institution, even if the entire system is not under scrutiny. Unlike many areas of public interest advocacy, there is no shortage of individuals willing to file corrections litigation challenging conditions of confinement in prisons. Prisoners have both the time and inclination to file litigation. Although most of these cases never make it past a motion to dismiss, some do lead to the appointment of extremely competent counsel. Thus, many correctional administrators view litigation as a fact of life that must be addressed.

However, litigation has not been uniformly effective in either promoting constitutional compliance or prompting systemic reform. The case studies provide a basis for offering several tentative explanations for this variation in response, although they are necessarily preliminary and exploratory.

First, litigation has been identified as having the most dramatic and far-reaching structural effects in the South, where prisons previously were modeled on the plantation system, and were self-sufficient and dependent on agriculture. In the South, the courts "repudiated a long-standing and deeply ingrained approach to prisons and replaced it with an alternative model, one that was in line with the dominant view of corrections officials and organizations across the nation." This observation may reflect a more fundamental pattern: litigation may be most effective in transforming institutions that deviate from a widely shared professional social norm.

Second, case studies and assessments of litigation in corrections and other areas highlight the importance of enlisting the support of crucial insiders within the targeted system to achieve lasting reform. Both supporters and critics of judicial intervention have noted the significance of this factor in achieving system reform. For example, Sheryl Dicker, the editor of a volume containing five cases of child advocacy efforts, concludes that "advocates must find a 'partner' inside government to achieve successful implementation of reforms. Gerald Rosenberg, who is generally skeptical of the capacity of courts to achieve significant reform, concludes that courts can be effective producers of significant social reform when "[a]dministrators and officials crucial for implementation are willing to act and see court orders as a tool for leveraging additional resources or for hiding behind." Joel Handler also observes that the "bureaucratic contingency" that thwarts much judicially mandated change can be overcome by forming alliances with crucial government agencies. Harris and Spiller identified "unwillingness or inability to comply on the part of one or more necessary actors" as one of two variables explaining noncompliance with court orders.

Although cooperation of crucial insiders is an important ingredient of successful implementation, it is not a variable that remains constant or unaffected by the courts. Judicial intervention frequently affects the stance of key decision-makers toward reform. Leaders who were sympathetic to litigation at the outset sometimes become more hostile as the litigation proceeds and the adversary process takes over. Some officials who were initially skeptical or hostile to judicial intervention become more supportive as a result of constructive interactions with judicial officers or recognition of potential benefits flowing from the litigation. In addition, new leaders and staff often accompany litigation. The dynamic character of the litigation process makes reliable predictions about the level of cooperation with and the likely success of court intervention difficult.

The strategy of judicial intervention is a third factor accounting for the differential success of litigation. I have argued elsewhere that a court's capacity to intervene effectively in correctional institutions depends, at least in part, on the approach adopted by the court to manage the compliance process. I identify the catalyst approach combining a deliberative remedial formulation process with the use of traditional sanctions to induce compliance as the approach most likely to lead to successful intervention, drawing on case studies to support this conclusion. Recent case studies confirm the significance of judicial approach in defining the court's potential. Case studies also suggest that approaches encouraging mediated remedies, such as the use of court-appointed officials to assist in developing and monitoring a decree, contribute to the success of judicial intervention.

Finally, the case studies suggest that progress has been made over the last twenty years in the development of creative and constructive approaches to judicial intervention, and that the use of these approaches enhances the likelihood of achieving institutional reform. Judges and litigators have developed more cooperative forms of fact-finding, remedial formulation, and monitoring that minimize the adverse effects of the adversary process and enhance the possibility of cooperative approaches to solving the problems identified through litigation or the threat of litigation. These approaches include: (1) the use of expert panels selected by the parties to perform fact-finding, assist in developing remedies and monitor compliance; (2) the use of court-supervised mediation to achieve a consensual remedy that addresses the problems underlying constitutional violations; (3) the use of existing oversight mechanisms in the enforcement stage, such as state regulatory agencies and the accreditation process; (4) the use of monitoring mechanisms that employ defendants' employees as compliance officers; and (5) consolidation of cases involving related institutions to avoid the tendency to displace problems to institutions not under the purview of a particular court.

II. THE CONTINUED NEED FOR CORRECTIONS LITIGATION

The corrections field has progressed considerably over the past twenty years, in part as a result of litigation. This progress, along with the limited role of litigation in corrections reform, poses the issue of the continued significance of corrections litigation in the next decade. Has litigation run its course?

There is strong evidence that litigation continues to play a crucial role in achieving and maintaining minimally adequate correctional institutions, and that this need will continue through the next decade. This Section summarizes the circumstances justifying the continued need for litigation concerning conditions and practices in correctional institutions.

A. Conditions in Corrections Institutions Continue to Deprive Inmates of Minimally Adequate Living Conditions

Conditions threatening the health and safety of inmates continue to plague many correctional institutions, even in institutions that have been subject to suit. Compliance with minimal standards on constitutional decency has yet to be achieved in many of the state institutions and systems currently under court order. In numerous cases lacking vigorous judicial enforcement, little progress toward achieving and developing systems for maintaining constitutional conditions has occurred. Overcrowding has undermined the progress toward compliance made in many jurisdictions, and conditions in many jails appear to be particularly poor.

The pressures of increasing population and limited budgets account for a significant portion of the recent deterioration of conditions in correctional institutions. Between 1980 and 1990, the number of people incarcerated in the United States doubled. At the beginning of 1991, "state and federal prisons were operating at 25.1 percent over capacity.... The National Council on Crime and Delinquency projects that by 1994, the state and federal prison population will reach one million, an increase of more than 200 percent since 1980. Jails and juvenile facilities are experiencing similar increases in population.

Overcrowding threatens to overwhelm the capacity of correctional systems to maintain minimally adequate living conditions. Case after case recounts the dramatic and devastating effects of overcrowding on the conditions in corrections institutions. The observations of the court in the Rhode Island prison litigation are typical: "Overcrowding at the ISC in Mr. Gordon's opinion, has overwhelmed the institution's maintenance and support services and, therefore, it represents 'an immediate and overt threat to the inmate population.' "

In many systems that have previously achieved compliance with court orders to improve conditions and programs, overcrowding has led to a recurrence of such basic problems as violence, inadequate service delivery, unsafe living conditions, and renewed activity by the courts in response to these conditions. Many defendants have responded to population increases by seeking to modify caps to allow facilities to house additional inmates even though those facilities have already been found to be constitutionally deficient at existing population levels.

The fiscal crisis currently facing state and local governments is an additional factor undermining the progress made toward achieving minimally adequate conditions in correctional institutions. Many states and localities have attempted to cut staff and slash operating and capital budgets for corrections, even in the face of court orders and increasing populations. In many cases, drastic judicial action has been needed to prevent states from cramming inmates into already overcrowded facilities with reduced staff and services.

Overcrowding is not the type of problem that corrections administrators ordinarily can remedy without outside support. In many instances, without pressure from the courts, they receive neither the legislative and executive support necessary to redirect correctional policy, nor the resources necessary to maintain adequate levels of service delivery.

B. No Effective Check on the Conditions in Correctional Institutions Other Than Litigation or the Threat of Litigation Has Emerged

Litigation has served to open correctional institutions to public scrutiny, to hold officials accountable for the institutions they run, and to create pressure to achieve and maintain constitutional prisons and jails. The pressures toward isolation and insulation, however, lurk on the horizon. External scrutiny and accountability are crucial to prevent prisons and jails from routinely subjecting inmates to the brutal conditions that characterized the isolated institutions of yesteryear. In most jurisdictions, effective methods of holding corrections accountable have not yet developed.

There is persuasive evidence that without litigation many correctional systems will insulate themselves from scrutiny and thus prevent the disclosure of inadequate conditions that is so crucial to correctional form.

Human Rights Watch investigators report that in some institutions, their visits were carefully managed, and they were unable to visit the areas and facilities that they had specifically requested. Indeed, the report relies heavily on reported cases for its description of conditions in correctional institutions. Similarly, much of the media coverage of prison and jail conditions in recent years concerns information and assessments obtained through litigation. Without litigation, the salutary role played by the media in exposing inadequacies in prison conditions will be diminished.

In addition, without the realistic threat of litigation, corrections advocates lack any effective means of influencing public officials to take seriously inmates' concern. Inmates lack political power to advocate effectively on their own behalf; in most states they are not allowed to vote, even after they have completed their sentences. The plight of criminal offenders rarely inspires effective political mobilization. At least for adult offenders, coalitions with the political clout to influence governors and legislators do not exist. Without external pressure to correct serious deficiencies, the dynamics of organizational stasis predispose responsible officials to avoid rocking the boat.

Nor is there persuasive evidence that the American Correctional Association ("ACA") or any other professional organization within the corrections field currently performs an effective oversight role in the absence of litigation. The American Correctional Association has created a set of standards for all correctional functions, and is currently in the process of auditing state and local agencies to assess their compliance with these standards and accrediting those that do. Although more than 100 facilities and programs sought accreditation in 1991, accreditation does not adequately assure that the institutions are constitutional. Moreover, the accreditation process lacks any sanctions for lack of accreditation. Indeed, corrections professionals themselves report that a major incentive for participation in the accreditation process is the avoidance of litigation. Litigation has been a necessary catalyst for involvement in the accreditation process in many instances of successful change through accreditation. Moreover, the accreditation process has not been able to hold the line against the pressures of limited budgets and increasing populations. In response to pressures on corrections administrators to manage their facilities with fewer resources for greater numbers of inmates, the ACA diluted the standards governing adequate living space. The National Prison Project and the American Bar Association provided the only organizational opposition to this move. "The power within the field of corrections augmented by the pressures of political arena will dilute the standards and the very meaning of accreditation."

Meaningful grievance mechanisms can permit correctional institutions to respond promptly to trouble spots and personnel problems, and can provide prompt resolution disputes without the necessity of litigation. To be effective, these mechanisms must include some form of independent review, participation by inmates and staff in their design and operation, short enforceable time limits, written responses with reasons for adverse decisions, and effective administrative oversight of the system. Some states have adopted grievance mechanisms that have been certified by the Department of Justice or the courts to comply with these general requirements.

However, grievance procedures do not provide an effective substitute for litigation concerning conditions of confinement in correctional institutions. Many grievance systems do not meet the standards required for accreditation under the Institutionalized Persons Act, and there is some question as to whether systems that have recently been certified in fact comply with the requirements of effective dispute resolution. Even those that do qualify are not generally designed to address systemic problems. They do not accept class-wide complaints, and do not empower corrections officials to involve other state actors whose participation is frequently necessary to address systemic problems such as overcrowding and poor living conditions. Similarly, other dispute resolutions internally administered by the corrections department, such as ombudsmen, deal primarily with individual problems, such as failure to deliver mail. Moreover, most grievance officers and ombudsmen depend on the administration for their position. This seriously limits their capacity to hold their departments to constitutional standards, particularly when additional resources are required to do so. Indeed, experts on dispute resolution state that alternative forms of dispute resolution, such as negotiation and mediation, have worked as agents of systemic reform in corrections only when linked in some significant way with litigation.

C. Litigation Has Only Begun to Address the Problems Facing Jail and Juvenile and Women's Institutions

The reform of jails has not progressed to the same extent as state correctional facilities over the past two decades. The combination of the decentralized and rural character of many jails insulates them from scrutiny. Inmates in jails remain incarcerated for relatively short time periods, and often leave the institution before their case can be heard or certified. Many jails, particularly in rural areas, remain untouched by litigation. Jails are more likely than prisons to subject inmates to the brutal, primitive conditions that characterized prisons twenty years ago. In many jurisdictions, jails are run by sheriffs whose background and primary concern is law enforcement and who typically lack the expertise and resources necessary to manage decent facilities.

Serious problems also persist in juvenile facilities. According to the Office of Juvenile Justice and Delinquency Prevention, by October 1989, only 34 of 56 participating states and territories had demonstrated compliance with the requirement of separation of juvenile and adult offenders. Similarly, although the largest state juvenile systems, such as Florida, California, and Texas, have been the subject of litigation, many institutions with extremely poor conditions have yet to be tackled. Despite the fact that a disproportionate number of children in juvenile justice institutions have a history of multiple problems, "the services they receive are likely to be insufficient and/or unresponsive to their needs." Moreover, juvenile justice advocates report that children are far less likely to complain about brutal conditions than adults.

Historically, litigation has rarely focused on the problems of incarcerated women. Until recently, women have been less likely to litigate, although there are indications that this reluctance is diminishing. In cases challenging conditions in both men's and women's institutions, the problems of women tend to be neglected, and court-ordered improvements are often not extended as fully to women's institutions. Furthermore, the population in women's facilities is growing at a much faster rate than men's institutions, and overcrowding problems in women's institutions are severe. Nonetheless, corrections advocates have also noted an increased public interest in addressing the problems facing incarcerated women.

Prisons: The Cruel and Unusual Punishment Controversy

PHILIP J. COOPER

Litigation launched by prisoners and detainees in the nation's jails has raised a variety of law and policy issues. Inmates may challenge facets of the conditions of their confinement, procedures used by prison officials, the operation of rehabilitation and release programs, or, particularly in the case of women inmates, the equality of their treatment relative to others. Judges face cases that raise individual grievances and suits that present large packages of issues. On some occasions, the broad attack across a range of conditions of confinement and prisons procedures issues is little more than a litigation too, a sort of barrage tactic. Often, however, the prison cases present several issues that really are very much interconnected, as when severe overcrowding overtaxes available medical care.

BASIC CONDITIONS OF CONFINEMENT

Many of the challenges to conditions of confinement developed in older facilities that were overcrowded and operating on extremely limited finances. Not surprisingly, the issues that arose in those cases were Eighth Amendment claims concerning overcrowding, safety, sanitation and plumbing conditions, clothing and personal hygiene, nutrition and food services, climate and ventilation, insect and rodent infestation, medical care, psychiatric treatment, and opportunity for exercise and recreation.

The argument that a correctional facility is seriously overcrowded, which results in conditions that are degrading, unhealthful, and unsafe, is one of the more common charges in prison and jail suits. Since the benchmark for evaluating cruel and unusual punishments is society's "evolving standards of decency" and other similarly open textured language, the problem for the judge has generally been just how to determine whether a particular prison is unconstitutionally overcrowded. In the first wave of cases, that was not a particularly difficult task since the overcrowding was so extreme and because the other conditions existing in the institutions were so bad that there was little question for any reasonably impartial observer. The second wave of cases, however, often involved new, relatively modern, or refurbished facilities. In these settings, the degree of crowding became more significant.

Source: Excerpted from Cooper, Phillip J. Prisons: The Cruel and Unusual Punishment Controversy. Ch. 8 in *Hard Judicial Choices: Federal District Court Judges and State and Local Officials.* New York: Oxford University Press, 1988.

Prison administrators point out that there may be a considerable difference between the ideal population of a prison and the point at which overcrowding is so severe as to merit the label cruel and unusual punishment. The three principal means of evaluating available space are the design capacity of the institutions, space standards generated by national corrections organizations or government bodies that are expressed in square feet of cell space per inmate (generally sixty to eighty square feet), and studies by responsible independent evaluators.

The rating information most often comes to the trial judges through introduction of expert testimony; submission of sets of recognized standards, with comparisons to the target institution; and judicial visits to the facilities, generally at the request of the plaintiffs. Judges frequently employ both the design capacity and square-foot measures, often interpreting those figures in light of reports issued by state agencies or national corrections groups. The experts' standards and evaluations, though, are sometimes contested.

While the Supreme Court has, as recently as 1978, relied upon standards promulgated by professional organizations, its most recent rulings have cautioned against according excessive constitutional significance to such measures. Justice Rehnquist warned in 1979, "[W]hile the recommendations of these various groups may be instructive in certain cases, they simply do not establish the constitutional minima; rather, they establish goals recommended by the organization in question." He did not go on to explain what criteria trial judges ought to employ. The Court has, however, recognized that judgments about overcrowding must comprehend the nature and duration of the confinement as well as the effect of other conditions existing in the prison. Housing a number of nonviolent offenders in relatively crowded conditions for short periods is not the equivalent of placing dangerous felons in overcrowded cells indefinitely with little out of cell time.

It is generally agreed that state and local governments have a duty to exercise reasonable care in protecting the safety of an inmate from physical harm at the hands of other inmates or because of institutional conditions, but it is extremely difficult to provide adequate security in that type of housing for the kind of inmates housed in maximum security prisons. In addition to claims of inadequate security, judges have also frequently encountered safety issues in the form of fire hazards. Fire safety is a complex matter in a correctional facility given the conflicting need for secure lock down of inmates, on the one hand, and the requirement to provide rapid egress from burning cell blocks, on the other. Compliance with modern fire standards is all the more complicated in older facilities that were constructed without regard for fire safety.

Similarly, the effort to assure a stable and acceptable climate, adequate ventilation, and minimally adequate light in a secure environment has also been a major problem in older facilities. The courts that have been asked to decide conditions of confinement cases consider these as important factors in their assessment of the "totality of the circumstances." Environmental factors of this sort are particularly important when facilities are substantially overcrowded.

Cases attacking facilities that are old and in poor condition or severely overcrowded have often presented evidence of inadequate plumbing, poor sanitation, and limited hygiene opportunity for inmates. A lack of adequate water, toilet, and washing facilities presents the kind of "shock to the conscience" that leads to adverse rulings against prison administrators. Moreover, judges have found that while these deficiencies do indeed present that kind of assault on basic human dignity, they also raise the likelihood of health threats brought on by inadequate sanitation. Where the buildings are extremely old, there may even be a threat to the structural integrity of the institution from leaking pipes. In some instances the inadequacies of the physical plant were accompanied by a refusal on the part of authorities to provide inmates with hygiene items like toothepaste or clean clothing. Courts facing the early conditions of confinement cases insisted on correction of these deficiencies.

Another factor frequently cited in conditions cases is nutrition and food services. Judges have generally refused to order that meals should be appetizing or that inmates are entitled to particular types and quantities of food, but they have considered whether there was food of adequate nutritional value prepared in sanitary conditions. These food service issues are often intermingled with questions of general sanitation and inmate hygiene since food is most often prepared by working prisoners. Like the personal hygiene questions, demands for adequate nutrition were answered swiftly during the first wave of conditions challenges. Nevertheless, rising populations during the 1970s threatened to reinvigorate the nutrition and food preparation issue in those prisons with aging facilities and inadequate equipment or kitchens that are difficult to maintain. Corrections administrators have also been called upon to deal with two added food service questions over the past decade. The first involves the need to provide medically mandated diets for ailing or aging inmates. The second demand arose when some inmates, particularly Black Muslims, asserted a religious bar to consumption of pork products, a prison staple since many facilities produce pork for internal use.

Those facilities with food service, sanitation, and hygiene deficiencies, not surprisingly, have occasionally presented serious insect and rodent infestations. Courts have considered the presence of those pests as indicators to be considered in examining other deficiencies. They have also regarded them important as potential health risks.

Prison conditions rulings uniformly insist upon the provision of basic medical care for inmates. The general principle that deprivation of basic care is cruel and unusual punishment was addressed in a series of rulings from the late 1960s on. The Supreme Court issued the authoritative pronouncement on the principle in 1976 in *Estelle v. Gamble*, which held that failure to provide care to inmates who are necessarily completely dependent upon the institution for their medical needs is an infliction of unnecessary suffering that serves no penological objective and is "inconsistent with contemporary standards of decency." What is not clear, as Justice Stevens observed in dissent, is precisely how lower courts are to implement the *Gamble* ruling, since the Court concluded that negligence or relative inadequacy of treatment is not sufficient to claim a constitutional violation. Rather, the inmate must "allege acts or omissions sufficiently harmful to evidence deliberate indifference to serious medical needs." Stevens argued that this standard focuses upon "the subjective motivation of persons accused of violating the Eighth Amendment rather than [on] the standard of care required by the Constitution."

The Court did say that it would not tolerate deliberate indifference to the medical needs of prisoners "whether the indifference is manifested by prison doctors in their response to the prisoner's needs or by prison guards in intentionally denying access to medical care or intentionally interfering with the treatment once prescribed." Indeed there have been a number of studies and a variety of judicial opinions that involved cases in which doctors, nurses, or inmate medical assistants either refused to take inmates' requests for care seriously or failed to pay attention to their particular medical needs. There have also been findings that medical personnel have not provided medical treatment or medicine that was prescribed for a prisoner.

The most common situation, however, is not one in which there is indifference or hostility but where a facility simply lacks adequate clinical facilities, staff, trained support personnel, medical recordkeeping, and prescription services. For jails and prisons lacking clinical space or equipment, the mode of treatment is often transportation to a prison medical facility or civilian hospitals near the institution. Transportation requires the availability of both vehicles and guards since such trips outside provide opportunities for escape. The inability to provide secure transportation because of personnel shortages among guards has sometimes meant lengthy delays in treatment. Where correctional institutions are located in remote parts of large states, the transportation problems become particularly acute.

There are two other troublesome clinical difficulties that judges have confronted in the prisons conditions litigation. First, in some installations judges have found only token psychiatric services even though substantial numbers of inmates need intensive treatment. Second, usually in jails cases but also in prisons suits, they find that though substantial numbers of inmates have severe alcohol or drug problems, the institutions often lack meaningful programs to deal first with withdrawal and later with treatment.

There is one other factor often considered part of the cruel and unusual punishment calculus, the availability of exercise or recreational facilities. Prison overcrowding can tax both facilities and personnel resources. As large populations exhaust exercise facilities and equipment, those unable to exercise find themselves with more lock down time and less opportunity to vent their energies. In jails, particularly small jails, the problem is often a lack of exercise areas. Where they do exist, jail exercise facilities may be enclosed areas on the roof or in the basement. Like larger prisons, jails are also limited by personnel shortages from affording inmates adequate exercise opportunities. A number of judges have considered access to exercise as a factor in their total conditions of confinement analysis. Judge E. Gordon West found "[c]onfinement for long periods of time without the opportunity for regular outdoor exercise does, as a matter of law, constitute cruel and unusual punishment. West faced a challenge to conditions of confinement of prisoners on Louisiana's death row:

> They live in cells measuring approximately 6 feet by 9 feet. The building is so situated that practically no sunlight ever enters the cells. . . . During each 24 hour period the inmate is allowed out of this small cell for only 15 minutes. During that time he may go down a closed in corridor to a shower room where he must bathe, wash clothes, and supposedly exercise, all in a matter of 15 minutes. The inmates who testified in this case have been living under this condition for as long as 9 years.

CHALLENGING CORRECTIONS PROCEDURES

In addition to challenges to the environment in which they are held, inmates frequently contest the formal and informal practices and rules enforced by corrections personnel. There are due process attacks on classification procedures, prison disciplinary practices, imitations on visits to inmates, and access to legal assistance. Equal protection charges are often lodged alleging racial discrimination. Also common are First Amendment claims concerning religious liberty and freedom of expression.

There are two important premises and one caveat underlying due process claims in prison cases. First, while a prisoner is deprived of his or her liberty to move about the community, there remains a wide range of confinement options that vary from extremely loose confinement in minimum security facilities with work release or home furlough programs to solitary confinement in maximum security prisons. Just because one has been sentenced to some sort of confinement, it is not the case that one may be made to suffer further loss of liberty as discipline without some form of due process protection, though the requisite procedures may be very informal by comparison with criminal trials. The Supreme Court has held: "[T]hough his rights may be diminished by the needs and exigencies of the institutional environment , a prisoner is not wholly stripped of constitutional protections when he is imprisoned for crime. There is no iron curtain drawn between the Constitution and the prisons of this country." Second, the Supreme Court has rejected the notion that inmates possess only privileges as opposed to rights, with only rights but not privileges protected by the requirements of due process of law. The question in these cases is whether corrections administrators are causing a serious injury to an inmate's life, liberty, or property. The caveat to be observed in due process cases is that the fact that inmates are entitled to minimum procedural protections and bars to arbitrary administrative action does not usually prevent corrections officials from using judgment in assigning prisoners to various facilities or punishing those who violate prison rules.

The process of classification of prisoners and detainees by type of offense and conduct has been contested. The manner in which one is classified often determines the nature of the correctional facility to which one is assigned. Higher classification means a great loss of liberty and the increased physical risks that come from assignment to maximum security prisons with the most dangerous inmates in a penal system. However, corrections officials retain substantial interests in maintaining security, preventing escape, and rehabilitating other prisoners that justify broad discretion in the classification of offenders charged to their custody. Federal courts have not held that there is a right to a certain type of classification. The Supreme Court has rejected the assertion that inmates are entitled to due process before they can be transferred from a medium security to a maximum security institution, though it has been determined that there are due process limitations on transfers of prisoners to mental hospitals.

The most frequent due process questions are those concerning prison discipline. The types of prison discipline that have been used over time vary from loss of minor privileges, loss of good-time credit (credit against one's sentence earned for time served without rules violations), punitive confinement (either complete lock down with other prisoners or solitary confinement), or in an earlier day, physical punishment. Corporal punishment has been generally banned, though corrections officers retain the authority to use the force necessary to control inmates. As late as the early 1970s, some judges encountered cases in which there was direct corporal punishment administered to prisoners. In others, indirect punishments like the use of mace and tear gas, chaining to the bars of one's cell, or restriction to bread and water for extended periods to physically weaken prisoners were struck down.

The Supreme Court addressed the availability of due process in prison discipline in a 1974 ruling, *Wolff v. McDonnell*. The Court rejected the assertion "that the procedure for disciplining prison inmates for serious misconduct is a matter of policy raising no constitutional issue." Recognizing that "there must be a mutual accommodation between institutional needs and objectives and the provisions of the Constitution that are of general application," the Court observed, "[p]rison disciplinary proceedings are not part of a criminal prosecution, and the full panoply of rights due a defendant in such proceedings does not apply." The Court concluded that inmates facing disciplinary action are entitled to written notice of the charges against them; to an opportunity to present evidence and make statements in their own behalf; to cross-examine witnesses, where doing so will not create a "risk of reprisal or undermine authority"; and to receive a written summary of the evidence and findings of the disciplinary board.

Apart from these core questions of prison discipline, federal courts have been asked to address three other problems. Where judges have been shown that prisoners were disciplined as a matter of retaliation, as in the case of one inmate who was sentenced to solitary confinement "in retaliation for his legal success," they have held in favor of the inmates. The second set of issues concerned inmates sentenced to solitary confinement. While those sentenced to solitary or administrative confinement are entitled to procedural due process in the disciplinary action, there is no constitutional ban on the use of solitary so long as it meets minimally adequate conditions of confinement standards. The third issue, and one that remains a continuing source of disagreement, is the use of rules that allow discipline for ambiguous offenses, such as "abusive language," "insolence," "sarcasm," "disrespect," or being "out of order." Since the first wave of litigation, most facilities have provided fairly elaborate books of institutional rules, though the conflict between the corrections officers' need for discretion and flexibility to maintain order and the inmates' demands that they not be punished for undefined and arbitrary offenses continues.

The remaining frequently raised due process complaint has to do with interference with inmates' access to federal courts. The Supreme Court has held for years that the state violates due process if it interferes with inmates' opportunities to file papers in pending litigation, including cases contesting the legality and conditions of their confinement. Of course, inmates who are illiterate, cannot afford attorneys, have little knowledge of legal details, or lack access to a law library in which to do research may have a right they cannot really exercise. Jailhouse lawyers, known as writ writers, became important people in prisons because they could help others prepare their cases. Justice Fortas, writing for the Court in 1969, held that corrections administrators, at least in the absence of an adequate legal assistance program, cannot prevent writ writers from assisting other inmates. Similarly, the Court has held that officials must provide adequate law libraries or assistance from persons trained in law.

The opportunity for visits from family and friends has been another difficult issue often presented as part of freedom of association protected by the First Amendment. Some judges found that, at least where family members are concerned, inmates do have a constitutionally protected right to visitation. The courts that have addressed the issue acknowledge corrections officials' need to regulate visitation rights to ensure security and order but note that such restrictions cannot be overly broad and must serve legitimate peneological objectives. Judge Kane struck down a rule prohibiting visits by friends on that ground.

The matter of freedom of expression, or perhaps more accurately communication, has been somewhat more complicated. These questions arose largely in cases concerning inmate demands to send and receive uncensored mail, press requests for interviews with prisoners, and inmate claims to a right to be able to receive books, periodicals, and newspapers. Until the first wave of prison suits, many systems had more or less complete censorship authority over incoming and outgoing mail, often limiting communications to a few people on an approved list and then only for those letters that could satisfy the censor. The purpose of the mail inspection was ostensibly to detect escape plans and catch contraband being shipped into the facility, but the practice was also employed to prevent inmates from dispatching complaints about the operation of institutions. The Supreme Court encountered the question in a case decided in 1974. In prohibiting across the board inspection and censorship, the Court managed to avoid declaring that inmates had First Amendment rights to freedom of speech or press. Instead, the Court found that government could not arbitrarily interfere with the free flow of communications otherwise available to the members of society. In this case, censorship interfered with the right of the addressees to receive the inmates' correspondence, quite apart from the inmates' right to send it. However, the Court left open some limited authority for officials to inspect for contraband and even to go further under carefully limited circumstances. In general, though, inmates are free to correspond.

Reporters followed up on the correspondence cases and argued that they had a similar right to access to interview inmates in prisons. The Court rejected those claims in favor of assertions by prison administrators that inmates would use the notoriety of the interviews for advantage within the inmate subculture. Correspondence is one thing, visits to jails with microphones and cameras might be something else. Many prisons do, however, have administrative rules which do allow on-camera and recorded interviews.

The receipt of magazines, newspapers, and books was also commonly censored on a variety of grounds, ranging from immorality for those items considered sexually explicit to radical political literature to anything administrators considered objectionable. Historically, prison libraries were often based upon donations gathered by church groups. In later times those same groups were called upon to help determine what was suitable reading material for the inmates. As lower courts began to strike down restrictions on reading material, many jurisdictions relaxed their rules. The Supreme Court, in its only ruling on the matter, did uphold as a security safeguard a so-called "publisher only rule" that prohibited inmates from receiving hardcover books except for those sent directly from a publisher, book club, or bookstore.

THE QUESTION OF REHABILITATION AND RELEASE

Inmates have raised a variety of issues that fall generally into a category of matters of rehabilitation and release. These include questions about adequacy of prison rehabilitation, education, vocational training, psychiatric care and counseling, and parole and probation. Parole questions are of importance to prisons cases in part at least because inmates' behavior within an institution is often related to their expectations about chances for parole. From another perspective, corrections studies have found anxiety, confusion, and frustration over the vagaries of parole decisions to be one of the inmates' leading complaints.

The Supreme Court has generally concluded that while the due process clause provides procedural protection for probationers or parolees whose status is revoked, it does not provide guarantees, procedural or substantive, for inmates seeking parole or commutation of their sentences. It is one thing to be granted liberty and then have it removed, according to the Court, but quite another to have a possibility to obtain one's liberty and be denied.

SPECIAL PROBLEMS OF WOMEN BEHIND BARS

The Supreme Court and other federal courts have taken a strong position insisting upon an end to racial discrimination in corrections under the equal protection clause of the Fourteenth Amendment. A less well known but very significant area of equal protection concern involves women in correctional institutions. It is in part precisely because women represent such a small percentage of inmates in a state system or county jail that they sometimes find themselves disadvantaged relative to male prisoners. The total numbers of women are often low, so that the per capita costs of their incarceration appear to be disproportionately high. States vary considerably in how they respond to the task of incarcerating women, ranging from contracting with other states for correctional services to incarceration in facilities adjoining men's institutions in order to take advantage of economies of scale, to the single independent state institution for women. Where the state women's prison is used, it tends to have a more diverse age group and distribution of offenses than men's institutions. However women are housed, they do have special needs for health care, clothing, and other services.

THE POLITICAL AND FISCAL DILEMMAS OF PRISON REFORM

In sum, like the mental health cases, prisons are total institutions which present a variety of questions that touch on important constitutional issues and involve a wide range of state laws, regulations, and administrative practices. Like the mental health cases, the judge called upon to decide prison reform suits must operate in a complex and conflict ridden environment. Though there are similarities between the mental health and prisons cases, there are also contrasts. The politics of corrections are quite different from mental health, as are some of the fiscal pressures that must be recognized by courts and accommodated by administrators.

THE POLITICS OF MYTH AND INTERNAL INSTABILITY

The President's Commission observed that corrections "is the part of the criminal justice system that the public sees least and knows least about." Perhaps as dangerous as the lack of knowledge is the belief in a number of myths about the system that simply do not comport with reality. Among the more common of these are the notion that few felons go to prison, prison sentences are getting shorter because judges are too liberal, one prisoner is more or less like any other, and it should not take much to maintain them in confinement. One of the most popular myths is the assumption that prisons are country clubs when they ought be harsh institutions and that they should be self-sufficient or profit making operations. There were dramatic efforts following the first wave of prison cases to improve prison conditions and practices both through litigation and by the efforts of corrections professionals along with the elected officials they serve. However, prison populations have risen dramatically, as have the costs of confinement. As the public demands more prison sentences of longer duration, the difficulty of meeting the needs will grow. The lack of knowledge and myths are likely to continue to frustrate the efforts of prison officials to make the public understand the severity of the problems in their corrections systems.

At the same time that corrections administrators were attempting to deal with these public pressures, they faced growing human relations tensions within the system. Conflict in the system fostered increased hostility between inmates and corrections officers. At one level, staffing shortages made it difficult to meet custodial needs quite apart from efforts to provide security and support for rehabilitation programs. Reactions to low pay and a lack of public respect led to increased union organizing efforts during the 1970s, which increased stresses within the corrections system. The same pressures led to high turnover rates at both the executive level and among line corrections officers. For example, in Colorado during the mid-1970s, there were "six different Wardens at the Penitentiary, four Directors of the Division of Corrections, and four Executive Directors of the Department. As a result, policies and practices [were] constantly changed, leaving prisoners and staff in a constant state of flux." Demands for affirmative action recruitment in corrections added another pressure to the complex human resource politics.

Several observers of the corrections process have noted that the 1970s witnessed the rise of increasing tensions between what they refer to as "the new inmate" and the "new corrections officer." The new inmate is more sophisticated in attacking the system, more disposed to issue those challenges, and increasingly aware of the complexities of organizational politics. The new corrections officer, it has been said, "sees himself as the victim of an unjust system—a system which is concerned more with protection of the rights of criminals, whom he may perceive as sub-human, than it is concerned with the rights of the God-fearing, upright citizens of his community. . . . He opposes prison reform as a threat to his physical security. He has organized his fellow officers in defense of his way of life." The fact that large correctional facilities are generally located in rural settings and often overwhelmingly administered by Caucasians, whereas the inmate population has substantial percentages of minority inmates predominantly from urban areas adds to the conflict. The rural locations often compound the difficulty of recruiting minority officers.

One additional variable to be added to the mix is the conflict that arises in corrections between states and localities. In a number of states, counties house backlogs of sentenced prisoners awaiting transfer to state facilities while simultaneously holding detainees awaiting trial and misdemeanor offenders serving short sentences. When state prisons become overcrowded, sentenced felons back up at the county level, thus presenting counties with long term overcrowding coupled with increased security demands to deal with the tougher inmates. Intergovernmental complexity affects not only contests for tax dollars, but is manifest in discussions of sentencing policy and other substantive issues. County sheriffs frequently find themselves on opposite sides from state corrections officials in legislative and budgetary battles.

MEETING THE FISCAL CHALLENGE

The politics of corrections, as with mental health, are often budgetary politics. What is clear from the case law is that virtually all of the judges who have issued corrections remedial decrees recognized the hardships faced by administrators attempting to obtain adequate operating funds, let alone the further burdens posed by the need to acquire capital funds for new construction and modernization of existing facilities. On the other hand, they will not permit constitutional violations to stand on financial justifications.

In addition to the obvious financial demands, corrections reform has presented two continuing controversies, First, corrections administration has had a continuing conflict between addressing costs of custody and the needs of rehabilitation programs. The internal politics of corrections have exacerbated the battles between the two sides as many administrators who have come up through the system from the ranks of guard have historically favored custody over rehabilitation. The second frustration, and one very much related to prison reform litigation, has to do with the financial demands of new construction required to replace outmoded facilities. This construction must be accomplished while simultaneously making improvements in the existing institutions needed to make them functional until the new buildings are completed. No administrator wishes to send good money into dying installations, but prisoners are legally entitled to minimally adequate conditions now, not at the end of the new construction work.

Like mental health administrators, correctional officials must assemble their budgets from a collection of state funds and federal grants. During the 1970s, at a time when financial demands were increasing because of increased prison populations and high rates of inflation, state governments fell upon financial hard times coupled with reductions in several important federal grant programs. Another similarity between mental health and corrections is the fiscal strain imposed upon the states and localities by adding bonded indebtedness to finance construction at a time of high interest rates.

CONCLUSION

This chapter has sketched the interactions of courts and administrators in corrections policy, with particular attention to the questions of conditions of confinement and prison practices at the heart of the corrections reform movement. An examination of judicial decisions directing change in corrections operations indicates how interrelated the pieces of prison reform are. Much like the mental health cases, one of the greatest challenges to judges called upon to decide prison suits is to deal with the overlapping issues they present.

Judicial Reform and Prisoner Control: The Impact of *Ruiz v. Estelle* on a Texas Penitentiary

JAMES W. MARQUART
BEN M. CROUCH

In December 1980 Judge William W. Justice (Eastern District of Texas) delivered a sweeping decree against the Texas Department of Corrections in *Ruiz v. Estelle*. That decree, a year in the writing following a trial of many months, was the culmination of a suit originally filed with the court in 1972. The order recited numerous constitutional violations, focusing on several issues. First, TDC was deemed overcrowded. To deal with the overcrowding problems, TDC erected tents, expanded furloughs, and in May 1982 even ceased accepting new prisoners for approximately ten days. Moreover, a "safety valve" population control plan passed by the legislature in 1983 and a liberalized "good time" policy have been used to expand parole releases. Nevertheless, overcrowding continues. A second issue was TDC's security

Source: Excerpted from Marquart, James W. and Ben M. Crouch. Judicial Reform and Prisoner Control: The Impact of *Ruiz v. Estelle* on a Texas Penitentiary. *Law and Society Review* 19 (4): 557–586, 1985.

practices. The judge ordered the prison administrators to sharply reduce and restrict the use of force by prison personnel. He also demanded the removal and reassignment of special inmates known as "building tenders" since the evidence clearly indicated that these inmates were controlling other inmates. To further increase security, the decree called for TDC to hire more guards and to develop a much more extensive inmate classification plan. Thirdly, the judge found health care practices, procedures, and personnel in need of drastic upgrading. A fourth shortcoming involved inmate disciplinary practices. Problems included vague rules (e.g., "agitation," "laziness"), the arbitrary use of administrative segregation, and a failure to maintain proper disciplinary hearing records. Fifth, the court found many problems with fire and safety standards in TDC. Finally, TDC was found to have unconstitutionally denied inmates access to courts, counsel, and public officials.

Since our concern in this paper is with the official and unofficial means of prisoner control that were ruled unconstitutional by the court, we limit our analysis to those parts of the court order (e.g., removal of building tenders and changes in security practices and personnel) relevant to that concern. To appreciate the effects of the order, we must first understand how Eastham was organized and how it operated prior to the court's intervention.

I. PRISONER CONTROL UNDER THE OLD ORDER

At Eastham, the staff maintained tight discipline and control through a complex system of official rewards and punishments administered by an elite group of prison officers. Basically, this control system rewarded those inmates who had good prison records with such privileges as good time, furloughs, dormitory living instead of a cell, and jobs other than field work. On the other hand, the staff severely punished those inmates who challenged the staff's definition of the situation. The most unusual and important element in controlling the prisoners in the old order centered on the staff's open and formal reliance upon a select group of elite inmates to extend their authority and maintain discipline. It was this latter system of prisoner control, called the "building tender (BT) system," that the court ordered TDC to abolish.

The Building Tender/Turnkey System

The staff employed a strategy of coopting the dominant or elite inmates with special privileges (e.g., separate bathing and recreational periods, better laundered uniforms, open cells, clubs or knives, "friends" for cell partners, craft cards) in return for aid in controlling the ordinary inmates in the living areas, especially the cell blocks.

Structure and Work Role. The BT system at Eastham involved three levels of inmates. At the top of the hierarchy were the "head" building tenders. In 1981, each of the 18 blocks had one building tender who was assigned by the staff as the "head" BT and was responsible for all inmate behavior in "his" particular block. Essentially, the head BT was the block's representative to the ranking officers. For example, if a knife or any other form of contraband was detected in "his" living area, it was the head BT's official job to inform the staff of the weapon's whereabouts and who had made it, as well as to tell the staff about the knife-maker's character. In addition, these BTs would help the staff search the suspected inmate's cell to ferret out the weapon. Because of their position, prestige, and role, head BTs were the most powerful inmates in the prisoner society. They acted as overseers and frequently mediated and settled disputes and altercations among the ordinary inmates.

At the second level of the system were the rank-and-file building tenders. In every cell block or dormitory, there were generally between three and five inmates assigned as building tenders, for a total of nearly 150 BTs within the institution. These inmates "worked the tank," and their official role was to maintain control in the living areas by tabulating the daily counts, delivering messages to other inmates for the staff, getting the other inmates up for work, cleaning, and reporting any serious misbehavior by inmates to the head BT who, in turn, told the staff. Another important duty of the BTs was the socialization of new inmates into the system. When new inmates arrived at a living area, BTs informed them of the "rules," which meant "keep the noise down, go to work when you are supposed to, mind your own business, and tell us [the BTs] when you have a problem." In addition to these tasks, the BTs broke up fights, gave orders to other inmates, and protected the officers in charge of the cell blocks from attacks by the inmates.

The third level of the building tender system consisted of inmates referred to as runners, strikers, or hitmen. Runners were not assigned to work in the blocks by the staff; rather, these inmates were selected by the BTs for their loyalty and willingness to act as informants. More importantly, runners served as the physical back-ups for the BTs. If a fight or brawl broke out, the runners assisted the BTs in quelling the disturbance. As a reward for their services, runners enjoyed more mobility and privileges within the block than the other inmates (but less than the BTs).

The final aspect of the building tender system consisted of inmates referred to as turnkeys, who numbered 17 in 1981. As mentioned earlier, the prison contained a large corridor known as the Hall. Within the Hall were several large metal barred doors, or riot barricades. Turnkeys worked in six-hour shifts, carrying on long leather straps the keys that locked and unlocked the barricades. They shut and locked these doors during fights or disturbances to prevent them from escalating or moving throughout the Hall. In addition to operating the barricades, turnkeys routinely broke up fights, assisted the BTs, and protected the prison guards from the ordinary inmates.

The building tender system functioned officially as an information network. Structurally, the staff was at the perimeter of the inmates society, but the building tender system helped the staff penetrate, divide, and control the ordinary inmates. BTs and turnkeys in turn had snitches working for them not only in the living areas but throughout the entire institution. Thus, the staff secured information that enabled them to exert enormous power over the inmates' daily activities. As mentioned earlier, the BTs and turnkeys were handsomely rewarded for their behavior and enjoyed power and status far exceeding that of ordinary inmates and lower ranking guards. Unofficially, these inmates maintained order in the blocks through fear, and they physically punished inmates who broke the rules.

The Staff and Unofficial Control

The staff at Eastham did not leave control of the prison totally in the hands of their inmates agents. In addition, the guards actively enforced "unofficial" order through intimidation and the routine use of physical force. Rules were quickly and severely enforced, providing inmates with clear-cut information about what they could and could not do, and who was boss (cf. McCleery, 1960). The unification or symbiotic relationships of these two groups—that is, guards as inside outsiders and inmates agents as elite outside insiders—precluded revolt at practically every level.

Intimidation. Inmates who challenged a guard's authority (e.g., by insubordination, cursing at him, or "giving him a hard time") were yelled at by guards or supervisors (sergeants, lieutenants, and captains). Racial epithets, name calling, derogation, threats of force, and other scare tactics were common. These methods, though physically harmless, ridiculed, frightened, or destroyed the "face" of the offending inmate.

Physical Force. Coercive force is an important means of controlling people in any situation or setting. At Eastham, the unofficial use of physical force was a common method of prisoner control. Inmates were roughed up daily as a matter of course. Within a two-month period, the first author observed over 30 separate instances of guards using physical force against inmates. Key informants told the researcher that this number of instances was not surprising. Indeed, as Marquart (1985) notes, fighting inmates was an important value in the guard subculture. Guards who demonstrated their willingness to fight inmates who challenged their authority were often rewarded by their supervisors with promotions, improved duty assignments, and prestigious labels such as "having nuts" or being a "good" officer. The willingness to use force was a rite of passage for new officers, and those who failed this test were relegated to unpleasant jobs such as cell block and gun tower duty. Those who refused to fight were rarely promoted, and many of these "deviant" officers eventually quit or transferred to other TDC prisons.

Generally, the physical force employed by ranking officers was of two kinds. First, some inmates received "tune-ups" or "attitude adjustments."

These inmates were usually slapped across the face or head, kicked in the buttocks, or even punched in the stomach. The intent of a "tune-up" was to terrorize the inmate without doing physical damage. More serious, but still a "tune-up" was the "ass whipping" in which the guards employed their fists, boots, blackjacks, riot batons or aluminum flashlights.

The second form of force was beatings. Beatings occurred infrequently and were reserved for inmates who violated certain "sacred" rules by, for instance, attacking an officer verbally or physically, inflicting physical harm on other inmates, destroying prison property, or attempting to lead work strikes, to escape, or to foment rebellion against the rules or officers. Inmates who broke these rules were defined as "resisting" the system and were severely injured—often suffering concussions, loss of consciousness, cuts, and broken bones.

The threat and use of force were an everyday reality under the old order, and the guards routinely used force to subdue "unruly" inmates (see Ninth Monitor's Report, 1983). Although rewards and privileges served as important official means of control, the prison order was ultimately maintained through the "unofficial" use of fear and terror. The staff ruled the penitentiary with an iron hand and defined most situations for the inmates. Those inmates who presented a serious challenge (e.g., threatening or attacking officers, fomenting work strikes) to the system were harassed, placed in solitary confinement, and sometimes beaten into submission.

II. EASTHAM IN TRANSITION

Although there were some efforts to ease overcrowding and to reform prison operations such as medical services, the dominant posture of TDC in 1981 and most of 1982, at all levels, was to resist the court order both through legal action and by noncompliance. Prison officials rejected the intrusion of the court as a matter of principle and particularly feared the consequences of relinquishing such traditional control measures as the BT system. Initially, TDC fought the BT issue. However, additional court hearings in February 1982 made public numerous examples of BT/turnkey perversion and brutality. In late May 1982, attorneys for the state signed a consent decree agreeing to dismantle the decades-old inmate-guard system by January 1, 1983.

Compliance

To comply with the decree, the staff in September 1982 reassigned the majority of the BTs to ordinary jobs (e.g., laundry, gym, showers) and stripped them of all their former power, status, and duties. Even BTs reassigned as orderlies or janitors in the living areas were not permitted to perform any of their old BT duties. Court-appointed investigators, called monitors, oversaw the selection of orderlies and kept close tabs on their behavior. These outside agents periodically visited Eastham and asked their own inmate informants to make written statements about any orderly misbehavior. Consequently, several inmate orderlies lost their jobs for fighting with and giving orders to the ordinary inmates; they were replaced by less quarrelsome ordinary inmates.

In addition to removing the BTs and turnkeys, TDC was ordered to hire more officers to replace the former inmate guards. Eastham received 141 new recruits during November and December 1982. The guard force was almost doubled. Guards were assigned to the barricades and had to learn from the former turnkeys how to operate them (e.g., how to lock and unlock the doors, what to do when fights broke out). More importantly, a guard was assigned to every block and dormitory. For the first time in Eastham's history (since 1917), guards had assignments within the living areas. Also for the first time, the guards maintained the security counts.

Compliance with the court order also required the TDC to quit using physical force as an unofficial means of punishment and social control. At Eastham, in early 1983, ranking guards were instructed to "keep their hands in their pockets" and refrain form "tuning up" inmates. In fact, guards were told that anyone using unnecessary force—more force that was needed to subdue an unruly inmate—would be fired. The staff at first believed this rule would be "overlooked" and that the TDC administration would continue to support a guard's use of force against an inmate. But in this they were disappointed. In March 1983, a ranking guard was fired and two others were placed on six months' probation for beating up an inmate. Another incident in April 1983 led to the demotions and transfers of three other ranking guards.

III. THE NEW ORDER

Changes in Interpersonal Relations between the Guards and Inmates

The implementation of these reforms resulted in three major changes within the prison community. The initial and most obvious impact of the *Ruiz* ruling has been on the relations between the keepers and the kept. Formerly, inmates were controlled through relentless surveillance and by a totalitarian system that created a docile and passive ordinary inmate population. In all interactions and encounters, the guards and their agents defined the situation for the ordinary inmates.

Now, however, with the abolition of the BT/turnkey system and the disappearance of "tune-ups" and "beatings," a new relationship between keepers and kept has emerged. It is characterized by ambiguity, belligerence, confrontation, enmity, and the prisoners' overt resentment of the staff's authority. Inmates today no longer accept "things as they are." They argue with the guards and constantly challenge their authority. Moreover, the guards now find themselves in the position of having to explain and justify the rules to the inmates.

Disciplinary reports show the contrast between the new (1983 and 1984) and the old (1981 and 1982) orders. We see from Table 1 that reported inmate threats towards and attacks on the guards increased by 500 percent and more over two years. Nevertheless, it is clear from these data, as well as from interviews and observations, that the behavior of inmates towards the staff become increasingly hostile and confrontational. Simple orders to inmates (e.g., "tuck your shirt in," "get a haircut," "turn your radio down") were often followed by protracted arguments, noncompliance, and such blistering verbal attacks from inmates as "fuck all you whores, you can't tell me what to do anymore," "get a haircut yourself, bitch," "quit harassing me, you old country punk," or "get your bitchy ass out of my face, this is my radio not yours."

In addition to, and perhaps as important as, these changes in the control structure, the social distance between the guards and prisoners has diminished. The "inmates-as-nonpersons" who once inhabited our prisons have become citizens with civil rights. In the past, inmates at Eastham, subjected to derogation and physical force and ignored by extra-mural society, saw little to gain from challenging the system. Recent court reforms, however, have introduced the rule of law into the disciplinary process. Inmates now have many due-process privileges. They can present documentary evidence, call witnesses, secure representation or counsel, and even cross-examine the reporting guard. They are in an adversarial position vis à vis their guards, which at least in some procedural senses entails a kind of equality.

TABLE 1
Selected Disciplinary Cases Resulting in Solitary Confinement: Direct Challenges to Authority from 1981 to 1984*

	1981	1982	1983	1984
1. Striking an officer	4	21	38	129
	(1.3)	(6.5)	(12.0)	(49.4)
2. Attempting to strike an officer	7	9	18	21
	(2.3)	(2.7)	(5.7)	(8.0)
3. Threatening an officer	4	5	38	109
	(1.3)	(1.5)	(12.0)	(41.8)
4. Refusing or failing to obey an order	90	65	72	213
	(30.6)	(20.1)	(22.8)	(81.7)
5. Use of indecent/vulgar language (cursing an officer)	11	14	89	94
	(3.7)	(4.3)	(28.2)	(36.0)
TOTAL	116	114	225	566
Population levels	2938	3224	3150	2607

*Numbers in parentheses indicate the rate per 1000 inmates. The population figures are based on the average monthly population at Eastham.

Reorganization within the Inmate Society

The second major change concerns a restructuring of the inmate social system. The purging of the BT/turnkey system and the elimination of the old caste system created a power vacuum. The demise of the old informal or unofficial rules, controls, and status differentials led to uncertainty and ambiguity.

The Rise of Inmate-Inmate Violence. Prior to *Ruiz* and the compliance that followed, inmate-inmate violence at Eastham was relatively low considering the types of inmates incarcerated there and the average daily inmate population. Table 2 illustrates the trends in inmate-inmate violence at Eastham. The data in this table clearly document a rise in serious violence between inmates. The most remarkable point here is that the incidence of violence increased while the prison population decreased by over 300 inmates.

When the BTs were in power, one of their unofficial roles was to settle disputes, disagreements, and petty squabbles among the inmates in the living areas. Inmates came to the BTs not only for counsel but to avoid discussing a problem with the guards. The disputes often involved feuding cell partners, love affairs, petty stealing, or unpaid debts. The BTs usually looked into the matter and made a decision, thereby playing an arbitrator role. Sometimes the quarrelers were allowed to "fight it out" under the supervision of the BTs and without the staff's knowledge. Inmates rarely took these matters into their own hands by attacking another inmate in a living or work area.

To avoid the labels of punk, rat, or being weak, inmates involved in personal disputes shy away from telling guards about their problems. With the BTs gone, this leaves the inmates on their "own" to settle their differences. The inmates' sense of justice—a revenge and machismo-oriented system

TABLE 2
Selected Inmate-Inmate Offenses Resulting in Solitary Confinement:
Weapons Offenses 1981–1984

	1981	1982	1983	1984
1. Fighting with a weapon	25	31	46	31
	(8.5)	(9.6)	(14.6)	(11.8)
2. Striking in inmate with a weapon	21	25	40	57
	(7.1)	(7.7)	(12.6)	(21.8)
3. Possession of a weapon	40	25	59	134
	(13.6)	(7.7)	(18.7)	(51.4)
4. Homicide	86	82	145	225
	(30.6)	(20.1)	(22.8)	(81.7)
TOTAL	116	114	225	566
Population levels	2938	3224	3150	2607

with characteristics of blood feuds—is given full sway. The system means that inmates are virtually "cornered" and forced to use serious violence as a problem-solving mechanism. Physical threats, sexual come-ons, stealing, and unpaid debts are perceived as similarly disrespectful and as threats to one's "manhood."

To many inmates, killing or seriously wounding a tormentor in response to a threat is justifiable behavior. At Eastham, violent self-help has become a social necessity as well as a method of revenge. Rather than lose face in the eyes of one's peers and risk being labeled weak, which is an open invitation to further victimization, many inmates see assaultive behavior as a legitimate way to protect their "manhood" and self-respect.

The Emergence of Inmate Gangs. As personal violence escalated, inmate gangs developed, partly as a response to the violence but chiefly to fill the void left by the BTs. Prior to 1982, only one inmate gang, the Texas Syndicate, or TS, existed at Eastham.

The presence of the gangs was not really felt or perceived as a security problem until late 1984. Prior to this time, the staff had identified and kept tabs on the gang leaders as well as on recruiting trends. The staff also uncovered several "hits," but violence did not erupt. Then, in November 1984, two ABs (Aryan Brotherhood) stabbed two other ABs; one victim was the AB leader. Early December saw four TS (Texas Syndicate) stab another TS in a cell block. Shortly thereafter, several members of the Texas Mafia murdered another TM in an administrative segregation block, a high security area housing inmates with violent prison records, known as gang leaders, and many gang members. In the final incident a TS leader at Eastham murdered a fellow TS member in the same segregation block as the previous murder, on January 1, 1985. Thus, gang-related violence has emerged not only at the prison, but within the gangs themselves.

Reactions of the Guards

The reforms have upset the very foundations of the guard subculture and work role. Their work world is no longer smooth, well-ordered, predictable, or rewarding. Loyalty to superiors, especially the warden, the job, and /or organization—once the hallmark of the guard staff at Eastham—is quickly fading. The officers are disgruntled and embittered over the reform measures that have "turned the place over to the convicts."

Fear of the Inmates. Part of the *Ruiz* ruling ordered TDC to hire hundreds of guards to replace the BTs. Eastham received 150 new guards between November 1982 and January 1983. For the first time guards were assigned to work in the living areas. It was hoped this increase in uniformed personnel would increase order and control within the institution. Contrary to expectations, the increase in inexperienced personnel and the closer guard-inmate relationships resulted in more violence and less prisoner control. As indicated earlier, assaults on the staff skyrocketed between 1981 (4) and 1984 (129). Additionally, one officer was taken hostage and three guards were stabbed by inmates at Eastham in 1984.

The traditional authoritarian guarding style at Eastham has been replaced with a tolerant, permissive, or "let's get along" pattern of interaction. The attitude currently prevailing among guards is summed up by the following guard's statement: "I don't give a damn about what they do, as long as they leave me alone. I'm here to do my eight hours and collect a pay check, and that's it."

"We've Lost Control." The rise in inmate-inmate violence, the emergence of violent gangs, the loss of traditional control methods, the combative nature of guard-inmate interactions, the derogation of guards, and the influx of inexperienced guards have contributed to a "crisis in control" for the guards. Many of the guards, especially the veterans, perceive the changes wrought in the wake of *Ruiz* as unjustified and undermining their authority. Indeed, as we see in Table 3, the total number of solitary confinement cases has skyrocketed since 1981.

The data reveal that the rate of serious disciplinary infractions (violence and challenges to guards' authority) rapidly increased after the reforms in 1983 despite a decrease in the inmate population. The rapid increase in rule violations has demoralized the guard staff to the point of frustration and resignation.

The traditional means of dealing with "unruly" prisoners have been abolished and replaced with more official, due process methods. Standards and guidelines for the guards' use of force have been implemented. Whenever a guard uses force to control an inmate for whatever reason (e.g., breaking up fights, taking an inmate into custody), the officer must submit a written report detailing all phases of the incident. When a use of force involves a scuffle, all parties are brought to the prison's hospital to photograph any injuries or abrasions. Forced cell moves are also videotaped. Documentation and accountability are musts for the guard force today. Furthermore, whenever physical force is used against inmates, Internal Affairs investigates the incident. Thus, the disciplinary process itself frustrates the line officers—so much that they often "look the other way" or simply fail to "see" most inmate rule violations.

TABLE 3
Inmates Sentenced to Solitary Confinement from 1981 to 1984

All offenses	487	404	889	1182
	(165.7)	(175.3)	(282.2)	(453.)
Population levels	2938	3224	3150	2607

IV. SOME CONCLUSIONS ON COURT REFORMS AND PRISONER CONTROL

The *Ruiz* ruling sounded the death knell for the old prison order in Texas. Legal maneuverings and a new prison administration have given increasing substance to the new order that *Ruiz* initiated. Table 4 summarizes the distinctions between the old, or inmate-dependent, order and the new, bureaucratic-legal order.

The transition towards a bureaucratic-legal order at Eastham permits much less autonomy. To increase central office control over TDC's many prisons, the new TDC administration (under Raymond Procunier) established, in 1984, regional directors to supervise more closely the wardens of individual units. As elsewhere, new policies to carry out court-ordered reforms have also reduced the discretion of all unit officials. Written directives regarding disciplinary or supervisory procedures emphasize legal standards

TABLE 4
A Summary Depiction of Eastham before and after Ruiz

	Inmate-Dependent Pre-Ruiz Era	Bureaucratic-Legal Order Post-Ruiz Era
1. Decision-making power	Decentralized—warden establishes many policies and procedures at the prison. Prison administrators enjoy a high degree of autonomy.	Centralized—warden carries out directives established in central TDC office. Less unit flexibility; prison officials allowed little autonomy.
2. Staff/inmate relations	Based on paternalism, coercion, dominance, and fear. Majority of the inmates are viewed and treated as nonpersons. Guards define the situation for the inmates.	Based on combative relations wherein guards have less discretion and inmates challenge the staff's authority. Guards fear the inmates.
3. Prisoner control apparatus	Internal-proactive control system based on information. Guards penetrate the inmate society through a system of surrogate guards. Organized violence, riots, mob action, and general dissent are obviated. Punishment is swift, severe, certain and often corporal. Control is an end itself.	External-reactive control system in which the guard staff operates on the perimeter of the inmate society. Loss of information prevents staff from penetrating inmate society; thus they must contain violence. Punishment is based on hearings and due-process considerations. Control mechanisms are means-oriented.
4. Inmate society	Fractured and atomistic due to the presence of BTs—official snitches.	Racially oriented with the emergence of violent cliques and gangs.

more than the traditional, cultural values that once defined prison objectives. The precedence of legal standards is especially evident in the "use of force" policy. Each time some physical means of control is used, a "use of force" report (a series of statements and photographs) must be completed and filed with the central office. Whenever a physical confrontation is anticipated (e.g., forced cell moves), the action is videotaped. The watchword is documentation. The bureaucratic-legal order also discourages informal relations between officers and inmates. Yet few staff-inmate links limit organizational intelligence and thus the ability to anticipate trouble.

The court-prompted reforms have created for prison officials a dilemma analogous to that experienced by police. Guards, like police, must balance two fundamental values: order and rule by law. Clearly, order can be maintained in a totalitarian, lawless manner. In a democratic society, order must be maintained under rules of law. Having been mandated to maintain control by constitutional means, Eastham prison officials face a problem that pervades our criminal justice system today.

Judicial Intervention: Lessons from the Past

JOHN J. DIIULIO, JR.

The rise of judicial intervention into penal systems has been part of a broader expansion of the courts' role in American government. In a few recent cases, the courts have shown some reluctance to intervene, and there is a hint of evidence that the problem of AIDS in prisons and jails may encourage judges to defer more readily to the wisdom of on-site corrections officials. But there is no reason to suppose that we are witnessing a return to the hands-off doctrine, in the 1990s and beyond, judges will continue to influence, and in many cases to dictate, how prisons and jails are organized and managed.

THREE VIEWS OF JUDICIAL INTERVENTION

As sentencing and demographic trends conspire to make continued growth in the nation's prison and jail populations, and institutional overcrowding, virtual certainties, it is most likely that judges will continue to intervene and act as wardens. Whether one welcomes or laments this prospect may depend not only on one's beliefs about the constitutional and moral propri-

Source: Excerpted from Dilulio, John J. Judicial Intervention: Lessons from the Past. Ch. 4 in *No Escape: The Future of American Corrections.* New York: Basic Books, 1991.

ety of judicial involvement in this area but also on one's assessment of the consequences of that involvement measured in terms of institutional safety, civility, and cost-effectiveness. There are three basic schools of thought on the impact of judicial intervention into prisons and jails.

One school argues that judges have emboldened the inmates, upset informal order-keeping arrangements among prisoners and between inmates and staff, and gutted basic custodial controls. Members of this school blame the courts for rising tides of prison violence. For example, Kathleen Engel and Stanley Rothman have argued that court-imposed reforms have increased prison violence by undermining the "complex relationships among inmates" that had "contributed to the maintenance of order and inmate solidarity." The notion that such informal cellblock alliances were once a bedrock of prison order is a vivid but wholly unsubstantiated sociological myth; riots and disturbances have occurred most often precisely where prison administrators have relied upon inmates to control other inmates and have failed to run things by the book. Especially in high security prisons, those prison managers have governed best who have governed most and most formally.

A second school maintains that activist judges have done no more than force prison administrators to operate in ways that secure rather than deny prisoners' rights. Advocates of this view credit the courts with improving prison and jail conditions. For example, the ACLU's National Prison Project led the litigation efforts that expanded court intervention into penal affairs; indeed, the organization spearheaded the use of special masters and monitors. One of the ACLU's primary objectives in this area has been to decrease the number of people behind bars and to force a greater use of ostensibly less harsh and restrictive alternatives to incarceration; hence, whether the actual impact on cellblock conditions is good, bad, unknown, or nonexistent, the organization counts as major victories instances of judicial involvement where population limits have been imposed and negative media attention has been focused on the prison gates.

Yet a third school believes that the courts have fostered a codification of correctional policies and procedures resulting in the bureaucratization of the institutions, which in turn has made prisons and jails more orderly and humane. This belief moves from a top-down conception of bureaucracy that focuses more on formal administrative trappings (bulky training manuals, elaborate central-office policy directives, uniform institutional training programs, and the like) than on the day-to-day work of line employees. By definition, those in a bureaucracy who perform the agency's critical tasks have little discretion; successful job performance is not highly contingent on the integrity, personality, wit, or any other special talents of the workers.

A TALE OF TWO STATES AND ONE CITY

None of the leading views of judicial intervention fares well when considered in the light of actual cases. There is a great deal of variance in the outcomes of judicial interventions into penal systems. Let us now explore three cases that illustrate the range of outcomes in relation to the intervening judge's modus operandi. As we shall see, the course and consequences of an intervention depend on many factors, but not surprisingly, the judge's role is primary.

THE *RUIZ* INTERVENTION IN TEXAS

Perhaps the single most controversial, publicized, and revealing instance of judicial intervention into a major prison system is *Ruiz vs. Estelle* in Texas. The case began in 1972, dragged on into 1987, and revolutionized the way Texas ran its prisons. Nobody had a more profound sense of what the intervention had wrought than Dr. George Beto.

During Beto's tenure and into the 1980s, the Texas prison system had been hailed as one of the nation's best; but during 1984 and 1985 a total of 52 inmates of Texas prisons were murdered, and over 700 were stabbed. More serious violence occurred during those two years than had occurred in the previous decade. As the disorder mounted, inmate participation in treatment and educational programs became erratic, the once immaculate inmate living quarters ceased to sparkle, and recreational privileges were curtailed.

What happened to the Texas Department of Corrections (TDC) was the product of at least two sets of related factors: a major flaw in the model of penal administration fathered by Beto and bequeathed to his successor, W. J. Estelle, and *Ruiz v. Estelle*, a landmark court case in which federal district judge William Wayne Justice brought about sweeping changes in TDC's philosophy, leadership, and day-to-day management practices while making the agency the *bête noire* of state policy makers and the press.

Beto, a tall, lean Lutheran minister with a doctorate in education, instituted what came to be known in corrections circles as the control model of penal administration. His control model emphasized inmate obedience, work, and education, roughly in that order. Every TDC prison was run as a maximum-security operation organized along strict paramilitary lines. Official rules and regulations were enforced rigorously. In the prison corridors, for example, clean-shaven, white-uniformed inmates were required to walk between lines painted on the floors rather than moving at random down the center. Talking too loud was a punishable offense. Punishment for rule violations, major and minor, was swift and certain. Rewards for good behavior came in the form of better work assignments, sentence reductions, and "trustyships." Each inmate spent his first six months doing backbreaking stoop labor, a cog in the machine of TDC's then enormously successful agribusiness complex. All inmates were required to attend school and, if illiterate, to learn how to read and write.

In return for watching the officers' backs, providing information, turning cell doors, tending to the physical upkeep of the institutions, and other duties, Beto's buildings tenders were officially rewarded with better food, job assignments, and other amenities. The building tender system was a calculated gamble aimed at turning the "natural" leaders of the society of captives into the official allies of the government of keepers.

When in 1972 Beto resigned amid pleas from all over the state that he remain as director of TDC, most of his control model had been well institutionalized: the paramilitary procedures, the liberal awarding of good time, the stress on inmate discipline, work, and education. The building tender system, however, was never a well-integrated part of the model. Beto and his top aides were aware that, without unremitting efforts to keep it honest, the building tender system could easily degenerate into the very system of inmate dominance and corrupt inmate-staff relations it was meant to forestall.

Under Beto's hand-picked heir, W. J. "Jim" Estelle, the number of TDC inmates increased by the thousands and the agency's prisons more than doubled to over two dozen institutions. Though in many respects a brilliant prisons man, Estelle was no "Walking Jim." Under Beto, the building tender system had been a sharpened knife wielded by a master chef in a calm kitchen. This knife was handed to Estelle who, by comparison, was a good short-order cook behind a busy counter. Estelle was a younger man with a mostly office bound style of executive leadership; word of abuses did not always trickle up to his headquarters in Huntsville, and there were no independent channels of information such as had enabled Beto and his aides to check on the veracity of reports from the field and caused them to notice when such reports were forthcoming.

Predictably, while most other parts of the control model survived and were strengthened under Estelle, the building tender system ran amok and became nothing more than a con-boss system in which selected inmates were allowed to carry weapons and were given illicit privileges for "keeping things quiet." In some instances, this meant administering beatings to fellow inmates who had defied an officer or refused to work. At a few TDC institutions, the administration became a virtual hostage to the building tenders, relying on them to perform many or most custodial functions. In at least one prison, the weekend staff consisted of only a dozen officers supervising some forty building tenders who made counts, searched cells, frisked other inmates, and administered harsh and arbitrary discipline.

In 1978, the state's first Republican administration in 105 years took the reins in Austin and wasted little time in shaking things up. With new appointees, the Texas Board of Corrections, a body once dominated by leading Texas businessmen who had never been anything but supportive of TDC, started to cast unprecedented split votes and to voice public criticism of the agency. Political pillars of TDC such as Texas State House Appropriations Chairman Bill "The Duke of Paducah" Heatly and H. H. "Pete" Coffield were passing from the scene. Meanwhile, the state's oil revenues were drying up, forcing Texas policy makers to scratch for ways to be even stingier than customary with financial support for public agencies. Estelle lacked the political instincts that had made Beto so successful with the state's political establishment; TDC lost its "sacred cow" status and was targeted for budget cuts.

Judge Justice Intervenes

In this context the case of *Ruiz v. Estelle* was litigated, beginning in 1972 shortly before Estelle's appointment. Inmate David Ruiz, a chronic offender who had been incarcerated many times, sent a handwritten petition to Judge William Wayne Justice of the Eastern District Court. In this petition, Ruiz charged that conditions in "the hole" were inhumane. Ruiz challenged conditions of confinement in TDC under section 1983 of the U.S. Civil Rights Act. In 1974, Judge Justice combined Ruiz's petition with those of seven other inmates, thereby framing a class action suit.

The trial began in 1978. In the preceding four years, Judge Justice had imposed a number of orders on TDC. In 1975, for instance, he prohibited prison authorities from censoring inmates' mail. In 1980 his 248-page memorandum opinion required scores of changes in the Texas prison system, among them: an end to the use of building tenders; a requirement that the agency double its officer force and retrain veteran officers; a revision in the procedures for handling inmate grievances; a complete overhaul of the prisoner classification system that would reduce the number of maximum-security designations; a division of the prison population into management units of not more than 500 each; a radical improvement in health delivery systems that would give inmates easy access to state-of-the-art medical treatment; and the provision of a single cell for each inmate. All the major issues in the case were decided wholly in favor of the plaintiffs.

In 1982, a decade after the litigation had begun, the U. S. Circuit Court of Appeals for the Fifth District upheld Justice's central findings about the unconstitutionality of conditions inside the Texas prisons, but overturned several provisions of the original order. At the same time, however, the panel chided TDC officials for failing to run better prisons and warned that the "implementation of the district court's decree can become a ceaseless guerrilla war, with endless hearings, opinions and appeals, and incalculable costs." The panel also warned Judge Justice and his team of monitors to "respect the right of the state to administer its own affairs so long as it does not violate the Constitution."

Unfortunately, neither the judge and his monitors nor the TDC officials fully heeded the panel's warnings. The litigation continued at full boil for three more years amid bitter charges and countercharges. Estelle was the proud director of a proud agency. He challenged TDC's critics on the bench and elsewhere to measure its performance in terms of safety, cleanliness, programs, and costs. Compared to prisons in California, Michigan, and many other major jurisdictions, TDC prisons had measured up favorably: For example, between 1973 and 1980 there was a total of 19 homicides in Texas prisons, while there were 139 in California; rates of prison assaults in Texas ran well below the national average while costs per inmate were the lowest in the country; and TDC boasted the only fully accredited prison educational system in the nation.

The judge, however, painted an unrelievedly bleak image of TDC while his staff acted in ways that were almost calculated to breed ill will, confusion, and low morale among the very persons—from the director to the junior officers in the cellblocks—who would ultimately have to translate the court's decree into administrative action. No matter how Estelle and his staff moved to bring the agency into compliance with the court's sweeping orders, public criticism and a barrage of new orders followed.

Estelle's defense of the agency, like the judge's attack, was undiscriminating, even desperate. He fought fiercely to protect Beto's control model and to shore up staff morale. By 1983, however, Beto himself recognized that the building tender system was a cancer ripe for the cutting, a rotten administrative crutch that TDC could and should drop at the judge's invitation in order to preserve and strengthen the rest of the system. These decisions, however, were not up to Beto. Under fire from the Board of Corrections, and having had the agency's budgetary requests rebuffed by a state legislature that was about to launch critical investigations into TDC's financial management, Estelle resigned in late 1983.

Estelle's replacement, Raymond Procunier, was a salty-mouthed man with a brash leadership style. Known in corrections circles as "the pro," Procunier had directed several major corrections agencies, usually leaving them in turmoil. But state leaders got from Procunier what they wanted: a promise to rush TDC into the latter stages of compliance with the judge's orders. After a brief honeymoon with his staff, Procunier fired employees who did not jump to cooperate, subjected officers to lie detector tests, and took other actions that undercut his popularity within the department. Within months of his arrival, political support for his administration crumbled as murders multiplied, inmate-on-officer assaults skyrocketed, programs were disrupted, costs escalated, prison gangs organized along racial and ethnic lines blossomed, and outside contractors were brought in to do the agriculture and other work once solely the province of TDC inmates.

What Beto and Estelle had taken twenty years to build, Judge Justice, aided and abetted by Estelle's successor and by grandstanding state policy makers eager to make fresh political hay and headlines out of the system's legal troubles, helped to put asunder, by making the task of formal prison governance inside Texas prisons much harder and personally more unrewarding.

THE *NEWMAN* AND *PUGH* INTERVENTION IN ALABAMA

In 1971, an Alabama inmate filed a lawsuit charging that six fellow inmates had died in the state prison hospital because of inadequate medical treatment. If anything, "inadequate medical treatment" is a euphemism here. Sick and dying Alabama inmates simply went unattended. Such medical facilities as existed were decrepit, understaffed, and without basic equipment. Maggots crawled through patients' festering wounds.

Moreover, Alabama corrections officers were extremely ill trained and undertrained. Within their ranks, there was no TDC-style esprit de corps or sense of mission, no well-practiced paramilitary security routine, and no tradition of openness to outsiders, including legislators, journalists, and extra departmental researchers. Whereas Texas prisons in the decades leading up to the *Ruiz* litigation had always enjoyed sufficient political and budgetary support, in the decades leading up to the *Newman* and *Pugh* intervention, Alabama prisons had been political and fiscal orphans.

Judges Johnson and Varner Intervene

In October 1972, Federal District Judge Frank M. Johnson found the Alabama prison system's medical facilities so poor as to be in violation of the Eighth Amendment's prohibition against "cruel and unusual punishments." He ordered major changes in medical facility staffing and other areas.

Initially, Johnson thought that these changes could and would be made within about six months. But his orders encountered fierce resistance from the Department of Corrections and many of the state's political leaders. As Judge Justice did in Texas, Johnson might have responded to this initial political and bureaucratic resistance by immediately bringing other parts of the prison system under his review, piling unmet order upon unmet order until the appeals court had its say. He did not.

Instead, Johnson remained focused on the medical issues, expressed his determination to see needed improvements made in the prison health care facilities, rolled with the verbal punches thrown at him by disgruntled agency and political officials, and simply let it be known that he would resort to contempt citations and other measures if some significant degree of compliance was not forthcoming. As a result, the department followed many of his orders and by 1974 the state's prison medical facilities had improved somewhat.

But the institutions remained violent, overcrowded, and plagued by other serious problems. Thus, in 1976 Judge Johnson assumed control of the entire Alabama prison system. He appointed a committee of thirty-nine Alabamans to offer "advice and consent" as he attempted to remedy the system's defects. But the state's political leadership simply would not budge on budgeting for the needed reforms.

By 1979, a showdown between the judge and the department and its political allies appeared imminent, but two things happened to avert it. First, Johnson moved to the appellate court, and Federal District Judge Robert E. Varner took the reins. Second Governor George C. Wallace, who was among those who rallied the department and the legislature against the judge and fought the intervention tooth and nail, left the office and was succeeded by Fob James.

Governor James saw the prison system's troubles as the product of poor management. Judge Varner, like Judge Johnson before him, was determined to make the necessary changes, with the department's consent and cooperation if at all possible but without it if absolutely necessary. Varner appointed James temporary receiver for the Alabama prison system. James appointed a new, reform-minded director of corrections, Robert Britton.

Britton had worked in TDC under none other than Dr. George Beto and considered Beto a great administrator. Britton's reputation as a no-nonsense Texas-style executive preceded him to Alabama and put him in favor with the prison rank-and-file. He immediately set about the task of building alliances with the state's political establishment, instituting officer training programs, improving food services and sanitation, and addressing other problems identified by the court. Judge Varner appointed Beto himself to serve on a four-member expert committee charged with overseeing implementation of the remaining court orders.

In December 1988, Beto's committee recommended that Judge Varner dismiss the seventeen-year-old suit, which he did. Most observers, including state officials who had initially opposed the judge's "interference," agreed that though the intervention had by no means perfected Alabama's prison system, it had helped to catalyze remarkable improvements at reasonable human and financial costs—or at least without the tragic explosion of murders and assaults, the utter demoralization of staff, and the other severe problems that had accompanied the *Ruiz* intervention in Texas.

THE RHEM INTERVENTION IN NEW YORK CITY

When the case of *Rhem* began in January 1972, everyone who mattered— the mayor, key corrections officials, and jail-beat journalists—knew that the Tombs was filthy, dilapidated, and unfit for human habitation, and that pretrial detainees there were repressively and routinely handled as dangerous maximum-security felons. Led by Mayor Abraham Beame, however, city officials stonewalled Judge Morris E. Lasker's decree to upgrade the jail.

In response, Lasker gradually turned up the heat. After granting the department numerous delays and threatening officials with contempt citations, in July 1974 he gave the city thirty days to deliver to his chambers a detailed plan to remedy the unconstitutional conditions at the jail. The "or else" in this ultimatum was hard for anyone to ignore: Plan and budget the needed reforms or the jail will close at once. The city appealed this improve-it-or-close-it decision, but the Second Circuit Court backed Lasker.

Eventually, Lasker brought the entire city jail system under his review. Under his direction, a new Tombs jail was built in Manhattan, and the corrections department improved its management practices there and on Rikers Island. After 1978, a complicated set of plaintiffs' attorneys and others became involved in the process of negotiating and implementing court-ordered reforms. But Lasker managed to keep nearly everyone focused on what he treated as their common objective: to bring the city's jails up to minimum constitutional muster by making them safe and civilized.

At the end of 1989, the jails remained under Lasker's supervision. In the previous years, he had fought many political and bureaucratic battles—including one to keep unpopular jail reforms on the agenda when the city was falling into bankruptcy—but in each case he prevailed and the jails in question improved markedly.

In contrast to Judge Justice in Texas, at no point in the intervention did Lasker bully or belittle corrections officials. Even when there was clear evidence of bureaucratic foot dragging and worse, the judge's response was measured and restrained. This made converts among many who had strongly opposed Lasker's efforts. For example, city corrections chief Benjamin Malcolm recognized that he had earned a contempt citation but was grateful to Lasker for not slapping him with one. As a result, Malcolm's attitude toward the court changed over the course of the intervention, causing him to revise his "early view of Lasker as a judge overstepping his boundary to that of a judge who had the guts and courage to stand up and keep the system in line."

TOWARD EFFECTIVE JUDICIAL INTERVENTION

My advice about how judges can best proceed is based on an analysis of exploratory studies that do not lend themselves to systematic comparisons. Unfortunately, the available empirical data on judicial intervention do not offer much in the way of natural experiments. And except as a mental experiment, we cannot hold everything else constant and see what would have happened if, say, Judge Lasker (or a more Lasker-like judge) had presided in the Texas as well as the New York City cases.

Just the same, there are four general lessons to be drawn from an analysis of the record of judicial intervention into prisons and jails from 1970 to 1989.

By now, the first and foremost of these lessons should be obvious: Intervening judges must proceed in a judicious manner, move in incremental steps, and avoid antagonizing the people who must translate their orders into administrative action in the cellblocks. They must seek to reform, not to revolutionize, the institutions, taking pains to preserve those organizational elements that are worth preserving. Judge Justice's mistake in Texas was in attempting to punish corrections officials for their real or perceived slights against his authority; Judges Johnson, Varner and Lasker managed both the symbols and the substance of their respective interventions more deftly. The political and bureaucratic resistance to judicial intervention was every bit as intense in Alabama and New York City as it was in Texas. But only Judge Justice reacted to the opposition in a way that even his most inveterate academic apologists admit created an atmosphere of distrust, in addition to deepening efforts to resist court-approved reforms.

The second lesson is that as judges attempt to make changes in the way prisons and jails are run, they should visit the institutions, make firsthand observations, and talk to inmates and staff. The ethic of a bench that confines itself to interpreting the laws is hardly appropriate for judges who make and oversee the implementation of laws; responsible activist judges must leave the serenity of their chambers. Judges will learn more from such field trips than they will from reading all the books, essays, and neatly typed depositions in the world. They will be in a far better position to predict and weigh the real costs and benefits of any court-induced changes and to appreciate the constraints under which prison administrators at all levels operate. They will be able to see for themselves whether institutional practices are in need of repair, and to judge whether cells are cramped, food is decent, health care is available, and so on.

The third lesson is that judges need to approach intervention with one eye on the dynamics of complex organizations. They need not trade their legal texts for monographs on organization theory (heaven forbid!), but they must understand the agencies they are seeking to reform as delicate human organisms. Infusing the members of any large, complex organization with a genuine sense of mission and identification with their agency is no easy task. Corrections is a dangerous, dirty, difficult and thankless profession.

More concretely, it means recognizing that administrative stability at the top of a corrections department is hard-won and precious. Between 1973 and mid-1987, in less than one-third of all corrections agencies did corrections commissioners enjoy an average tenure of five years or more; in over one-third they held office for an average of three years or less. Judges should try not to exacerbate this problem of fluctuating executive leadership, for it is largely responsible for the fact that prisons and jails have been ill managed, undermanaged, or not managed at all. And they should recognize how truly difficult is the task of the line corrections officer even when performed under the most stable and supportive conditions; we would all be better off if most judges (and all professionals) had the practical wisdom, public-spiritedness, and professional integrity of the average prison or jail worker.

The fourth, final, and most general lesson is that intervening judges should make a broader application of the idea that prisons and jails must be governed in ways that make them constitutional. In the Madisonian formulation of *The Federalist*, constitutional government springs from the recognition that "men are not angels"; those who rule must be strong enough to control the governed, but obliged to control themselves. Prison and jail managers are the government of the institution. They must be given enough formal authority to govern inmates who are most decidedly not angels. At the same time, however, they must be subjected to internal and external checks and balances: professional standards, peer review, legislative inquiries, media scrutiny, openness to extra departmental researchers, and, last but not least, responsible judicial intervention and oversight.

CHAPTER **3**

Contemporary Correctional Institutions as People Processing Organizations

Prison can be seen as a unique form of society, with its own distinctive set of social and cultural arrangements that include a dominant social structure, a special set of goals, norms and values, and a primitive yet serviceable economy. In attempting to explain this phenomenon, early scholars focused on universal and distinctive characteristics of prisons. For example, Clemmer (1940) was among the first to specify the "inmate code," and he coined the term "prisonization" to characterize the process of acculturation to that code. Sykes (1958) described the "pains of imprisonment" that derive from institutions that punish and control through isolation. Goffman (1961) described prisons as "total institutions," a special class of organizations that are designed to transform people socially and psychologically. Finally, Ohlin (1960) described how "goal conflict" stemming from opposing mandates of treatment and custody is a salient characteristic of prisons.

Later on, scholars began to investigate the complexity and diversity of inmates and prison settings. For example, scholars began to argue that inmate behavior results both from an "importation" of personal dispositions as well as from a process of "adaptation" to prison society. Jacobs (1977) subsequently described the importance of race and gang membership in the social organizations of prisons. Meanwhile, Toch (1977) introduced the concept of prison "niches," which are subenvironments with distinctive attributes, and developed instruments for measuring salient characteristics of prison settings. Finally, Zamble and Porporino (1988) identified the various psychological coping strategies that inmates use to deal with the problems of prison life.

The readings in this section develop the theme of the uniqueness of prisons, which is found in the early prison literature, while extending the emphasis on complexity and diversity, which is found in the later prison literature. The perspective looks beyond prisons as a class of institutions to investigate more closely specific types of prisons, specific groups of inmates, and specific features of prison operation. In addition, the manners in which prisons affect people and people affect prisons are examined. The readings also include contrasting perspectives, which emphasize ways in which prisons are similar to other organizations and social institutions. To highlight the real-world implications of various perspectives, issues of prison administration are discussed in many readings.

The first reading, by Elaine Lord, a prison superintendent, deals with women's prisons. The author discusses the distinctive characteristics of female inmates as they relate to treatment, other forms of programming, and prison administration. The next reading addresses special management inmates, specifically, the victim-prone inmate, the inmate troublemaker, and the mentally ill inmate. The focus of discussion is on the problems these inmates present and on ways to address these challenges. The third reading, by David Cooke, a forensic psychologist, discusses how prison settings influence everyday behavior. The discussion centers on Barlinnie, a special unit in the Scottish prison system designed to deal with violent inmates. The next article describes how the influx of young gang members into the California prison system adversely affected the quality of prison life. The fifth reading, by Susan Philliber, reviews the literature on correctional officers with regard to role conflict, career paths, guard subcultures, and officer prisonization. The following reading, by Nancy Jurik, describes how organizational factors and individual attitudes impact employment opportunities for women, a problem that transcends prison settings. The final reading, by John DiIulio, a political scientist, discusses ways to improve prison administration by emphasizing what prisons have in common with forms of government. The author suggests that prisons should be thought of as minigovernments rather than as minisocieties.

NOTES

Clemmer, Donald 1940. *The Prison Community*. New York: Holt, Rinehart and Winston.

Sykes, Gresham M. 1958. *The Society of Captives*. Princeton, NJ: Princeton University Press.

Goffman, Irving. 1961. *Asylum: Essays on the Social Situation of Mental Patients and Other Inmates*. New York: Anchor Books.

Ohlin, Lloyd. 1960. "Conflicting interests in correctional objectives." In Richard A. Cloward et al., *Theoretical Studies in the Social Organization of the Prison*. New York: Social Science Research Council. Pp. 111–29.

Jacobs, James B. 1997. *Stateville: The Penitentiary in Mass Society*. Chicago: University of Chicago Press.

Toch, Hans. 1977. *Living in Prison: The Ecology of Survival*. New York: Free Press.

Zamble E. and F. J. Porporino. 1988. *Coping, Behavior and Adaptation in Prison Life*. New York: Springer-Verlag.

A Prison Superintendent's Perspective on Women in Prison

Elaine M. Lord

Over and over during recent years, we hear of the ever-burgeoning numbers of incarcerated women. This trend is reflected across the nation at both the state and local levels. The American Correctional Association's (ACA) Task Force on the Female Offender (1990) notes that the female population has had a greater percentage increase than has the male population each year since 1981. The Bureau of Justice Statistics, in its 1991 *Special Report: Women in Prison*, notes that the number of women under state and federal prison jurisdiction had grown by more than 27,000 since 1980, an increase of more than 200%. In looking at state prison systems, the report finds that the rate of growth for female inmates exceeded that for males in each year since 1981. In fact, from 1980 to 1989, the male state prison population increased by 112% whereas the female population increased 202%. In New York State alone, the number of women under state custody more than tripled during the period from 1982 to the end of 1990, increasing from approximately 800 to 2,700, according to the New York State Department of Correctional Services (DOCS, 1991:2).

Immarigeon and Chesney-Lind (1992) point out that, even in the face of a rapidly growing prison population, women still represent only a small proportion (roughly 5%) of that population. Further, women commit far fewer serious or violent offenses than do men, and they return to prison at a lower rate. These authors argue, along with other researchers, that female offenders commit crimes that, although unacceptable, pose little threat to the physical safety of the community (p. 9). Despite the fact that the woman offender population was growing at a faster rate than the male offender population, the growth has never been found to be related to the seriousness of women's offenses.

The numbers of women caught up in the criminal justice system for property crimes and drug possession accounted for the increased growth of women in custody. The nation's "war on drugs," coupled with changing law enforcement and judicial practices with regard to drugs, played a major part

Source: Excerpted from Lord, E. M. "A Prison Superintendent's Perspective on Women in Prison." *The Prison J.* 75(2), June 1995, pp. 257–269.

in this dramatic change. In other words, women are not being sent to prison in increasing numbers because they are committing more, or even more serious, crimes but rather because we made a change in the way we do business. In fact, the proportion of women in prison for violent crimes has actually dropped (Immarigeon & Chesney-Lind, 1992:3).

IMPACT OF INCARCERATION ON WOMEN AND CHILDREN

The ACA's Task Force on the Female Offender in 1990 found that the average woman offender is responsible for young children and is usually a single parent/primary caretaker of the children. The average woman offender comes from a single-parent home and often has other incarcerated family members. The most difficult consequence of imprisonment for women is to endure the pain of separation from their children. Many women feel tremendous guilt over this separation, and children, in their way, wonder what they have done to create a situation where their mothers are taken or sent away. It is clear that both mothers and children grapple with how to maintain their bonds while separated. They discuss sending kisses through the mail or watching the same moon at night, and some run away to talk to their mothers. Children just do not give up on their mothers because they are in prison.

It is important to support parenting by listening to mothers, by getting mothers talking about their experiences, by providing educational experiences about parenting issues, and by providing opportunities for mothers to talk to teachers and school counselors. In the visiting room, it is important to provide child caregivers so that a woman can have some time outside of a child's hearing to discuss problems/issues with other adults or perhaps to have some individual time with one of her children. The play area, which takes up one third of the visiting room, provides a more normal setting for a mother and child. And because a mother's absence has so deep an impact on a child, mothers now tape-record stories to send to their children so that they can be played whenever the children are lonely or just to help them sleep.

However, if we are ever going to effectively intervene in the intergenerational connections of crime, abuse, drugs, and incarceration, we must recognize that these are families at risk. To effect change and enhance the healthy nurturing potential of these mother/child relationships, we must face that this can occur only in the context of consistent relationships and cannot occur in isolation. These relationships cannot thrive on 2 hours a week or a month, and they cannot thrive on 1 week a year—they cannot thrive in prison. Everything that we are doing in prison to address family issues we can do better in free society and at considerably less cost. And maybe even more basic, why is it necessary to separate these women from their children? A free society should strive to use the least restrictive response to transgression. For most women and children, this is certainly not prison. It is important to remember that parenting is a learned skill. Birthing is biological, mothering is not. And, all too frequently, these mothers come from families that were themselves in crises or that are still in crises—that were mired in poverty, drugs, violence, and homelessness. We need to divert funds from prisons that are exorbitantly expensive and move those funds to assist families with young children at risk before they are caught up in the criminal justice system.

Women's Experiences of Family Violence and Drug Abuse

Two thirds of incarcerated women ran away from home at some time as children, and about one fourth attempted suicide previously. About 65% of incarcerated women were victims of severe and prolonged physical and sexual abuse primarily as children, but for many continuing into adulthood. For most of these women, the abuse occurred before the age of 14 and was perpetrated by a male member of the family. Three quarters had histories of alcohol abuse, and one half had histories of drug abuse. Many had previously participated in drug and alcohol treatment programs (ACA Task Force on the Female Offender, 1990:17–19).

As a result of their experiences, some women may replicate the violence they have experienced, whereas others may numb themselves or seek a false aura of power with drugs. Drug use, then, is a manifestation and, again, we must look beyond the substance abuse itself to the real story. Drug use becomes a way to numb pain, to take oneself out of a painful and hopeless world. The drug use, in and of itself, is not the problem that needs to be addressed but is only a symptom—of feelings that must be kept in check to ensure survival. In fact, research has shown a link between violent victimization experiences and alcohol and drug use among women (Miller, Downs, & Joyce, 1993:1). This is currently a population that is in large measure finding its way to prison. Yet, residential drug treatment costs between $17,000 and $20,000 per year, and outpatient treatment costs $2,700 per year. All of these figures are well below costs of imprisonment for these same women coupled with foster care costs for their children. Prison costs between $20,000 and $30,000 per year, whereas foster care adds another $4,000 to $14,000 per year, excluding administrative costs. Miller and her coauthors suggest that "women who use drugs should be placed in treatment programs specifically designed for dealing with the woman and her children. This can be accomplished at a fraction of the cost of incarceration" (p. 7). Certainly, treatment programs are designed as such—for substance abuse treatment. Prisons, on the other hand, are designed to keep inmates out of the community at large. Prisons may have substance abuse programs, but they are not the main business of the prison. Security takes precedence over all other functions and absorbs the majority of the funding. Thus a drug program in prison functions in and around the daily regime of security. In prison, it will always remain a secondary function to security. That is simple reality.

We need to be more honest with ourselves that the vast majority of women receiving prison sentences are not the business operatives of the drug networks. We need to stop deluding ourselves that we are putting pushers in prison. The glass ceiling appears to operate for women whether we are talking about legitimate or illegitimate business. Women sell drugs in small quantities to maintain their own habits, or sometimes, they move large amounts of drugs as "mules" for males who control sophisticated drug businesses. They are very small cogs in a very large system, not the organizers or the backers of illegal drug empires. This, coupled with a growing mood among the American public reportedly concerned about early intervention with troubled kids and more drug treatment in preference to more prisons, should give us the opening needed to look at better and more cost-effective ways of dealing with women offenders.

Women's Health

The costs of medical care in prison have risen dramatically with the advent of the AIDS crisis. One out of every five women entering the New York State prison system is HIV+. Every correctional agency is dealing with an increasingly sick and debilitated population. Now, just as we have become more able to deal with AIDS, we have begun to struggle with rising but related problems associated with tuberculosis and increases of sexually transmitted diseases and gynecological problems that may be related to HIV infection in women. Studies have shown that women come into prison with more medical needs than do men. They are sicker, have had more recent and serious injuries, have had little previous health care, and have little knowledge of their own bodies.

The costs of medical care in prisons are climbing steadily as the population of those imprisoned gets sicker. Not only do huge amounts of funds get expended for direct medical care, staff, and equipment, but security costs always accompany such care inside and outside of prisons. Thus, when an inmate must go out to a hospital, security staff must accompany the inmate, adding yet more to the costs. Prison systems are now getting into the business of operating their own hospitals to reduce costs—still an expensive proposition. In addition, prisons for women have added concerns relating to pre- and postnatal care that must be addressed. And gynecological and obstetrical services are scarce in almost every jurisdiction. Yet, if the population of women in prison is less dangerous and is less apt to flee custody, it would appear appropriate that we investigate other alternatives for pregnant women who are now flooding our prisons. So, too, we know that the first year of an infant's life is critical to the formation of a bond between mother and child. At Bedford Hills, women and babies stay in a nursery unit, and most mothers leave prison with their babies. I question why Bedford Hills has so long been an anomaly, but I also suggest that most women even at Bedford Hills could be placed in an alternative community setting with their infants at significantly less cost. Most of the pregnant women coming into prison are young first offenders in need of intensive drug treatment. They are often babies having babies who need support and guidance as well as increased linkages with the community, not increased isolation.

Mental Illness

Greater and greater numbers of women appear to be entering correctional systems at the present time with prior histories of psychiatric hospitalization and/or suicide attempts. In fact, recent trends to deinstitutionalize populations in mental health facilities and facilities for the mentally retarded seem to be creating a shift in who houses whom, and our hospitals are now in our prisons. A month does not seem to go by now without a woman getting off the arriving bus with immediate needs for psychiatric intervention. Women are being received with 8, 10, 28, or even 32 prior psychiatric commitments. Bedford Hills receives women whose permanent residences are listed as psychiatric centers.

Just as men have long been overrepresented in our prisons, women were overrepresented in our mental institutions. Obviously, recent cutbacks in funding for the mentally ill are throwing large numbers of women in need into the streets, and this change is being reflected over time in our prison system as they make their way from one institutional system to another. There are in reality few community supports for persons with serious mental health needs. Women leaving mental institutions often find themselves alone and often become homeless. As they make their way from the streets to shelters, they often stop taking prescribed medications and self-medicate with street drugs that are easily accessible. It is only a matter of time, then, before they become caught up in the criminal justice system.

I am not suggesting that women need to be back in mental institutions, and certainly not in prisons, but rather that we need to develop new methods of supporting those women who need support short of hospitalization. Certainly, congregate living or other types of supportive programs have not been explored adequately in this country, and these can be both more effective and less costly when designed to take into account the actual needs of women. Women need safe places, and there are not many of them in our urban areas.

DIFFERENCE

... [W]omen "do time" differently from how men do time. Men concentrate on "doing their own time," relying on their feelings of inner strength and their ability to withstand outside pressures to get themselves through their time in prison. Women, on the other hand, remain interwoven into the lives of their significant others, primarily their children and their own mothers, who usually take over the care of the children. Yet, the inmate generally continues in a significant caretaking role even while incarcerated. All anyone has to do to see a major difference is to observe prison visiting rooms to see the difference. A woman's most frequent visitors are grandma with the kids, whereas a man's are his wife and the kids. In American society, we trap ourselves when making "special" arrangements—in essence, we try to make everything identical for different groups and then decide what is special that needs to be addressed about one group. Generally, this gets us into trouble.

I cringe when I hear about the "special" needs of women—and, in my case, of incarcerated women. In America, we have gotten caught up in arguments of equality but seldom can define equality or even identify *equal to what*. In the case of prisoners, equal generally means equal to men prisoners. Maybe what we should be addressing is the inequality of women. Why? Why don't we make it a policy to do programs for mothers and then add programs for fathers....

The problem with understanding equality in terms of identicalness is simply that the sexes are not identical. Men and women are different, even in terms of the crimes they commit, their roles, their risks of being violent, their victims, their risks of recidivism. Yet, to make women "equal," many jurisdictions have gone on building programs to make women's prisons like or equal to men's prisons. Prison security classification systems are designed for male prisoners who present substantially different risks to society and to the prison managers. It is almost unknown to create classification systems for women that would factor in their own particular realities and characteristics. Rather, to be "equal," we simply use instruments designed to assess the dangerousness of men and overbuild or oversecure for women at significant cost but little real gain in increased safety.

Europeans suggest that we in America are getting caught in the precedent of our case law because we have not clearly defined *equal to what*. In the Netherlands, women in prison are not in uniform whereas men are. The Dutch simply explain that women are not escape risks whereas men are much more likely to attempt to escape. Further, they indicate that if a woman does escape, everyone knows where to find her: She will simply go home. Therefore, they see no need to treat men and women identically in terms of prison uniforms, and they are clear that any legal challenge relating to equality would not even be a consideration in a Dutch court. In America, in the case of prison uniforms, the facts are the same: Women do not present much of an escape risk. However, the system that instituted a policy similar to that of the Dutch would find itself confronted with equality arguments.

REFERENCES

Immarigeon, R., and M. Chesney-Lind. *Women's Prisons: Overcrowded and Overused.* 1992. San Francisco: National Council on Crime and Delinquency.

Miller, B. A., W. R. Downs, and K. Joyce. *Victimization of Drug Women*. Paper presented at the Fourth International Conference on the Reduction of Drug Related Harm, Rotterdam, March, 1993.

The Special Management Inmate

RICHARD A. McGEE
GEORGE WARNER
NORA HARLOW

OVERVIEW

Simply in being atypical, the Special Management Inmate poses problems for the prison administration. Prisons must handle large numbers of people in standardized ways if they are to stay within their budgets and if equity issues are not to be raised.

The needs of special inmate groups also may compete directly with those of the general population—efforts to meet the needs of special groups may have costs for the majority of prisoners, even if these are only "opportunity costs" of programs or services that otherwise could have been provided. Prison administrators must decide just how much attention will be paid to special needs and problems.

WHO IS THE SPECIAL MANAGEMENT INMATE?

Inmates in the first group—those requiring special handling for their own protection—include inmates whose physical, mental, or personality weaknesses make them likely targets of more aggressive inmates, as well as those whose past actions or behaviors have left them open to revenge. In the former category are the mentally retarded, the passive homosexual, the physically small or effeminate, and the socially inadequate; in the latter are witnesses and informers, former police or former correctional officers, inmates with gambling or narcotics debts, gang dropouts or members in trouble with the gang; and inmates whose crimes are particularly offensive. Especially notorious offenders (those spotlighted by the media) also may need to be

Source: Excerpted from McGee, Richard A., George Warner, and Nora Harlow. "The Special Management Inmate." Prepared for the National Institute of Justice, U.S. Department of Justice by the American Justice Institute under subcontract to Abt Associates Inc., contract number J-LEAA-011-81-2-sub-AJI, March 1985.

protected from inmates hoping to gain some fame of their own through an attack on a prominent individual.

Inmates whose special management needs arise from their threat to the safety of others include those who have committed a specific in-prison offense or rule violation, as well as those who have demonstrated a more general tendency to endanger others or disrupt institutional order. In the latter category are habitual troublemakers, racial agitators, gang leaders, traffickers in drugs or other contraband, sexual aggressors, inmates with a history of assault or possession of weapons, and high escape risks.

Mentally ill or abnormal inmates may be found in either of the above categories, since they often are victimized by other inmates and their mental or emotional problems may lead them to threaten others. But even if they do not endanger themselves or others, those with mental problems may require special treatment if they are to function in the general population, and at least for short periods they may need to be separated from the mainline.

THE SEGREGATION DILEMMA

Segregation is a common response to the problems presented by the Special Management Inmate. Whether for punishment, for treatment, or for their own or others' safety, those who present special problems commonly are handled separately from the general population. The separation of special inmates may simplify their management and minimize their impact on the general population. In the short run at least, segregation seems to benefit everyone.

But segregation itself can be a source of problems for the prison administration. First, separate handling is costly—not only do staffing ratios tend to be higher in segregated housing, but special line movements, separate feeding and exercising, increased security measures, and the like add directly to the costs of running the institution. Based on staff costs alone, it has been estimated that segregation is seven times as expensive as a general population unit.[1]

Separate handling of special groups also tends to deprive the general population. The operation of segregated housing has opportunity costs in terms of increased security, programs, or amenities that otherwise could have been provided on the mainline. And the need to restrict the general population while segregated inmates are moved or afforded special access inconveniences the majority of inmates for a few.

Recent judicial developments add new costs to the decision to segregate the Special Management Inmate. The current trend, at least for certain classes of segregated inmates, is to require conditions and services essentially equal to those available in population.[2] In most prisons this greatly complicates the management of both mainline and segregated populations, who often must share facilities without coming into contact with one another. Generally also, this places further strains on the prison budget.

THE HIGH COSTS OF LABELING

Prison managers must identify the special inmate if his needs and those of the institution in general are to be met. But in so doing they invoke a phenomenon commonly associated with labeling in other areas: The act of naming the problem often makes it worse.

Inmates assigned to protective custody present the most obvious example. Once officially labeled as unable to protect themselves, or confirmed in their status as "faggot" or "snitch," many inmates find it difficult or impossible to return to the mainline. For most prisons the result is a growing population of inmates in protective custody and a continual search for suitable housing for them.

Labeling has similar costs for other special inmate categories. The mentally ill may be seen by staff and other inmates as more "crazy" after a stay at the state mental hospital than before. The individual coming out of disciplinary segregation may find it hard to avoid both further conflicts with other inmates and additional terms in segregation once he has been defined as a troublemaker.

Unfortunately, it is often much easier to have a special label applied than it is to remove it, in part because it is easier to admit an inmate to a special program than it is to send him out again. As the chief psychiatrist of one departmental treatment unit observed, "It takes a phone call to get a man in here and an act of Congress to get him out."

THE CONTEXT OF DECISION-MAKING

The state prison is embedded within a political and bureaucratic system that includes not only the corrections apparatus, but the rest of the state government, from the courts, legislature, and elected executives to related departments such as mental health and regulatory agencies dealing with finance, personnel, or public works. Decisions made in all of these settings will help to determine what the prison administrator can do in dealing with the Special Management Inmate.

Transfer of mentally ill inmates to state hospitals, for example, depends to a large degree on state laws and the commitment policies of the mental health department. A new staff training program may require the approval of the corrections director, the legislature, and the state personnel office. A plan to alter or move the disciplinary detention unit may run into problems with the law, the courts, or the department of finance.

A few of the more important constraints on decision-making at the institutional level are departmental goals and policy, correctional standards and case law, plant design, budget, institutional role, and institutional "climate."

DEPARTMENTAL GOALS AND POLICY

Any prison administrator must work within parameters set by the corrections department. With respect to the Special Management Inmate, this may mean that procedures such as those governing the operation of segregation units are essentially dictated by policy handed down by the department. In other cases, policy may be phrased to allow variation at the institutional level. For example, in Oregon, where departmental policy permits officers to informally discipline inmates in less serious cases, officers at the Oregon State Correctional Institution are allowed by institutional management to do so, while those at Oregon State Prison are not.

CORRECTIONAL STANDARDS AND CASE LAW

In combination, standards and case law influence prison policy and procedure in many areas affecting segregation. These include not only conditions of confinement, but also the ways an inmate can be placed in and removed from special housing; by whom and how often his status must be reviewed; and how staff assigned to segregation units will be selected, trained, and supervised. Court intervention in disciplinary procedures and housing and programming requirements over the past decade or so, plus the more than 40 standards affecting Special Management Inmates in the American Correctional Association manual alone, suggest the extent to which prison managers are constrained in the handling of these types of inmates.

A prison may be operating under a court order that greatly restricts what management can do. (An injunction occasionally may have the opposite effect, freeing up the system and enabling innovation where change of any kind had been difficult to push through.) But even where no court order is currently in effect, decision-making will usually be influenced by what departmental lawyers believe to be safe and correct.

Case law also has tended to require that conditions in protective custody and administrative segregation be demonstrably different from those in the disciplinary unit and/or that they be similar to those provided the general population. ACA and Justice Department standards reflect this orientation,[3] and prison systems hoping to avoid litigation are well advised to heed them.

PLANT DESIGN

The physical plant is not the most important limiting factor, since some very good programs have been run out of shockingly inadequate facilities. With good staff, some prison managers claim, virtually anything is possible.

But plant design is an enabling or constraining influence on many aspects of prison life. The existence of several housing units with their own yards and mess halls permits incompatible inmates to be handled safely in the same institution without resort to segregation. California Mens Colony has this capacity; New York's Auburn Correctional Facility does not. The difference in safety, at least as perceived by staff and inmates, can be striking.

A well-designed, small facility also enables prison management and staff to know inmates well, to anticipate problems before they escalate into crises, to regulate and monitor inmate movement and activities, and to maintain a level and kind of staff-inmate communication that contributes to a positive institutional climate. There is no doubt that plant design is, in all but the most exceptional cases, a critical component of successful handling of Special Management Inmates.

BUDGET

Fiscal resources available to the institution and the prison system are a fundamental determinant of a manager's options in dealing effectively with special needs. Virtually any new program or policy will have costs reflected in some line item—costs that will have to be absorbed through cuts in other areas or by increases in the overall budget. Occasionally, a program has been implemented with minimal or no new fiscal costs (as when inmate activity groups meet "after hours" in unused space with volunteer staff supervision), but such opportunities are uncommon. More often, some hard decisions must be made involving choices between existing programs for one group and new programs for another.

Staff training is an area that is often sacrificed when the budget tightens. More than one corrections department has turned to the training budget for funds to maintain programs or functions considered more critical or to meet more urgent needs. Training is an investment in the future, and fiscal pressures tend to force an orientation, however shortsighted, to the here and now. Ways must be found to protect and even expand funds for training staff who work with Special Management Inmates.

INSTITUTIONAL ROLE

. . . In California, with 12 facilities, the Medical Facility at Vacaville is designed to handle the medically and psychiatrically abnormal; Folsom and San Quentin routinely take the "heavier" cases; and the Mens Colony accepts onto its mainline those inmates who elsewhere would have to be locked up for their own safety. The number and variety of facilities within the California system even allows the separation of warring gangs into their "own" institutions.

The ability to transfer inmates from one institution to another can simplify management of both (or all) populations. But once institutional role has been established, it is often difficult to change. Other components of the system come to depend on the institution to perform its accepted function, and an institutional climate develops that tends to perpetuate itself. Management may nudge the institution in one direction or another, as sometimes occurs when a new administrator succeeds in "loosening up" the prison or "tightening it down." But, to some extent, management options are defined—for better or for worse—by the culture and historical traditions of the institution.

INSTITUTIONAL CLIMATE OR CHARACTER

There is an undeniable character associated with any prison that is hard to define and even more difficult to control, yet it importantly affects what can be done within the institution. Climate and role are closely, perhaps indistinguishably, related. It is not clear whether certain institutions come to play certain roles because they are suited by climate, or whether a particular character develops as a result of the role the facility plays within the prison system.

Whatever the source of institutional character, most prison administrators acknowledge that some of their most successful policies, procedures, and programs might not work in an institution whose climate does not support them. Few would expect, for example, to create a "safe house" or sanctuary in a strife-torn prison dominated by gangs. The flagrant homosexual or transsexual can walk the mainline only in very special settings. In a medically oriented facility, the therapeutic atmosphere clearly increases staff and inmate tolerance for abnormal behavior.

ELEMENTS OF AN EFFECTIVE RESPONSE

With some oversimplification of a very complex area, our observations suggest that an institution and/or system dealing effectively with the special management inmate is characterized by the following:

- There is room within the prison system for some functional specialization at the institutional level and sufficient cooperation among units to permit inmate transfers in appropriate cases.

- The mission of the individual institution is clear (management has articulated a distinctive purpose for the facility, which is reflected in a coherent body of policies and procedures and a consistent and widely understood set of goals).

- Top management provides strong, clear, but not overbearing leadership of the entire institution.

- Responsibility is delegated (the institution "runs itself" because middle managers are given significant latitude within the areas for which they are responsible).
- Management has sufficient control over staff selection, assignment, training, and discipline to insure competent handling of special-needs inmates.
- Inmate complaints or grievances are heard and dealt with effectively and in a timely fashion; the system is one that inspires their confidence.
- Lines of communication are multiple, varied, and two-way (inmates as well as staff can easily and effectively make themselves heard, and management knows what is going on everywhere in the institution).
- Management and staff visibility on the yard and in inmate housing and work areas is high; staff and inmates talk to each other.
- Incentives and rewards motivate the kinds of behavior (both staff and inmate) that management wants to encourage.
- Rules may be strict and expectations for behavior high, but people are treated fairly and with respect, and management is perceived as caring about those who live and work there.
- A range of disciplinary options is available, and management is flexible enough to devise appropriate punishments in individual cases without excessive resort to segregation; staff are trained in the use of alternatives to disciplinary reports.
- There are written guidelines for the use of force, mechanical restraints, and medication; formal criteria and procedures for assignment to any kind of segregation; and regular reassessment of status for inmates placed in special categories.
- There are varying levels of structure for inmates who require temporary or transitional control or care.
- Custodial officers are recognized as human service providers and work cooperatively with professional staff, expanding mental health and program resources.
- Inmates are involved in meaningful work and/or other activities—idleness is low.
- Activities that lead to victimization—e.g., contraband, gambling, homosexual behavior—are controlled.
- Plant design allows for effective supervision of all inmate activities and all areas used by inmates, and vulnerable inmates are not assigned to less supervised areas.
- Institutional climate is relaxed enough to allow some inmate responsibility and self-determination, and some "normalization" of the prison

experience, at least to an extent compatible with security and other institutional needs.

In other words, effective handling of the Special Management Inmate assumes effective management of the institution generally, a high-quality staff, and a facility that, if not ideal in physical layout, is at least not totally inadequate or so dilapidated and obsolete in design that nothing but "warehousing" of inmates is possible. It also assumes that the institutional climate or culture is amenable to reasonably normal relationships among inmates and between inmates and staff.

NOTES

1. George Sullivan. "Challenge: Abort Protective Custody," unpublished paper, Salem, Oregon State Correctional Institution (1983).
2. Courts have held that inmates in protective custody must be provided programs and services roughly equivalent to those available on the mainline (e.g., *Blaney v. Commissioner*, Mass. C.A. No. 43373), and standards for administrative segregation require that conditions of confinement be substantially similar to the general population, with restrictions only for demonstrable security or health reasons. American Correctional Association, *Model Correctional Rules and Regulations*. (College Park, MD, ACA Correctional Law Project, 1979).
3. Ibid.

Prison Violence: A Scottish Perspective[1]

DAVID J. COOKE

RISING PRISON VIOLENCE

The last decade saw a substantial increase in the level of violence in Scottish prisons. The prison system was wracked by a series of lengthy and highly visible hostage-taking incidents, the rate of assaults doubled and the level of aggressive and hostile behaviour by prisoners was high.[2] The prison system was under stress.

Source Excerpted from Cooke, David J. "Prison Violence: A Scottish Perspective." *Forum on Corrections Research* 4(3): September 1992, pp. 23–30.

EXPLANATIONS FOR THE VIOLENT INCIDENTS IN SCOTTISH PRISONS

Clements's contention . . . that we must consider not only the prisoner's characteristics but also the setting in which he or she is placed, has greater congruence with contemporary psychological accounts of violent behaviour. Difficult prisoners are only difficult in certain settings. By understanding these settings, we can reduce prison violence.

In the rest of this article, it is argued that major benefits can be derived by identifying those characteristics of a regime that influence the level of prison violence. First, a case study is presented to demonstrate the potential power of changing regime factors. Second, the literature on violence in prisons and secure hospitals is explored for clues concerning which regime factors may be important.

THE BARLINNIE SPECIAL UNIT: A CASE STUDY

In the Scottish context, powerful evidence supporting the view that changing regime characteristics can influence the level of prisoner violence comes from the Barlinnie Special Unit. This Unit was established in 1972 because of concerns about the increasing level of violence in Scottish prisons. A radical approach was adopted. The regime plan was based on three underlying principles: first, the need to reduce the traditional hostility between staff and prisoners; second, the need to increase the autonomy of prisoners; and third, the need to provide a forum in which feelings of anger, hostility and frustration could be expressed and conflicts resolved.[3]

An evaluation of prison records demonstrated that if the behaviour of a group of 25 prisoners had remained the same in the Special Unit as it had been in the referring prison, then the number of assaults in the Special Unit would have been 105. Only two assaults have occurred.

Similarly, when serious incidents are considered—i.e., attempted escapes, hunger strikes, "smash-ups," hostage takings, dirty campaigns, barricading and self-mutilation—the expected frequency was 154, but only 9 such incidents have occurred. The fact that the inmates' behaviour changed so quickly after they were transferred to the Unit suggests that changes in the regime, rather than changes in the psychological characteristics of the individual prisoners, were responsible.[4]

THE ADVANTAGES OF CONSIDERING REGIME FACTORS

In any attempt to understand and limit institutional violence, there are certain advantages to giving greater emphasis to regime factors. First, changing the way in which we run institutions may be easier than changing the psychological characteristics of the people we contain in those institutions. Rice and colleagues[5] argued that explaining the violence of psychiatric patients merely in terms of their psychopathology severely limits what staff can do to reduce violent behaviour. Others have argued—and evidence from the Barlinnie Special Unit supports this argument—that antisocial behaviour can be reduced more effectively by making environmental changes rather than attempting to make psychological changes.[6]

Second, changing situational factors may be the only method available for reducing violent behaviour. Many aggressive individuals in prisons have an aversion to psychologists and psychiatrists and will not co-operate with them during treatment.

Third, increasing our understanding of the determinants of prison violence, and thereby our control over its level (we hope), should make prison environments safer not only for those who have to live there, but also for all those who work there.

WHICH REGIME FACTORS ARE IMPORTANT?

With our current state of knowledge, it seems impossible to answer the question posed above: which regime factors are important? Rather, all that we can do is identify the areas that merit further study.

A common theme in this diverse literature is that the characteristics of the staff, who deliver the regime or the treatment to inmates, have central importance in determining the level of violence in an institution. The evidence available implicates four elements, namely staff-inmate communication, staff training, staff experience and staff morale.

Staff-Inmate Communication

Not surprisingly, the behaviour of staff appears to have a substantial influence on the behaviour of prisoners. This is not a new idea. In 1844, the Inspector of Prisons for Scotland stated:

> in some prisons an unusual degree of good conduct is induced, and the number of punishments kept low, by the personal influence of the officers, and by their care in reasoning with prisoners before resorting to punishment.[7]

The British literature provides some empirical support for this contention. Zeeman and colleagues[8] demonstrated that prisoners' alienation— the absence of staff-inmate communication—had a powerful influence on inmates' behaviour.

Davies and Burgess[9] examined the rates of violence in one prison under the management of four different governors (wardens). They attributed the reduced rate of violence under one governor to the fact that he had introduced staff-inmate committees and meetings. These meetings not only increased contact between staff and prisoners, providing both groups with, at times, mutual goals, but also reduced the level of tension by providing an appropriate channel for dealing with grievances.

The apparent success of the Barlinnie Special Unit has in part been attributed to the quality of the staff-inmate relationships.[10] Perhaps the most convincing view comes from the best-known ex-mate of the Special Unit—Boyle:

> What made the Unit unlike any other place was the way staff and prisoners were allowed and encouraged to sit down and talk together. This was the single most important factor of the Unit.[11]

In North America, Love and Ingram argued that the comparatively low rate of prisoner-on-prisoner violence at Federal Correctional Institution Butner could be attributed to the manner in which staff related to prisoners:

> Without some of the traditional mechanisms of coercion to exercise control over prisoners, staff at Butner FCI are disposed to a more objective and equal treatment of prisoners, i.e., towards a more "professional" orientation.[12]

Thus, the notion that staff-inmate relationships are central to reducing institutional violence is an old principle which seems to have some empirical support. How can good relationships be achieved?

Staff Experience and Staff Training

Hodgkinson and colleagues[13] demonstrated that nurses in the training grades are assaulted more often than expected, while nursing assistants are assaulted less often than expected.

Davies and Burgess[14] found parallel results with prison officers. Officers with less experience were more likely to be assaulted than officers with more experience, regardless of their age. It has been argued that older prisoners are more likely to assault younger officers because they do not like taking orders from them, but the contention was not substantiated by this study. Length of experience was the critical factor.

Why is experience important? In both studies, it was argued that the experienced staff adopted a different approach to prisoners as compared with the inexperienced staff. It appeared that those in the training grades, or those with less experience, were assaulted more often because they were less circumspect and more confronting. In addition, lack of experience may make prison officers and nurses less competent at observing and judging the mood of a prisoner or patient.

All is not lost. Further evidence from the literature on institutional violence indicates that if front-line staff are trained to be more subtle and flexible, or to use more appropriate behaviours in their approach to inmates, there is a subsequent reduction in the rate of assault.[15] Lerner and colleagues expressed this point eloquently: "Officers need to understand offenders in order to know when to confront and when to support, when to be directive and when not to, when to trust and when not to, when to recommend psychotherapy and when not to, when not to set rules (and which rules)."[16]

Staff Morale

The concept of staff morale is difficult to operationalize, yet there are clues in the literature which suggest that poor staff morale may influence the aggressive behaviour of inmates.

In the psychiatric literature, Lion and colleagues[17] have contended that lowered staff morale and heightened inter-staff conflicts are conspicuous features of epidemics of violence.

Qualitative research suggests that violence among prisoners may occur when staff members feel alienated from management and when they are riven with internal dissension and splitting.[18] A study of Bathurst Jail in Australia—a jail noted for its attempts to improve the quality of relationships between staff and prisoners—found that when prison staff demonstrated their dissatisfaction by holding a 31-day strike, the prisoners became increasingly antagonistic and aggressive.[19]

Others[20] have insisted that high staff morale is "fundamentally important" in ensuring that the level of assaults in psychiatric units is minimized. Kingdon and colleagues[21] argued that staff morale can be maintained and enhanced if junior staff feel properly supported by senior staff.

One practical step toward enhancing staff morale has been suggested by Maier.[22] He suggests that staff who deal with violent inmates must have "me-time," a time during which they have the opportunity, either privately or in groups, to disclose and discuss their feelings of fear and anger toward those in their charge.

VISITORS

Glaser[23] contended that maximizing contact between prisoners and non-criminal persons from outside the prison could have a significant effect on recidivism rates. Access to visitors may have other positive benefits. Units such as Bathurst and the Barlinnie Special Unit allow prisoners to have visits seven days a week with no limit on the duration or frequency of these visits. Whatmore,[24] the forensic psychiatrist who helped establish and run the Barlinnie Special Unit, has argued that personal visitors can act as both a significant control over violent behaviours and a stimulus for change and maturation.

CROWDING AND TRANSIENCY

As mentioned above, the one feature of prison regimes that has been extensively examined—a feature that is comparatively easy to measure—is overcrowding. Overcrowding may influence aggression in a variety of ways: through the inability to control or avoid unwanted interaction or stimulation, through fear and through the lack of any means of maintaining personal identity. In overcrowded conditions, staff are often unable to protect individual prisoners from a major difficulty of confinement—being with other prisoners.

Unfortunately, the literature gives no clear answers. Some authors find that violence in prisons is inversely related to the amount of living space available to each prisoner.[25] In a psychiatric hospital, Dooley[26] attributed the elevated rate of violence on a Sunday to the increased number of patients in the recreational areas on that day. In his comprehensive review of this literature, Diethfield[27] concluded that a relationship probably exists between acts of violence and overcrowding, but that the relationship is frequently difficult to detect because it is influenced by the characteristics of the prisoners and those of the regime.

The mix of prisoners can be critical. Quay[28] developed a behavioural classification of prisoners designed to distinguish between predators and victims, or "heavies" and "lights." He advocated that these different types of prisoners should be separated and held in different types of regime. Quay reported that the rate of inmate-staff and inmate-inmate assaults dropped significantly in a large maximum-security penitentiary during the four years after inmates were separated on the basis of this classification system. This study provides suggestive evidence that there are certain "toxic mixes" of prisoners and that concentration rather than dispersal of "difficult" prisoners may reduce the level of prison violence.

Quay's work may explain an apparent contradiction in the literature. Authors such as Glaser,[29] Whatmore[30] and Robson[31] suggest that prisoners who are living in smaller groups are less likely to engage in offences against prison discipline. In contrast, Farrington and Nuttall,[32] after reviewing the literature, concluded that there was no empirical evidence to support the view that prisoners in large prisons were more likely than those in smaller prisons to engage in violent behaviour. Their findings may apply to the generality of prisoners but not to "difficult" prisoners: Whatmore and Robson argued that the most difficult prisoners should be held in small groups.

Ellis[33] and Porporino[34] have cogently argued that it is not crowding per se that is critical, but rather the rate of turnover or transiency of the prison population. In a swiftly changing population, normal social structures are not developed; challenges in the prisoner hierarchy are more frequent; natural wariness of new and potentially dangerous prisoners is exaggerated; normal prison trading relationships in drugs, money, tobacco and gambling are more risky; and prison officers behave in a more disciplinarian manner.

Change is threatening. Porporino[35] emphasized the difficulty in making simple generalizations in this field: he demonstrated empirically that transiency appeared to be the critical variable producing the apparently paradoxical result that the most crowded prisons were the least violence-prone because they had the lowest transiency rate.

It should be noted that transiency and overcrowding, although undesirable, need not necessarily lead to an increase in assault rates. Pelissier[36] monitored the rapid doubling of a prison population and found no increase in the rate of offences against prison discipline. What appears to have been of critical importance in this case is the care and attention taken in the management of change, in particular the care taken in ensuring that the regime and programs did not suffer adversely.

QUALITY OF THE REGIME: STIMULATION AND FRUSTRATION

The Woolf report[37] recognized that the physical conditions in which prisoners are held—deteriorating Victorian buildings, three to a cell, no in-cell sanitation—can contribute to the frustration of prison life which can lead to violence. Megargee[38] argues that the general frustrations of prison life—as exemplified by closed visits, letters going missing, lack of work, limited access to education and poor food—act as a significant situational determinant of violence.

King,[39] in an attempt to explain the lower rates of assault in an American maximum-security prison as compared with an English one, indicated that one critical factor was the quality of the American regime—more out-of-cell activities, greater disposable income, more frequent visits and in-cell televisions. Behaviour may be improved not only because the quality of prison life is enhanced but also because prisoners have more to lose.

Ideally, daily activities should be purposeful and not imposed merely to fill time. In the Barlinnie Special Unit, no formal routine of activities is imposed because the subcultural norms that the prisoners bring to the Unit are antiwork. However, prisoners are provided with resources and encouraged to pursue their own interests and set their own level of stimulation. Most engage in constructive activity.

Robson,[40] describing the regime at Bathurst Jail, emphasized the importance of meaningful activities—most notably trade training and education—to improve the morale and behaviour of prisoners.

LEVEL OF SECURITY AND CONTROL

Prison systems under stress frequently resort to high levels of control. The Scottish system responded in this manner following the spate of riots in the late 1980s. Whether, in the long term, this is the most effective strategy is open to doubt.[41]

Paradoxically, high levels of overt security and control may increase the probability of violence. Ward,[42] describing the effects of strict security in an American prison, found that the greater the security measures imposed, the greater the violence that occurred. Bidna[43] found that the implementation of strict security in Californian prisons—called "lock down"—resulted in an increased rate of stabbings in high-security institutions. Unfortunately, once again we are dealing with conflicting results, for Bidna also found that the lock-down produced a reduction in stabbings in a general prison. King[44] contended that the lower rates of assaults in an American prison compared with an English prison could be attributed, in part, to higher levels of control and observation; American prisoners felt safer. The optimum level of control will depend on the population.

Why is the level of control important? Because much violent behaviour is predicated on the desire to "save face." Felson and Steadman[45] argued that when the "saving of face" is a critical concern, the behaviour of one antagonist is a powerful determinant of the behaviour of the other. Aggression escalates in a trial of strength. Thus, if prison management provides an overly rigid, inflexible and authoritarian style of management, prisoners may resort to violence as a means of saving face, to show that they can resist the regime.

Evidence from regimes where control is diffuse supports this view.[46] In the Barlinnie Special Unit, prisoners are responsible for their daily routine, they can influence the day-to-day running of the regime and they can be involved in making decisions about their own progress and that of their peers. It is important to emphasize that authority is still maintained by the prison staff. However, the control is less overt and less likely to stimulate resistance.

PRISON MANAGEMENT AND ADMINISTRATIVE UNCERTAINTY

One response to the recent problems in Scottish prisons has been an emphasis on improved management. Proactive strategic planning has replaced reactive management.[47] DiIulio,[48] in his classic comparative study of American prison systems, argues that low rates of disturbance flow from good quality prison management. Good management should reduce the uncertainty that surrounds the life of prisoners; uncertainty produced by inconsistencies in the ways in which rules are applied, uncertainty about how to achieve parole, uncertainty in the many things that have significance for those in prison.[49]

Empirical evidence supports this view. Schnell and Lee[50] found that the introduction of a clear unambiguous time-out procedure for disruptive inmates led to a significant decrease in behavioural offences including violence. Ward[51] reported that the 120 stabbings within a six-month period in Folsom Prison could, in part, be attributed to the chaotic administration of that prison. Gentry and Ostapiuk[52] emphasized the importance of clear, unambiguous boundaries for staff and patients, showing that the consistent application of clear and fair rules reduced the tension caused by uncertainty. James and colleagues[53] found that 39% of the variance in violent incidents in a psychiatric ward could be attributed to a change in management practice which resulted in the use of temporary, rather than permanent, staff; staff transiency can be as disruptive as prisoner transiency.

An impressive demonstration of the effectiveness of good prison management is reported by Pelissier:[54] even the rapid doubling of an institution's population can be achieved with proper proactive planning.

CONCLUSION

The costs of prison violence are high. If we continue to focus on the intrinsic psychological characteristics of "difficult" prisoners, we have little hope of damming the rising tide of prison violence. We must focus on regime factors. Yet, as this brief review illustrates, there are no easy answers. Easy remedies are always suspect. Menkin noted: "There is always an easy solution to every human problem—neat, plausible and wrong."

Nonetheless, there are some clues. Regimes that are properly managed, which reduce uncertainty and population change; regimes that are not repressive but ensure the safety of prisoners; regimes that contain prisoners in clean and sanitary conditions, where meaningful contact with the outside world is facilitated; regimes that are administered by well-trained prison officers who have pride in their occupation; regimes with these qualities are likely to have a positive effect on prison violence.

NOTES

1. The views expressed in this article are those of the author and do not necessarily represent the views of the Scottish Home and Health Department.

2. D. J. Cooke, A. Walker, and W. Gardiner, "Behavioural Disturbance in Barlinnie Prison," *The Prison Service Journal*, 80 (1990): 2–8. See also D. J. Cooke, "Violence in Prisons: The Influence of Regime Factors," *The Howard Journal of Criminal Justice*, 30 (1991): 95–109.

3. P. B. Whatmore, "Barlinnie Special Unit: An Insider's View," in A. E. Bottoms and R. Light (eds.), *Problems of Long-Term Imprisonment* (Aldershot: Gower, 1987). See also J. Boyle, *A Sense of Freedom* (London: Handbooks, 1977). And

see D. J. Cooke, "Containing Violent Prisoners: An Analysis of the Barlinnie Special Unit," *British Journal of Criminology*, 29 (1989): 129–143.

4. For a fuller discussion, see Cooke, "Containing Violent Prisoners: An Analysis of the Barlinnie Special Unit."

5. M. E. Rice, G. T. Harris, and V. L. Quinsey, *Controlling Violence in Adult Psychiatric Settings* (Penetanguishene, Ont.: Penetanguishene Research Reports, 1991).

6. R. B. G. Clarke, "Delinquency Environment as a Dimension," *Journal of Child Psychology and Psychiatry*, 262 (1985): 515–523.

7. Inspector of Prisons for Scotland, *1844 Annual Report* (Her Majesty's Stationery Office, n.d.) p. 5.

8. E. C. Zeeman, C. S. Hall, P. J. Harrison, G. H. Marriage, and P. H. Shapland, "A Model for Prison Disturbances," *British Journal of Criminology*, 17 (1977): 251–263.

9. W. Davies and P. W. Burgess, "The Effects of Management Regime on Disruptive Behaviour: An Analysis within the British Prison System," *Medicine, Science and the Law*, 28 (1988): 243–247.

10. Whatmore, "Barlinnie Special Unit: An Insider's View." See also D. J. West, "The Clinical Approach to Criminology," *Psychological Medicine*, 10 (1980): 619–691. And see M. Fitzgerald, "The Telephone Rings: Long-Term Imprisonment," in A. E. Bottoms and R. Light (eds.), *Problems of Long-Term Imprisonment* (Aldershot: Gower, 1987).

11. Boyle, *A Sense of Freedom*, p. 11.

12. C. T. Love and G. L. Ingram, "Prison Disturbances: Suggestions for Future Solutions," *New England Journal on Prison Law*, 8, 2 (1982): 393–426, p. 409.

13. P. Hodgkinson, L. McIvor, and M. Phillips, "Patients' Assaults on Staff in a Psychiatric Hospital: A 2-Year Retrospective Study," *Medicine, Science and the Law*, 25 (1985): 288–294.

14. W. Davies and P. W. Burgess, "Prison Officers' Experience as a Predictor of Risk of Attack: An Analysis within the British Prison System," *Medicine, Science and the Law*, 28 (1988): 135–138.

15. J. A. Infantino and S.Y. Musingo, "Assaults and Injuries Amongst Staff With and Without Training in Aggression Control Techniques," *Hospital and Community Psychiatry*, 36 (1985): 1312–1314. See also M. E. Rice, G. T. Harris, G. W. Varney, and V. L. Quinsey, *Violence in Institutions: Understanding, Prevention and Control* (Toronto: Hans Huber, 1989). And see Rice, Harris, and Quinsey, *Controlling Violence in Adult Psychiatric Settings*. See also P. C. Kratcoski, "The Implications of Research Explaining Prison Violence and Disruption," *Federal Probation*, 52 (1988): 27–32. And see M. L. Lanza, H. L. Kayne, C. Hicks, and J. Milner, "Nursing Staff Characteristics Related to Patient Assault," *Issues in Mental Health and Nursing*, 12 (1991): 253–265. And see D. J. Cooke, P. J. Baldwin and J. Howison, *Psychology in Prisons* (London: Routledge, 1990).

16. K. Lerner, G. Arling, and S. C. Baird, "Client Management Classification Strategies for Case Supervision," *Crime and Delinquency*, 32 (1986): 254–271, p. 255.

17. J. R. Lion, D. Madden, and R. L. Christopher, "A Violence Clinic: Three Years' Experience," *American Journal of Psychiatry*, 133 (1976): 432–435.

18. Ibid. See also Cooke, "Violence in Prison: The Influence of Regime Factors."

19. K. Mahony, "Effects of the February 1984 Prison Officer Strike. Bathurst Gaol Evaluation Study." Unpublished report.

20. D. G. Kingdon and E. W. Bakewell, "Aggressive Behaviour: Evaluation of a Non-Seclusion Policy of a District Psychiatric Service," *British Journal of Psychiatry*, 153 (1988): 631–634.

21. Ibid.

22. G. J. Maier, "Relationship Security: The Dynamics of Keepers and Kept," *Journal of Forensic Sciences*, 31 (1986): 603–608. See also G. J. Maier, L. J. Stava, B. R. Morrow, G. J. Van Rybroeck and K. G. Bauman, "A Model for Understanding and Managing Cycles of Aggression Among Psychiatric Inpatients," *Hospital and Community Psychiatry*, 38 (1987): 520–524.

23. G. Glaser, "Six Principles and One Precaution for Efficient Sentencing and Correction," *Federal Probation*, 48 (1984): 22–28.

24. Whatmore, "Barlinnie Special Unit: An Insider's View."

25. E. I. Megargee, "Population Density and Disruptive Behaviour in a Prison Setting," in A. K. Cohen, A. F. Cole, and R. G. Bailey (eds.), *Prison Violence* (Lexington, D.C.: Heath, 1976). See also P. H. Nacci, H. Teitelbaum, and J. Prather, "Population Density and Inmate Misconduct Rates in the Federal Prison System," *Federal Probation*, 41 (1977): 27–38.

26. E. Dooley, "Aggressive Incidents in a Secure Ward," *Medicine, Science and the Law*, 26 (1986): 125–130.

27. J. Ditchfield, *Control in Prison: A Review of the Literature* (London: Her Majesty's Stationery Office, 1991).

28. H. O. Quay, *Standards for Adult Correctional Institutions* (Washington, DC: Federal Bureau of Prisons, 1983).

29. Glaser, "Six Principles and One Precaution for Efficient Sentencing and Correction."

30. Whatmore, "Barlinnie Special Unit: An Insider's View."

31. R. Robson, "Managing the Long Term Prisoner: A Report on an Australian Innovation in Unit Management," *Howard Journal*, 28 (1989): 187–203.

32. D. P. Farrington and C. P. Nuttall, "Prison Size, Overcrowding, Prison Violence and Recidivism," *Journal of Criminal Justice*, 8 (1980): 221–231.

33. D. Ellis, "Crowding and Prison Violence: Integration of Research and Theory," *Criminal Justice and Behavior*, 11 (1984): 277–308.

34. Porporino, "Managing Violent Individuals in Correctional Settings."

35. Ibid.

36. B. Pelissier, "The Effects of a Rapid Increase in a Prison Population: A Pre- and Post-Test Study," *Criminal Justice and Behavior*, 18 (1991): 427–447.

37. Woolf, Prison Disturbances April 1990: Report of an Inquiry.

38. E. I. Megargee, "Psychological Determinants and Correlates of Criminal Violence," in M. E. Wolfgang and N. A. Weiner (eds.), *Criminal Violence* (Beverly Hills, CA: Sage, 1982).

39. R. D. King, "Maximum-Security Custody in Britain and the USA: A Study of Gartree and Oak Park Heights." *British Journal of Criminology*, 31 (1991): 126–152.

40. Robson, "Managing the Long Term Prisoner: A Report on an Australian Innovation in Unit Management."

41. Porporino, "Managing Violent Individuals in Correctional Settings."

42. D. A. Ward, "Control Strategies for Problem Prisoners in American Penal Systems," in A. E. Bottoms and R. Light (eds.), *Problems of Long-Term Imprisonment* (Aldershot: Gower, 1987).

43. H. Bidna, "Effect of Increased Security on Prison Violence," *Journal of Criminal Justice*, 3 (1975): 33–46.

44. King, "Maximum-Security Custody in Britain and the USA: A Study of Gartree and Oak Park Heights."

45. R. B. Felson and H. J. Steadman, "Situational Factors in Disputes Leading to Criminal Violence," *Criminology*, 21 (1983): 59–74.

46. Robson, "Managing the Long Term Prisoner: A Report on an Australian Innovation in Unit Management." See also Cooke, "Containing Violent Prisoners: An Analysis of the Barlinnie Special Unit."

47. Scottish Prison Service, *Organising for Excellence: Review of the Organisation of the Scottish Prison Service* (Edinburgh: Scottish Prison Service, 1990).

48. J. J. DiIulio, *Governing Prisons: A Comparative Study of Correctional Management* (London: Collier Macmillan, 1987).

49. King and McDermott, "'My Geranium Is Subversive': Some Notes on the Management of Trouble in Prison."

50. J. F. Schnell and J. F. Lee, "A Quasi-experimental Retrospective Evaluation of a Prison Policy Change," *Journal of Applied Behavioral Analysis*, 7 (1974): 483–496.

51. Ward, "Control Strategies for Problem Prisoners in American Penal Systems."

52. M. Gentry and E. G. Ostapiuk, "The Management of Violence in a Youth Treatment Centre," *Clinical Approaches to Aggression and Violence: Issues in Criminological and Legal Psychology No. 12* (Leicester: British Psychological Society, 1988).

53. D. V. James, N. A. Fineberg, A. J. Shah, and R. G. Priest, "An Increase in Violence on an Acute Psychiatric Ward: A Study of Associated Factors," *British Journal of Psychiatry*, 156 (1990): 846–852.

54. Pelissier, "The Effects of a Rapid Increase in a Prison Population: A Pre- and Post-Test Study."

Changes in Prison Culture: Prison Gangs and the Case of the "Pepsi Generation"

GEOFFREY HUNT
STEPHANIE RIEGEL
TOMAS MORALES
DAN WALDORF

This article examines recent changes in prison life. Information collected from a series of in-depth interviews with a sample of California ex-prisoners suggests an important corrective both to the criminal justice literature and to those sociological accounts which have attempted to explain the culture of prison life. The interview data reveal that a serious deterioration in the quality of life has taken place inside California prisons, and that this change results from influences emanating from within the prison as well as from external factors.

Since Clemmer (1958) published the *Prison Community* in 1940, sociologists and criminologists have sought to explain the culture of prisons. A key debate in this literature centers on the extent to which inmate culture is either a product of the prison environment or an extension of external subcultures. Those in the former camp, such as Sykes and Messinger (1977), Cloward (1977), and Goffman (1961), have argued that the inmate social system is formed "as a reaction to various 'pains of imprisonment' and deprivation inmates suffer in captivity" (Leger and Stratton, 1977:93). These writers saw the prison as a total institution in which the individual, through a series of "status degradation ceremonies," gradually became socialized into prison life. Analysts such as Irwin and Cressey (1977) challenged this view of prison life, arguing that it tended to underestimate the importance of the culture that convicts brought with them from the outside. They identified two dominant subcultures within the prison—that of the thief and the convict—both of which had their origins in the outside world.

Our interview material did not clearly support one or the other of these opposing views and instead suggested that other dynamics of prison life were key to understanding inmates' experiences. Salient in inmate interviews was a greater degree of turmoil than was common to prison life in the past. The reasons for this turmoil were complex and included newly formed gangs, changes in prison population demographics, and new developments in prison policy, especially in relation to gangs. All these elements coalesced to cre-

Source: Excerpted from Hunt, Geoffrey, Stephanie Riegel, Tomas Morales, and Dan Waldorf. "Changes in Prison Culture: Prison Gangs and the Case of the 'Pepsi Generation'." *Social Problems* 40(3):398–409, 1993.

ate an increasingly unpredictable world in which prior loyalties, allegiances, and friendships were disrupted. Even some of the experienced prisoners from the "old school" were at a loss as to how to negotiate this new situation. Existing theories were not helpful in explaining our findings for the current dynamics could not be attributed solely to forces emanating from inside the prison or outside it.

THE ESTABLISHED CALIFORNIA PRISON GANGS

According to various accounts (Camp and Camp, 1985; Davidson, 1974; Irwin, 1980; Moore, 1978; Porter, 1982), the first California prison gang was the Mexican Mafia—a Chicano gang, believed to have originated in 1957 in the Dueul Vocational Institution prison. This Chicano group began to intimidate other Chicanos from the northern part of the state. The non-aligned, predominantly rural Chicanos organized themselves together for protection. They initially called themselves "Blooming Flower," but soon changed their name to La Nuestra Familia. Like the Mexican Mafia, La Nuestra Familia adopted a military style structure, with a general, captains, lieutenants, and soldiers. However, unlike the Mexican Mafia, La Nuestra Familia had a written constitution consisting of rules of discipline and conduct.

The Texas Syndicate, a third Chicano gang, followed the model of the Mexican Mafia and La Nuestra Familia and utilized a paramilitary system with a president at its head. Its members are mainly Mexican-American inmates, originally from Texas, who see themselves in opposition to the other Chicano groups, especially those from Los Angeles, who they perceive as being soft and too "Americanized."

Both black and white prisoners are also organized. The general view on the origins of the Black Guerilla Family (B.G.F.)—the leading black gang— is that it developed as a splinter group of the Black Family, an organization reportedly created by George Jackson. The authorities were particularly wary of this group, both because of its revolutionary language and reports that its members, unlike those of other gangs, regularly assaulted prison guards.

The Aryan Brotherhood—the only white gang identified in California prisons—originated in the late 1960s. It is said to be governed by a 3-man commission and a 9-man council who recruit from white supremacist and outlawed motorcycle groups. According to prison authorities, it is a "Nazi-oriented gang, anti-black [which] adheres to violence to gain prestige and compliance to their creed" (Camp and Camp, 1985:105).[1]

The available sociological literature on older prison gangs is divided on the issue of their relationship to street gangs. On the one hand, Moore in discussing Chicano gangs argues that they were started by "state-raised youths and 'psychos'" (1978:114) inside the prisons, while Jacobson sees them as an extension of street gangs. Although Moore sees the gangs as initially prison inspired, she describes a strong symbiotic relationship between the street and the prison. In fact, she notes that once the gangs were established inside the prisons, they attempted to influence the street scene. "The Mafia attempted to use its prison-based organization to move into the narcotics market in East Los Angeles, and also, reputedly, into some legitimate pinto-serving community agencies" (1978:115).

Chicano and Latino gangs. Among Chicanos, the Nortenos and the Surenos are the most important groupings or gangs. These two groups are divided regionally between the North and South of California, with Fresno as the dividing line.[2] Although regional loyalties were also important for the Mexican Mafia and La Nuestra Familia, the regional separation between North and South was not as rigid as it is today for Surenos and Nortenos.

In addition to the Nortenos and the Surenos, two other groups were mentioned—the New Structure and the Border Brothers. Our respondents provided differing interpretations of the New Structure. For instance, some noted it was a new Chicano group made up of Nortenos which started in San Francisco, while others implied it was an offshoot of La Nuestra Familia. Opinions differed as to its precise relationship to La Nuestra Familia.

The Border Brothers are surrounded by less controversy. Their members are from Mexico, they speak only Spanish and, consequently, keep to themselves. Most of our respondents agreed this was a large group constantly increasing in size, and that most members had been arrested for trafficking heroin or cocaine.

Although, there was little disagreement as to the Border Brothers' increasing importance, which was partly attributed to their not "claiming territory," there was, nevertheless, some dispute as to their impact on the North/South issue. Some respondents saw the Border Brothers as keeping strictly to themselves.

> The Border Brothers don't want to have anything to do with the Surenos Nortenos—they keep out of that 'cause it's not our fighting and all of that is stupid. . . . Either you are a Chicano or you're not. There is no sense of being separated (Case 3).

Others predicted that in the future, the Border Brothers will become involved in the conflict and will align themselves with the Surenos against the Nortenos.

> It used to be Border Brothers over there and Sureno and Norteno, stay apart from each other. . . . But now what I see that's coming out is that the Border Brothers are starting to claim Trece now.[3] What I think is going to happen to the best of my knowledge, is that the Surenos instead of them knockin' ass with the Nortenos, they're going to have the Border Brothers lock ass with the Nortenos due to the fact that they're south and all that. Maybe in a few years we will see if my prediction is true or not (case 36).

Black gangs. The Crips, originally a street gang from South Central Los Angeles, is the largest of the new black gangs. It is basically a neighborhood group.

I: So the Crips is more a neighborhood thing than a racial thing?

R: Oh yeah! That's what it stems from. It stems from a neighborhood thing. There's one thing about the Crips collectively, their neighborhoods are important factors in their gang structures (Case 5).

The Bloods are the traditional rivals of the Crips. Although, like the Crips, they are a neighborhood group, they do not attribute the same importance to the neighborhood.

They're structured geographically in the neighborhood, but it's not as important as it is for the Crips. Only in LA is it that important. Bloods from LA, it's important for them but they don't have as many neighborhoods as the Crips. But anywhere else in Southern California the neighborhoods are not that important. Only in LA (Case 5).

The 415s is a third black prison gang emerging recently. The group is made up of individuals living within the 415 San Francisco Bay area telephone code.[4] Although the group's visibility is high, especially in the Bay area, the organization appears to be loosely structured, so much so that one of our respondents suggested that the 415s were more an affiliation rather than a gang.

All of these gangs are said to be producing a significant impact on prison life. Whereas previously there were four or five major gangs, today there are nine or ten new groupings, each with its own network of alliances and loyalties. These crosscutting and often conflicting allegiances have a significant impact on prison life. They produce a confusing, disruptive situation for many prisoners and can even produce problems for existing friendships. As one Puerto Rican respondent noted, "When I first started going to the joints . . . it wasn't as bad to associate a guy from the North and the South. It wasn't that big of a deal" (Case 39). But as the fragmentation increased and dividing lines became more rigid, this type of friendship was much less acceptable. According to many of our respondents, another consequence of fragmentation was an increase in intraethnic conflict, especially amongst the black population.

Back then there was no Crips, there was no Bloods, or 415s. It is a lot different now. The blacks hit the blacks. When the blacks at one time were like the B.G.F. where the blacks would stick together, now they are hitting each other, from the Crips, to the Bloods, to the 415, are pretty much all enemies (Case 39).

The picture provided by our respondents is one of an increasing splintering of prison groupings. Allegiances to particular groups, which had previously seemed relatively entrenched, are now questioned. Friendships developed over long prison terms are now disrupted, and where previously prisoners made choices about joining a gang, membership has now become more automatic, especially for Chicanos. Today, what counts is the region of the state where the prisoner comes from; if he comes from South of Fresno, he is automatically a Sureno, if he is from North of Fresno, he becomes a Norteno.

PEPSI GENERATION

Respondents not only described the conflict arising from the new divisions within the prison population, but also attributed this conflict to new prison inmates. They emphasized that the new generation of prisoners differed from their generation—in their dress, attitudes, and behavior toward other prisoners and the prison authorities. Respondents described themselves as convicts who represented the "old school."

> In my point of view there is what is called the old school. . . . And the old school goes back to where there is traditions and customs, there is this whole thing of holding your mud, and there is something you don't violate. For instance you don't snitch, you are a convict in the sense that you go in and you know that you are there to do time. And there is two sides. There is the Department of Corrections and there is you as the convict (Case 34).

A convict, in this sense, was very different from the present day "inmate" who they described as not having

> a juvenile record or anything like that, and so that when they come in they have no sense of what it is to do time. . . . The inmate goes in there and he goes in not realizing that, so that they are doing everybody else's number or expect somebody else to do their number. Which means for instance, that if they can get out of something they will go ahead and give somebody up or they will go against the code. Say for instance, the food is real bad and the convict would say, look we have to do something about this so let's make up a protest about the food and present it to the warden. And the convict will go along with it because it is for the betterment of the convicts. The inmate will go and go against it because he wants to be a good inmate and, therefore, he is thinking about himself and not the whole population (Case 32).

The prisons were full of younger prisoners who were described disparagingly by our respondents as "boys trying to become men," and the "Pepsi Generation," defined as

> the young shuck and jive energized generation. The CYA [California Youth Authority] mentality guys in a man's body and muscles can really go out and bang if they want. They are the youngsters that want to prove something—how tough and macho and strong they are. This is their whole attitude. Very extreme power trip and machismo. The youngsters want to prove something. How tough they are. And there is really very little remorse (Case 16).

According to our respondents, the "Pepsi Generation" went around wearing "their pants down below their ass" (Case 40) and showing little or no respect for the older inmates, many of whom had long histories of prison life which normally would have provided them with a high degree of status. Disrespect was exhibited even in such seemingly small things as the way that the younger prisoners approached the older inmates.

> They'll come up and ask you where you are from. I had problems with that. They come with total disrespect. It seems like they send the smallest, youngest punk around and he comes out and tries to jam you. You know, you've been around for a long time, you know, you've got your respect already established and you have no business with this bullshit. . . . And here you have some youngster coming in your face, talking about "Hey man, where you from" (Case 2)?

This view was graphically corroborated by a 38 year old Familia member who described the young inmates in the following way:

> They're actors. Put it this way, they're gangsters until their fuckin' wheels fall off. . . . I'm a gangster too. But there is a limitation to everything. See I can be a gangster with class and style and finesse and respect. Get respect and get it back. That's my motto, my principle in life. Do unto another as you would like do have done to you. These kids don't have respect for the old timers. They disrespect the old men now (Case 36).

The "younger generation" was not only criticized for its disrespect, but for its general behavior as well. They were seen as needlessly violent and erratic and not "TBYAS"—thinking before you act and speak.

> I think they're more violent. They are more spontaneous. I think they are very spontaneous. They certainly don't use TBYAS. I think their motivation is shallower than it was years ago (Case 16).

Their behavior had the effect of making prison life, in general, more unpredictable, a feature many of our respondents disliked.

> They have nothing but younger guys in prison now. And ah, it has just changed. I don't even consider it prison now anymore. I think it is just a punishment. It is just a place to go to do time. Which now since there are so many children and kids in prison it is hard to do time now. It is not like it used to be where you can wake up one morning and know what to expect. But now you wake up and you don't know what to expect, anything might happen (Case 12).

INMATE CULTURE REASSESSED

Inmate's picture of prison life is of increasing uncertainty and unpredictability: more traditional groupings and loyalties are called into question as new groups come to the fore. Whereas previously, prisoners believed a clear dividing line existed between convicts and authorities, today they see this simple division disintegrating. This occurs because, in their attempt to control the spread of prison gangs, authorities introduced a series of measures which contained the gangs, but also unexpectedly created a vacuum within the organizational structure of the prison population—a vacuum soon filled by new groups. Group membership was taken from newer inmates, who, according to our respondents, had not been socialized into the convict culture. The dominance of these groups soon led to an environment where the rules and codes of behavior were no longer adhered to and even the more experienced prisoners felt like newcomers. Moreover, the ability of prisoners to remain nonaligned was hampered both by developments amongst the prisoners and by the actions of the authorities. For example, a Norteno arrested in the South and sentenced to a southern prison would find himself in a very difficult and potentially dangerous situation.

> You'll see some poor northern dude land in a southern pen, they ride on [harass] him. Five, six, seven, ten deep. You know, vice versa—some poor southern kid comes to a northern spot and these northern kids will do the same thing. They ride deep on them (Case 2).

Study respondents portrayed prison culture as changing, but the change elements they identified were both inside and outside the institution. The available theoretical approaches, which have tended to dichotomize the source of change, fail to capture the complexity and the interconnectedness of the current situation. Furthermore, the information we received produced no conclusive evidence to prove whether or not the street scene determined the structure of gangs inside the prison or vice versa. For example, in the case of the Crips and the Bloods, at first glance we have a development which supports the approaches of Jacobs (1974) and Irwin and Cressey (1977). The Crips and the Bloods originated in the neighborhoods of Los Angeles and transferred their conflicts into the prison environment. In fact, according to one respondent, once in prison, they bury their intragang conflicts in order to strengthen their identities as Crips and Bloods.

> Even when they are "out there" they may fight amongst themselves, just over their territory. . . . But when they get to prison they are wise enough to know, we gotta join collectively to fend off everyone else (Case 5).

However, although the Crips and Bloods fit neatly into Jacobs' perspective, when we consider the case of the 415s and the Nortenos and the Surenos, we find their origins fit more easily into Cloward's (1977) alternative perspective. According to two accounts, the 415s began in prison as a defense group against the threatening behavior of the Bloods and the Crips.

> It [the 415s] got started back in prison. In prison there is a lot of prison gangs . . . and they were put together a lot. They got LA—gangs like the Bloods and the Crips, and they are putting a lot of pressure on the people

from the Bay area. And we all got together, we got together and organized our own group (Case G189).

Originally, the Nortenos and Surenos existed neither on the streets nor in the adult prisons but within the California Youth Authority institutions. Gradually this division spread to the adult prisons and soon became powerful enough to disrupt the traditional loyalties of more established gangs. Furthermore, in-prison conflicts soon spread to the outside and, according to information from our San Francisco study, Norteno/Sureno conflicts are beginning to have a significant impact on the streets.

CONCLUSION

As Irwin (1980) noted over ten years ago, prisons today are in a turmoil. From both the Department of Corrections perspective and the interview material, it is clear that the prison system is under immense pressures. As the prison population expands and the Department of Corrections attempts to find more bed space, the problems within the prisons multiply.[5] The impact of this situation on the inmates is clear from the interviews—they complain about the increased fragmentation and disorganization that they now experience. Life in prison is no longer organized but instead is viewed as both capricious and dangerous.

For many, returning to prison after spending time outside means being confronted by a world which they do not understand even though they have been in prison many times before. Where once they experienced an orderly culture, today they find a world which operates around arbitrary and ad hoc events, and decisions seem to arise not merely from the behavior of their fellow prisoners but also from prison authorities' official and unofficial decisions. Where before they understood the dominant prison divisions—prisoners versus guards and black versus white inmates—today they find new clefts and competing allegiances. The Chicanos are split not only between the Mexican Mafia and La Nuestra Familia but also North versus South. A relatively unified black population is divided into different warring camps of Crips, Bloods, and 415s.

The world portrayed by our respondents is an important corrective both to the criminal justice literature, which portrays prison life in very simplistic terms, and to those theoretical approaches which attempt to explain prison culture solely in terms of internal or external influences. Our interviews have shown that the linkages between street activities and prison activities are complex and are the result of developments in both arenas. Therefore, instead of attributing primacy to one set of factors as opposed to the other, it may be more useful and more accurate to see the culture and organization of prison and street life as inextricably intertwined, with lines of influence flowing in both directions.

NOTES

The data for this paper were made possible by funding to the Home Boy Study from the National Institute of Drug Abuse (ROI-DA06487), administered by Mario de la Rosa, Ph.D. The authors are grateful to the anonymous *Social Problems* reviewers of this paper. Correspondence to: Hunt, Institute For Scientific Analysis, 2719 Encinal Ave., Alameda, CA 94501.

1. In addition to these five major groupings, other gangs, including the Vanguards and the Venceremos, are referred to in the literature. Today these groups seem to have disappeared altogether or may in some cases have been incorporated into other gangs. For a further discussion of California gangs, see Castenedo (1981), Conrad (1978), and a report by EMT Associates, Inc. (1985) to the California Department of Corrections. For information on prison gangs in other parts of the United States, see Beaird (1986), Buentello (1984), Crist (1986), Fong (1990, 1991), Jacobs (1977), and Lane (1989).

2. There was some disagreement as to the precise dividing line between North and South. Although Fresno was often cited, others said Bakersfield was the dividing line.

3. The term Trece has a number of meanings especially amongst Chicanos in Los Angeles where it refers to "eme," or "m" the 13th letter in the Spanish alphabet. "Eme" is also used to describe the Mexican Mafia.

4. It should be noted that during 1992, telephone area codes in the Bay area were changed to two codes—415 and 510. The gang's name refers to the period when one code covered the entire Bay area.

5. One can but speculate as to what effect the estimated 5,000 arrests in Los Angeles as a result of recent riots will have on the correctional system.

REFERENCES

Beaird, L. H. 1986. "Prison Gangs." *Corrections Today* 48 (July):12, 18–22.

Buentello, S. 1984. "The Texas Syndicate." Texas Department of Corrections. Unpublished report.

Camp, G. M., and C. G. Camp. 1985. *Prison Gangs: Their Extent, Nature and Impact on Prisons.* U.S. Department of Justice, Office of Legal Policy, Federal Justice Research Program, Washington, DC.

Castenedo, E. P. (compiler). 1981. *Prison Gang Influences on Street Gangs.* Sacramento, CA: California Department of Youth Authority.

Clemmer, D. 1958. *The Prison Community.* New York: Rinehart and Co.

Cloward, R. 1977. "Social Control in the Prison." Pp. 110–132 in *The Sociology of Corrections,* ed. R. G. Leger, and J. R. Stratton. New York: John Wiley and Sons.

Conrad, J. 1978. "Who's in Charge? Control of Gang Violence in California Prisons." In *Report on Colloquium on Correctional Facilities,* 1977, ed. N. Harlow. Sacramento, CA: Department of Corrections, 1978.

Crist, R. W. 1986. "Prison Gangs: Arizona." *Corrections Today* 48 (July):13, 25–27.

Davidson, R. T. 1974. *Chicano Prisoners: The Key to San Quentin.* Prospect Heights, IL: Waveland Press, Inc.

EMT Associates, Inc. 1985. "Comparative Assessment of Strategies to Manage Prison Gang Populations and Gang Related Violence." Vols. 1–8. Sacramento, CA: California Department of Corrections. Unpublished report.

Fong, R. S. 1990. "The Organizational Structure of Prison Gangs: A Texas Case Study." *Federal Probation* 54:1.

Fong, R., and S. Buentello. 1991. "The Detection of Prison Gang Development: An Empirical Assessment." *Federal Probation* 55:1.

Goffman, E. 1961. *Asylums*. Garden City, NJ: Anchor.

Irwin, J. 1980. *Prisons in Turmoil*. Boston: Little, Brown and Company.

Irwin, J., and D. Cressey. 1977. "Thieves, Convicts, and the Inmate Culture." Pp. 133–147 in *The Sociology of Corrections*, ed. R. G. Leger, and J. R. Stratton. New York: John Wiley and Sons.

Jacobs, J. 1974. "Street Gangs Behind Bars." *Social Problems* 21:395–409.

Lane, M. P. 1989. "Inmate Gangs." *Corrections Today* (July):98–128.

Leger, R. G., and J.R. Stratton. 1977. *The Sociology of Corrections. A Book of Readings*. New York: John Wiley and Sons.

Moore, J. W. 1978. *Homeboys: Gangs, Drugs, and Prison in the Barrios of Los Angeles*. Philadelphia: Temple University Press.

Porter, B. 1982. "California Prison Gangs: The Price of Control." *Corrections Magazine* 8:6–19.

Sykes, G. M., and S. L. Messinger. 1977. "The Inmate Social System." Pp. 97–109 in *The Sociology of Corrections*, ed. R. G. Leger, and J. R. Stratton. New York: John Wiley and Sons.

Thy Brother's Keeper: A Review of the Literature on Correctional Officers*

SUSAN PHILLIBER

RESEARCH ON ROLE CONFLICT

There is no lack of essays describing the role conflict experienced by COs. It has been argued that this situation is inevitable because COs are in the middle, between administrators and inmates (Cheatwood, 1974).

Source: Excerpted from Philliber, Susan. "Thy Brother's Keeper: A Review of the Literature on Correctional Officers." *Justice Quarterly*, 4(1): 9–37, 1987.

*This is a revision of a paper presented at the annual meetings of The American Society of Criminology, Atlanta, October 1986. The author is grateful to John Klofas, John Hepburn, James Marquart, Peter Wickman, Lucien Lombardo and Ben Crouch, and to several corrections officers at Eastern New York Correctional Facility for their comments and suggestions.

Some research concentrates on the institutional variables that predict role conflict. Hepburn and Albonetti (1980) found role conflict to be greater in minimum-security settings; Zald (1962) reported that institutions with mixed treatment and custody goals spawned more role conflict than institutions concerned only with security.

The staff member's duties in the prison may also be related to the presence of role conflict. Treatment staff have been found to suffer more role conflict than custody staff (Hepburn and Albonetti, 1980), but the amount of inmate contact does not seem related to this problem (Whitehead and Lindquist, 1986a) although some writers insist that keeping an appropriate distance from inmates will lessen such conflict (Peretti and Hooker, 1976).

Some authors advocate a team approach to jobs in the prison in order to lessen role conflict (Piliavin, 1966; Ward and Vandergoot, 1977). Hepburn and Albonetti (1978) argue that a well-implemented team system, as opposed to just any team system, reduces role conflict among custodial personnel. Others, however, report that their attempts to introduce a system of overlapping roles in the prison did not change perceptions about the utility of counseling or orientations toward custody (Piliavin and Vadum, 1968).

Attributes of the officers themselves are also related to role conflict. Poole and Regoli (1980a) report that a "sense of calling to the field" is related negatively to this problem. Among sergeants, they find that commitment to a professional ideology reduces role conflict, work alienation, and anomia (1983). Whitehead and Lindquist (1986b), however, find no relationship between professional orientation and role conflict.

The data on what role conflict may cause, in turn, are somewhat stronger than the data on what factors promote role conflict. Direct relationships have been found between role conflict and stress (Cullen et al., 1985; Whitehead and Lindquist, 1986a), punitiveness (Hepburn and Albonetti, 1980), custody orientation (Poole and Regoli, 1980b), tedium (Shamir and Drory, 1982), and burnout (Manning, 1983). Role conflict is related negatively to job satisfaction (Hepburn and Albonetti, 1980) and to beliefs that COs should be supportive, that inmates can be rehabilitated, and that prison can rehabilitate (Shamir and Drory, 1981). Role strain appears to be related negatively to the perception of both intrinsic rewards (chance to try new things, use existing skills, freedom to plan work) and to extrinsic rewards (pay, job security, kind of people one works with) on the job (Hepburn and Jurik, 1986). Overall, role difficulties in prisons appear to take a rather serious toll.

In spite of all this, Toch and Klofas (1982) found "no evidence of 'role conflict' among officers, of unendurable strain, cognitive dissonance or experienced pressure of conflicting goals" (43–44). Indeed, several of the studies included fail to report the univariate distributions of their role variables.

Several other observations about this literature seem to be justified. First, the body of knowledge about role conflict among corrections officers is not accumulating as systematically as it might because these authors are not all studying the same thing. This research does not differentiate carefully between the conflict felt by officers because they have several different roles to perform and the conflict felt between officers and others because they each have different tasks in corrections. In addition, some research seems to deal primarily with role confusion; in these studies, officers often complain about lack of administrative guidance and support (Jacobs, 1978; Willet, 1983).

Moreover, the researchers hardly seem to recognize that even individuals' role problems may take different forms. Shamir and Drory (1982), on the other hand, differentiate between role conflict, role ambiguity, and role overload. Although all these role difficulties may exist for COs and for prisons, they are not the same; more careful distinction seems important.

As one offshoot of this confusion, the solutions that are suggested for conflicts between staff members seem likely to aggravate individual role conflict. Some writers, for example, have advocated broadening the roles of both treatment and custody personnel to lessen the conflict between them (Hepburn and Albonetti, 1978; Johnson, 1976, 1977; Johnson and Price, 1977). Yet how does such a suggestion square with the finding that role conflict is less in custody-oriented settings, where everybody knows exactly what the job is about? At the moment, the suggestions for relieving interrole conflict seem destined to increase intrarole conflict.

Another potential problem in these studies, mentioned by only a few authors (Shamir and Drory, 1981), is the possibility that our assumptions about causal order are askew. Attitudes toward punitiveness or belief in the rehabilitative potential of inmates may cause rather than result from role conflict.

THE CAREER PATH OF CORRECTIONS OFFICERS

In describing what he calls "the brutal scheme" for guards, Wicks (1980:1) writes:

> Watching their initial entrance into the prison can be quite an experience. The hope on their faces, the positive anxiety of their motivated gait—at first, it's all there.
>
> Then, slowly and almost methodically, the smiles wane, the expectations atrophy, and the desires to perform in a positive fashion succumb to escapist fantasy and verbally acknowledged skepticism. . . . After six months to a year the period of hope and enthusiasm should almost be all over.

Can we document this portrait with research findings? Although the requisite longitudinal data for career studies of corrections officers are rare (cf. Crouch and Alpert, 1982; Willet, 1983), the literature contains some eloquent descriptive accounts of the socialization processes for new guards (Crouch and Marquart, 1980). In addition, we can gain some indications of what happens to the CO over time by reading those cross-sectional studies which include measures like "months employed" or "experience as a CO." Age is another possible surrogate measure for career stage, although it is less desirable because some officers enter their occupation later in life.

In fact, the correlations of age with other variables are perplexing. Crouch and Alpert (1982) report no relationship between age and punitiveness; Jurik (1985) reports a positive relationship between age and favorable attitudes toward inmates; Toch and Klofas (1982) report a negative relationship between age and custody orientation. Whitehead and Lindquist (1986a) report that age among COs is related negatively to stress and burnout. Thus older COs seem to be about as punitive as any other age group, more oriented toward custody, more favorable toward inmates, and less stressed and burned out than younger COs. This confusing picture may be a result of the poor correlation between age and variables such as years of service, education, or other likely predictors of these factors.

Length of time as a CO has been found to be related negatively to favorable attitudes toward inmates (Jurik, 1985), to belief in the rehabilitative potential of inmates (Shamir and Drory, 1981), and to the number of disciplinary reports filed (Poole and Regoli, 1980b). Length of service is related positively to stress (Cullen et al., 1985), to custody orientation (Poole and Regoli, 1980b), and to perceived legitimacy of inmate social protest (Hepburn, 1984).

Some authors argue that these relationships involving age and tenure do not follow the linear patterns on which popular statistics rely so heavily. Instead it appears that variables such as custody orientation (Toch and Klofas, 1982) and cynicism (Regoli, Poole, and Shrink, 1979) follow a curvilinear pattern over the career of the corrections officer. In this model, the youngest officers, with their relative naiveté, and the oldest officers, with a seasoned acceptance of their lot, display the fewest negative symptoms and attitudes. Mid-career officers, on the other hand, whose illusions are gone but for whom relief is nowhere in sight, suffer the greatest problems.

This area of research would profit from longitudinal data and from control over other variables. Age and time on the job are likely to be related to one another, but are not the same. The distinction between the two variables is illustrated in Jurik's sample (1985), in which age was related positively to favorable attitudes toward inmates while number of months employed was related negatively. Similarly, Cullen et al. (1985) found that length of experience was related positively to stress, while Whitehead and Lindquist (1986a) reported age as related negatively to stress. Such research may be potentially expensive, but longitudinal data from a sample of COs over time seem likely to yield the information necessary to disentangle these and other variables.

IS THERE A GUARD SUBCULTURE?

Whether or not a guard subculture actually exists, some guards' statements make it clear that they think it should exist, especially if it implies solidarity. As one officer pleads:

> Practice comradeship. It is important that a corrections officer be able to trust and depend on fellow officers. A show of uniformed and unified force is important not only for your sake, but is essential to your credibility as a guard force, both to the inmates and to the administration (Ward, 1981:52).

Another CO asserts that the uniform worn by guards is an important symbol of being united as "the solidary brotherhood of the wearers of the uniform (Howton, 1969:67).

Part of the difficulty in learning whether a guard subculture exists lies in knowing how to measure such a subculture. Duffee (1975) used measures of differences in organizational goals among guards, administrators, and inmates as indicators that the guards constituted a subculture. Klofas (1984) argued later that even though Duffee had found such differences, they were not sufficient evidence of a subculture.

Other data that might suggest a subculture are drawn from a study showing that guards socialize together after work (Esselstyn, 1966). One might argue, however, that these data are not particularly strong, nor does after-work interaction in itself validate a subculture. The simulation by Haney, Banks, and Zimbardo (1973), although not concerned with subcultures per se, shows that when students were placed in the guard role, they quickly developed a set of distinctive attitudes and behaviors. Marquart (1986) produced compelling evidence that superiors teach and reward lower-ranking officers for the use of various techniques for controlling inmates. Perhaps these studies constitute evidence of a subculture. Other studies refer to the guard subculture but do not measure whether one exists (Crouch, 1980; Crouch and Marquart, 1980).

It is difficult, however, to come away from the research by Klofas and Toch (1982) with the impression that anything approaching solidarity exists among COs. The data produced by these authors demonstrate pluralistic ignorance among guards: although most of them are not particularly punitive toward inmates, they believe that most of their fellow guards are punitive. In fact, those who are highly custody-oriented are a minority in prisons but believe that everyone agrees with them.

Lombardo (1985) has produced one of the most careful definitional discussions of whether a guard subculture exists. He argues that it does not for the following reasons: COs are not recruited to the job for task-related purposes, they do not set their own goals, they are not interdependent, they do not have democratic organization or participation in decision making, they work in a competitive atmosphere of distrust, and they have poor communication. In spite of this skepticism, Lombardo (1986) is currently gathering longitudinal data on whether a guard subculture develops among officers in a new prison.

Similarly, Hepburn (1984) doubts the existence of a subculture because variables such as perceived legitimacy of inmate social protest are related to education and length of employment among guards. This finding suggests variation, not unanimity, among COs and change over time. Poole and Regoli (1981) insist that a guard subculture is absent because working alone is common and is encouraged among guards. Klofas (1984) argues that differences both within and between groups must be considered in a definitive evaluation of whether a subculture exists among COs. Because opinions about inmates vary widely within the group and only slightly between COs and other groups, Klofas doubts that the subculture concept will prove as useful among prison guards as in studies of the police.

On balance, it appears that the hard evidence for the existence of a guard subculture is still lacking. This area of research would be strengthened by more clarity in both the theoretical and the operational definitions of subculture.

THE PRISONIZATION OF CORRECTIONS OFFICERS

Perhaps nothing is so vivid to the prison newcomer as the fact that all is not as it appears from the outside. In spite of public impressions that prisons are governed securely by armed guards who make all decisions and maintain control, many studies have documented the "real" way in which prisons operate.

One of the repeated findings in this literature is that inmates and guards make deals with each other to maintain the peace. Inmates obtain privilege and status, and in exchange they help guards to maintain order. This system in the extreme is presented vividly by Marquart and Roebuck (1986), who describe the "snitch" system in Texas prisons. These adaptations and the impact of guard work on those who perform it have also been described perceptively by inmates (Jackson, 1970; Chang and Armstrong, 1972; Griswold et al., 1970).

Work by Hepburn and Crepin (1984) suggests that these informal systems are more complicated than they appear. COs' perceptions that they depend on inmates to get their jobs done seem to lead to accommodating relationships between the two groups, as traditionally suggested. On the other hand, when COs perceive that they have little institutional authority and thus find themselves dependent upon inmates for their personal safety, the result seems to be increased repression rather than accommodation. Lombardo (1981) found that officers who report less social distance from inmates wrote more, rather than fewer, reports on those inmates.

Thomas (1984) provides a look into the prison "mesostructures" that help guards, whether accommodating or repressive, to deal with contradictory and changing instructions from administrators. He argues that the mesostructure can actually cause the means and ends which are part of the formal structure to become "uncoupled" so that they no longer perform in expected ways.

Other researchers have also pointed out the informal arrangements made by guards to cope with prison organizational and role problems. Hartman (1969) describes various status games that keepers play to "cool out" inmates. Crouch (1980a) details two different guarding styles in the same prison, each involving behaviors not officially sanctioned by administrators. Kalinich (1980) argues that guards are sometimes a corrupt part of the inmate contraband economy; McEleney (1985) shows how guards use such techniques as lockdowns to control both inmates and administrators. Hewitt, Poole, and Regoli (1984) documented selective enforcement of prison rules as a control technique used by COs. These creative arrangements might be seen as an adaptation by guards and inmates to many of the problems outlined above.

Guards also victimize inmates in a variety of ways (Bowker, 1981; Stotland, 1976; Toch, 1977). Techniques include harassment as well as physical, sexual, economic, social, and psychological victimization. Many of these behaviors are considered common among inmates, but not among their guards.

In perhaps the most ironic finding, several authors have documented that some guards try to help inmates surreptitiously, even at the expense of bending rules (Johnson, 1976, 1977; Lombardo, 1981; May, 1976a; Toch, 1978). Most of these authors regard this behavior as characteristic of only a minority of guards; Lombardo (1981) notes that guards are much more likely to help inmates with institutional problems than with personal difficulties.

Thus, a variety of guard behaviors may reflect the impact of the prison environment on the keepers. Some may be necessary, some are healthy, and some blur the line between inmate and guard.

REFERENCES

Bowker, L. H. 1981. *Prison Victimization*. New York: Elsevier.

Chang, D. H., and W. B. Armstrong (eds.). 1972. *The Prison: Views from the Inside*. Cambridge, MA: Schenkman Publishing Co.

Cheatwood, A. D. 1974. "The Staff in Correctional Settings: An Empirical Investigation of Frying Pans and Fires." *Journal of Research in Crime and Delinquency* 11, 2:173–79.

Crouch, B. M. 1980. "The Book vs. the Boot: Two Styles of Guarding in a Southern Prison." Pp. 207–24 in *The Keepers*, ed. B. Crouch. Springfield, IL: Charles Thomas Publishers.

Crouch, B. M., and G. P. Alpert. 1980. "Prison Guards' Attitudes Toward Components of the Criminal Justice System." *Criminology* 18, 2 (August):227–36.

———. 1982. "Sex and Occupational Socialization Among Prison Guards: A Longitudinal Study." *Criminal Justice and Behavior* 9, 2 (June):159–76.

Crouch, B. M., and J.W. Marquart. 1980. "On Becoming a Prison Guard." Pp. 63–106 in *The Keepers*, ed. B. Crouch. Springfield, IL: Charles Thomas Publishers.

Cullen, F., B. Link, N. Wolfe, and J. Frank. 1985. "The Social Dimensions of Correctional Officer Stress." *Justice Quarterly* 2, 4 (1985):505–33.

Duffee, D. 1975. "The Correctional Officer Subculture and Organizational Change." *Journal of Research in Crime and Delinquency* 12:155–72.

Esselstyn, T. C. 1966. "The Social System of Correctional Workers." *Crime and Delinquency* 12, 2:117–24.

Griswold, H. J., M. Misenheimer, A. Powers, and E. Tromanhauser. 1970. *An Eye for an Eye.* New York: Holt, Rinehart and Winston.

Haney, C., C. Banks, and P. Zimbardo. 1973. "Interpersonal Dynamics in a Simulated Prison." *International Journal of Criminology and Penology* 1:69–79.

Hartman, C. 1969. "The Key Jingler." *Community Mental Health* V, 3:199–205.

Hepburn, J. 1984. "The Erosion of Authority and the Perceived Legitimacy of Inmate Social Protest: A Study of Prison Guards." *Journal of Criminal Justice* 12:579–90.

Hepburn, J., and C. Albonetti. 1980. "Role Conflict in Correctional Institutions: An Empirical Examination of the Treatment-Custody Dilemma Among Correctional Staff." *Criminology* 17, 4 (February):445–59.

———. 1978. "Team Classification in State Correctional Institutions: Its Association with Inmate and Staff Attitudes." *Criminal Justice and Behavior* 5, 1 (March):63–73.

Hepburn, J., and A. E. Crepin. 1984. "Relationship Strategies in a Coercive Institution: A Study of Dependence Among Prison Guards." *Journal of Social and Personal Relationships* 1:139–57.

Hepburn, J., and N. Jurik. 1986. "Individual Attributes, Occupational Conditions, and the Job Satisfaction of Correctional Security Officers." Paper presented at annual meetings, American Society of Criminology, Atlanta (October).

Hewitt, J. D., E. Poole, and R. M. Regoli. 1984. "Self-Reported and Observed Rule Breaking in Prison: A Look at Disciplinary Response." *Justice Quarterly* 3:437–48.

Howton, F. W. 1969. "Bureaucracy, Summary Punishment and the Uniform: Notes on the CO and His Work." *Criminologica* 7, 8:59–67.

Jackson, G. 1970. *Soledad Brother.* New York: Coward Press.

Jacobs, J. B. 1978. "What Prison Guards Think: A Profile of the Illinois Force." *Crime and Delinquency* 25 (April):185–96.

Johnson, R. 1987. *Hard Time.* Monterey, CA: Brooks/Cole Public Co.

———. 1976. "Informal Helping Networks in Prison: The Shape of Grass-Roots Correctional Intervention." *Journal of Criminal Justice* 4:53–70.

———. 1977. "Ameliorative Prison Stress: Some Helping Roles for Custodial Personnel." *International Journal of Criminology and Penology* 5:263–73.

Johnson, R., and S. Price. 1981. "The Complete Correctional Officer: Human Service and the Human Environment of Prison." *Criminal Justice and Behavior* 8, 3 (Sept.):343–73.

Jurik, N. C. 1985. "Individual and Organizational Determinants of Correctional Officer Attitudes Toward Inmates." *Criminology* 23, 3:523–39.

Kalinich, D. B. 1980. *Power, Stability and Contraband: The Inmate Economy.* Prospect Heights, IL: Waveland Press, Inc.

Klofas, J. M. 1984. "Reconsidering Prison Personnel: New Views of the Correctional Officer Subculture." *International Journal of Offender Therapy and Comparative Criminology* 28:169–75.

Klofas, J. M., and H. Toch. 1982. "The Guard Subculture Myth." *Journal of Research in Crime and Delinquency* 19, 2 (July):238–54.

Lombardo, L. X. 1986. "The Development of the Correctional Officer Subculture at a New Maximum Security Institution." Paper presented at annual meetings, American Society of Criminology, Atlanta (October).

———. 1985. "Group Dynamics and the Prison Guard Subculture: Is the Subculture and Impediment to Helping Inmates?" *International Journal of Offender Therapy and Comparative Criminology* 29:79–90.

———. 1981. *Guards Imprisoned: Correctional Officers at Work*. New York: Elsevier.

Marquart, J. W. 1985. "Prison Guards and the Use of Physical Coercion as a Mechanism of Prisoner Control." *Criminology* 24, 2:347–66.

Marquart, J. W., and J. B. Roebuck. 1986. "Prison Guards and Snitches: Social Control in a Maximum Security Institution." Pp. 158–76 in *The Dilemma of Punishment*, ed. K. C. Haas, and G. P. Alpert. Prospect Heights, IL: Waveland Press, Inc.

May, E. 1976. "A Day on the Job—In Prison." *Corrections Magazine* 6 (December).

McEleney, B. L. 1985. *Correctional Reform in New York*. New York: University Press of America.

Peretti, P. D., and M. Hooker. 1976. "Social Role Self Perceptions of State Prison Guards." *Criminal Justice and Behavior* 3, 2 (June):187–95.

Piliavin, I. 1966. "The Reduction of Custodian-Professional Conflict in Correctional Institutions." *Crime and Delinquency* 12 (April):125–34.

Piliavin, I., and A. Vadum. 1968. "Reducing Discrepancies in Professional and Custodial Perspectives." *Journal of Research in Crime and Delinquency* 5 (January):35–43.

Poole, E. D. and R. M. Regoli. 1983. "Professionalism, Role Conflict, Work Alienation, and Anomia: A Look at Prison Management." *The Social Science Journal* 20, 1 (January):63–70.

———. 1981. "Alienation in Prison: An Examination of the Work Relations of Prison Guards." *Criminology* 19, 2 (August):251–70.

———. 1980a. "Examining the Impact of Professionalism on Cynicism, Role Conflict, and Work Alienation Among Prison Guards." *Criminal Justice Review* 5, 2 (Fall):57–65.

———. 1980b. "Role Stress, Custody Orientation and Disciplinary Actions: A Study of Prison Guards." *Criminology* 18, 2 (August):215–26.

Regoli, R. M., E. D. Poole, and J. L. Shrink. 1979. "Occupational Socialization and Career Development: A Look at Cynicism Among Correctional Institution Workers." *Human Organization* 38, 2:183–87.

Shamir, B., and A. Drory. 1981. "Some Correlates of Prison Guards' Beliefs." *Criminal Justice and Behavior* 8, 2 (June):233–49.

———. 1982. "Occupational Tedium Among Prison Officers." *Criminal Justice and Behavior* 9, 1:79–99.

Stotland, E. 1976. "Self Esteem and Violence by Guards and State Troopers at Attica." *Criminal Justice and Behavior* 3, 1:85–96.

Thomas, J. 1984. "Some Aspects of Negotiated Order, Loose Coupling, and the Mesostructure in Maximum Security Prisons." *Symbolic Interaction* 7, 2:213–31.

Toch, H. 1977. *Living in Prison.* New York: Free Press.

———. 1978. "Is a Correctional Officer by Any Other Name a 'Screw'?" *Criminal Justice Review* 3, 2:19–35.

Toch, H., and J. Klofas. 1982. "Alienation and Desire for Job Enrichment Among Correction Officers." *Federal Probation* 46 (March):35–44.

Ward, L. H. 1981. "Corrections Officers Today." *Corrections Today* 43,1 (Jan./Feb.):52.

Ward, R. J., and D. Vandergoot. 1977. "Corrections Officers with Caseloads." *Offender Rehabilitation* 2, 1 (Fall):31–38.

Whitehead, J. T., and C. A. Lindquist. 1986a. "Correctional Officers' Job Burnout: A Path Model." *Journal of Research in Crime and Delinquency* 23, 1 (February):23–42.

———. 1986b. "Correctional Officer Professional Orientation: A Replication of the Klofas-Toch Measure." Paper presented at annual meetings, Academy of Criminal Justice Sciences, Orlando, FL (March).

Wicks, R. J. 1980. *Guard! Society's Professional Prisoner.* Houston: Gulf Publications.

Willet, T. C. 1983. "Prison Guards in Private." 1983. *Canadian Journal of Criminology* 25, 1:1–17.

Zald, M. 1962. "Power Balance and Staff Conflict in Correctional Institutions." *Administrative Science Quarterly* 6 (June):22–49.

Organizational Barriers to Women Working as Corrections Officers in Men's Prisons

NANCY C. JURIK

This analysis of the experiences of female officers in men's prisons illustrates the interplay between individual characteristics and organizational context in producing and reinforcing workplace attitudes and behavior. In addition, the study identifies some key barriers to organizational reform. Such identification is important because attempts to equalize work opportunities involve organizational change.

Source: Excerpted from Jurik, Nancy C. "An Officer and a Lady: Organizational Barriers to Women Working as Corrections Officers in Men's Prisons." *Social Problems* 32(4):375–88, April, 1985.

ORGANIZATIONAL BARRIERS TO FEMALE CORRECTIONAL OFFICERS

Despite improved opportunities, female officers experienced great difficulties surviving and advancing in the Western D.O.C. While as a group correctional officers faced many common problems, female officers faced additional barriers not confronted by their mail counterparts. These women overwhelmingly attributed the resistance they experienced at work to the biased attitudes and behavior of individual male officers and supervisors:

> The major problem for women officers is male staff. We expect it from the inmates . . . but the male officers make demeaning remarks! If you say something, they pout in a corner (female officer).

And, in fact, several male officers and supervisors did acknowledge some prejudice regarding women employed in men's prisons.

Both male and female officers expressed concern about women's reliability in violent situations. These fears appeared to be rooted in three popular beliefs about women. One objection centered on the "greater physical weaknesses" of women. Although there were no height and weight requirements for male or female security officers in the Western D.O.C., it was still commonly believed that women were not capable of functioning in dangerous situations.

> They are just not strong enough to struggle with a six-foot inmate. Then I get hurt trying to make sure they aren't beaten to death (male officer).

Another objection focused on the "mental weaknesses" of women.

> This place works on your mind after a while. Women just can't take that kind of strain. Most of them will crack (male officer).

A final set of concerns focused on the sexual identity and behavior of female officers. There was considerable fear that women might become emotionally involved with inmates.

> The first thing I always ask about an officer is "Who owns him?—Me or the inmate?" Women sometimes go soft on the inmates. We had one who got involved. She started bringing stuff in to him. She got dirty (i.e., smuggled contraband to inmates) (male supervisor).

At first glance, the suspicions surrounding female officers appeared to be a manifestation of the biased attitudes held by *individual* male staff and supervisors. Researchers frequently attribute these sentiments to childhood and adult gender-role socialization (see Wilson, 1982). However, further analysis of my data revealed that this explanation was only part of the story. Barriers to female correctional officers also include those set up by the organizational structure of the Western D.O.C. Such barriers include tokenism, conflicting organizational goals, external environmental conditions, informal organizational structures, and inadequate strategies for institutionalizing correctional reforms.

Tokenism

The suspicion surrounding female officers stemmed in part from the relatively small numbers of women who occupied security positions in men's prisons. Kanter (1977:206–42) defines "tokens" as members whose social type constitutes a minority within the organization. She observes three perceptual phenomena associated with the presence of "tokens," each of which has consequences for their organizational positions: (1) they are highly visible and so capture a disproportionate share of others' awareness; (2) their presence polarizes the differences between tokens and dominants; and (3) their attributes become distorted to fit the dominants' stereotypes about tokens.

At the time of this study, the percentage of female officers assigned to men's prison facilities in Western D.O.C. ranged from zero to 26 percent. In the two newer male prison facilities, approximately 26 of the correctional officers were women; in the older facilities approximately seven percent were women. In one facility, there were no women at all. In interviews, it was readily apparent that female officers perceived their heightened visibility in men's prisons:

> We need only the most qualified women. There are so few women that every incompetent one hurts all the others who come after her (female supervisor).

> If a woman falls short, she's censored, ostracized, talked about, whereas ten incompetent men are not noticed (female officer).

In addition to the barriers posed by tokenisms, the following organizational-level problems *indirectly* limited the integration and advancement of female officers in Western D.O.C. by thwarting the implementation of the new service orientation and blocking accompanying reforms in personnel hiring and promotional practices.

Service and Security as Conflicting Organizational Goals

As noted frequently in the prison literature, correctional security workers must continually confront a variety of conflicting and ambiguous organizational directives (Cressey, 1966; Fox, 1982). Simultaneous efforts to achieve the goals of social control and inmate service or rehabilitation often collide. Within the Western D.O.C., the service philosophy was never intended by the administration to replace or compromise the security function of the correctional system. It was hoped that, in the long run, the two would complement each other (i.e., more active and satisfied inmates would be less likely to cause altercations). However, in practice, these expectations had little chance of succeeding. On one hand, rational management of security matters required that officers treat all inmates alike and enforce rules in a consistent manner. On the other hand, inmate service and program responsibilities required that officers pay attention to individual needs and tailor inmate activities accordingly. In addition, inmate involvement in programs sometimes required a loosening of certain institutional security constraints. For example, increased inmate movement within and outside of the prison was necessary to allow participation in educational programs. Such movement posed additional security problems for prison facilities which were already understaffed and overcrowded. When such conflicts arose, security concerns frequently predominated.

> I agree with the administration's idea of combining security and treatment responsibilities. But it fell through. I do not see any difference today. Now they are trying to keep officers in the same units every day to do both counseling and security. It's a good idea, but officers get burned out so fast. They can't do both jobs. Security winds up being all most can handle (female supervisor).

While stereotypic feminine qualities were seen as an asset in the more service-oriented prison environment, these same attributes were a liability in the more security-oriented environment.

> The male officers and even the supervisors tend to think that brute strength is all they can count on. In a pinch, women will be relegated to a worthless role (female officer).

> One night my sergeant said there were only three officers on the yard and he didn't know what they would do if there was trouble. He said that he wasn't counting me because I was a female (female officer).

In the long run, inmate programs and services might have lessened the danger in Western D.O.C. facilities thereby complementing security functions. However, in the short run the staff perceived these different goals as conflicting. When security concerns predominated to the exclusion of the service dimension—as was frequently the case in Western D.O.C.—the role of women in the male correctional environment was viewed more negatively. Co-workers and supervisors suspected that women were too weak physically and emotionally to handle potentially explosive situations.

Extra-Organizational Conditions

A number of external factors greatly exacerbated prison overcrowding and staff shortages which, in turn, increased the level of danger in the facilities. During 1982 and 1983, serious financial constraints were placed by the state on the hiring of new program staff. Further, determinant sentencing laws and other efforts by the state to "crack down" on crime resulted in larger-than-expected increases in the prison population. Although a new institution was added in 1981, the expanding inmate population quickly filled that facility as well as others in the system. By the end of 1982, many of the facilities were operating significantly above capacity levels. Simultaneously, the turnover rate among correctional officers was so high (40 percent per year) that many shifts were understaffed. In a dangerous, crowded environment, new service-oriented programs were not implemented effectively. Given these tensions, officers' security responsibilities preempted their program-related functions.

> At first, the department was trying to develop rehabilitation programs. Now with all the overcrowding we face, it's mostly a matter of caretaking. We just don't have the resources to hire programs staff (male trainer).

These problems combined to reduce the number of programs available to inmates and diminish the security staff-to-inmate ratio to levels which all personnel described as dangerous. This level of danger bolstered suspicions regarding female officers' competence.

> The male officers don't trust us as back-ups. The supervisors and administrators don't think that women can maintain order in the prisons now because they're crowded and dangerous. They are afraid women would be the first hostages (female officer).

Informal Organizational Structure

A third barrier to the implementation of the correctional reforms was posed by the informal organizational structure of the Western D.O.C. The obstacles which informal work structures pose to women entering non-traditional occupations are frequently noted in the literature (Martin, 1980; O'Farrell and Harlan, 1980). The conflict between security and service functions—and the dangerous, overcrowded conditions in these facilities—intensified hostile reactions. While most of the newer staff supported the change in philosophy, there was a significant amount of resistance on the part of many of the "old-guard" (pre-1978) supervisors and line staff—most of whom were men.

> This emphasis on the *service* functions of officers makes it seem like we're maids or something. We have less power than the inmates now. The change in our job title underlines that . . . *service officers*! That's a joke! (male officer).

Resistance to the service philosophy reinforced suspicions surround the ability of women to perform adequately as correctional officers in men's prisons. These opponents expressed resentment regarding the interference of the central office in hiring, evaluation, and promotional decisions.

> To meet their quotas, they've hired a lot of female officers who just aren't qualified. They've got women working in places they just shouldn't be. . . . They should not be in the yard or in housing. They are much more likely than a man to get hurt (male officer).

In addition, the combination of these old-guard hostilities with the informal rules governing advancement further limited the opportunities available to female officers in two ways. First, in the absence of adequate formal opportunities for power and advancement, informal connections and favors became increasingly important to department staff. Women and other minorities are generally disadvantaged by these informal advancement structures (see Kanter, 1977:264).

> Advancement is contingent on several factors. One of the most important is still the superior's hidden selection criteria. Certain people are primed for promotion by giving them special assignments and increasing their educational opportunities. That depends on your connections and relationships with those higher up. . . . It's who you know. Women don't usually fare too well. The higher ups are men, of course (female administrator, formerly a line officer).

Second, major changes in departmental philosophy and the entry of a new group of workers encountered great hostility from old-time employees who felt that they had benefited from the informal occupational culture of the status quo.

> A lot of male officers see us as a threat. They think if we do the job well, then somehow it takes away from their abilities. So, they try to burn women out or to "backstab" (female officer).

Therefore, the perceived threat was not caused solely by a fear of outsiders disrupting the subculture's solidarity (as argued by Martin, 1980:138–57). It was also due to a perceived threat to promotional advancement in an organization where such opportunities were scarce.

Inadequate Implementation Strategies

The failure of Western D.O.C. departmental administrators to be aware of and plan for the resistance of the informal subculture severely hampered their ability to implement new reform-oriented policies effectively. Strategies helpful in facilitating acceptance of organizational change have been frequently discussed in the policy implementation literature (see Aronson, et al., 1984:453–86; Jurie, 1984). Yet, in Western D.O.C., there was no program designed to facilitate implementation. No plans existed to counteract resistance. There were, for example, no training seminars for mid-management. There were no specific incentives for cooperation or careful communication of changes to the various management levels. Staff had no input on proposed changes, nor were the personal benefits of the changes made apparent to them. Similarly, there was no systematic plan of negative sanctions for failure to conform to new policies.

> Nobody asked us how we felt about any of these changes. Half the time we don't even know why things are changed. We just have to pass the rules

down to the line staff. Sometimes, we know a policy won't work. Those making the policy may have never even worked with inmates (male supervisor).

Administrative policies should reflect more communication from the bottom to the top. There should be more accountability of the line staff to insure and encourage more consistent performance. Policy implementation depends too much upon who is in the chain of command, whether that individual likes the policy or not (female officer).

Because of these inadequacies, both the institutionalization of the new service philosophy and the integration of new female recruits were thwarted.

The whole issue of women working in housing areas has not been dealt with at the administrative level. Little was done to prepare for the entry of women officers into male prisons. Administrators need to be aware of these issues. They should support those new female staff and not just throw them in there (female supervisor).

Without plans to counteract informal resistance to its new policies, Western D.O.C. placed itself in the position of dictating rather than negotiating reform. The discretion held by mid-management and line-staff made the institutionalization of administrative reform policies quite difficult (see Lipsky, 1980). Intimidation, aggressiveness, and informal opportunity arrangements continued to permeate the organizational structure of the Western D.O.C. and to reinforce the skepticism surrounding female officers. As a result, the relatively few female officers bore the burden of "proving themselves" in the face of suspicious staff:

It's an aggressive environment. You have to act macho to make it. If you don't do that, it's hard to make them believe you're competent, and you'll never get anywhere in the job. But even then, they say that you're "hard" (female officer).

IMPACT OF ORGANIZATIONAL BARRIERS ON FEMALE OFFICER ADVANCEMENT

The inadequate institutionalization of departmental reform policies affected the career progress of female officers at several crucial points—in training, work assignments, and performance evaluation. These organizational problems limited the availability and coherence of *training* programs offered to correctional officers. Officers were forced to rely on informal instruction by colleagues on the job. These problems also reinforced the importance of supervisor discretion in allocating *work assignments* and conducting officer *performance evaluations*. At each of these three points in the officer's career path, the suspect status of female officers, combined with the predominance of traditional security functions and informal opportunity structures, limited the integration and advancement opportunities available to female officers.

Pre-employment Experience and Training

As a group, women entered correctional employment with less "anticipatory socialization" than male recruits. For example, among those officers surveyed, only 38 percent of the female officers compared to 68 percent of the males reported any previous employment in either corrections or a related occupation. None of the women had served in the military. In contrast, 46 percent of the men reported military service records.

On-the-job training should have provided recruits with the requisite skills for their work. Such training was especially crucial for recruits who had no previous employment experience in that field. As we have seen, women were much more likely to fall into this inexperienced group. In the Western D.O.C., training had the additional important function of disseminating and institutionalizing the new service-oriented correctional philosophy adopted by the administration. As explained earlier, the adoption of a service-oriented philosophy established an area in which it was perceived that women could make a major contribution. However, the organizational problems discussed in the preceding section limited the effectiveness of training programs in three ways.

First, because of a rapidly growing inmate population and consequent staff shortages, many officers did not receive formal training prior to their first day of work. Attending in-service training courses became a problem for similar reasons. These difficulties occurred despite departmental policies which specified that each officer had to complete a minimum of 80 training hours per year.

> At the main facility, they don't go to work without first attending the academy. Here, we've been understaffed since we opened and a lot of our officers haven't ever been to the academy (male training coordinator).

In the survey, 33 percent of the officers reported that they had never attended any entry-level training program offered by the department. In addition, 21 percent stated that they had received less than ten hours of in-service training during the year preceding the survey.

Second, it was difficult to develop a coherent and relevant training program because officer performance standards were inadequately specified, another result of the ambivalent incorporation of the new correctional philosophy. The ambiguity and conflict surrounding the necessary duties of correctional officers resulted in diverse, and sometimes inconsistent, themes in department training programs. Some classes emphasized physical abilities while others focused primarily on management and communication skills.

> Our training makes them touch. We let them know what it is like to have urine thrown in their face. They can't be shocked on their first day of work. We prepare them (training officer).

> The important thing for them to learn is that they are people managers. They must be able to communicate. We no longer have the manpower to

force the inmates to do what we want. We have to know how to manage them (training coordinator).

Finally, the manner in which training was conducted frequently prevented officers and supervisors from taking it seriously. Training was provided outside the prison work units. As a consequence, trainers had little direct authority over the correctional officers and virtually no influence over supervisors in the units.

> If they (captains) don't want to let the guys off for training, there's not much I can do about it. Going through channels and complaining, well, that takes a long time (trainer).

Moreover, much of the training neglected the social control-oriented reality of the officer's work day.

> What the trainers say is so different from what my supervisor tells me to do on the unit. It sounds good in the class, but I am not allowed to use it at work. A lot of it wouldn't work anyway (male officer).

Because, as a group, they came to the department with less related experience, inadequate training forced female officers to become more dependent on the informal training offered to them by veteran officers. These veterans were most likely to be male officers. Lacking adequate training, female recruits initially reaffirmed male co-workers' expectations that women were less capable officers.

> Everybody goes out and they are scared. They will make mistakes. But when you're a woman, they remember. You represent other women who will come after you. You're a woman making a mistake . . . not just another new officer (female officer).

Without adequate training in management techniques, communication skills, and crisis intervention strategies, line officers were not able to implement alternatives to more traditional tactics of intimidation as a form of inmate control. Physical strength and mental aggressiveness persisted as valued abilities for line security staff. Given stereotypes about women held by the majority of male staff, women remained less valued officers when such skills were deemed important.

Work Assignments

The duties assigned to officers had a tremendous impact on their occupational role learning. Although the majority of correctional officers had the same rank, the activities they performed varied greatly. Officers' assignments affected their attitudes toward work, the department, and themselves. More importantly, however, assignments frequently determined later chances for advancement, because type and variety of experience gained by line officers at work heavily influenced their future evaluations for promotion. Interview and survey data indicated that in most men's prisons within the Western D.O.C. the range of work assignments allocated to female officers was more limited than those of their male counterparts. In the absence of specific regulations assuring equal assignment allocation, some supervisors used their discretion to restrict the tasks performed by female officers.

Although it was departmental policy to extend equal work opportunities to women, there were no formal policies regulating the placement of female officers in particular work areas. Duties were assigned primarily through supervisor preferences. The frequency with which they were changed and the criteria for determining who received which assignment were determined by the supervisor of each unit.

Some superintendents and supervisors opposed the assignment of women to duties in cellblocks, housing units, and yards. Objections to such assignments centered on perceived physical weaknesses of female officers. However, inmate rights to privacy were also utilized as a justification for restricting women's work assignments. There was considerable disagreement as to the validity of this explanation. A training coordinator comments facetiously:

> There is no problem with women in the yard, in living quarters, if they are not correctional officers. I can come and go as I please with no questions asked. That uniform does something. They are not supposed to see the men nude then (female trainer).

As a result of such limitations, female officer assignments were concentrated in control room, visitation, and clerical areas.

> My captain once said—he was serious—"Women in corrections are great. Every control room should have some" (female officer).

In the survey responses, the work assignment checked by the largest percentage of male officers as "consuming most of my time" was yard duty (51 percent). In contrast, the modal work assignment for female officers was control room duty (39 percent).

The interpretation of work assignment policy varied both over time within the same prison, and across different institutions.

> When I first worked here, female officers worked every area that men did. Our current administrator won't allow women in the housing area—he says it's a violation of inmate privacy. Now women are pretty much confined to control booths, visitation, property or central communications units (female officer).

Restrictions in routine work assignments were significant because they ultimately limited the promotional possibilities for female officers. Without experience working in the yard and in housing, women found it difficult, if not impossible, to be promoted either to higher security levels or into the counseling officer track.

> The one thing an officer does not want to do is work the control room and work it extremely well. Their supervisor will never want to let them move anywhere else. . . . They'll go nowhere in the department, nowhere up, that is (male supervisor).

There were job assignments which were viewed by some supervisors as "appropriate" duty positions for women such as clerical work or duty in the control room or mail room. This information was communicated to female officers.

> Some sergeants don't make any bones about telling you that women don't belong in security positions with the residents (male inmates). . . . Or after you're there for a while, you see what positions they let women in (female officer).

These allocation patterns served to encourage "intra-sex" competition for the valued assignments:

> One of the most powerful positions a female officer can hold is in central communications. Another good place is in transportation. The women know that and they compete with each other for what they can get. The men don't mind that. . . . I mean we can't compete with them. Women wind up telling on each other . . . (by) passing incidents to the sergeant (female officer).

Ironically, in addition to their effect on promotional decisions, restrictions in female work assignments fueled the resentment of male officers for the "special treatment" given to women.

> I work here typing all day. I hate it. Then the guys come in, the other officers, and they say, "How do you rate being in here out of the hot sun, in this nice air-conditioned room!" They are irritated that I make the same wages they do and get the "cush" jobs! (female officer).

In absence of specific guidelines for greater integration of female officers, an informal network of opportunity took over. Their duty assignments were dependent on the attitudes of their supervisors.

> I guess I should be grateful in one sense. My captain said, "Hey, I'm gonna get you out of here and in the yard!" At that time, women did not work the yard in that unit. I went out. I had a very liberal lieutenant and sergeant and *I worked the yard*! I was there during the food riot. I found out I could do the job. Now my major says, "I wouldn't put you in the yard unless you had a man next to you." So now I work in his office . . . answer his phone (female officer).

This informal opportunity network most often worked to the disadvantage of women working in men's prisons. The suspect status of female officers, combined with the discretionary nature of duty assignment, prevented them from obtaining the experience and recognition which were vital to promotion. Without the opportunity for such experience, their abilities were never fully demonstrated; their suspect status was merely reaffirmed.

Performance Evaluations

The annual performance evaluations of correctional officers became part of their permanent work records within the department. These evaluations were conducted by supervisors according to broad departmental guidelines. Later, these evaluations were scrutinized carefully when officers applied for promotions. Despite formal attempts to substitute universalistic for particularistic criteria in these reviews the ambiguous and discretionary nature of the guidelines lead to inconsistent evaluations of officers.

> Recognition? It depends on who your lieutenant and captain are, especially for women. It's how "in" you are. . . . You can work your bippy off and get passed over for someone you know isn't worth table salt (female officer).

In the absence of clear directives, supervisors' ratings were more easily influenced by their stereotyped views of women as seductive or weak.

> My first time on yard duty, a resident came up and asked me a question and I was written up. On my performance evaluation, it said: "Over-familiar with residents" (female officer).

The subjectivity inherent in the officer review process was, in part, a side-effect of both the inadequate institutionalization of the service philosophy and the conflicting nature of correctional work. A content analysis of the departmental performance evaluation form for correctional service officers revealed the continued emphasis on security to the exclusion of service responsibilities. Out of the 18 categories of responsibilities evaluated, only one dealt with any service function performed by officers for inmates—that of administering first aid in an emergency situation. Communication skills, conflict diffusion or other service-related functions were not addressed. Eight categories related to line officers' responsibilities to follow orders and show respect for superiors. The remaining categories dealt with such issues as report writing, care of state property, control and direction of inmates, and proficiency in the use of firearms. The continued prevalence of para-military custodial and security functions supported traditional stereotypes of prison guards and indirectly accentuated the perceived weaknesses of female officers.

Even if performance ratings were based on universal standards, most officers felt that their use in promotions and other decisions was permeated by favoritism. Such perceptions reinforced beliefs that evaluations and promotions of women were based either on physical appearance or on the promise of sexual favors. Male officers resented this alleged favoritism. Female officers, in turn, feared retaliation if they responded negatively to sexual harassment from supervisors.

> When this male investigator tried to kiss me at work, I didn't tell anyone. It's not good to make waves that way. Your supervisors think you're just trying to cause trouble (female officer).

When women were promoted, they often felt a need to prove their qualifications and disprove the innuendoes of "sexual" favoritism.

> Our captain was known for hiring and promoting women officers. When he moved me into administrative duties, a lot of the guys there said, "She's just another one of the captain's harem." After a few months, I was able to prove that I was competent *and* that I was not screwing the boss (female officer).

Without clear and uniform standards for officer evaluations, female officers were again dependent on the goodwill of individual supervisors. If gender stereotypes entered their performance evaluations, they had little formal recourse. Grievance procedures required employees to file with their immediate supervisors. If the superior was the subject of the grievance, this requirement presented a serious obstacle to the grievance process. Given the subjectivity of the review process, it was extremely difficult to document the degree to which the evaluations of particular employees were biased. Finally, the subjectivity of the process also ignited male co-worker hostilities because they believed that positive evaluations and promotions of female officers were often "sexually motivated."

REFERENCES

Aronson, D., C. T. Dienes, and M. C. Musheno. 1984. *Public Policy and Police Discretion.* New York: Clark Boardman Company.

Cressey, D. 1966. "Contradictory Directives in Complex Organizations: The Case of the Prison." Pp. 349–73 in *Prison Within Society*, ed. L. Hazelrigg. New York: Doubleday.

Fox, J. 1982. *Organizational and Racial Conflict in Maximum Security Prisons.* New York: D.C. Heath.

Jurie, J. D. 1984. *Policy Implementation.* Unpublished doctoral examination. Arizona State University, Tempe.

Kanter, R. M. 1976. "The Impact of Hierarchical Structures on the Work Behavior of Women and Men." *Social Problems* 23:415–30.

Lipsky, M. 1980. *Street-level Bureaucracy: Dilemmas of the Individual in Public Services.* New York: Russell Sage Foundation.

Martin, S. E. 1980. *Breaking and Entering: Policewomen on Patrol.* Berkeley: University of California Press.

O'Farrell, B., and S. Harlan. 1982. "Craftworkers and Clerks: The Effect of Male Coworker Hostility on Women's Satisfaction with Nontraditional Jobs." *Social Problems* 29:252–63.

Wilson, N. K. 1982. "Women in the Criminal Justice Professions: An Analysis of Status Conflict." Pp. 359–74 in *Judge Lawyer Victim Thief*, ed. N. H. Rafter, and E. A. Stanko. Boston: Northeastern University Press.

The Prison as a Constitutional Government

JOHN J. DIIULIO, JR.

There is nothing inherent in the nature of prisons or their clientele that makes better prisons impossible. There is nothing about spending more money, hiring more staff, erecting modern buildings, increasing hours of formal training, or reducing inmate populations that makes better prisons inevitable. Low levels of order, amenity, and service in prisons are neither expressions of amorphous social forces (internal or external) nor by-products of public apathy or the insensitivity of corrections officials. Poor prison conditions are produced by observable and, it appears, remediable defects in the way that prisons are organized and managed. If one is interested in improving the quality of prison life, then the best way to think about the prison is not as a mini-society but as a mini-government. What James Madison argued with respect to the government of society at large applies with equal force to the government of the prison. Prison managers must effect a government strong enough to control a community of persons who are most decidedly not angels. At the same time, however, prison managers must be subject to a vigorous system of internal and external controls on their behavior, including judicial and legislative oversight, media scrutiny, occupational norms and standards, rigorous internal supervision and inspections, ongoing intra-departmental evaluations, and openness to outside researchers.

Based on our explanatory study of correctional institutions in three states, it appears that there is some relationship between administrative structure and prison conditions. The proper unit of analysis, however, is less the corrections agency as a whole and more the prison itself; not who reports to whom at headquarters but who works how in the institutions. Contrary to the argument made in much of the existing literature, the best hypothesis seems to be that higher-custody prisons that are organized along bureaucratic, even paramilitary, lines and operated strictly "by the book" will have less violence than those that are organized and run more loosely. A corollary to this hypothesis is that reliance on inmates to control other inmates—whether via building tenders, inmate council representatives, con bosses, prison gang leaders, or other such inmate-staff arrangements—is a recipe for compromising security and violating laws. Where higher-custody prisons are concerned, those govern best who govern most and most formally.

Source: Excerpted from DiIulio, John J., Jr. "The Prison as a Constitutional Government." Chapter 6 in *Governing Prisons: A Comparative Study of Correctional Management*, pp. 235–263. New York: Free Press, 1987.

In a more highly bureaucratized prison, officers would behave according to a manageable number of simple operational rules. Theirs would be a tight, stable, uniform routine of monitoring inmate movement, frisking inmates, searching cells, and so on. Officer training would take place in an abbreviated "boot camp" where this routine would be memorized and practiced, physical training and self-defense arts would be mastered, and the basic principles of security management, from key control to riot control, would be learned. Preservice educational requirements would be minimal.

In the genuine prison bureaucracy, officers would be more "impersonal" in their relations with inmates, but that is the same as saying that they would be less able to discriminate against inmates whom they disliked. They would be more "restrictive," but that would make even-handed treatment of inmates more imperative and the threats to security less acute. In short, a prison bureaucracy would involve organizational patterns of superordination and subordination that minimize the exercise of arbitrary power or inequality in prisons. Uniformed prison workers at all but the highest levels would be neither professionals nor craftsmen but bureaucrats in the same sense that soldiers are bureaucrats.

In much of the literature, any case for more highly structured forms of prison administration is ruled out of bounds by such observations as the following:

> While bureaucratic forms support accountability functions essential to a correctional program in meeting its control obligations, the same forms restrict the highly adaptive and infinitely varied kinds of organizational response which are essential to a dynamic treatment process.

> The prison is often an extreme example of bureaucracy as managers sometimes try to control people as easily and effectively as they would a manufactured commodity. . . . The extreme preoccupation of many wardens and staff with rules, power, and coercion is responsible for . . . poor communication, poor morale . . . and self-protectiveness on the part of the staff. . . . Inmates are forced to develop their own lifestyle in their own world in order to retain any sort of self-integrity.

Just the reverse, however, may be true: bureaucratic prisons may foster higher staff morale, better inmate programs, and a more safe and civilized prison environment. But, unless and until far more empirical research is completed, we will not know what, if any, relationship exists between administrative structure and prison conditions. Even if we knew that prison bureaucracy was best able to produce high levels of order, we would still need to know whether bureaucratizing (or militarizing) the prison beyond a given point would improve (or worsen) the overall quality of prison life, and whether this administrative form is superior for both lower- and higher-custody institutions.

CORRECTIONAL LEADERSHIP AND ADMINISTRATIVE STABILITY

To be well governed, it would appear that prisons need not only bureaucratic bodies but stable, nonbureaucratic heads. If the prison is to be a constitutional government, then corrections executives must lead and prison wardens must manage both behind the walls and beyond them. They must make frequent on-site institutional tours (not "visits") and become hostages neither to second-hand reports nor to what one prison official called "iron bars of paperwork." At the same time, they must make frequent and constructive contacts with their organization's outside "coaches, customers, and critics."

Our study revealed the important degree to which corrections executives can influence the philosophical cast, sense of mission, institutional procedures, and political strength of corrections departments. If the person who directs the prison system does not make a sensible estimate of the problems with which he and his subordinates must wrestle, if he is unable to garner and institutionalize political support for the agency, or if his tenure is too short for him to do anything more than announce his departure, then there would appear to be little hope for the kinds of administrative measures necessary to effect and to sustain a high quality of prison life. Even with a correctional philosophy that can be translated first into policy decrees and then into a bureaucratic routine of administrative action, no prison system will perform well unless it can successfully manage those political and other pressures that make for administrative uncertainty and instability. As California's Richard A. McGee observed, "all of the debating in the world will not solve corrections problems without some analysis of the political contexts in which these [publicly] supported agencies have their being."

At this stage, it is impossible to generalize about the kinds of persons who would make successful prison executives. Nor is it yet possible to generalize about the characteristics most common to successful prison wardens or superintendents. There are, however, a few broad observations that may be worth considering. First, successful prison directors and institutional managers are not here today, gone tomorrow. They are in office long enough to learn the job, make plans, and implement them. Second, they are highly "hands-on" and proactive. They pay close attention to details and do not wait for problems to arise but attempt to anticipate them. While they trust their subordinates and do their share of paperwork, they keep themselves focused on the prisons and what is actually happening inside of them. At the same time, they recognize the need for outside support. In short, they are strangers neither to the cellblocks nor to the aisles of the state legislature. Third, they act consciously to project an image of themselves that is appealing to a wide range of people both inside and outside of the organization. Fourth, they are dedicated and fiercely loyal to the department and see themselves as keepers engaged in a noble and challenging (if mostly thankless) profession.

Even if there were fifty-one such correctional leaders ready and able to assume control of our prisons, it would mean little unless those jurisdictions where prison directorships are still political plums did something to de-politicize their corrections departments. So long as prison directors change every few years and prison wardens play musical chairs, the kind of correctional leadership and administrative stability necessary to better prisons will not be forthcoming.

Nowhere in the world of public or private management do administrators at all levels face the type of thorny problems confronted on a daily basis by prison workers. They operate in a world where normal, everyday objects must be viewed as potentially lethal weapons. A sergeant in a California prison delighted in showing visitors a "book of horrors," a photographic catalogue of inmate weapons and those who made (or were victimized by) them: sharpened plastic combs stuck into bars of soap and used as knives; bullets concealed in a mattress (discovered by a metal detector); a prisoner's "ki-ester stash" (a homemade gun which the inmate had concealed in his rectum and used during an escape attempt); a shampoo bottle with a wick used as a flame thrower and the charred bodies of those inmates on whom it was used; inmates with weapons in their hair (blacks in their tight braids, whites in their pony tails); and so on.

Those who work in prisons must doubt inmates' motives and look beneath the surface of superficially positive developments. For instance, a Michigan prison administrator spoke of one of the system's newer religious sects as a budding prison gang: "They're not a religion but a pressure group, a racket with a cover. They extort money, sell job assignments. But as a religion they are given rights which enable them to organize and operate freely."

Following personal interviews, former TDC director W. J. Estelle provided a written discourse on prison management in which he concluded: "Now in seven rambling pages I have told you nearly everything I've absorbed over 32 years ... although I neglected a few pedestrian items such as clearing the count, contraband control, public speaking, budget preparation, construction management, effective application of anhydrous ammonia, use of portable fuel storage tanks, etc. ...." Clearly, corrections is unlike any other occupation. At a minimum, to be at all successful in the field requires a willingness to spend a great deal of time inside prisons. Only there can one learn the real ropes of the trade, including some sense of the unique emotional and other job stresses shared by prison workers.

Having conceded so much to the uniqueness of the prison workers' task, we should also point out that prison workers have tended to exaggerate it by overstating both the dangers and the overall difficulty of what they are paid to do. Unlike police, firemen, and other public servants who perform vital and often dangerous tasks, what prison workers do is hidden physically from public view and has only rarely captured the public imagination in a favorable way. The popular stereotypes of prison workers, particularly correctional officers, are most unflattering and wholly unjustified. Stressing the dangers of their work and the "powder keg" theory of governing inmates is a way for prison workers to enhance their self-image, add a bit of color and romance to an otherwise monotonous occupation, and, they believe, garner the appreciation of the rest of us. In addition, by perpetuating the myths about inmates and prison governance discussed in chapter four, prison authorities can deflect responsibility for unsafe, unclean, and unproductive prisons away from themselves and onto everything from villainous judges to impersonal social, political, and economic forces over which nobody, let alone the prison staff itself, has much apparent control.

Corrections is by no means a dismal profession. Prison workers perform what is arguably one of the most essential functions of the sovereign state. They are most likely to succeed in raising their status if they act so as to raise the quality of prison life. They can begin by discarding self-defeating myths about prisons in favor of a shared vision of good prison government.

If our correctional agencies can attract and hold onto able executives, talented managers, and conscientious workers, if they can operate according to a realistic management philosophy and are given sufficient (though not necessarily ample) resources, and if they can develop a sense of mission, an esprit de corps, and learn to manage their power over convicted criminals with common sense and compassion, then our correctional institutions will probably be safer, cleaner, less idle, more productive, and maybe even cost less to operate. In short, prisons can be governed well or ill. We need to learn much more about how to govern them well with the human and financial resources at hand.

The only finding of this study that, to me at least, seems indisputable, is that, other things being equal, dedicated, security-conscious prison management will yield more in the way of prison order, amenity, and service than less dedicated, more lax prison management; in short, prison management matters. The quality of prison management is influenced mainly, though not solely, by the prison's political environment, its correctional leadership, and its correctional philosophy. Some keepers do their jobs more sensibly and with better results than others, but all of them deserve our admiration and respect for performing an illiberal task in a liberal polity.

A paramilitary prison bureaucracy, led by able institutional managers and steered by a talented executive, may be the best administrative response to the problem of establishing and maintaining higher-custody prisons in which inmates and staff lead a calm, peaceful, and productive round of daily life. Prison workers can simultaneously share a sense of mission, identify with each other, care about the inmates, and perform well a vital service to the people of the law-abiding and tax-paying community.

THE MORALITY OF IMPRISONMENT

Even if we knew for sure how to make prisons more safe and sound, many would still oppose imprisonment or view it as a necessary evil. Liberals tend to believe that prisons are by their very nature oppressive and inhumane; conservatives tend to believe that they cost too much and punish too little. The first complains that prisons brutalize; the second complains that they coddle. To some, knowing that prisons can be improved via better management is like knowing that the guillotine can work better provided that it is well oiled; to others, a concern for anything beyond warehousing convicts bespeaks too much compassion for remorseless offenders and too little for their innocent victims. Both groups view the prison as a morally bankrupt institution.

I disagree entirely. It is possible to justify the expenditure of human and financial resources necessary to effect (or inch toward) decent conditions behind bars. Good prisons are prisons where levels of order, amenity, and service are indisputably high. Such institutions are not only possible but desirable. They represent the best moral option for a people that wants to be both just and merciful towards its convicted criminals.

The prison is not, as Hawthorne phrased it, the black flower of civilization. Instead, it is evidence of a civilization which seeks to treat all but its most murderous citizens in a spirit of hopefulness and compassion. Imprisonment is a public ideal, and that ideal, like any other, will go unrealized where it is unmet by citizens willing and able to cooperate toward its fulfillment. In the famous words of Dostoevsky, the degree of civilization in a society can be judged by entering its prisons. It is not enough, therefore, to erect prison walls; the morality of imprisonment is unassailable, but the moral standing of any actual prison will depend on its quality of life.

CONCLUSION: THE DUTY TO GOVERN

It is easy to think of alternatives to imprisonment and to pursue magic cures for the ills of America's correctional complex. It is much harder to get down to the nitty-gritty business of finding and implementing ways to improve conditions for the hundreds of thousands of people who live and work in our prisons. The former is an exciting enterprise that is in vogue; the latter is a tremendous undertaking that seems hopeless. The first stimulates general ideas and frees us to look ahead; the second immerses us in the particulars of prison management and forces us to learn from our mistakes. The former enables us to theorize about how well we will employ new or additional resources; the latter constrains us to discover and apply practical ways of doing better with what is at hand.

The government's responsibility to govern does not end at the prison gates; nor, for that matter, does its ability. Whether government can or should run cost-effective railroads, engineer economic prosperity, or negotiate us to international bliss may all be open questions. But government can and should run safe, humane, productive prisons at a reasonable cost to the taxpayers. No self-respecting government would abdicate or excuse itself from so central a duty. Prisons are a public trust to be administered in the name of civility and justice. Governing prisons is a public management task that we can learn to perform much better.

CHAPTER 4

Contemporary Prisons as Process: Correctional Intervention

In the previous section, we saw that prisons can be viewed as unique societies unto themselves, having their own social and cultural arrangements. In this section, we approach prisons as mirrors of the larger societies they serve. The reflection, however, is a contorted one, since offenders are disproportionately drawn from the lowest strata of society. At their worst, inmate populations are violent, illiterate, drug-addicted, disease-ridden, malnourished and under-socialized. From this perspective, prisons are a microcosm of the ignoble side of society, containing its worst failures.

Prisons are required not just to take inmates sent by the courts but to take them as they are in whatever shape they are in. Many inmates are multiple-problem individuals, with criminality being only one node in a connate and experiential web of social and psychological deficits. Thus, when it comes to programs, prisons tend to be full-service institutions, offering a gamut of programs, many of which are comparable to those available in the larger society.

Prisons offer programs that address the needs and problems of inmates for a variety of reasons. The most basic rationale is that the law requires prisons to protect the physical and emotional well-being of inmates and to maintain their safety. The legal standard for prison programming is not especially high, involving mostly essential medical services. Humanitarian rationales for prison programs are also advanced, usually by pointing to the extensive history of social adversity that characterizes most inmates. This rationale, however, can be undercut by pointing to similarly situated law-abiding citizens and by arguing that, all other things being equal, limited resources should be directed toward those who are not criminal and therefore more morally deserving. These arguments often are resolved by advancing the principle of least eligibility which dictates that inmates are entitled only to the same level of services as the least eligible members of free society.

The most common, and, at least in the abstract, the most compelling and expansive rationales for inmate programs are based on utilitarian grounds. Generally, two arguments are advanced. First, prison programs reduce recidivism, and they result in a net benefit to society when the costs of programming are balanced against the savings that accrue from prevented crimes. Second, idle inmates being a warden's nightmare, prison programs are a key element in maintaining institutional control. Both of these arguments are subject to scientific verification, and evaluations of the effectiveness of prison programs play a critical role in assessing these arguments.

Finally, prisons are "people-processing" institutions made up of three stages—input, throughput, and output. Prisons have no control over their input, which is determined by the legislature and the courts, and they have only limited control over their output, usually by means of early release programs that are tied to prison behavior. In contrast, prisons have great control over their throughput. Consequently, the things that prisons do to, with, and for inmates define the character of these institutions.

This section begins with the problem of infectious diseases in inmate populations. The first two readings deal with AIDS, which is probably the most contentious and costly health care issue of the century. The first reading, based on research by the U.S. Department of Justice, Bureau of Justice Statistics, presents epidemiological estimates of the prevalence of AIDS in inmate populations. The second reading, by Michael Kirby, commissioner of the World Health Organization, discusses several highly controversial proposals for dealing with HIV-positive inmates, including mandatory screening, the distribution of condoms, and access to sterile needles for intravenous drug use. The third reading deals with tuberculosis, which is a problem of increasing concern in the criminal justice system.

The fourth reading, by Tim Brennan, discusses the prison classification process. Classification procedures are a way of making sense of the great diversity in inmate populations, and this reading concentrates on classification for security purposes rather than for treatment.

The next four readings deal with the most common types of inmate programs—alcohol and drug treatment programs, education programs, and prison industries. The first of these readings by Helen Annis looks at the characteristics of effective alcohol and drug treatment programs. Next, Timothy Flanagan and Kathleen Maguire review the social and economic arguments for and against prison industry programs, and they present a model for full prison employment. Subsequently, T. A. Ryan discusses the link between literacy programs and reintegration. Lastly, Friedrich Lösel discusses the characteristics of effective correctional programs.

The section ends with a reading on the inmate disciplinary process, which operates as a mini criminal justice system within prison systems.

HIV in Prisons

Peter M. Brien
Allen J. Beck

TRENDS IN HIV INFECTION IN U.S. PRISONS

At year's end 1994, 22,713 inmates in state and federal prisons were known to be infected with the human immunodeficiency virus (HIV). In 1991, 16,921 state prisoners were HIV positive; in 1994, 21,749 were HIV positive, a 29% increase. The Federal Bureau of Prisons held 630 HIV-positive inmates in 1991 and 964 in 1994, a 53% increase.

Between 1991 and 1994 the number of HIV-positive inmates grew at about the same rate as the overall prison population (29% compared to 26%). As a result, the percentage of all prisoners infected with HIV rose from 2.2% in 1991 to 2.3% in 1994. HIV-positive inmates comprised 2.3% of the state prison population in 1991 and 2.5% in 1994. In federal prisons HIV-positive inmates were 1.0% of all prisoners in 1991 and 1.1% in 1994.

HIV-infected inmates are concentrated in a small number of states. New York and Florida house the largest number of HIV-positive inmates. In 1994 these two states held nearly half of all HIV-positive inmates in the nation. New York had the highest percentage of inmates known to be HIV positive (12.4%), followed by Connecticut (6.6%), Rhode Island (3.8%), Maryland (3.7%), and New Jersey (3.6%).

Seven states reported having fewer than 10 cases of HIV-positive inmates in their prisons. Vermont reported no HIV-positive inmates. Twenty-six states reported that fewer than 1.0% of their inmate population were HIV positive.

Texas reported the largest growth in the number of HIV-positive inmates, from 615 in 1991 to 1,584 in 1994. Substantial increases were also reported in Florida (an increase of 881 inmates), Connecticut (366), and North Carolina (351).

CONFIRMED AIDS CASES IN U.S. PRISONS

At the end of 1994, 4,849 confirmed AIDS cases were in U.S. prisons—4,478 state inmates and 371 federal inmates. Of the remaining HIV-positive inmates, 2,492 showed symptoms of HIV infection and 14,988 were asymptomatic.

Source: Extracted from "HIV in Prisons." *Bureau of Justice Statistics Bulletin*. Washington, D.C.: U.S. Government Printing Office, 1996.

The number of prison inmates with confirmed AIDS has nearly tripled since 1991, when there were 1,682. The number of inmates with lesser or no symptoms of HIV infection grew by 13%.

COMPARISON TO THE U.S. RESIDENT POPULATION

At the end of 1994, the rate of confirmed AIDS in state and federal prisons was more than 7 times higher than in the total U.S. population. Approximately 0.52% of all prisoners had confirmed AIDS, compared to 0.07% of the U.S. population.

Over the last 3 years, the available data indicate that the rates for confirmed AIDS cases have been much higher in prisons than in the general population. In 1993 the incidence of AIDS was over 8 times greater inside prisons than in the general population. The rate of AIDS infection in 1992 was about 9.5 times higher for prisoners than the general population, and in 1991, the AIDS-infection rate was over 6.5 times higher inside prisons than in the general population.

AIDS-RELATED DEATHS IN STATE PRISONS

In 1994, 955 state inmates died of Pneumocystis carinii pneumonia, Kaposi's sarcoma, or other AIDS-related diseases. These AIDS-related deaths comprised over a third of all deaths of state prisoners.

The rate of death because of AIDS is about 3 times higher in the prison population than in the total U.S. population age 15 to 54. Between 1991 and 1993 about 1 in every 3 prisoner deaths was attributable to AIDS-related causes, compared to 1 in 10 deaths in the general population.

In every year since 1991, "AIDS-related causes" has been the second leading cause of death for state prisoners behind "illness and natural causes." For every 100,000 state inmates in 1994, 104 died of AIDS-related causes. The number of AIDS-related deaths in prison has increased 84% since 1991, making AIDS the fastest rising cause of state inmate deaths.

In 1994 AIDS-related causes accounted for over half of all inmate deaths in New York (60%), Connecticut (60%), Florida (56%), Massachusetts (54%), and New Jersey (51%). Fifteen states reported having no AIDS-related deaths, and 8 states reported only 1 AIDS-related death.

HIV Infection of Male and Female State Inmates

At the end of 1994, there were 19,762 male and 1,953 female state inmates infected with HIV—2.4% of all male and 3.9% of all female state inmates. The rate of HIV infection was higher for women than men in every region and in most states.

Since 1991 the number of male state inmates infected with HIV has increased 22%, while the number of female inmates infected has increased at a much faster rate—69%.

In three states more than 10% of female inmates were known to be HIV positive—New York (20%), Connecticut (15%), and Massachusetts (12%). New York (12%) was the only state in which more than 10% of the male inmates were known to be infected with HIV.

HIV-testing Policies

Each state, the District of Columbia, and the Federal Bureau of Prisons test their inmates for HIV based on certain criteria. Most jurisdictions (45 out of 52) test inmates if they have HIV-related symptoms or if the inmates request a test. Twenty-six states test inmates after they are involved in an incident, and 15 states test inmates who belong to specific "high-risk groups."

Seventeen states test all inmates who enter their facilities. Three of these states (Alabama, Missouri, and Nevada) and the Federal Bureau of Prisons also test inmates upon their release.

Rhode Island, Utah, and Wyoming test all inmates currently in custody. New York, Hawaii, and the Federal Bureau of Prisons test inmates selected at random.

AIDS Recommendations and Prisons in Australia

MICHAEL KIRBY[1]

What can be done to protect prisoners from infection with HIV whilst in prison? About some matters there need be little debate. Few observers would dispute the need to:

- provide information, education, and training to prisoners and to prison officers, administrators, and all those responsible for prisons about the special risks of HIV/AIDS in the prison context;

- provide facilities for antibody testing on a voluntary basis whenever a prisoner reasonably wishes to undergo the test;

Source: Extracted from Kirby, Michael. WHO Global Commission, AIDS Recommendations and Prisons in Australia. In *HIV/AIDS and Prisons*, edited by Jennifer Norberry, Matt Gaughwin, and Sally-Anne Gerull, pp. 7–22. Canberra: Australian Institute of Criminology, 1991.

- provide for strict confidentiality in the results of the test and for counselling both before and after testing is conducted. Discovery of seropositivity, particularly in a prison environment with a lack of support that may be available outside, adds to the need for understanding and assistance to prisoners found to be HIV positive. Prolonged periods of idleness, and the absence of the distractions available to a person pursuing an ordinary life in the community, mean that the impact of knowledge of seropositivity will be even greater in the case of a prisoner than otherwise;

- pay attention to tattooing by unsterile tattooing equipment which is another special concern in the Australian prison culture. It provides a reason for the provision of bleach or other cleaning materials so long as in-house tattooing occurs;

- provide facilities for treatment, including AZT, therapy, and therapeutic counselling from prison medical staff to seropositive prisoners. Such staff should be provided with information about HIV/AIDS with the latest medical and non-medical supports available to persons infected; and

- collate appropriate data for the purpose of tracing the problem and constantly reviewing policies. Epidemiological data on the incidence of HIV among prisoners, provided on a purely statistical footing, should be pooled and distributed to correctional authorities throughout the country. Personal identifiers should be removed from such data.

Fortunately, certain studies including some on South Australian prisons, reveal relatively high levels of accurate knowledge about HIV and its modes of transmission within prisons (Gaughwin, et al., 1990:63). Clearly, prison journals should be used and prisoners themselves consulted on ways in which information can be effectively disseminated in the prison environment to ensure necessary behaviour modification.

TESTING, CONDOMS, AND BLEACH?

Mandatory Screening

This leaves three issues of controversy upon which there is no unanimity. The first is whether compulsory testing of prisoners should be supported. Its introduction in New South Wales was accompanied by considerable debate including, apparently, within the government. There is a tendency with AIDS to resort to mandatory screening. The government is then seen to be acting. It is usually directed at powerless, voiceless groups (such as prisoners, overseas migrant applicants, and members of disciplined services). It has the colour of a medical response to a medical problem. We remember the widespread useful testing for tuberculosis. It is relatively cheap. It has some epidemiological utility. It may also provide prisoners with some proof in the event that they later wish to bring an action for negligent care against the government or prison authorities.

The arguments in favour of mandatory testing of all prisoners for purely statistical data are strong. But, as introduced in Australia, identifiers have not been removed. Confidentiality has not been observed. In some prisons, the prisoners are segregated and lose valuable rights. In others, their confidences have been betrayed, as when one prison officer told a family member that his father would take a time to get to the interview room because he was "in the AIDS wing." Testing leads to no cure. Unless accompanied by strict confidentiality (which is difficult anyway to maintain in a prison environment) it leads to discrimination, hatred, and even retaliation out of fear. Unless a strict policy of separate prisons and segregation is adopted, the testing leads, effectively, nowhere. As well, it is subject, unless constantly repeated, to the defects of false positives and negatives and to the window period. It may lead to false confidence about HIV status. It does not have the advantage which "encouraged" voluntary testing presents as a first step in personal responsibility and behaviour modification which are essential for the containment of the HIV epidemic—especially in the artificial environment of prisons.

Whilst, therefore, I understand the political forces which lie behind compulsory testing of prisoners, I do not believe that it can be justified as an effective strategy against the spread of HIV in prisons, at least as presently undertaken. It is, I regret to say, politically attractive in part because it is cheap and has little consequence but involves doing something. I consider that the WHO guidelines which exclude such involuntary screening show greater wisdom.

Condoms

The provision of condoms in prisons has been opposed by prison officers' associations. In New South Wales, they even threatened to go on strike if any condoms were distributed in prisons (*Sydney Morning Herald* 14 June 1990). As a result of this threat it was agreed that the proposal would be "kept on ice" for the time being. The *Sydney Morning Herald* reported that it was understood that "Ministers feared that any unexpected confrontation with prison officers would seriously jeopardize legislation aimed at introducing compulsory AIDS testing for all New South Wales prisoners."

A number of arguments are raised against the provision of condoms in prisons. Some of them are based upon the assertion that homosexual activity does not exist. This is a factual issue. It appears to defy such anecdotal and research information as is available. In some cases it is opposed on the basis that the provision of condoms would condone sexual activity, to the decline of prison discipline. However, in many of the responses to the AIDS epidemic, authorities have had to face cold reality. In the name of the higher good of preventing the spread of a deadly condition, which should certainly not be acquired whilst a person is the responsibility of a State in a prison, steps have been taken which, even recently, would have been considered unthinkable. The most obvious of these involves the needle exchange scheme.

It is said that prison officers should not be demeaned by handing out condoms. I entirely agree. Such a procedure would, in any case, greatly discourage their use. Condoms should be readily available from medical services. At the least they should be available from vending machines or prison stores. Prisoners cannot walk into a pharmacy and purchase them, as ordinary citizens may. They should not, by reason of their imprisonment, be exposed to the risk of a deadly condition which can be avoided (or the risk greatly reduced) by the use of condoms.

Then it is said that condoms will break and are not suitable to anal intercourse. New and safer condoms have been developed. Furthermore, it is not only for anal intercourse that condoms should be used. Condoms reduce the risk of sexually transmitted diseases spreading by other means of sexual intercourse. No one suggests that condoms are a complete answer to sexual transmission of HIV. But they clearly reduce the risk very substantially. They would not be likely to be used in violent sexual acts, for example, rape in prison. But for reducing the transmission of HIV in prisons at least by consensual sexual activity, condoms should in my opinion be made available free of charge. Whilst it is true that there is some risk that they may be used for secreting drugs or other objects, it is necessary in HIV prevention to balance risks. One thing is sure about HIV: once acquired there is no cure. In most, if not all, cases it leads to death. I therefore find myself in agreement with the leader of the *Sydney Morning Herald:*

> [T]here are more private ways of distributing condoms. In other countries condoms are simply sold across the counter in prison canteens or from vending machines. For six years, NSW Prison Officers have maintained that they will not accept the State-sanctioned introduction of condoms. This obstruction is a major political problem ... there is ... a fear that condoms would be used to conceal contraband in body cavities. This is indeed a risk. But it is less serious than the dangers of the spread of AIDS in NSW prisons and its implications for society outside the prisons (14 June 1990).

IV Drug Use

The most controversial issue is whether sterile syringes should be made available to prisoners or, at the least, bleach and other cleaning materials to reduce the risk of spreading HIV through unsterile needles infected with contaminated blood. That risk is greater in the prison context because of the likelihood that, if illicit drugs are available, they will be administered with equipment which must be repeatedly used and shared amongst many users. To the subcultural forces which promote sharing of unsterile needles in civilian society, is typically added the imperative of unavailable alternatives in the prison context. It is not as if the prisoner can participate in the needle exchange scheme which has been introduced. He or she, if addicted, will usually have access only to imperfect equipment: just the kind likely to provide the perfect vehicle for the spread of contaminated blood.

I can understand the attitude of politicians and prison officers who resist the notion of providing sterile needles or even cleaning materials in a prison context. To many this would seem the final abandonment of the "war against drugs" and in a disciplined context. It would appear, in an environment designed to uphold the law, to condone illegal drug use: a contradiction in terms. Many of these arguments were presented by analogy, when the proposal for needle exchange was made. In a rare and bold move with bipartisan support, governments in Australia, New Zealand, and elsewhere have concluded that the risks of HIV/AIDS, and the usually fatal result of the infection, require radical and even unpalatable steps to be taken.

It is my belief that in due course even more radical steps will be needed as the AIDS epidemic penetrates Western societies by the vectors of drug-infected heterosexual males and females. Already we are beginning to see serious calls to address the problems of drug addiction by the techniques of public health rather than the imperfect mechanisms of law and order (for example, Australian Parliament, 1989; Wodak, 1990; Kaplan, 1988). But this will remain a long-term strategy—one of great significance for the prison system. In the short-term, in prisons, as in society, connections must be tolerated precisely because HIV once acquired has such devastating, horrible consequences. Offenders are imprisoned as punishment and not for punishment. They certainly do not go to prison to be exposed to the risk of acquiring a fatal condition there. Unless governments and prison administrators can absolutely guarantee a totally drug-free environment, it is their plain duty to face up to the risks of the spread of HIV infection by the use of unsterile injecting equipment in prisons. If it is too much to adopt a similar exchange system (unused for used needles), at the very least cleaning bleach should be provided in discreet ways for use by prisoners. Such provision must be backed up by education about the great dangers of IV drug use today. It must be supported by the expansion of methadone and drug rehabilitation programs both within prison and afterwards (Strang, 1990; Victorian Ombudsman reported in *The Age* 20 July 1990). Again, I agree with the *Sydney Morning Herald* leader of 14 June 1990:

> Dr Alex Wodak, Director of the St Vincent's Hospital Drug & Alcohol Service said this week [that] prisoners [should be supplied with] condoms and provided with bleach for cleaning needles. It is advice to which [the Minister] should listen.

CONCLUSIONS

The World Health Organization has provided sensible guidelines. It is unfortunate that Australian politicians and prison administrators have not adhered to them. Not enough has been done to spread and repeat educational messages to the constantly changing prison population. Political gestures, such as mandatory testing, have been made with little practical utility in addressing the real problems of HIV infection in prison. Prisoners found to be infected are not isolated. The only advantage of this testing is that it will provide evidence upon which prisoners will be able to rely in actions against governments in negligence in other respects to HIV acquired in prison. I rather doubt that this was the policy which lay behind the strategies of mandatory testing of prisoners. As is usually the case, those strategies are based either on ignorance or prejudice or real indifference to the true problems of containing the AIDS epidemic.

In the potential incubator of prisons, those true problems derive from the established modes of transmission of the HIV virus. These are by IV drug use and advice, education, and counselling (including to the point that the highest protection exists in avoiding entirely risky activities) must be given. But for those who cannot, or will not, take such advice, practical steps must also be taken. These include the availability of condoms and of cleaning agents or bleach to prisoners.

NOTES

1. Personal views only. This address is an adapted and updated version of the South Australian Justice Administration Foundation Oration 1990 Annual Oration, "AIDS Strategies and Australian Prisons."

REFERENCES

Australian Parliament. Parliamentary Joint Committee on the National Crime Authority 1989, *Rethinking Drug Policy*, Canberra.

Gaughwin, M. D. et al. 1990. "Preventing Human Immunodeficiency Virus (HIV) Infection Amongst Prisoners: Prisoners and Prison Officers' Knowledge of HIV and Their Attitudes to Options for Prevention." *Community Health Studies* 14(1):61–4.

Kaplan, J. 1988. "Taking Drugs Seriously." *The Public Interest* 92:32.

Strang, H. 1990. "AIDS in Prisons." *National AIDS Bulletin* 4(6):42–4.

Wodak, A. 1990. "Heroin Legalisation: Totem and Taboo Revisited." *Modern Medicine of Australia* 33(5):76–85.

World Health Organization. 1987. Consultation on Prevention and Control of AIDS in Prisons (6–18 November), WHO, Geneva.

Tuberculosis in Correctional Facilities

THEODORE M. HAMMETT
LYNNE HARROLD
with the assistance of
JOEL EPSTEIN, J.D.

INTRODUCTION AND SUMMARY

Infectious diseases are of increasing concern to correctional health care professionals and correctional administrators. Inmate populations contain disproportionate numbers of persons of low socio-economic status, individuals with problems of substance abuse, and people with generally high-risk and unhealthy lifestyles and poor access to medical care. As in the community beyond the walls of prisons and jails, such groups are much more susceptible to a range of infectious diseases, including HIV/AIDS, tuberculosis (TB), hepatitis B and C, syphilis, gonorrhea, and other sexually transmitted diseases.

The problem of infectious diseases in correctional facilities is, of course, not only a correctional problem. While there is great and legitimate concern about the spread of such diseases within correctional facilities, it is of at least equal concern that the vast majority of inmates return to the community where they may contribute to sharply rising epidemic curves. According to a recent estimate by the U.S. Centers for Disease Control and Prevention (CDC), as many as 133,000 persons with TB infection may be released to the community each year from federal and state correctional facilities.

Tuberculosis presents particularly serious problems, as well as intervention opportunities, for correctional institutions. Prisons and jails, like other congregate facilities, are high-risk settings for the spread of tuberculosis infection. Living conditions are invariably crowded, and many buildings have antiquated systems with poor ventilation and air circulation. Inmates are already more susceptible to TB infection and TB disease because of factors associated with their high-risk lifestyles and inadequate access to health care services, as well as increased prevalence of HIV/AIDS among them. Finally, the appearance of multidrug resistant tuberculosis (MDR-TB) raises the threat of an often untreatable disease spreading in a closely confined population.

Source: Extracted from Hammett, Theodore and Lynne Harrold, with the assistance of Joel Epstein. "Tuberculosis in Correctional Facilities." *Issues and Practices in Criminal Justice Series*. U.S. Department of Justice, Office of Justice Programs, National Institute of Justice. Washington, DC: U.S. Government Printing Office, 1994.

On the other hand, it is more feasible to screen inmate populations, as well as to ensure that they complete a course of preventive therapy or treatment for TB disease, than it is to carry out such interventions with high-risk populations in the community. Data from health departments funded by CDC to provide nationwide TB skin testing and preventive therapy in correctional facilities show how effective such programs can be in retaining patients. Of almost 10,000 inmates eligible for screening in six correctional facilities, 99.9 percent received the skin test, 99.7 percent had their tests read, 91 percent of those with positive results were referred for follow-up medical evaluation, 85 percent of those referred actually received follow-up evaluation, and 94 percent of those recommended for preventive therapy and able to complete the course of therapy within their sentences actually completed it. Almost 30 percent more inmates than drug treatment center clients (66 percent) completed the preventive therapy.

In view of growing concern about tuberculosis in prisons and jails, as well as the spreading realization that more intensive TB control interventions in inmate populations make sense both for the health of this population and for the public health, the Centers for Disease Control and Prevention and the National Institute of Justice (NIJ) cosponsored a national survey of tuberculosis and tuberculosis control in correctional facilities. The survey was conducted by Abt Associates Inc. in conjunction with the seventh survey of FHV/AIDS in Correctional Facilities.

Survey respondents reported 1,177 inmates under treatment for TB disease (805 in state/federal prison systems and 372 in city/county jail systems). Eighty-five percent of cases were among men and 15 percent among women. Some have suggested that these numbers are suspiciously low, but the resulting point prevalence rate of 121 cases per 100,000 inmates is in the expected range, based on independently reported incidence rates from other prison studies. Correctional systems reported 45 current and 140 cumulative cases of drug-resistant TB; 76 of the cumulative drug-resistant cases (54 percent) were resistant to both isoniazid (INH) and rifampin (RIF), the two leading TB drugs. Inmate cases of drug-susceptible TB were reported from all regions and drug-resistant cases were reported from most regions, although distributions were uneven with a bicoastal emphasis.

Survey results reveal 53,000 TB-infected inmates in the responding correctional systems (48,000 in 33 state/federal prison systems and 5,000 in 16 city/county jail systems). The infection rate (based on total inmates) was 10 percent among men and 11 percent among women. However, many correctional systems participating in the survey were unable to supply this information. There were about 2,400 reported TB skin test conversions in the two years before the survey, although many systems were unable to provide these data. In particular, many jail systems do not screen for TB infection or conduct repeat screening because of the generally short inmate stays.

Based on responses from about 65 percent of the participating systems, 43 current cases of TB disease were reported among correctional staff. Two of the cases were drug-resistant. In addition, 605 staff were estimated to be TB-infected, including 79 skin test convertors over the past two years.

In general, the TB control policies of most correctional systems appear to follow most of the CPC's recommendations. Areas of high compliance with recommended policies include the following: coordination of TB control programs and tracking of TB cases; screening of inmates for TB infection, particularly among state/federal systems; providing chest X-rays for skin-test positive inmates and sputum smear/culture examination for inmates with TB symptoms; conducting drug susceptibility studies on all cultures positive for TB; duration of treatment for TB disease for HIV-negative inmates; provision of directly observed therapy for inmates with TB disease; identification, tracking, and screening of close contacts of potentially contagious TB cases in state/federal systems, particularly for close contacts in the same facility as the index case; offering preventive therapy to most recommended categories of inmates; duration of preventive therapy for HIV-negative inmates; and provision of training on TB to correctional and medical staff.

Areas in which compliance with CDC recommendations is less widespread include the following: screening of city/county inmates for TB infection (although such programs may be impractical in jails due to short stays and rapid turnover); screening of staff for TB infection; testing of HIV-infected inmates for anergy (i.e., they may be nonreactive on skin tests requiring an immune system response), which may produce false negative skin test results; isolation of all potentially contagious TB cases in negative pressure isolation rooms; duration of treatment for TB disease for HIV-infected inmates; identification, tracking, and screening of close contacts—particularly in jail systems—and contacts in facilities other than the current facility of the index case; offering preventive therapy to close contacts; duration of preventive therapy for HIV-infected persons; and providing TB education to inmates.

Classification for Control in Jails and Prisons

Tim Brennan

THE ROLES OF INSTITUTIONAL CLASSIFICATION

Classification is a key process in solving many of the problems of jails and prisons. This section describes various primary and subsidiary roles performed by control classification systems in jails and prisons.

Source: Excerpted from Brennan, Tim. "Classification for Control in Jails and Prisons," in *Prediction and Classification in Criminal Justice Decision Making*, edited by Don M. Gottfredson and Michael Tonry, pp. 323–334. Chicago: University of Chicago Press, 1987.

INMATE, STAFF, AND PUBLIC SAFETY

A high priority goal for jails and prisons is to provide a safe environment for all inmates and staff. This necessitates the valid identification and classification of violent offenders and their separation from likely victims. Both inmate and staff safety are linked to identification, classification, and supervision of dangerous inmates. Alexander (1982) indicates that this goal has first-order priority in most institutional classification approaches. Failure to separate predators from victims is likely to result in victimization and an unsafe, anxiety-provoking environment. Identification and separation of these types is coupled with higher supervision of the dangerous or high-risk offenders. Suicide screening procedures similarly attempt to identify prisoners having a high risk for suicide and highlight their need for appropriate surveillance and treatment.

Public safety also depends on valid classification of levels of dangerousness. Such classifications are coupled with security constraints and release recommendations to minimize escape, erroneous community placements, and serious recidivism. Classification decisions that release apparently high-risk inmates to the community often become a focus of public controversy (Bottoms, 1973). Discretionary release into the community of persons who then commit serious offenses can produce intense media attention, public scorn, and strong criticism of the classification procedures used in jails and prisons.

CLASSIFICATION FOR REHABILITATION AND REINTEGRATION

Reintegration of inmates often is pursued by placing them into educational or vocational programs in the communities near the institution. In this instance, classification must balance public safety with the goals of offender rehabilitation and reintegration. Correct classification aims to protect the prisoner's rights to avoid deterioration of social skills, to have access to rehabilitation programs, and to be placed in the least restrictive environment. This minimizes the isolation of inmates from the outside community while simultaneously achieving the often opposing goal of public protection. A good classification system will provide a rational basis for balancing such objectives. Mistakenly classifying offenders as high risk may restrict an inmate's participation in rehabilitative programs and thereby undermine the goals of rehabilitation and treatment.

EQUITY, FAIRNESS, AND CONSISTENCY

These classification goals are important to both inmates and corrections staff. Poor classification can undermine all three of these goals. The goal of consistency requires classification methods that attempt to minimize subjectivity and bias and use reliable data. Newer objective classification approaches aim to constrain or limit the extremes of subjective discretion, bias, and prejudice.

PROVISION OF APPROPRIATE SERVICE

Classification is a basic mechanism for identifying the various vocational, educational, physical, and mental health needs of inmates. This identification helps protect offenders from "deliberate indifference" to certain treatment needs (e.g., medical, drug and alcohol, and psychiatric problems) and protect their right to receive minimally adequate treatment (National Institute of Corrections, 1981). The courts have seen classification as a means of ensuring consistent and equitable allocation of housing and program resources. Valid classification is a primary buttress to the right to be reasonable, protected from violent assault or the fear of violence. Neither inmates nor staff want the anxiety of "surprises." Thus classification has a critical role in reducing anxiety by creating an orderly, predictable, and controlled environment.

EFFICIENCY AND RATIONALITY IN RESOURCE UTILIZATION

Correct classification is crucial for avoiding waste. Correct "matching" of inmates with agency resources is the foundation of efficient resource allocation. For example, erroneous overclassification of inmates into inappropriately, high security, or custody levels constitutes systematic waste of assets. Similarly, when needed services are withheld from an eligible inmate, the results may be violence, escape, failure to rehabilitate, or lawsuits. Thus both positive and negative errors can produce waste, extra costs, and reduced efficiency.

Valid classification becomes even more crucially important when there are severe resource shortages. A recent National Institute of Corrections (1984) report asserts, "the increasing demand for both security and program resources, coupled with the probability that the availability of both will decrease, calls for an especially efficient and effective classification decision that will make the most advantageous use of physical, financial and human resources" (p. 9).

MANAGEMENT PLANNING

Classification is a tool for coherent planning of budgets, staffing, programs, and physical space requirements (Fowler and Rans, 1982). Planning in jails and prisons is generally based on enumeration of inmate population characteristics, sizes, and trends. Glaser (1974) has described the use of classification for enumeration and accurate estimation of population structures and trends. By providing more accurate planning data than do global population estimations, classification systems can forecast differentiated levels of need for various resources and services and can provide more accurate and detailed estimations of resource requirements.

In virtually all instances where jails and prisons have introduced objective classification systems, the new systems showed that planning for new construction was based on erroneous assumptions. Enormous financial savings resulted because planners had consistently overestimated the need for expensive maximum security cells and underestimated the need for minimum security space (Levinson, 1982; Austin, 1983).

SOCIAL CONTROL AND DISCIPLINE

Classification serves several social control functions that are not immediately obvious (Hobbs, 1975). It is intricately involved in maintaining the stability and order of the institution through consistent and appropriate processing decisions. It governs distribution of various rewards and punishments. It is critical in minimizing discord, maintaining orderliness, and generating consistent inmate expectations and predictions that help allay the anxiety generated by the presence of many deviant individuals.

Social control concerns will usually prioritize community and institutional goals above the concerns of inmates. Control classifications identify and label threatening individuals and impose constraints or barriers on them. Such restraints not only separate but may stigmatize certain individuals.

Classification is strongly linked to the control and management of inmates' behavior since it governs access to rewards and may circumscribe privileges. For example, misbehavior is often "punished" by reclassifying the person to a less privileged level, while good behavior is rewarded by reclassification into custody levels having greater privileges.

The line classification officer plays a critical role in regulating inmate behavior (Prottas, 1979). Institutional expectations for good or bad behavior are conveyed and enforced via the classification process. If subjective discretion is allowed, the authority and power of the lineworker is enhanced. Officers may informally escalate the degree of harshness resulting from classification decisions in order to manage difficult or ambiguous situations. Such discretionary escalation is more easily imposed when procedures are traditional, subjective, and informal. Under these circumstances, classification is used, in effect, as a tool to achieve discipline and control.

INSTITUTIONAL ORDER

Institutions deal with "classes of clients" since bureaucratic responses must always be standardized. Prisons and jails cannot plan for, provide responses to, or cope easily with innumerable individualized distinctions and cannot deal with all possible contingencies (Prottas, 1979; Lipsky, 1980). Classification is a main mechanism for creating simplicity and order out of the diversity of most inmate populations. Such simplification is a preliminary step to the planning, selection, and design of standardized institutional responses.

Until individuals are classified, bureaucracies are unable to deal with them (Prottas,1979; Lipsky, 1980). All bureaucratic actions or decisions require that the new "inmate" be defined. In jails and prisons the initial classification transforms "citizens" into "inmates," who are then eligible for appropriate institutional housing, treatment intervention, and program placement.

Classification contributes to bureaucratic orderliness by making inmate movement, rehousing, and transfers predictable and consistent. Alexander (1982) has noted that unpredictability and disorganization tend to undermine personal relations and trust, which undermines most of the other goals of corrections. Classification aims to reduce disorder and uncertainty by eliminating arbitrariness, vagueness, unclear criteria, bias, subjectivity, and prejudice from most inmate processing and movement decisions.

COMMUNICATION

Both staff and inmates require accurate understanding of the various labels used to describe inmates. When these names are vague or inconsistent, communication can break down, expectations and predictions do not hold up, and institutions lapse into disorganization. Anxiety rises with inability to communicate justifications for classification decisions. Valid and rational classification decisions help to provide a sense of predictability, which in turn allays anxiety. Meaningless labels and unpredictable decisions come from unclear criteria, unclear decision rules, informal discretion, and high heterogeneity among "classes" of inmates that are presumed to be homogeneous.

MONITORING AND ACCOUNTABILITY

Classification has recently been recognized to be fundamental for monitoring goal achievement. Fowler and Rans (1982:23) suggest that classification systems and data they produce can indicate whether goals and policy objectives are being achieved.

Effective monitoring depends on whether appropriate data are designed, collected, and used. Information that indicates achievement of the various policy goals of a jail or prison can, in theory, be routinely and accurately collected. Top managers have responsibility for the design, support, and monitoring of such data collection. Yet such accountability procedures have often been undermined by both poor management skills and the prevalence of classification that is subjective, informal, and undocumented. If data are available that indicate the extent to which each major policy is achieved, accountability becomes possible. This function of classification can be threatening to both line and administrative staff and may therefore provoke resistance and sabotage at both levels (Prottas, 1979).

PROTECTION FROM LIABILITY

Many jail and prison personnel are starting to realize that good classification is a means of avoiding public embarrassment, maintaining good public relations, and avoiding costly litigation. Errors can devastate the public image of a facility. Valid classification is a main instrument in avoiding such errors. In addition, objective classification provides documentation and justification for decisions. Thus it provides more protection against litigation than informal approaches that are deficient in both documentation and justifications—the basic prerequisites for protection in legal disputes.

If a jail or prison, however, has introduced objective classification and then does not properly implement it or fails to follow established procedures, it becomes in fact more vulnerable to litigation. This is because it then becomes easier to demonstrate that agency personnel failed to follow official procedures. Thus it behooves institutional personnel to be adequately trained and to follow established procedures carefully.

In summary, there are a variety of roles of institutional classifications that can support the needs of inmates, staff, institutions, and the public. Objective classification systems offer advantages over more traditional systems in fulfilling most of these goals.

REFERENCES

Alexander, J. 1982. "Security Classification in New York State." In *Classification as a Management Tool: Theories and Models for Decision Makers*, ed. L. Fowler. College Park, MD: American Correctional Association.

Austin, J. 1983. "Assessing the New Generation of Prison Classification Models." *Crime and Delinquency* 29:561–76.

Bottoms, A. E. 1973. "Methodological Aspects of Classification in Criminology." In *Collected Studies in Criminological Research: Methodological Aspects of Classification in Criminology*, vol. 10. Strasbourg: Council of Europe.

Fowler, L., and L. Rans. 1982. "Classification Design Implementation: Technologies and Values." In *Classification as a Management Tool: Theories and Models for Decision Makers*, ed. L. Fowler. College Park, MD: American Correctional Association.

Glaser, D. 1974. "The Classification of Offenses and Offenders." In *Handbook of Criminology*, ed. D. Glaser. Chicago: Rand McNally.

Hobbs, N. 1975. *Issues in the Classification of Children.* Vol. 1. San Francisco: Jossey-Bass.

Levinson, R. B. 1982. "The Federal Prison System's Security Designation/Custody Classification Approach." In *Classification as a Management Tool: Theories and Models for Decision Makers*, ed. L. Fowler. College Park, MD: American Correctional Association.

Lipsky, M. 1980. *Street-Level Bureaucracy.* New York: Russell Sage.

National Institute of Corrections. 1981. *Prison Classification: A Model Systems Approach.* Washington, DC: National Institute of Corrections.

———. 1984. *Jail Classification.* Washington, DC: National Institute of Corrections

Prottas, J. 1979. *People-Processing.* Lexington, MA: Lexington.

Effective Treatment for Drug and Alcohol Problems: What Do We Know?

HELEN M. ANNIS

Claims for the effectiveness of treatment for drug and alcohol problems differ dramatically. A recent overview of alcoholism-treatment outcome studies documented widely differing claims, ranging from a better than 90% recovery rate reported by a free-standing hospital facility to a 7% abstinence rate reported by the Rand Corporation for U.S. federally funded facilities.[1] What accounts for such divergent findings on treatment effectiveness? Can the content of different programs vary so radically that some produce a 90% abstinence rate while others generate only a 7% abstinence rate?

Such variant claims of outcome effectiveness are likely to be a function of factors other than the treatment as such. For example, the 90% recovery rate referred to clients who had successfully completed a 28-day residential program and had maintained active involvement in a one- to two-year aftercare program; within this highly selected group of clients, more than 90% had "continuous sobriety" or were "currently sober" but had experienced relapses while still in aftercare. In contrast the 7% recovery rate reported for clients of government-funded facilities referred to successive male admissions who were continuously abstinent for 4.5 years following treatment. In addition to obvious differences in sample selection and attrition, definition of successful outcome and length of the follow-up interval—any one of which could explain the widely discrepant outcome rates observed—the treatment programs may well have differed in the characteristics of the

Source: Excerpted from Annis, Helen M. "Effective Treatment for Drug and Alcohol Problems: What Do We Know? *Forum on Corrections Research* 2(4):18–30, 1990.

client populations served. Extreme caution therefore is required in interpreting reported outcome rates.

Although most studies on the effectiveness of alcohol- and drug-treatment programs have been conducted outside the correctional system, the results of these studies are relevant to understanding the role of: (a) client characteristics; (b) program length, setting and intensity; (c) treatment methods; (d) client treatment matching; and (e) relapse prevention strategies with offender populations. Each of these areas is reviewed below.

CLIENT CHARACTERISTICS

There are numerous studies exploring the importance of client characteristics in treatment outcome. How do the outcomes of male and female alcoholics compare? Although it is frequently asserted that female alcoholics have poorer prognoses than male alcoholics, reviews of the empirical literature reveal that alcoholic men and women do not differ in treatment outcome rates.[2] However, positive response to alcohol and drug treatment has been associated with several client characteristics other than sex: being married, employed, of a high social class, financially secure, socially active and well adjusted to work and marriage, and having little history of arrest. Unfortunately, these positive prognostic characteristics are not typically found in offender populations.

In fact, poor treatment outcome has been associated with client characteristics that are prominent in offender groups: aggressiveness, high rates of attempted suicide, organic brain syndrome and sociopathic personality. Work by McLellan and his colleagues[3] with both alcohol- and drug-dependent clients indicates that the severity of psychiatric symptomatology is an important factor in predicting response to treatment; alcohol- and drug-dependent clients with low psychiatric severity at admission have achieved good outcomes across a variety of treatments, whereas those with high psychiatric severity have shown little improvement and uniformly poor outcomes. Offenders with a dual diagnosis (a psychiatric diagnosis and a diagnosis of alcohol or drug abuse and dependence) are likely to respond poorly to substance-abuse programming.

In summary, it is important to recognize that:

1. client characteristics have played a major role in predicting response to alcohol- and drug-treatment programming;
2. some offenders can be expected to have a number of poor prognostic characteristics; and
3. any comparison of outcome rates across treatment programs must take into account differences in the characteristics of the offender populations served.

PROGRAM LENGTH, SETTING, AND INTENSITY

In the past few years, there has been much interest in how the intensity and duration of treatments and treatment settings affect outcomes. Spiraling health-care costs have stimulated an assessment of the effectiveness of traditional methods of service delivery compared with lower-cost alternatives. Specifically, questions have been raised about the required length of residential treatment, the cost effectiveness of residential versus day treatment, and out-patient alternatives.[4]

Findings from well-controlled clinical trials have been remarkably consistent in reporting no advantage for lengthy or intensive treatment programming. For example, residential alcoholism treatment lasting one to two weeks has been found to produce results comparable to treatment lasting several months. Furthermore, random controlled trials at the Donwood Institute in Toronto, Ontario,[5] and the Butler Hospital in Providence, Rhode Island,[6] demonstrated equally positive outcome results for clients in day-treatment programs and those in more costly residential treatment. These studies suggest that factors other than treatment length and setting should receive greater attention in the design of future substance-abuse treatment programming.

Another question that has been raised is whether treatment on an out-patient basis may be as effective as residential treatment for alcohol and drug abusers. In a large-scale evaluation of clients discharged from federally funded alcoholism-treatment facilities in the United States, the Rand Corporation found no differences in outcome for clients treated in out-patient programs and those in residential programs. Similarly, the Drug Abuse Reporting Program (DARP), involving 44,000 clients from 52 federally supported drug abuse treatment centres throughout the United States, reported that for opioid addicts, other drug-abusing adults, and youth clients (19 and under), there was an out-patient treatment option (methadone maintenance or drug-free out-patient counseling) that was equally as effective as or more effective than residential treatment. The results from these large-scale evaluations must be interpreted with caution, however, because clients who self-select to enter residential or out-patient treatment may differ in important but unrecognized prognostic characteristics.

Fortunately, a number of random controlled trials reported in the literature permit a direct comparison of the general effectiveness of outpatient and residential services. In these trials, alcoholics or other substance abusers were randomly assigned to out-patient counseling or to residential treatment. A number of such studies have been conducted in probation and parole systems. For example, 74 delinquent, drug-abusing adolescents within the San Francisco Juvenile Probation Department were randomly assigned to in-patient treatment or to the usual out-patient probationary care.[7] In-patient treatment averaged 132 days and consisted of psychodynamically oriented psychotherapy, community meetings, family therapy, recreational therapy, psychodrama, and an onward school program. Follow-up at one year after admission showed no difference on a variety of outcome measures, including alcohol and drug use and social functioning between the adolescents receiving in-patient treatment and those receiving the usual out-patient probationary services. Similar results were reported in a study of adult parolees with a history of opiate abuse.[8] Parolees randomly assigned to parole services or an experimental halfway house program showed no differences in the rate of new criminal convictions or in the number of drug-free weeks in the community during the first year following release from incarceration.

The weight of evidence from these and other well-controlled trials is clear. Out-patient treatment for substance abuse can produce outcomes essentially equivalent to those of residential treatment at substantially lower cost.

TREATMENT METHODS

Are some treatment methods more effective than others? This question is currently the subject of some controversy in the field of substance abuse treatment. Bill Miller, a prominent scientist in the field, argues that certain treatment methods such as aversion therapy, behavioural self-control training, social skills training, stress management, marital and family therapy, and a community reinforcement approach have demonstrated specific effectiveness, particularly in the treatment of alcoholics. (Ironically, Miller notes that these methods are not currently employed in most treatment programs.)

In contrast, other investigators conclude that differences between treatment methods have demonstrated relatively little effect on long-term outcomes. Although statistically significant outcome differences are occasionally reported for different treatment methods, the magnitude of these differences is usually small. Whereas client characteristics at treatment intake typically account for about 30% of the outcome variance, treatment variables account uniquely for only 6% to 7% of the variance, with additional variance being shared with the predictive value of client characteristics. Clearly, much remains to be learned about improving treatment programming.

CLIENT-TREATMENT MATCHING

Despite the controversy about the impact of treatment variables on outcome, there is a growing consensus in the field that the search for a single, universally effective treatment approach is misguided. It is now widely acknowledged that there is broad heterogeneity among alcoholics, cocaine abusers, and other substance abusers, and that a client with one set of characteristics may respond favourably to one type of treatment or treatment setting, whereas a client with another set of characteristics may respond more favourably to another treatment approach. The attempt to match clients to treatments in order to improve outcome results is referred to as client-treatment matching or the matching hypothesis. Although the development of empirical evidence of matching effects is in its infancy, there is general agreement that the differential assignment of clients with drug and alcohol problems to different treatments has the potential to substantially improve outcome results.

Over the past few years, the promise shown by a variety of pharmacological agents in the treatment of cocaine abuse has generated much excitement. The agents studied have included desipramine, lithium, bromocriptine, and other psychotropic drugs. Recently, prominent researchers in the area have cautioned that the development of a single, definitive treatment for all cocaine abusers now appears no more likely than it has for opiate abusers or alcoholics. Progress is being made, however, in defining appropriate matches of pharmacological agents to types of cocaine abusers. Studies to date have used DSM-III Axis I symptomatology and have tended to be non-blind, non-placebo preliminary trials. Early data suggest that some pharmacological agents may be effective for specific diagnostic subpopulations of cocaine abusers. For example, methylphenidate, a substitute medication that shares cross-tolerance with cocaine, has been found effective only in the treatment of the 5% of cocaine abusers who have a clearly established attention-deficit disorder. Similarly, non-cyclothymic cocaine abusers have shown no benefit from lithium, whereas lithium has been associated with cessation of cocaine abuse and reduced cocaine craving in cyclothymic patients. Larger samples and double-blind controlled trials are needed to substantiate these findings.

In order to demonstrate a differential treatment response or matching effect, it is necessary to study clients who vary on a particular characteristic under two or more treatment conditions. A simple case is illustrated in the figure: client type "A" has a positive outcome under treatment "X" but a poor outcome under treatment "Y," whereas the reverse is true of client type "B." In this example, a matching effect would still be demonstrated if client type "B" showed a similar outcome under treatments "X" and "Y," and client type "A" continued to show a better outcome under treatment "X."

The search for patient-treatment matching effects requires the reliable assessment of patient variables on the one hand, and treatment variables on the other. More progress has been achieved in the conceptualization and assessment of salient characteristics of patients than in the measurement of treatment variables; nevertheless, advances are being made in the evaluation of certain aspects of treatment environments. The table lists some patient and treatment variables that have received attention in the alcohol- and drug-abuse treatment literature in relation to patient-treatment matching.

A recent review of substance abuse treatment literature by this author located 15 studies that provide evidence of successful client-treatment matching effects.[9] One of these studies, conducted on an offender population drawn from Monteith Correctional Centre in Northern Ontario, demonstrated the importance of a personality variable in the differential assignment of alcoholic inmates to a highly confrontational form of addiction treatment. One hundred fifty incarcerated male alcoholics with a high or low self-image were randomly assigned to 224 hours of intensive, confrontational group psychotherapy or to institutional care. Alcoholic inmates with a high self-image showed a better outcome in the group therapy than in institutional care, whereas the reverse was true of alcoholic inmates with a low self-image. For those with a low self-image, the group therapy program apparently had a detrimental effect.

A study conducted at the Addiction Research Foundation in Toronto demonstrated that an alcoholic client's risk profile can provide a powerful guide for differential treatment assignment. Seventy alcoholics participating in an employee assistance program were randomly assigned to relapse-prevention therapy or to more traditional counseling on an outpatient basis. Each client was classified as having either a "generalized profile" (i.e., similar drinking risk across all categories of risk situations) or a "differentiated profile" (i.e., greater drinking risk in some types of situations than others). At six months, follow-up results showed no difference across the two treatment conditions in typical quantity of alcohol consumed daily by clients with generalized profiles; however, clients with differentiated profiles showed substantially better outcomes under relapse-prevention treatment than under traditional counseling. The results were significant, both statistically and clinically: the client-treatment matching effect accounted for over 30% of the outcome variance.

RELAPSE-PREVENTION STRATEGIES WITH OFFENDER POPULATIONS

The prevention of relapse is increasingly being recognized as a central problem in the treatment of alcoholism and other substance abuse. One influential theoretical framework that has been applied to the problem of relapse is Albert Bandura's cognitive-social learning approach. In Bandura's theory of self-efficacy, the critical distinction between initiation and maintenance strategies heralded a significant conceptual development for the addiction treatment field. The maintenance of behavioural change had been largely neglected in alcoholism and other substance-abuse programming. However, attention has recently focused on the development of relapse-prevention treatment strategies explicitly designed to foster the maintenance of behavioural change.

The Addiction Research Foundation in Toronto has been evaluating a cognitive-social learning approach to relapse prevention. The relapse-prevention model essentially involves a highly individualized analysis of the client's drinking or drug-use behaviour over the previous year to determine the high-risk situations experienced by that client. A 100-item self-reported questionnaire called the Inventory of Drinking Situations (IDS)[10] has been developed to assess drinking within the eight categories of relapse situations identified in the work of Allan Marlatt:[11] unpleasant emotions, physical discomfort, pleasant emotions, testing personal control, urges and temptations, conflict with others, social pressures to drink, and pleasant times with others. The IDS subscales have received positive reports on reliability, content, and external validity, and a client classification system based on the profile of IDS subscores has been shown to be associated with age, sex, and consumption-related variables. A parallel questionnaire for drugs other than alcohol, the Inventory of Drug Taking Situations (IDTS), is currently undergoing psychometric evaluation.

In the cognitive-social learning approach to relapse prevention, the first step in the development of an individually tailored treatment plan is the assessment of a client's high-risk situations. Treatment focuses on encouraging the client to engage in homework assignments designed to develop alternative coping responses in high-risk situations for relapse. Mastery experiences in successfully implementing alternative behaviours to drinking or drug use in these situations have a powerful impact on the client's cognitive appraisal of 9 personal coping abilities, resulting in an improved perception of self-efficacy and a change in future drinking or drug-use behaviour.

Based on clinical trials conducted at the Addiction Research Foundation in Toronto,[12] a two-phase approach to relapse prevention is recommended: phase I to concentrate on strategies known to be powerful in the initiation of a change in drinking or drug-use behaviour, and phase II to focus on strategies with greater potential for the long-term maintenance of this change. Phase I uses powerful induction aids, such as avoidance of drinking or drug use situations, coercion, hospitalization, protective conditions like sensitizing drugs (e.g., Antabuse), involvement of a spouse or responsible collateral, and a directive role by the therapist.

In phase II, the maintenance phase, all external aids are gradually withdrawn as the focus shifts to promoting client self-inferences that are consistent with those known to facilitate generalization and maintenance of behavioural change. The major challenge is to create assignments (i.e., real-life cue exposure conditions) in which clients succeed in controlling their drinking or drug use in formerly problematic situations. A hierarchy of risk situations is established: The use of external aids established in phase I is reduced as the therapist gradually transfers the responsibility for risk anticipation and the planning of coping strategies to the client. Multiple assignments are given across a variety of the drinking or drug-use risk situ-

Patient-Treatment Matching

Patient Variables	Treatment Variables
1. General	
Sociodemographic (e.g., age, sex, marital status, social stability, family history of alcoholism/drug abuse)	Setting (e.g., in-patient, out-patient, day treatment)
Environmental Resources (e.g., finances, social supports)	Intensity/duration (e.g., brief advice, long-term therapy)
Neuropsychological Status (e.g., type and degree of neuropsychological deficit)	Method (e.g., disulfiram, relaxation therapy)
Personality (e.g., self-esteem, locus of control, MMPI profile, psychiatric diagnosis, psychiatric severity)	Therapist (e.g., directive, non-directive professional, peer)
	Goal (e.g., abstinence, moderation)
	Context (e.g., group, individual treatment system)
2. Alcohol/Drug Specific	
Consumption (e.g., years of excessive drinking/ drug taking, quantity, frequency)	
Dependence (e.g., degree of alcohol/drug dependence symptomatology, presence of physical withdrawal)	
Expectancies/Outcome Beliefs (e.g., self-efficacy, belief in disease concept)	
Situational Antecedents (e.g., types of high-risk situations)	

Adapted from Annis, H. M. "Patient-Treatment Matching in the Management of Alcoholism," in C. P. O'Brien (ed.), *Treatment of Chemical Dependence*. NIDA Research Monograph 90 (Washington, DC: National Institute on Drug Abuse, 1988).

ations in the client's hierarchy, and all major risk situations are involved in homework assignments before treatment is terminated in order to promote client self-attribution of control. The goal of treatment is to enhance client self-efficacy in all identified areas of drinking and drug-taking situations.

These relapse-prevention counseling methods are currently being used with some offender groups in the Ontario correctional system. Institutional settings provide a particular challenge for the application of these procedures. Ideally, institution-based programs combine the use of therapy sessions—which are designed to help inmates identify their high-risk situations for the use of alcohol and other drugs and to rehearse alternative coping responses—with the use of temporary absence passes to allow planned entry into high-risk situations in the community. Probation and parole services can provide a good counseling setting for the implementation of relapse-prevention procedures if the reporting of a slip in alcohol or drug use does not automatically result in a disciplinary sanction.

The United States Federal Bureau of Prisons recently implemented a large-scale clinical research trial of relapse-prevention procedures to evaluate a new residential therapeutic community program for men and women who are within 18 months of release from prison. In this controlled, multisite prison trial, involving over 6,000 inmates with drug-abuse problems, inmates assigned to the new program will be assessed on the IDS and the IDTS to establish their alcohol or drug-use risk profiles. These profiles will be used as a clinical tool for developing an individualized relapse-prevention treatment plan. The program's effectiveness will be evaluated on the basis of self-efficacy, drug use, criminal behaviour, occupational and social functioning, and mental and physical health over a five-year follow-up period.

CONCLUSION

Our increased understanding of effective treatment for drug and alcohol problems is reflected in the evolution of question-guided clinical investigation in the field. More simplistic questions about the effects of patient characteristics on outcome and the comparative effectiveness of treatments varying in duration, intensity, setting, and method are leading to a greater focus on more complex questions about client-treatment interaction effects and the development of client-specific relapse-prevention strategies. Fundamental to this evolution has been an acknowledgment of the tremendous heterogeneity among alcoholics and other substance abusers, and of the great diversity of possible treatment approaches.

Evidence to date suggests that under certain conditions, matching can yield a major improvement in client outcome. Studies with a strong theoretical orientation in the choice of client-treatment variables have tended to produce the most dramatic effects of matching, accounting for 16% to 30% of the treatment outcome variance. These results are extremely encouraging. Clearly, much remains to be learned about the most salient characteristics of clients with alcohol and drug problems and how they can be matched to theoretically relevant treatment structures. Nevertheless, current evidence strongly suggests that treatment outcome results for substance abusers will improve substantially with our growing knowledge of the optimal matching of clients to treatment alternatives and of the application of relapse-prevention strategies that are designed to promote improved maintenance of treatment gains in the community.

NOTES

1. Emrick, C. D., and J. Hansen, "Assertions Regarding Effectiveness of Treatment for Alcoholism," *American Psychologist* (1983):1078–1088.

2. Annis, H. M., and C. B. Liban, "Alcoholism in Women: Treatment Modalities and Outcomes," in O. J. Kalant (ed.) *Alcohol and Drug Problems in Women. Research Advances in Alcohol and Drug Problems*, vol. 5. (New York: Plenum Press, 1980).

3. McLellan, A. T., L. Luborsky, G. E. Woody, C. P. O'Brien, and K. A. Druley, "Predicting Response to Alcohol and Drug Abuse Treatments: Role of Psychiatric Severity," *Archives of General Psychiatry* 40 (1983):620–625.

4. For reviews of this literature, see: Annis, H. M., "Is Inpatient Rehabilitation of the Alcoholic Cost-Effective? Con Position," *Advances in Alcohol and Substance Abuse* 5 (1986):175–179; Miller, W. R., and R. K. Hester, "Inpatient Alcoholism Treatment: Who Benefits?" *American Psychologist* 41 (1986):794–805; and Wilkinson, D. A., and G. W. Martin, "Intervention Methods for Youth with Problems of Substance Abuse," in H. M. Annis and C. S. Davis (eds.), *Drug Use by Adolescents* (Toronto: Addiction Research Foundation, in press).

5. McLachlan, J. F. C., and R. L. Stein, "Evaluation of a Day Clinic for Alcoholics," *Journal of Studies on Alcohol* 43 (1982):261–272.

6. McCrady, B., R. Longabaugh, E. Fink, R. Stout, M. Beattie, and A. Ruggieri-Authelet, "Cost Effectiveness of Alcoholism Treatment in Partial Hospital Versus Inpatient Settings after Brief Inpatient Treatment: 12-Month Outcomes," *Journal of Consulting and Clinical Psychology* 54 (1986):708–713.

7. Amini, F., N. J. Zilberg, E. L. Burke, and S. Salasnek, "A Controlled Study of Inpatient vs. Outpatient Treatment of Delinquent Drug Abusing Adolescents: One Year Results," *Comprehensive Psychiatry* 23(5) (1982):436–444.

8. Miller, D. E., A. N. Himelson, and G. Geis, "Community's Response to Substance Misuse: The East Los Angeles Halfway House for Felon Addicts," *The International Journal of the Addictions* 2(2) (1967):305–311.

9. Annis, H. M., "Patient-Treatment Matching in the Management of Alcoholism," in L.S. Harris (ed.), *Problems in Drug Dependence*, Research Monograph 90 (Rockville, MD: NIDA, 1988).

10. Annis, H. M., *Inventory of Drinking Situations* (Toronto: Addiction Research Foundation, 1982).

11. Marlatt, G. A., and J. R. Gordon, *Relapse Prevention: Maintenance Strategies in the Treatment of Addictive Behaviors* (New York: Guilford Press, 1985).

12. Annis, H. M., and C. Daipis, "Relapse Prevention," in R. K. Hester and W. R. Miller (eds.), *Handbook of Alcoholism Treatment Approaches* (New York: Pergamon Press, 1989).

A Full Employment Policy for Prisons in the United States: Some Arguments, Estimates, and Implications

TIMOTHY J. FLANAGAN
KATHLEEN MAGUIRE

WHY SHOULD PRISONERS WORK?

Regarding the utilitarian aspects of prisoner employment, the case is best stated in the negative. That is, it is wholly inefficient, inhumane, unproductive, and perhaps counterproductive to allow a large number of employable individuals to languish in inactivity: "[T]he failure to provide productive activity for prisoners which could reduce correctional operating costs not only confers no benefit on the prisoners, it imposes a substantial burden on the public" (Hawkins, 1983:121). Corrections expenditures have been the fastest growing segment of state budgets during the 1980s, and by 1990 many states faced massive deficits; failure to utilize a potential revenue source cannot be justified in these circumstances. Increased employment of inmates in prison industrial programs could yield both "in-house" and extra-departmental benefits. Putting more inmates to work in carefully planned and effectively managed activities holds much promise for improving the fiscal situation for correctional departments over time. It would allow revenues to be funneled to important correctional programs that may have suffered as a result of lean state budgets. Also, a portion of the monies could be returned to industrial programs, thereby enhancing the profit base and contributing to the recovery of the initial costs of expanding prison shops.

Improvement and expansion of inmate employment also could affect the aggregate economic welfare of states by reducing the strain that correctional expenditures traditionally have placed on state budgets.[1] Additional economic benefits include the potential for inmate employees to pay taxes, provide financial support to dependents, and contribute to victim compensation funds.

In addition to these economic advantages, increased employment of inmates in industrial programs might enhance the stability and improve the atmosphere of the institutional environment. Efficiently run programs could reduce idleness and provide routine and structure for daily activities. Zamble and Porporino (1988) contended that prison environments place individ-

Source: Excerpted from Flanagan, Timothy J. and Kathleen Maguire. "A Full Employment Policy for Prisons in the United States: Some Arguments, Estimates, and Implications." *Journal of Criminal Justice* 21(2):117–130, 1993.

uals in a "behavioral deep freeze" that may reduce already deficient inmate coping skills. Consistent involvement in meaningful activities may improve inmate adjustment and coping ability. There is growing empirical support for the proposition that involvement in prison work programs is related to reduced inmate misconduct (Petersilia and Honig, 1980; Flanagan, et al., 1988; U.S. Department of Justice, 1991; Maguire, 1992).[2]

Prisoner habilitation comprises the second major justification for the expansion of inmate work programs. Note the use of the term habilitation rather than the more commonly used term, rehabilitation. Rehabilitation implies restoration to a previous state. Habilitation, in contrast, involves a process of learning or equipping with skills. Most inmates enter prison with little education and few or no skills.[3] Many have sketchy or nonexistent work records and minimal discipline. Prison programs that expose inmates to the "world of work" hold promise for instilling self-discipline and responsibility as well as teaching time and resource management. Prison work programs also can communicate to offenders the important message that there are rewards to be gained through legitimate employment. Prison time ought to be utilized to yield a more tractable, trainable, and employable individual—one who has obtained at least a modicum of skills and work habits to use upon release.

The final justification for employing prisoners is grounded in humanitarian principles. As long as American society is committed to the widespread use of long-term incarceration, basic notions of human dignity require that useful and productive activities be provided to inmates. Involvement in meaningful activities can reduce tensions, aid the individual in coping with the harshness of the institutional environment, and give prisoners a sense of self-worth. At least a portion of individual self-concept is linked to how an individual's time is spent. Prison work programs can allow inmates to retain a sense of self-respect also by enabling them to provide for themselves and perhaps offer financial assistance to dependents. Moreover, prison industries can provide transferable employment experience to prepare offenders to join the conventional work force upon release.

There is strong public support in the United States for the principle that prisoners should work. In a 1982 Gallup poll, 94 percent of those surveyed felt that it was a "good idea" to "require prisoners to have a skill or learn a trade, to fit them for a job before they are released from prison." Eighty-three percent felt that "keeping prisoners busy constructing buildings, making products and performing services that the state would have to hire other people to do" was a good idea. Eighty-one percent favored paying prisoners for their work but requiring inmates to pay two-thirds of their wages to their victims or to the state for the cost of maintaining the prison (Gallup, 1982, cited in Flanagan, 1989). Cullen and Travis, after collecting additional public opinion data, concluded that "many Americans are convinced of the beneficial if not curative nature of putting inmates to work" (1984:53).

Although Americans support the *proposition* that prisoners should work, application of the principle has led to a historical record ranging from short-lived successes to unmitigated failures. This dismal history is partially due to (1) an abiding and pervasive belief in the "principle of least eligibility," which is often masked when opinion polls are taken during times of economic prosperity or when the wording of questions oversimplifies the issue,[4] and (2) the inherent constraints on running a business within the confines of a correctional facility.

LIMITATIONS OF EMPLOYING PRISONERS

Several practical limitations relating to the prison environment itself have hobbled the development of prison work programs; chief among these is that prisons were not designed to be factories. Correctional facilities often lack the physical plant to expand industrial programs significantly. Moreover, during times of prison overcrowding, basic housing concerns are likely to take precedence over the allocation of additional space to employment programs. However, a 1992 survey on prison construction showed that 27 states and the Federal Bureau of Prisons were planning for new facility construction to take place during the next three years. This represents opportunities to design prisons in a way that gives high priority to prisoner employment (Perk-Davis, 1992).

In addition to architectural and spatial problems, the prison work day is problematic. It is punctuated by numerous intrusions that serve the superordinate goal of security; these include regular counts, call-outs for visitation or medical, legal, or counseling sessions, and lockdowns. Inmate turnover as well as difficulty in attracting and retaining civilian supervisors also are common problems (Flanagan, 1989:153). Finally, facility administrators and correctional officers have always been, and will continue to be, judged against a primary standard of facility security, and proposals to expand prison labor programs will be circumscribed by the supremacy of security interests.

A number of economic and political concerns also have limited the scope of prison labor programs. A survey of correctional industry directors reported that the lack of resources to develop new programs was among the top three problems facing industry managers (Greiser, Miller, and Funke, 1984). Many correctional facilities are old, as is their industrial equipment; the cost of updating equipment and implementing new programs is often prohibitively high for strained corrections budgets. Capital for investment may be available from the private sector, but state-use laws and other restrictive legislation enacted by many states and the federal jurisdiction limit the market for prison goods, thereby limiting the appeal of the corrections arena for private investors. Finally, faced with the expansion of prison work programs, unionized and local labor opposition is likely to surface once again, as it did in the early part of the twentieth century, when organized opposition virtually emasculated inmate labor:

> The fears of private business and organized labor about unfair competition from prison labor and the principle of least eligibility that continues to dominate public attitudes toward correctional reform are tremendous political and social obstacles to legal change (Flanagan, 1989:154).

However, it is important to distinguish between the overall labor market, in which total labor may be in excess, and lower-spectrum jobs, for which there is often a lack of available workers.[5] It is more plausible that prison industry programs and releasees trained in these programs would compete for employment at the lower end of the spectrum. Thus, the salience of the displacement issue will vary with economic conditions.

FULL EMPLOYMENT

Full employment does not mean that every citizen holds a job. Some citizens are not members of the labor force due to age, infirmity, choice (e.g., for child-rearing), or other reasons. Moreover, full employment of labor force participants is not attainable. Labor economists distinguish several types of unemployment. The most familiar one is called *deficient-demand unemployment*, which arises from an "inadequate total demand for labor" (Reynolds, Masters, and Moser, 1987:423). In the prison context, several developments over the course of the twentieth century have reduced demand for prisoner employment, so it is clear that much of the vast unemployment in contemporary American prisons is deficient-demand unemployment. *Structural unemployment* occurs when there is a mismatch between the skills possessed by labor force participants and the needs of employers (Bellante and Jackson, 1979). If the changing nature of work requires a better educated and more highly skilled work force, for example, and if the characteristics of available workers do not meet these needs, then some portion of the unemployment rate is attributable to these structural deficiencies. The educational and skill deficiencies that mark prisoner populations may be a real obstacle to full employment in prisons. Finally, residual or *frictional unemployment* arises "from normal turnover in the labor market and the fact that finding new jobs takes time" (Reynolds, Masters, and Moser, 1987:423). Consequences of prison administrative procedure such as frequent interinstitutional transfers and extended reception status in some facilities may promote higher levels of frictional unemployment in prisons than in the larger society.

Full Employment in Prisons

State and federal prisons in the U.S. contain a disproportionate number of young, minority males with limited education and negligible skills and work experience. As a result, the proportion of inmates available for labor force participation will be greatly affected by how participation in educational programs in prisons is regarded. If inmates with primary program assignments in vocational training, adult basic education, or high school equivalent educational programs are regarded as *outside* of the prison labor force, then labor force participation rates in prisons will be much lower than in the free community. Ironically, correctional systems that offer a rich variety of such educational programs and encourage inmates to participate in the programs will have lower labor force participation than program-starved systems in which work, regardless of its training content, is promoted. Alternatively, if education in prison is viewed as a program that operates in conjunction with a work requirement, or as a program in which inmates must actually *earn* the privilege to participate through work, then labor force participation will be much higher.

Another important definitional issue is whether institutional maintenance work should "count" as labor in prisons. Critics of this practice point to abundant evidence of featherbedding in institutional maintenance assignments (the proverbial "six men on a broom") and argue that these experiences do not amount to "labor" in any meaningful sense. On the other hand, these assignments are critical to the orderly operation of the prison, *can* be transformed into jobs that mirror trades in the free economy that employ Americans, and can employ significant numbers of prisoners. Moreover, in the free economy factories employ both production workers and maintenance workers, and they pay employees differential wages based on the skill requirements and labor supply for the various job categories.

If it is assumed that educational programs are not a substitute for work in prisons but an adjunct to prison labor and that institutional maintenance jobs can be transformed into legitimate jobs, up to 90 percent of the inmates of adult prisons should be regarded as prison labor force participants. This figure is henceforth referred to as a component of the *Optimal model* of prison employment. An alternative model in which educational programming is regarded as an alternative to institutional work and institutional maintenance jobs are considered "make work" would limit effective labor force participation in adult prisons to about 30 percent of the prisoner population. This is called the *Minimal model* of prison employment.

After estimates of labor force participation are established, it is necessary to estimate prison employment and unemployment rates. As mentioned above, a 100 percent employment rate is impossible to achieve. Moreover, aspects of prison population management such as interinstitutional transfers may increase frictional unemployment, and characteristics of prisoners such as illiteracy and aggressive behavior may contribute to structural unemployment. Notwithstanding these potential problems, the *Optimal model* of prisoner full employment assumes that unemployment within the prison labor force need not exceed 10 percent. The *Minimal model* assumes that characteristics of the prison as a workplace and deficiencies of the inmate labor force would create unemployment rates of up to 50 percent, even within the circumscribed labor force of the *Minimal model*. Multiplying the labor force participation rates by the target employment rates under the two models yields what will be called "Effective Prisoner Employment Rates" (EPERs) of 80 percent in the *Optimal model* and 15 percent in the *Minimal model*. Note that while the EPER of 15 percent is labeled "minimal," it represents a 50 to 90 percent *increase* in the rate of prisoner employment over current levels in most prisons. The optimistic estimates imply a tenfold increase in employment rates of prisoners.

ECONOMIC IMPLICATIONS

Economist Robert Greiser estimated that 50,000 inmates were employed in correctional industries in the late 1980s, and U.S. correctional industries generated $800 million in sales. Greiser estimated that the average value of production per inmate was "well below $20,000 *which is less than one-fourth that of the production per worker in the private sector*" (1989:22). The *Optimal model* would yield 658,400 employed prisoners (at an EPER of 80 percent, given a state and federal prison population of 823,000). If production value per inmate remained constant (at its very low level), correctional industries' production under the *Optimal model* would increase to more than $13.2 billion. If production value per worker in correctional industries doubled (to an amount that still would be less than half that of free world workers), the total Gross Prison Product (GPP) would exceed $26 billion, and free world-like production value would approach $53 billion, which is equivalent to the Gross National Products (GNP) of Greece, Peru, and Thailand in 1987.

Under the *Minimal full employment model*, which assumes a 15 percent EPER, 123,450 inmates would be employed in state and federal prisons, which is more than double the current number. At current correctional industry production values, these inmate workers would produce $2.469 billion per year; if the average value of production reached levels comparable to those for free world workers, correctional industry output would exceed $9.8 billion per year (more than the GNP of Sudan in 1987). To place these estimates in larger context, the Gross Prison Product produced under even the most optimistic model would be less than one percent of America's Gross Domestic Product (GDP).[6]

Another way to assess the economic implications of prison full employment is to examine prison production in relation to the cost of correctional services. Total expenditures for correctional services at the federal, state, and local levels in the U.S. in 1988 were $19.1 billion (Maguire and Flanagan, 1991). In other words, if the average value of production per worker in correctional industries doubled (it would still be less than half of that in the private sector), the aggregate value of correctional production output under the *Optimal full employment model* would exceed the cost of correctional services. Of course "output" here is actually the *value added* by prisoner labor, or the total output minus the cost of inputs such as raw materials and capital costs. If the average value of production per worker in prisons rose to free world values, the value of prison production in 1989 under the *Optimal model* would have exceeded $52 billion, or more than twice the level of total correctional expenditures. Even the least optimistic full employment model would yield a GPP that would be more than 10 percent of the cost of governmental correctional expenditures.

Another way to measure the impact of prison full employment is to calculate the share of the total American work force that would be attributable to prisoners.[7] Under even the most optimistic model, the 658,400 inmate workers would represent *only one-half of one percent* of all employed Americans. Since prison populations are overwhelmingly male, the sex-specific comparison indicates that under the most optimistic prison full employment model, the number of male inmates in the prison labor force would be equivalent to about one percent of all males in the civilian work force aged 25 to 64 and less than 1 percent of employed male Americans.

CIVILIAN JOB DISPLACEMENT

One of the greatest fears about expansion of prison employment programs and perhaps the most important reason for resistance to such expansion is the argument that inmate workers will displace workers in the free society. Moreover, since these free world workers have committed no crimes and support the state through tax payments that fund prisoners' food, shelter, medical care, and programs, the argument is made that prison labor programs are a form of "double taxation" on displaced workers. These claims are based on the belief that since prisons pay inmate workers minuscule wages, these correctional industries enjoy a distinct and unfair competitive advantage. Coupled with state-use statutes that *require* governmental agencies to procure products and services from prison vendors whenever possible, even the low level of industrial output of contemporary prison labor is seen as a threat. "Full employment" of prisoners would, of course, be anathema to persons who make these claims.

However, it is not clear that prison industries and prison-based services displace workers in the free society. Federal Prison Industries, Inc. (FPI), the most successful of all correctional industries programs in the United States, was created in 1934 by legislation that required *simultaneously* that FPI "employ the greatest number of those inmates . . . who are eligible to work as is reasonably possible" and that "competition with private industry and free labor" be reduced "to a minimum" (FPI, 1990, citing 18 U.S.C., 4121–29). How to achieve these dual objectives is not always clear. The restriction of sale of prison-made products to governmental customers was seen as an important limit on the capacity of correctional industries to compete with private firms. When these laws were passed in the post-Depression era, however, few could have anticipated the massive expansion of government employment at all levels that has occurred in the United States since about 1965. What was once seen as a small customer has become the most voracious consumer—of tens of thousands of products ranging from paper clips to motor vehicles. The ability of manufacturing firms to "break into" the government market can mean the difference between financial growth and Chapter Seven bankruptcy proceedings. It is worth noting, however, that as a percentage of the market, prison-made goods comprise only a minute portion of goods and services procured by government each year. Some estimates have indicated that correctional industries tap less than 3 percent of the state-use market with their products (Greiser, 1989; Greiser, Miller, and Funke, 1984).

Critics of prison labor programs often fail to take into account that the private sector is an important supplier of the raw materials and equipment used in prison shops, so prison-based industries may create jobs for these suppliers. Perhaps adding the criterion of "high input usage" to the requirements of labor intensiveness and low competitive impact would enhance prison industry's economic appeal further. In addition, prison-based industries are not fully inmate-operated; these enterprises employ civilian supervisors, transport workers, financial staff, and others. For example, Federal Prison Industries employs 2,000 civilian foremen (Greiser, 1989). Others have pointed out that the fear of worker displacement as a result of prison industries recalls a time when the economic structure of American life was much simpler and more fragile than it has been in the latter half of the twentieth century (Cullen and Travis, 1984; Goodman, 1982). Finally, others have pointed out that the "cheap labor" advantage in prison-based industries is being undermined by a model that calls for real-world wages, with deductions against prisoner wages for room and board, victim restitution, family support, and postrelease savings.

NEW MODELS AND THE FUTURE OF PRISON EMPLOYMENT

In summary, approaching the issue of prison employment with an open mind and an appreciation of the beneficial effects of honest work for offenders allows us to think about a variety of methods for increasing and improving such work opportunities. The greatest economic impact of expanded prison work programs will be on the correctional system itself. Production of goods and services behind prison walls holds the promise of checking the spiraling cost of corrections, providing discipline and work experience to offenders who lack these attributes, making funds available for offenders' families and for restitution to crime victims, and providing offenders with an *earned* fund to support the transition from institutional to community life. Ripple effects on suppliers, support personnel, and civilian employment also may be beneficial. Most importantly, productive prisons may yield more than economic benefits—they may contribute to greater independence among ex-offenders rather than dependence on government assistance programs or illicit activities. In short, we can make our prisons the centers of productivity that we envision they should be by carefully pursuing a policy of full employment for American prisons.

ACKNOWLEDGMENTS

A previous version of this article was presented at the annual meeting of the Academy of Criminal Justice Sciences, March 1991. The authors wish to thank Robert C. Greiser, Ph.D., Federal Bureau of Prisons, and William J. McGuire, Ph.D., Federal Home Loan Bank of Cincinnati for their helpful comments.

NOTES

1. For example, the New York State Department of Correctional Services, Division of Industries has operated at no net expense to the state since 1986. The industry program not only has covered all costs associated with manufacturing and sales but also has covered the costs of vocational and security staff associated with the industry program.

2. While studying prison inmates in California, Petersilia and Honig (1980) observed the highest rates of misbehavior among those not involved in prison work programs. Flanagan et al. (1988) found that industry participants had significantly lower infraction rates than nonparticipants and that this relationship maintained when the sample was divided into adjustment risk groups. The Federal Bureau of Prisons (U.S. Department of Justice, 1991) found that industrial and vocational program participants accrued fewer and less serious misconduct reports than a matched comparison group. Maguire (1992) found that when samples of industry participants and nonparticipants were divided into two groups of high rate infractors, industry participation was significantly related to lower rates of rules violation even when preprogram misconduct rates were controlled.

3. A 1986 national survey of state prison inmates revealed that 62 percent of prison admissions held less than a high school diploma, and 31 percent were unemployed prior to arrest (Maguire and Flanagan, 1991).

4. Several decades ago Bames and Teeters clarified this issue when they wrote that "the public believes, in theory at least, that prisoners should work–and work hard. It is actually ambivalent about the matter; when jobs are plentiful, prisoners should work but during periods of recession, criminals should not take jobs from law abiding citizens" (1959:522).

5. The U.S. Bureau of Labor Statistics has reported that as of November 1989, the fastest declining occupations were in lower-spectrum industries such as electronic equipment assemblers, telephone and cable line installers and repairers,

machine operators, garment workers, and hand packagers. Among the many reasons for this decline are the lack of workers trained in these skills and the availability of cheaper labor outside U.S. borders. Prisoners could be trained in such occupations while incarcerated in order to help boost these sagging industries and bring back to the U.S. jobs lost to foreign countries.

6. The Gross Domestic Product for the United States in 1991 was $5,739.7 billion.

7. U.S. Department of Commerce population figures for 1989 were used for all calculations.

REFERENCES

Bames, H. E., and N. K. Teeters. 1959. *New Horizons in Criminology* (3rd ed.). Englewood Cliffs, NJ: Prentice-Hall.

Bellante, D., and M. Jackson. 1979. *Labor Economics: Choice in Labor Markets*. New York: McGraw Hill.

Cullen, F., and L. F. Travis. 1984. "Work as an Avenue of Prison Reform." *NFJ Crim and Civ Con* 10(1):45–64.

Federal Prison Industries, Inc. 1990. *Request for Proposals for Independent Market Study*. Washington, DC: Federal Bureau of Prisons. Mimeographed. (26 December).

Flanagan, T. J. 1989. "Prison Labor and Industry." In *The American Prison: Issues in Research and Policy*, eds. L. Goodstein and D. L. MacKenzie. New York: Plenum Press.

Flanagan, T. J., T. P. Thornberry, K. E. Maguire, and E. F. McGarreil. 1988. *The Effect of Prison Industry Employment on Offender Behavior: Report of the Prison Industry Research Project*. Albany: Hindelang Criminal Justice Research Center, State University of New York.

Goodman, S. 1982. "Prisoners as Entrepreneurs: Developing a Model for Prisoner Run Industry." *Boston Univ Law R* 62:1163–95.

Greiser, R. C. 1989. "Do Correctional Industries Adversely Impact the Private Sector?" *Federal Probation* 53:1824.

Greiser, R. C., N. Miller, and G. S. Funke. 1984. *Guidelines for Prison Industries*. Washington, DC: U.S. Department of Justice, National Institute of Corrections.

Hawkins, G. 1983. "Prison Labor and Prison Industries." In *Crime and Justice: An Annual Review of Research*, vol. 5, eds. M. Tonry and N. Morris. Chicago: University of Chicago Press.

Maguire, K. 1992. "Prison Industry: The Effect of Participation on Inmate Disciplinary Adjustment." Unpublished dissertation, Albany, State University of New York.

Maguire, K. and T. J. Flanagan, (eds.). 1991. *Sourcebook of Criminal Justice Statistics 1990*. U.S. Department of Justice, Bureau of Justice Statistics. Washington, DC: USGPO.

Perk-Davis, S. 1992. "The Good, the Bad, and the Ugly." *Corrections Compendium* 27(4):1, 5–18.

Petersilia, J., and P. Honig. 1980. *The Prison Experience of Career Criminals.* Santa Monica, CA: The Rand Corporation.

Reynolds, L. G., S. H. Masters, and C. H. Moset. 1987. *Economics of Labor.* Englewood Cliffs, NJ: Prentice Hall.

U.S. Department of Commerce, Bureau of the Census. 1991. *Statistical Abstract of the United States* (111th ed.). Washington, DC: U.S. Department of Commerce.

U.S. Department of Justice, Bureau of Justice Statistics. 1992. *Prisoners in 1991.* NCJ-134729. Washington, DC: U.S. Department of Justice (May).

U.S. Department of Justice, Federal Bureau of Prisons. 1991. *Post Release Employment Project: Summary of Preliminary Findings.* Washington, DC: U.S. Department of Justice.

Zamble, E., and F. J. Porporino. 1988. *Coping, Behavior, and Adaptation in Prison Inmates.* New York: Springer-Verlag.

Literacy Training and Reintegration of Offenders

T.A. RYAN

Results of studies over the last two decades clearly indicate that offenders who were functionally illiterate upon entering the prison system may be successfully reintegrated into society if they participate in literacy programs during incarceration.

What constitutes an effective literacy training program to prepare offenders for reintegration? There is no single answer to this question, and no one program has been singled out and proven universally effective. However, a common denominator of all effective literacy programs for offenders is that they do not conceptualize literacy as "readin', writin' and 'rithmetic." Instead, they define functional literacy broadly. They are holistic programs that link basic communication and computation skills with development of the total person.

GOALS OF LITERACY TRAINING

More than 15 years ago, Ryan et al.[1] identified four goals for literacy programs designed to prepare offenders for successful reintegration into society.

Source: Excerpted from "Literacy Training and Reintegration of Offenders." *Forum on Corrections Research* 3(1):17–23, 1991.

Self-Realization Goal

In achieving self-realization, offenders develop the knowledge, skills, and attitudes needed to realize their potential and gain heightened self-awareness, a realistic and positive self-concept, a value system congruent with the larger society, and feelings of self commensurate with their potential abilities. Trudnak[2] noted that functionally illiterate students are commonly unmotivated and demoralized, reflecting low self-esteem. The Council of Europe Select Committee of Experts on Education in Prison[3] recently emphasized the key benefits of literacy programs in helping offenders develop a sense of responsibility, self-determination, an ability to manage stress, and an ability to counteract negative aspects of prison life.

Self-fulfillment equips offenders with decision-making and problem-solving skills that promote the development of cognitive and critical reasoning skills.

Economic Efficiency Goal

Many offenders lack the knowledge, skills, and attitudes needed to manage family financial planning and to support themselves and their dependents at living standards above poverty level. Economically efficient individuals should be able to gain and maintain employment and to support themselves and their families with minimal or no assistance from private or pubic welfare.

In designing a literacy program for the Commonwealth of Virginia correctional system, Yurek and Yurek[4] recognized that literacy skills are essential to acquiring and maintaining employment. Inmates must increase comprehension skills needed for job search, job training, and on-the-job performance. Through literacy training, they should become aware of career options and develop a belief in themselves and their capacity for a better future as a result of gainful employment upon release.

Social Relationship Goal

By developing social relationships, offenders acquire the knowledge, skills, and attitudes needed to cope with social situations and to relate to others according to realities, expectations, and societal norms. The goal is to develop behaviour patterns that equip inmates to function effectively in home and community settings and to implement teaming and cooperation skills.

In our rapidly changing information age, the goal of social relationships requires a broad interpretation. Socialization of the individual must be one of the desired outcomes of literacy training. The social relationship goal should result in behaviour changes in inmates that allow them to interact with society in a manner not likely to be perceived as antisocial or deviant. This resocialization of offenders prepares them for successful reintegration into society.[5]

Civic Responsibility Goal

The goal of civic responsibility refers to preparing offenders to contribute in an organized, law-abiding way to the welfare of the group. Functionally illiterate inmates need to become aware of, and participate in, law-making, governance, and local community issues and affairs. They need to be informed about political issues and knowledgeable about legal standards of behaviour. This goal is consistent with the objective of literacy programs to prepare inmates to be productive, law-abiding citizens who will remain crime-free upon release.

MEANS FOR ACHIEVING LITERACY GOALS

It is impossible to describe any one literacy training program that would be universally effective in preparing functionally illiterate offenders for successful reintegration into society. Nevertheless, it is possible to design effective programs, and not necessarily by trial and error.

The staff in each correctional facility are responsible for designing literacy programs that address the needs of the offenders and that are relevant to social, economic, and political trends. The design of literacy programs must take into account the interests, aptitudes, and educational achievement levels of inmates, as well as their level of social and moral development and their capacity for problem solving, decision making, thinking, and reasoning.

RESEARCH ON LITERACY PROGRAMS RELEVANT TO REINTEGRATION

Over the last two decades, a considerable body of research on literacy programs has developed. In this context, functional literacy is defined in its broadest sense: it refers to the development of the whole person through the acquisition of cognitive, decision-making, problem-solving, and social skills in conjunction with the mastery of basic communication and computation skills.

Research has generally been conducted in three major areas: (a) the effect of educational programs on recidivism; (b) the characteristics of programs deemed effective in preparing inmates for reintegration; and (c) components of effective programs.

RESEARCH ON RECIDIVISM

At the outset, it should be noted that there are limitations to the extent to which one may describe the relationship between reduced recidivism and participation in correctional education programs as causal.

Wolford[6] asserted that the practice of measuring the impact of correctional education and other institutional programs on recidivism remained questionable. He observed that education was but one component in a comprehensive change process for offenders.

McCollum[7] stated that no responsible correctional administrator fantasized that education and training were the sole determining factors in postrelease behaviour.

In their review of research studies on the effectiveness of prison education programs, Linden and Perry[8] observed that relatively few conclusive studies had been reported.

Although most evaluations showed that inmates had made substantial improvement in learning, the change did not necessarily have an impact on postrelease employment and recidivism.

According to Deppe,[9] a popular misconception of correctional education is to assume that education is the answer to inmates' problems and that employment is the ultimate aim of corrections.

Coffey[10] noted that the impact of correctional education on postrelease behaviour was as yet undetermined and that quality education coupled with work experience and gradual release had never been conclusively tested.

RESEARCH ON CHARACTERISTICS AND COMPONENTS OF EFFECTIVE LITERACY PROGRAMS

Despite the questions about whether correctional education can be related to recidivism, some reported studies suggest a positive impact on the successful reintegration of offenders.

Schumacker, Anderson, and Anderson[11] reported results of a study comparing a group of adult parolees who had received vocational and academic training, another group who had received only vocational training while incarcerated, and a control group who had received no training. A sample of 845 subjects was randomly selected and, after attrition, reduced to 760. The vocational and vocational/academic groups reported the highest employment rates and lowest criminal activity after 12 months of follow-up, whereas the control group had the highest rate of criminal activity. "Vocational completers," those who had finished a vocational course of instruction, had a higher employment rate and fewer arrests upon release. Those who had received at least a general equivalency diploma had a higher employment rate and lower criminal activity rate after 12 months than releasees who did not have a general equivalency diploma.

Based on an assessment of correctional education in nine correctional facilities, Rice[12] identified program variables affecting rates of postrelease employment: degree of community and interagency involvement, inmate offence, type of instructional methodology, procedures for course development and implementation, intake and release procedures, and types of support services.

After reviewing files of 238 ex-inmates of the Vienna Correctional Center, Illinois, Anderson[13] concluded that vocational training and education did improve postrelease success and ability to retain employment. He noted that as grades increased, so did length of employment.

Lee[14] reported on an analysis of data from 1930 to 1977 comparing offenders who participated in educational programs with those who did not. The study revealed a significant relationship between correctional education participation and lowered recidivism rates in Minnesota.

Stevens[15] studied two groups of offenders in Georgia to investigate the relationship between inmate demographic characteristics, participation in a general educational development program, and recidivism. One group consisted exclusively of inmates who had participated in the education program (N = 2,000). The second group was a stratified random sample of inmates who had not participated. According to the results, recidivism among those who successfully completed the program was significantly less than for those who failed and those who did not participate.

To study the effects of participation in a vocational education program on recidivism, Shuman[16] selected four 50-member groups from Delaware correctional institutions: two experimental groups who had received training and two control groups who had not received training. Results revealed that the rate of recidivism for the groups who had received vocational training during incarceration was significantly lower than for the control groups.

In a four-year follow-up of 320 adult male felons discharged from West Virginia correctional institutions, Mace[17] found a strong negative relationship between recidivism and participation in prison education programs.

EXAMPLES OF EFFECTIVE LITERACY PROGRAMS

The following brief program descriptions illustrate components of literacy programs that have been reported to be effective for preparing adult inmates for reintegration.

Norwegian Program

The Norwegian Program is a household management course for inmates in Norway, which addresses problems they encounter when released from prison with meagre finances, no permanent residence, and no secure social environment. Through 120 hours of group instruction, the course seeks to assist in the process of reintegrating offenders into a non-supportive outside environment. Topics include nutrition, hygiene, social life, and financial planning. Inmates develop realistic budgets reflecting the circumstances they will encounter upon release.[18]

CHARACTERISTICS OF EFFECTIVE LITERACY PROGRAMS FOR REINTEGRATION

An analysis of the research on literacy programs reveals that effective programs have a significant number of common characteristics:

- The content reflects the diversity of human experience, is meaningful and relevant to the inmates, and addresses real-life concerns and issues such as family, sexuality, children, violence, assertiveness, and substance abuse.

- The content provides information that inmates need for their return to society, including material on employment, unemployment, housing, transportation, welfare, social security, vocational rehabilitation, education, and health care.

- The content of programs for young parents with custody of dependent children addresses child care, parenting, nutrition, health and hygiene, and family planning.

- Courses for inmates with limited English proficiency recognize cultural differences and provide language instruction.

- The programs integrate basic skills development with life skills development.

- The programs and achievements of inmate students are monitored.

- The learning environment is structured and supportive, providing opportunities for inmate students to apply and practice skills in the context of functional, real-life settings and situations.

- The programs use individual and group methods, a range of techniques, educational technology, and resources from community groups, business, and industry.[19]

Canadian Literacy Project

The Correctional Service of Canada launched a basic literacy project in response to the emphasis on functional literacy initiated by the Solicitor General of Canada in 1988. The adult basic education (ABE) curriculum design for the Prairie Region included communications, numeracy, natural sciences, and human sciences. The curriculum was accompanied by annotated reference booklets on ABE methods and materials, ABE and materials, and ABE assessment.[20]

Mandatory Literacy Program

The Mandatory Literacy Program has been implemented in a number of U.S. state correctional systems. The concept of mandatory literacy training originated with the United States Federal Bureau of Prisons, which initially set the sixth-grade achievement level, measured by the Stanford Achievement Test, as the standard for mandatory participation in literacy training. If federal inmates tested below the standard, they were required to enroll in a literacy program for 90 days. While these inmates could withdraw after 90 days, they could not be promoted above entry-level labour grade in prison industries or institutional work assignments if they did not meet the sixth-grade standard. The standard subsequently was raised to eighth grade and, again in 1990, to high-school completion or equivalency for inmates to qualify for top jobs in prison industry or work assignments. The requisite participation time was also increased, from 90 days to 120 days.[21]

Huntington Prison Literacy Project

The Huntington Prison Literacy Project is a successful, inmate-managed Laubach literacy program at Pennsylvania State Correctional Institution. Initially, inmates identified six priority areas for consideration in development of the program: organizational dynamics, selection and training of tutors, student-tutor relationships, maintenance of tutor interest, selection and use of supplementary materials, and learning problems. Inmate tutors were trained in a six-session workshop, during which the priority topics were discussed, case studies were reviewed, and results of research conducted by professional staff were reported.[22]

Oklahoma Prison Literacy Project

The Oklahoma Prison Literacy Project started in 1986, when a literacy task force studied the literacy needs of the inmate population and identified ways to meet these needs. The task force recommended the development of a state-wide literacy effort by all correctional facilities. The project was a joint effort of the Department of Corrections, the Department of Education, and the Department of Libraries. The Department of Corrections allowed staff who were apprentice trainers and supervisors the time to attend training sessions. The Department of Education furnished funds for the purchase of literacy workbooks and materials and enlisted school principals as literacy directors at each institution. The Department of Libraries supplied start-up kits for each facility, recruited literacy volunteers, provided an honorarium for each participating trainer, and paid the travel expenses of trainers. Members of 15 local literacy councils volunteered to work on the project. The Oklahoma Pardon and Parole Board declared its full support of the project and agreed that parole hearings would give favourable consideration to inmate participation in the program. This linkage with parole gave credence to incorporating reintegration concepts into the curriculum.[23]

Life Skills Programs

Ryan[24] described the Individualized Life Skills Program, which was developed for the Georgia correctional system over a three-year period involving extensive research. The program was open-ended, with short modules of instruction to facilitate use of performance contracting and contingency management. Three themes—health education, family and civic skills, and consumer education—were designed for incorporation into the regular adult basic education program.

Use of Technology

Designed to give participants a sense of involvement and motivation, a sophisticated delivery system of radio, television, and computer-assisted instruction was developed and implemented in Bexar County Detention Center, Texas. The jail annex contained a closed-circuit radio and television system that could broadcast to all cell blocks. Integrated into the system was the PLATO computer-assisted instructional system, an interactive program with four component categories: records, communications, courses, and noninstructional activities. According to pre- and posttests, the system resulted in higher scores in spelling and arithmetic computations and problem solving.[25]

Cognitive Development

Ventre[26] described a program, based on Kohlberg's theory of cognitive-moral development, which focused on the process of thinking about moral issues rather than on moral values as such. Kohlberg's theory established a hierarchy of levels of thinking about moral issues. The curriculum involved the presentation, in different formats, of subject area dilemmas and various options and responses to the dilemmas.

Self-Esteem Model

One experimental study analyzed the effects of a mathematical educational model to develop self-esteem in male inmates.[27] Conducted at Louisiana State Prison, this research project examined subjects who were within 12 months of discharge, had an IQ of at least 80, and could read at first grade level. Groups of five were tutored in 45-minute sessions twice a week for 18 weeks. According to the study findings, the educational model enhanced self-esteem while improving mathematical skills.

Educational Support Program

The Educational Support Program,[28] conducted in South Carolina from 1984 to 1987, provided offenders with linkage between education in the institution and continued education in the community upon release. Designed to ease the transition from prison to the community and to facilitate successful reintegration into society, the program helped adult female offenders to further their education, develop and enhance job skills, and improve self-concepts and self-esteem. The primary components of the program were intake, education (from literacy training to postsecondary education), support services, placement, and follow-up. Support services included intensive individual counseling, career guidance, group counseling, tutoring, and referral to community agencies. Weekly group counseling sessions addressed values clarification, decision making, parenting, money management, leisure and recreation, communication, interpersonal skills, crisis management, legal issues and the law, and health and hygiene. The offenders also attended group sessions on job-search techniques, job readiness, and on-the-job attitudes and performance.

Norwegian Followup Model Program

Begun in 1985, the Norwegian Followup Model Program also addressed the need to link education in prison with continued education in the community after release. When they entered prison, inmates developed educational plans which included continued education in the community. Small followup classes, held in several communities in Norway, established a clear link between education in prison and education in the community. A pilot project, involving 100 + 200 inmates in three prisons, was reported to be successful.[29]

BENEFITS OF LITERACY TRAINING IN ADULT PRISONS

The costs of providing literacy training to adult offenders are far outweighed by the benefits—to prison management, inmates, and society in general.

According to the American Correctional Association Committee on Offender Programs,[30] prisons are safer for staff, offenders, and visitors if inmates are productively engaged in literacy training that promotes mental and physical health. Moreover, literacy training facilitates the offender's ability to read and understand prison rules.

Based on a review of the literature, Enocksson[31] concluded that the education of inmates should result in their increased employability. Because work is of prime importance in adult life, inmates who fail to develop employable skills will be more likely to engage in repeated crime than inmates who achieve functional literacy and develop job skills. Successful completion of literacy training programs contributes to offenders' sense of self-worth and accomplishment and thus increases their motivation to succeed in the outside world.

The results of a study of Black inmates in Illinois led Black[32] to conclude that prison education could have significant rehabilitative effects on inmates lacking education and functioning at poverty level. In addition, once Black inmates experienced success in the educational program, their feelings of hostility and inadequacy were replaced by feelings of self-pride and self-worth.

According to the Select Committee of Experts on Education in Prison,[33] inmates with literacy problems deserve special attention because they suffer acutely. Their prospects for work within the prison and upon release are severely limited, their self-respect and self-confidence are impaired, and their social life may be curtailed. Inmates who successfully complete literacy programs are better prepared to cope with personal problems.

It is in society's best interest to make the prison population productive. To do so requires making offenders functionally literate. The American Correctional Association Offender Program Committee[34] has forecast that with the general population growth, the retirement of more workers, the expansion of the economy, the creation of more jobs, and the drop in the birth rate, there will be a demand for more workers. Society needs to capitalize on the economic contribution of inmates, most of whom will return to society. Those who leave prison unchanged and functionally illiterate will continue to commit crimes. Literacy, job skills, and life skills are needed to help reduce recidivism.

CONCLUSION

This era of increasing industrial, technological, and informational complexities demands more specialization and higher levels of performance. The acquisition of basic skills is the first and most significant step for functionally illiterate offenders to assume a place in the free world of today and tomorrow.

Trujillo[35] noted that the most desirable objective in adult basic education was the preparation of adults to function at their fullest capacities. Literacy training for inmates has been emphasized as a means to accomplish this objective. In fact, vocational training, higher education, and other avenues for social and economic advancement have little meaning for those who have yet to acquire basic literacy skills. A literacy program with a holistic approach must prepare offenders to develop new life perspectives, become aware of family, social, and civic responsibilities, develop the skills to maintain gainful employment, and change attitudes from defeatism and rejection to self-confidence, self-worth, and pride.

If inmates are to be successfully reintegrated, corrections must address the major challenge posed by the relatively limited participation of inmates in literacy training. Research has documented the problem of underenrollment, which plagues far too many prison education systems. Given the substantial proportion of functionally illiterate adult inmates, it is shocking, frightening, and unacceptable to find only a relatively small proportion participating in literacy programs in prison. There is a critical need to overcome the hurdles that discourage many inmates from taking advantage of education.

A study by Glover and Lotze[36] revealed that although educational programs were available to all inmates in New York prisons, many inmates did not participate. In a comparison of inmates who attended school and those who did not, program participants were found to be older and serving longer terms. This finding raises a serious concern: younger inmates, most of whom are not career criminals, may be released in relatively short times, and they must be functionally literate in order to reintegrate into society successfully.

The Select Committee of Experts on Education in Prison[37] observed that throughout Europe, the proportion of the population with serious literacy problems was far higher in prisons than in the community. In a study conducted in France, the proportion of illiterate inmates was three times that of the general population, even though literacy had been defined very narrowly. In Canada, Collins[38] estimated that 65% of federal inmates were functionally illiterate, according to School and College Ability Test scores. In the United States. estimates of functional illiteracy in prison populations range from 40% to 75%, depending largely on the definition of illiteracy.

Given the international statistics, 40% to 75% of adult inmates in institutions are functionally illiterate, and as many as three-quarters of the prison population do not participate in literacy programs—it is clear that there is a serious problem of underenrollment in literacy programs.

Every nation has a responsibility to prepare a significant number of functionally illiterate offenders for successful reintegration and at the same time protect society against them until they are able to function productively in the free world. These offenders cannot and will not achieve the goal of successful reintegration until they overcome the handicaps of personal, economic, social, and civic deficiencies.

We can and must meet the challenges by replacing the concept of "caging" offenders with the concept of educating offenders and promoting literacy training for men and women in correctional institutions throughout the world. We can and must continue to ensure that jails, prisons, and reformatories provide literacy training programs that will prepare offenders to return to society as productive, responsible, socially acceptable, and economically self-sufficient citizens contributing to the well-being of their communities.

A major challenge to the research community is the need for more conclusive research and well-designed evaluative studies, particularly on mandatory literacy training, and well-conceived and structured holistic education programs for adult inmates.

NOTES

1. Ryan, T. A., et al. *Model of Adult Basic Education in Corrections.* (Honolulu: University of Hawaii, 1975).

2. Trudnak, D. M. "The Letter: A Successful Reading-Writing Strategy for Adult Basic Education Instruction in Correctional Institutions." *Journal of Correctional Education* 41(3) (1990):116–117.

3. Select Committee of Experts on Education in Prison, Council of Europe. *Final Activity Report on Education in Prisons.* Unpublished manuscript (Strasbourg: The Council, 1989).

4. Yurek, E. T., and F. G. Yurek. "Increased Literacy Through Unison Reading." *Journal of Correctional Education* 41(3) (1990):110–114.

5. Hill, L. R. "An Adult Basic Education Curriculum." Pp. 420–424 in T. A. Ryan, ed., *Education for Adults in Correctional Settings*, vol. II, (Honolulu: University of Hawaii, 1975).

6. Wolford, B. "Correctional Education." Paper presented at the meeting of the American Criminal Justice Society, 1982, Washington, DC.

7. McCollum, S. G. "What Works: A Look at Effective Correctional Education and Training Experiences." *Federal Probation* 41 (1977):32–35.

8. Linden, R., and L. Perry. "Effectiveness of Prison Education Programs." *Journal of Offender Counseling, Services and Rehabilitation* 6(4) (1982):43–57.

9. Deppe, D. A. "New Model for Correctional Education." In L J. Hippchen, ed., *Holistic Approaches to Offender Rehabilitation* (Springfield, IL: Charles C. Thomas, 1982).

10. Coffey, O. D. "American Prison as an Educational Institution: Issues in Correctional Education for the 1986s." Pp. 134 in L. Leiberg, ed., *Employment Crime and Policy Issues* (Washington, DC: American University Washington College of Law, 1982).

11. Schumacker, R. E., D. B. Anderson, and S. L. Anderson. "Vocational and Academic Indicators of Parole Success." *Journal of Correctional Education* 41(1) (1990):8–13.

12. Rice, E. *Assessment of Quality Vocational Education in State Prisons* (Chapel Hill, NC: System Sciences, Inc., 1980).

13. Anderson, D. B. "Relationship Between Correctional Education and Parole Success," *Journal of Offender Counseling, Services and Rehabilitation* 5(3) (1981):13–25.

14. Lee, H. K. "System Dynamic Study of a Criminal Justice System and an Appraisal of Its Correctional Education." Doctoral dissertation, 1981, University of Minnesota.

15. Stevens, R. D. *Effects of Selected Demographic Characteristics on General Educational Development (GED) Participant Success and Recidivism within*

Georgia Correctional Facilities (Ann Arbor, MI: University Microfilms, 1981).

16. Shuman. C. C. *Effects of Vocational Education on Recidivism of Formerly Incarcerated Individuals* (Ann Arbor, MI: University Microfilms, 1976).

17. Mace, J. L. *Effect of Correctional Institutions' Education Programs on Inmates' Societal Adjustment as Measured by Post-Release Recidivism* (Ann Arbor, MI: University Microfilms, 1978).

18. Select Committee of Experts on Education in Prison, Council of Europe. *Final Activity Report on Education in Prisons*. Unpublished manuscript (Strasbourg: The Council, 1989).

19. Council of Chief State School Officers, Educational Resource Center on Educational Equity. "A Concern About Adult Literacy." *Concerns* 31 (1990):1–3.

20. Collins, M. "A Basic Literacy Project for the Correctional Service of Canada: Curriculum Design as a Strategy for Staff Development." *Journal of Correctional Education* 40(2) (1989):51–54.

21. McCollum, S. G. "Mandatory Programs for Prisons: Let's Expand the Concept." *Federal Probation* 54(3) (1990):33–35.

22. Correctional Education Association. *Learning Behind Bars: Selected Educational Programs from Juvenile, Jail, and Prison Facilities*. (Laurel, MD: The Association, 1989.)

23. Ibid.

24. Ryan, T. A. "The Individualized Adult Life Skills System." *Journal of Correctional Education* 33(3) (1982):27–33.

25. Diem, R. A., and J. F. Knoll. "Technology and Humanism: New Approaches in Correctional Education." *Journal of Correctional Education* 33(1) (1981):4–6.

26. Ventre, R. J. "Cognitive Moral Development in the Prison Classroom," *Journal of Correctional Education* 33(3) (1982):18–26.

27. Roundtree, G. A., D. W. Edwards, and S. H. Dawson, (1982). "Effects of Education on Self-Esteem of Male Prison Inmates." *Journal of Correctional Education* 32(4) (1982):12–18.

28. Ryan, T. A. "A Transitional Program for Female Offenders." In S. Duguid, ed. *Yearbook of Correctional Education* (Burnaby, British Columbia: Simon Fraser University, 1989).

29. Select Committee of Experts on Education in Prison, Council of Europe. *Final Activity Report on Education in Prisons*. Unpublished manuscript (Strasbourg: The Council, 1989).

30. American Correctional Association. *Literacy: A Concept for All Seasons* (Laurel, MD: The Association, 1988).

31. Enocksson, E. "A Review of the Value of Education and Training in Penal Institutions," *Journal of Offender Counseling, Services and Rehabilitation* 5(1) (1980):5–18.

32. Black, A. (1984). "Role of Education in Prison and the Black Inmate." Pp. 307–314 in D. Georges-Abeyis, ed., *Criminal Justice System and Blacks* (New York: Clark Boardman Co., Ltd., 1984).

33. Select Committee of Experts on Education in Prison, Council of Europe. *Final*

Activity Report on Education in Prisons. Unpublished manuscript (Strasbourg: The Council, 1989).

34. American Correctional Association. *Literacy: A Concept for All Seasons* (Laurel, MD: The Association, 1989).

35. Trujillo, T. M. "An Adult Basic Education Curriculum." Pp. 383–394 in T. A. Ryan, ed., *Education for Adults in Correctional Settings* (Honolulu: University of Hawaii, 1975).

36. Glover, J. W., and E. W. Lotze. "Prison Schooling: Who Gets Educated?" *Journal of Correctional Education* 40(3) (1989):108–114.

37. Select Committee of Experts on Education in Prison, Council of Europe. *Final Activity Report on Education in Prisons*. Unpublished manuscript (Strasbourg: The Council, 1989).

38. Collins, M. "A Basic Literacy Project for the Correctional Service of Canada: Curriculum Design as a Strategy for Staff Development." *Journal of Correctional Education* 40(2) (1989):51–54.

Effective Correctional Programming: What Empirical Research Tells Us and What It Doesn't

FRIEDRICH LÖSEL[1]

GENERAL EFFECTIVENESS

All meta-analyses on offender treatment suggest that offenders who receive some kind of psychosocial treatment tend to do better than those who do not. This conclusion cannot be attributed solely to reliance on selected positive results because various meta-analyses have also included unpublished research reports.

The overall effect of such treatment is relatively small. On average, offender treatment tends to reduce recidivism by approximately 10 percentage points. However, even such a small effect can produce significant cost savings.[2] Further, many recognized and praised medical treatments produce similar results.[3] Methodological studies also suggest that the potential upper limit of such reductions is actually between 30 percentage points and 40 percentage points.[4]

Source: Excerpted from Lösel, Friedrich, "Effective Correctional Programming: What Empirical Research Tells Us and What It Doesn't," *Forum on Corrections Research*, Vol. 8(3), pp. 33–37.

TYPE OF TREATMENT

There are remarkable differences in the effectiveness of different types of programming. Intervention based on empirically valid theories of criminal behaviour that address criminogenic needs (the need principle) and account for offender learning styles and characteristics (responsivity) produce greater results.[5] Successful programs also tend to be either behavioural, cognitive-behavioural, or multi-modal.

Unstructured casework, counseling, and psychodynamic, insight-oriented, and nondirective approaches tend to have less impact. The same is true of pure punishment, deterrence measures (such as boot camps), or measures with no educational or psychosocial component (such as diversion). Some of these less-appropriate programs have even been found to have negative effects.

PROGRAM INTEGRITY

Various studies suggest that high program integrity can lead to better offender outcomes. However, if the program is inappropriate to begin with, integrity will not improve outcome.

Low program integrity may be caused by things like weak program structure, lack of a manual, insufficient staff training, organizational barriers, staff resistance to proper program implementation, incidents that lead to political changes, unsystematic changes to the program, and lack of a basic philosophy of criminality and treatment.[6]

Of course, any form of programming is largely individual and cannot be completely standardized. It is, however, important to continually monitor areas such as program development, organizational structure, staff selection and training, communication, and decision-making rules.

METHODOLOGICAL CONSIDERATIONS

A large portion of the variances in treatment outcome can be attributed to methodological variations between studies.[7] One should, therefore, be cautious about generalizing the results of a single study.

The criteria used to measure program effects are particularly important. Behavioural and more objective measures of criminality and recidivism tend to produce smaller effect findings than measures of institutional adaptation, attitudes, or personality change. Reliable criteria and longer follow-up periods are also associated with smaller effects.

In many studies, measures of intermediate goals (such as personality change) tend to be too unspecific for sound prediction of future criminality.

This suggests the need for thorough assessment of offender development before, during, and after program participation.

LOCATION

Community-based programming tends to produce greater results than programming delivered in custody. However, some institutional programs have produced positive results.[8]

The negative impact of incarceration depends on personal, situational, and organizational characteristics that can be addressed at least partially by programming. Many offenders have hazardous lifestyles, so institutions may be a stabilizing influence. However, these arguments should not be misunderstood as a plea for custodial programs. Custody should be a last resort. Systematic risk and dangerousness assessments have proven useful in making placement decisions[9] and should be continually improved.

OFFENDER CHARACTERISTICS

A focus on simple offender variables like age, sex, or type of offence does not normally produce particularly strong results. It is more effective to assess high-risk personality disorders (such as psychopathy),[10] specific criminogenic needs, and responsivity.[11] Antisocial cognitive styles, lack of social skills, impulsivity, and verbal and neuropsychological problems indicate a risk of persistent offending.[12]

Such characteristics are relevant not only to treatment characteristics, but also to the fit between offender and program. For example, while roleplaying and interpersonal skills training may help "ordinary" offenders,[13] they can be counterproductive for primary psychopaths. Learned skills can be misused, which could result in treated offenders recidivating more frequently than untreated offenders.[14]

RISK AND PROGRAM INTENSITY

The risk principle suggests that high-risk offenders need intensive treatment, while low-risk offenders should not receive too-intensive (and costly) programming. However, very high-risk offenders are difficult to change, even through intensive treatment.

The best way to understand the relationship between risk and treatment failure is to imagine the letter "u," where the top of one end of the "u" represents high risk and the top of the other end represents low risk. The fit between risk and service level is most important at the bottom of the "u"—the broad middle range of offender risk.

Program intensity can also be influenced by other factors. For example, psychopathic offenders tend to express less motivation and effort,[15] putting them at risk of receiving less intensive treatment or of dropping out of the program.

ORGANIZATIONAL AND STAFF CHARACTERISTICS

Unfortunately, little systematic research has been done on the impact of organizational characteristics such as facility climate, prison regime, or relationship with other services. However, institutional features vary widely.[16] A regime that is emotionally and socially responsive, well-structured, norm-oriented, and controlling can be important not only to program interaction but also to future nonoffending.[17]

The impact of staff characteristics is also rarely investigated. Yet, psychotherapy research indicates that the personal variables of a therapist are very important to effective intervention.[18] Effective treatment requires well-selected, specifically trained, highly motivated, and continuously supervised staff. Staff attitudes and competence that do not match the aims and content of a program may not only lower treatment integrity, they may also hinder its effectiveness.

NATURAL PROTECTIVE FACTORS

Some individuals can cope relatively well without professional help. Cognitive and social competencies, an "easy" temperament, success at school or in hobbies, attachment to a stable reference person, social support from outside the family, and accepting/responsive or demanding/controlling educational styles can help protect an individual.[19]

Correctional programs do not generally account for such natural protective factors. However, young offender programming and early intervention in at-risk groups have shown that working with young offenders and their families is particularly effective.[20]

Unfortunately, this is much more difficult to accomplish with offenders who are older or in custody. Their natural environment is often heavily disturbed and they frequently lack personal and social factors that could help in decreasing criminality. Depending on the context, some of these factors (such as support from a deviant peer group) could even have a negative effect.[21] Despite these realities, efforts should be made to integrate such natural protectors into programming.[22]

RELAPSE PREVENTION

Various types of programming are relatively successful in the short term, but fail over the long term. However, the positive changes offenders achieved in these programs could be preserved by additional or relapse-prevention programming.[23]

Although the necessity for effective after-care is unquestioned, there is little research on the combination of treatment and relapse-prevention measures. Practical problems such as resource allocation also must be solved.[24]

DISCUSSION

Empirical evaluations of correctional programs have more to offer than do fashionable crime policy trends.

Although many inconsistencies and blind spots remain in the research, there are clearly some concepts that are key to effective correctional programming:[25]

- realistic expectations of results;
- theoretically sound concepts;
- dynamic offender risk assessment that matches the service level;
- appropriate targeting of specific criminogenic needs;
- awareness of the consequences of applying reinforcement;
- teaching self-control, thinking, and social skills;
- matching program type, offender, and staff;
- thorough selection, motivation, training, and supervision of staff;
- acceptance/reward and structure/control within the institutional regime;
- neutralization of criminogenic social networks;
- strengthening of "natural" protective factors;
- high program integrity;
- selection and assessment of adequate intermediate treatment goals;
- assessment and monitoring of offender behavioural change; and
- relapse-prevention and after-care programming.

NOTES

1. Bismarckstr. 1, 91054 Erlangen, Germany.

2. R. Prentky and A. W. Burgess, "Rehabilitation of Child Molesters: A Cost-benefit Analysis," *Child Trauma I: Issues and Research*, A. W. Burgess, ed. (New York: Garland, 1992): 417–442.

3. M. W. Lipsey and D. B. Wilson, "The Efficacy of Psychological, Educational and Behavioural Treatment," *American Psychologist*, 48 (1993): 1181–1209.

4. For example, large proportions of nonrecidivism in control groups, unreliability of treatment and outcome measures, and dichotomization of variables reduce the potential effects.

5. D. A. Andrews and J. Bonta, *The Psychology of Criminal Conduct* (Cincinnati: Anderson, 1994).

6. C. R. Hollin, "The Meanings and Implications of Program Integrity," *What Works: Reducing Reoffending*, J. McGuire, ed. (Chichester: John Wiley & Sons, 1995): 195–208. See also F. Lösel, "Working with Young Offenders: The Impact of Meta-analyses," *Clinical Approaches to Working with Young Offenders*, C. R. Hollin and K. Howells, eds. (Chichester: John Wiley & Sons, 1996): 57–82.

7. Lipsey, "Juvenile Delinquency Treatment: A Meta-analytic Inquiry into Variability of Effects." For a comparison with other studies see F. Lösel, "The Efficacy of Correctional Treatment: A Review and Synthesis of Meta-evaluations."

8. D. A. Andrews, I. Zinger, R. D. Hoge, J. Bonta, P. Gendreau, and F. T. Cullen, "Does Correctional Treatment Work? A Clinically Relevant and Psychologically Informed Meta-analysis." See also F. Lösel, "Increasing Consensus in the Evaluation of Offender Rehabilitation? Lessons from Recent Research Synthesis," *Psychology, Crime & Law* 2 (1995): 19–39.

9. J. Bonta, D. A. Andrews, and L. L. Motiuk, *Dynamic Risk Assessment and Effective Treatment*, Paper presented at the annual meeting of the American Society of Criminology, Phoenix, 1993. See also J. Bonta and L. L. Motiuk, "Classification to Halfway Houses: A Quasi-experimental Evaluation," *Criminology* 28 (1990): 497–506. And see J. Bonta and L. L. Motiuk, "Inmate Classification," *Journal of Criminal Justice* 20 (1992): 343–353.

10. R. D. Hare, "Psychopathy: A Clinical Construct Whose Time Has Come," *Criminal Justice and Behavior* (in press).

11. Andrews and Bonta, *The Psychology of Criminal Conduct*.

12. T. Moffitt, "Adolescence-limited and Life-course-persistent Antisocial Behavior: A Developmental Taxonomy," *Psychological Review* 100 (1993): 674–701.

13. R. R. Ross and E. A. Fabiano, *Time to Think: A Cognitive Model of Delinquency Prevention and Offender Rehabilitation* (Johnson City: Institute of Social Sciences and Arts, 1985).

14. M. E. Rice, G. T. Harris, and C. A. Cormier, "An Evaluation of a Maximum Security Therapeutic Community for Psychopaths and Other Mentally Disordered Offenders," *Law and Human Behavior* 16 (1992): 399–412.

15. J. R. P. Ogloff, S. Wong, and A. Greenwood, "Treating Criminal Psychopaths in a Therapeutic Community Program," *Behavioral Sciences and the Law* 8 (1990): 181–190.

16. J. Bonta and P. Gendreau, "Reexamining the Cruel and Unusual Punishment of Prison Life," *Law and Human Behavior* 14 (1990): 347–372. See also R. Moos, *Evaluating Correctional and Community Settings* (New York: John Wiley & Sons, 1975).

17. Moos, *Evaluating Correctional and Community Settings*. See also F. Lösel, "Protective Effects of Social Resources in Adolescents at High Risk for Anti-

social Behavior," *Cross-national Longitudinal Research on Human Development and Criminal Behavior*, H. J. Kerner and E. G. M. Weitekamp, eds. (Dordrecht: Kluwer, 1994): 281–301. And see M. Rutter, B. Maughan, P. Mortimore, and J. Ouston, *Fifteen Thousand Hours: Secondary Schools and Their Effects on Children* (London: Open Books, 1979).

18. F. J. Porporino and E. Baylis, "Designing a Progressive Penology: The Evolution of Canadian Federal Corrections," *Criminal Behaviour and Mental Health* 3 (1993): 268–289. See also F. Lösel and T. Bliesener, "Psychology in Prison: Role Assessment and Testing of an Organizational Model," *Criminal Behavior and the Justice System: Psychological Perspectives*, H. Wegener, F. Lösel, and J. Haisch, eds. (New York: Springer-Verlag, 1989): 419–439.

19. F. Lösel and T. Bliesener, "Some High-risk Adolescents Do Not Develop Conduct Problems: A Study of Protective Factors," *International Journal of Behavioral Development* 17 (1994): 753–777. See also M. Rutter, "Resilience in the Face of Adversity: Protective Factors and Resistance to Psychiatric Disorder," *British Journal of Psychiatry* 147 (1985): 598–611. And see M. Stouthamer-Loeber, R. Loeber, D. P. Farrington, Q. Zhang, W. van Kammen, and E. Maguin, "The Double Edge of Protective and Risk Factors for Delinquency: Interrelations and Developmental Patterns," *Development and Psychopathology* 5 (1993): 683–701.

20. R. E. Tremblay and W. Craig, "Developmental Crime Prevention," *Building a Safer Society: Strategic Approaches to Crime Prevention*, M. Tonry and D. P. Farrington, eds. (Chicago: The University of Chicago Press, 1995): 151–236. See also H. Yoshikawa, "Prevention as Cumulative Protection: Effects of Early Family Support and Education on Chronic Delinquency and Its Risks," *Psychological Bulletin* 115 (1994): 28–54.

21. D. Bender, *Psychische Widerstandsfähigkeit im Jugendalter: Eine Längsschnittstudie im Multiproblem-Milieu* [Resilience in Adolescence: A Longitudinal Study in Multiproblem Milieus], Doctoral dissertation, University of Erlangen-Nürnberg, 1995. See also F. Lösel, *Resilience and Protective Functions in Adolescence*, Keynote address at the Fifth Biennial Conference of the European Association for Research on Adolescence, Li'ege, Belgium, 1996.

22. L. L. Motiuk, "Using Familial Factors to Assess Offender Risk and Need," *Forum on Corrections Research* 7, 2 (1995): 19–22. See also Porporino and Baylis, "Designing a Progressive Penology: The Evolution of Canadian Federal Corrections."

23. D. R. Laws, *Relapse Prevention with Sex Offenders* (New York: Guilford Press, 1989).

24. T. Exworth, "Compulsory Care in the Community: A Review of the Proposals for Compulsory Supervision and Treatment of the Mentally Ill in the Community," *Criminal Behaviour and Mental Health* 5 (1995): 218–241.

25. For a more comprehensive overview see P. Gendreau, "The Principles of Effective Intervention with Offenders," *Choosing Correctional Options That Work: Defining the Demand and Evaluating the Supply*. A. T. Harland, ed. (Thousand Oaks, CA: Sage, 1966).

Discipline

TIMOTHY J. FLANAGAN

All prisons and jails must create mechanisms to maintain order and safety. Prison discipline takes many forms. These include rigid rules that encompass all aspects of conduct, institutional policies concerning movement and access to specific areas, procedures that regulate the importation of goods into the prison, regulations covering visiting, telephone and mail, and many others. Prisons construct elaborate and comprehensive regimes in support of the objective of a well-ordered and disciplined society of convicts.

The great debate among the early designers of penitentiary systems in the United States was essentially a conflict about the best way to achieve prison discipline. The Pennsylvania system featured solitary confinement at all times during the entire sentence. The proponents of the Pennsylvania model argued that complete isolation from the contaminating influence of other inmates best served the interests of prison discipline and reform. The architects of the Auburn-style congregate prisons, in contrast, permitted group labor during the day but required isolation in single cells at night. Moreover, all forms of communication among prisoners were strictly forbidden, whether at work, during meals, or while moving within the institution. As David J. Rothman observed, "To both advocates of the congregate and the separate systems, the promise of institutionalization depended upon the isolation of the prisoner and the establishment of a disciplined routine" (1971:82).

During most of their history, American prisons have relied on a system of rewards and punishments to maintain order. In the earliest American state prisons, from the 1820s through the Civil War, isolation, silence, hard labor, and cruel corporal punishments were the primary instruments of prison discipline. By the middle of the nineteenth century, American penologists had begun to experiment with a number of reward-based sanctioning systems. These systems included the concept of custody-grading, a scheme where the prisoner could move through stages of confinement in which the intensity of supervision was reduced, certain privileges could be earned, and the amount of trust granted to the inmate was gradually increased.

The reward-based behavioral control system was enhanced in the 1870s with the adoption in American reformatories of the indeterminate sentence, discretionary release authority, and good time systems. These developments permitted inmates to influence, through their prison behavior, the amount of

Source: Excerpted from Flanagan, Timothy J., "Discipline," in *Encyclopedia of American Prisons*, edited by Marilyn D. McShane and Frank P. Williams III. New York: Garland Publishing Co., 1996, pp. 161–165.

time that they would actually serve. Simultaneously, these methods, which were first developed in the New South Wales (Australia) and Irish prison systems, provided prison administrators with a powerful technique with which to control inmate behavior. In addition to working toward lower-custody housing, better work assignments, improved commissary and recreational privileges and other benefits, inmates' good behavior would result in "good time credits" deducted from the sentence. Conversely, violation of prison rules could result in the denial of these privileges, time in solitary confinement, or the reduction of good time credits. The latter penalty is in most respects the most severe, because it increases the time spent in confinement prior to release. Early release is the foremost goal of virtually all inmates.

THE PRISON JUSTICE SYSTEM

In many respects, the prison justice system mirrors the characteristics of the larger criminal justice system. The uniformed correctional staff perform a policing function within the prison. In some prisons, correctional officers are referred to as "the police" by inmates. The inmate rule book and the disciplinary procedure manual serve as the penal code and the criminal procedure code of the prison. Like a state penal code, the inmate rule book defines certain behavior as violations of the "law" of the prison, and specifies a range of penalties that may accompany a finding of guilt. The disciplinary procedure manual delineates the process through which allegations of violations are adjudicated and penalties imposed.

Like their counterparts outside prison, correctional officers exercise broad discretion in enforcing the institutional rule book (Poole and Regoli, 1980). No prison could manage the adjudication of every minor rule violation that might be charged. Moreover, writing up large numbers of "tickets" may be taken as evidence of an officer's inability to handle inmate conduct in a competent manner.

The categories of behavior that are proscribed in most inmate rule books are broad, so the officer's characterization of the offense may depend on the context in which the offense occurred. For example, verbal jousting between staff and inmates may be acceptable on a one-on-one basis, but an inmate's verbal harassment of an officer in a crowded yard might be "written up" as insolence, harassment, or a similar offense. An American Bar Association survey of institutional rule books in forty-four jurisdictions found that the written rules are "so vague and indefinite that it is difficult to differentiate between what may be permissible conduct and what might constitute a violation" (ABA, 1974:12). Prison rule books contain many of these "wastebasket categories" (Johnson, 1966), such as disrespect toward staff, in which the offender's demeanor may play a critical role.

Inmate rule books typically classify infractions according to seriousness, and provide for differential processing of violations. For example, minor infractions (which may result in a reprimand or loss of privileges for a brief time) may be adjudicated by a sergeant or lieutenant, while more serious violations may require a proceeding before an institutional "court." Many facilities provide for prehearing detention (analogous to serving time in jail prior to trial) pending adjudication of the charge. The institutional "court" is variously referred to as the disciplinary hearing, adjustment hearing, or superintendent's proceeding.

In the larger criminal justice systems, many studies have documented the attrition of cases as they pass through the stages of the criminal justice system. Some cases are declined for prosecution by the district attorney, others are dismissed at the initial appearance before a magistrate, and still others are turned back by grand juries or not sustained in the preliminary hearing. In sharp contrast, studies of case processing in the prison justice system show that nearly all cases charged are found guilty. In fact, some researchers have concluded that rather than being an adjudicatory process, the prison justice process is primarily dispositional in nature (Harvard Center for Criminal Justice, 1972). That is, once a disciplinary infraction is charged, the primary decision made by disciplinary committees is the meting out of punishment.

The fact that few disciplinary charges are dismissed (and few are reduced via plea bargaining) may simply indicate that correctional officers are selective in writing "tickets." An alternative view is that disciplinary courts, which are staffed by correctional agency employees, are reluctant to dismiss charges because of the belief that the inmate "must have done something" to warrant the officer's formal intervention. Also, reluctance to dismiss charges may reflect the view that such dismissals will undermine prison discipline and the authority of correctional staff. Kassebaum, Ward, and Wilner observed that dismissal of a disciplinary charge "implies that the reporting staff was wrong. For the morale of the rank and file correction officers, such inferences cannot be permitted" (1971:53).

Like the sentencing judge, the disciplinary committee or hearing officer has a broad range of sanctions to choose from, and discretionary authority to choose among these alternatives. These sanctions range from a simple reprimand with an accompanying entry in the inmate's file, to cell or work assignment changes, payment of restitution, confinement to cell (called "keep lock" in some systems), loss of good time credits, or a combination of sanctions. Referral of the case for outside prosecution is also an alternative for serious crimes, but relatively few prison crimes are referred to prosecutors. Twenty years ago the American Bar Association found that there was little correspondence between the severity of prison rule infractions and the penalties available in prison rule books, but revisions of institutional rules in recent years have made the penalty structure more commensurate with the severity of the infraction. Flanagan (1982) studied sentencing in prison disciplinary hearings and found the same factors that are associated with sentencing outcomes in the criminal justice system—severity of the offense and the prior disciplinary record of the offender.

WHO VIOLATES PRISON RULES?

Offenses against prison rules are not uniformly distributed among prisoners. A nationwide survey of state prison inmates conducted by the Justice Department in 1986 found that 53 percent of inmates had been charged with a rule violation (Stephan, 1989). Moreover, the average number of rule violations per inmate per year was 1.5. The Justice Department study did not distinguish between serious violations, such as assault, and minor violations. The study found that younger inmates, prisoners held in maximum security facilities, recidivists, men, and inmates who used drugs prior to imprisonment were more likely to violate prison rules than were other prisoners. Some studies have reported that blacks are more likely to be involved in prison rule violations, while others have found no race-based differences in infraction rates (Flanagan, 1983). Additional research has focused on psychological inventories, crowded conditions, and other factors as predictors of prisoner behavior.

The Justice Department survey also found that 94 percent of prisoners charged with rule infractions were found guilty, and that solitary confinement or segregation and loss of good time were the most frequently imposed punishments. Other penalties, in decreasing order of frequency, included confinement to cell or quarters, loss of entertainment or recreational privileges, loss of commissary privileges, reprimand, extra work, loss of job assignment, loss of visiting privileges, higher custody level within the facility, and transfer to another facility.

LEGAL ISSUES IN PRISON DISCIPLINE

Prior to the 1970s, courts typically took a "hands off" approach to the operations of prisons. In nearly all facets of prison administration, including the disciplinary process, judges deferred to the expertise and good faith of correctional administrators. Jones and Rhine observed that "a central justification for the 'hands off' doctrine was a fear on the courts' part that interfering in prison administration would undermine prison discipline and order" (1985:48). Under this view, "Prison officials had unlimited discretion to summarily enforce the myriad rules and regulations . . . and to mete out punishment without regard for an inmate's innocence or guilt" (1985:51).

The "hands off" perspective gave way in the 1970s, as courts became willing to examine correctional policies and practices. The landmark Supreme Court case on prison discipline was *Wolff v. McDonnell* (1974). The court in *Wolff* reasoned that inmates charged with a serious infraction of prison rules have a clear "liberty interest" in the outcome of disciplinary hearings. Further, the *Wolff* majority found that such interests are protected by the due process clause of the Fourteenth Amendment of the U.S. Constitution. At the same time, the court recognized the interest of the state in operating safe, secure, and orderly prisons. In attempting to reach a balance of these interests, the Court

> specified the following as the requisite ingredients of the disciplinary due process hearings: 1. Advance written notice of the charges against the prisoner must be given to him at least 24 hours prior to his appearance. . . . 2. There must be a written statement by the fact finders "as to the evidence relayed and the reasons for the disciplinary action." . . . 3. The inmate facing disciplinary proceedings "should be allowed to call witnesses and present documentary evidence in his defense when permitting him to do so will not be unduly hazardous to institutional safety or correctional goals." . . . 4. Counsel substitute (either staff, or where permitted, a fellow inmate) should be allowed where an illiterate inmate is involved, or where the complexity of the issue makes it unlikely that the inmate will be able to collect and present the evidence. . . . 5. The prison disciplinary board must be impartial (Jones and Rhine, 1985 quoting *Wolff v. McDonnell*).

Researchers who have examined the impact of *Wolff* and subsequent decisions on the prison disciplinary process conclude that judicial intervention in this area of correctional management has been beneficial. Jones and Rhine studied the disciplinary process in New Jersey prisons and concluded, "In contrast to the situation before *Wolff*, where disciplinary processes were loosely structured, and governed by substantial, and often unreviewable discretion, prison disciplinary systems are now much more formal, rational and legal in structure" (1985:103).

CONCLUSION

The challenge of operating safe, secure, and orderly prisons has never been greater than in the 1990s. Correctional issues such as overcrowding, longer sentences, increasing frequency of mental health problems among inmates, and gang membership make maintenance of prison discipline a Herculean task. Moreover, evolving constitutional standards and greater access to courts mean that correctional administrators can be sure that every policy, procedure, and decision is likely to be challenged in administrative or judicial appeals. The structure of prison rules and the procedures for rule enforcement can assist prison officials in socializing offenders to limits on their behavior and to the process of rewarding good behavior and sanctioning misconduct. When conducted professionally, the prison disciplinary process is a critical component of humane prisons in which people can live and work.

REFERENCES

American Bar Association. 1974. *Survey of Prison Disciplinary Practices and Procedures.* Washington, DC: American Bar Association.

Flanagan, T. J. 1982. "Discretion in the Prison Justice System: A Study of Sentencing in Prison Disciplinary Proceedings." *Journal of Research in Crime and Delinquency* 19(2): 216–237.

———. 1983. "Correlates of Institutional Misconduct among State Prisoners: A Research Note." *Criminology* 21(1): 29–40.

Harvard Center for Criminal Justice. 1972. "Judicial Intervention in Prison Discipline." *Journal of Criminal Law, Criminology and Police Science* 63 (2): 200–228.

Johnson, E. H. 1966. "Pilot Study: Age, Race and Recidivism as Factors in Prisoner Infractions." *Canadian Journal of Corrections* 8 (October): 268–283.

Jones, C. H., Jr. and E. Rhine. 1985. "Due Process and Prison Disciplinary Practices: From *Wolff* to *Hewitt*." *New England Journal on Criminal and Civil Confinement* 11(1): 44–122.

Kassebaum, G., D. A. Ward, and D. Wilner. 1971. *Prison Treatment and Parole Survival: An Empirical Assessment.* New York: John Wiley.

Poole, E. D. and R. M. Regoli. 1980. "Race, Institutional Rule Breaking and Disciplinary Response: A Study of Discretionary Decision Making in Prison." *Law and Society Review* 14(4): 931–946.

Rothman, D. J. 1971. *Discovery of the Asylum: Social Order and Disorder in the New Republic.* Boston: Little-Brown and Company.

Stephan, J. 1989. *Prison Rule Violators.* Bureau of Justice Statistics Special Report. Washington, DC.: United States Department of Justice.

CHAPTER 5

The Modern Jail

Jails are invariably described in the most disparaging terminology by justice reformers. These community-based institutions confine a highly diverse admixture of persons awaiting trial for serious and nonserious offenses, persons serving time for misdemeanors, persons awaiting transfer to state prison systems, mental health facilities, and other settings, and others. Perhaps the most distinct characteristic of jails, in comparison with prison systems, is the high rate of turnover of the inmate population. Counts of one-day populations in jails indicate that more than one-half million Americans are confined in these institutions on a single day, but, these facilities process as many as 13 to 16 million admissions during the course of a calendar year.

Another distinguishing characteristic of the jail is that this institution is inextricably linked with the monetarily driven pretrial release decision. That is, accused persons with economic resources are able to buy pretrial liberty in cases involving all but the most severe offenses, but the poor are required to serve the pretrial period in confinement. In addition to the direct punishment of deprivation of liberty that the jail represents, pretrial detention imposes economic, family, employment, and other hardships on offenders prior to conviction. Jails are also linked with the American criminal justice system's difficulty in providing speedy trial for persons accused of crime. If criminal cases were disposed more swiftly, many of our concerns about jail populations and jail services would be lessened.

Jails have traditionally been viewed as short-term detention settings, so they have always lacked the array of programming and services available in state prisons. Many of these facilities are old, understaffed, and lack even rudimentary education, work, training, or counseling programs for inmates. Observers of the jail argue that the lack of mental health resources in jails is especially dangerous, because in urban areas these facilities are the primary gateway into the mental health system. These concerns, and the uncertainty associated with criminal adjudication and sentencing, make jails a highly tenuous environment that challenges the adaptive resources of inmates and staff.

John Irwin argues that these characteristics of the jail environment are purposive; they are designed to comprise an institution charged with processing society's "rabble." In Irwin's view atrocious jail conditions are intended to convey society's rejection of its outcasts. Backstrand, Gibbons, and Jones's article challenges this assumption of Irwin's critique of the jail. Their study of two jails found that a high proportion of persons admitted to jails are serious law violators, and not just the disenfranchised and marginal of society as Irwin claims.

John Klofas's article argues that jails are best understood as part of the network of social, political, and economic organizations that make up communities. Klofas points out that wide variation in quality of physical environments, administration, staff professionalism, health care, and many other aspects of jail operations raises important questions about standards and control in correctional administration. He notes that the courts are ill suited to perform a supervisory role over local correctional facilities. In some jurisdictions, state agencies provide a measure of oversight and regulation toward the objective of uniform and humane jail administration.

Several of the contributors in this section address the question of the future of jails, and the possibility of significant improvement in jail administration and management in the future. All agree that the historical neglect of jails and chronic underfunding of these facilities represent major obstacles to jail reform. More importantly, lack of concern about jails on the part of citizens is perhaps the most serious impediment to improving this rapidly expanding component of the American criminal justice system.

Prison and Jail Inmates at Midyear 1996

DARRELL K. GILLIARD
ALLEN J. BECK

At midyear 1996 an estimated 1,630,940 persons were incarcerated in the Nation's prisons and jails. Federal and State prison authorities and local jail authorities held in their custody 615 persons per 100,000 U.S. residents. Prisoners in the custody of the 50 States, the District of Columbia, and the Federal Government accounted for two-thirds of the incarcerated population (1,112,448 inmates). The other third were held in local jails (518,492).

Source: Excerpted from *Prison and Jail Inmates at Midyear 1996*, by Darrell K. Gilliard and Allen J. Beck, Ph.D., U.S. Department of Justice, Bureau of Justice Statistics, NCJ-162843, January 1997.

On June 30, 1996, 1,164,356 prisoners were under Federal or State jurisdiction (includes prisoners in custody and persons under the legal authority of a prison system but who are held outside its facilities). The total increased 5.3% from midyear 1995. The States and the District of Columbia added 54,549 prisoners; the Federal system, 4,256.

Local jail authorities held or supervised an estimated 591,469 offenders. Twelve percent of these offenders (72,977) were supervised outside jail facilities in programs such as community service, work release, weekend reporting, electronic monitoring, and other alternative programs.

Thirty-nine percent of the growth in the prison populations during the 12 months ending June 30, 1996, was accounted for by California (10,954), the Federal system (4,256), Pennsylvania (4,095), and North Carolina (3,853). During this 12-month period, the total prison population increased at least 10% in 13 States. Nebraska reported the largest increase (16.0%), followed by Montana (15.2%), North Carolina (14.4%), Oregon (14.1%), Wisconsin (13.9%), and Pennsylvania (13.7%).

Two States and the District of Columbia experienced a decline in their prison population. The District of Columbia had the largest decline, −6.9%; followed by New Hampshire, −0.7%, and Connecticut, −0.2%.

TABLE 1

Number of Persons Held in State or Federal Prisons or in Local Jails, 1985, 1990–96

	Total inmates in custody	Prisoners in custody		Inmates held in local jails	Incarceration rate*
		Federal	State		
Year					
1985	744,208	35,781	451,812	256,615	313
1990	1,148,702	58,838	684,544	405,320	461
1991	1,219,014	63,930	728,605	426,479	483
1992	1,295,150	72,071	778,495	444,584	508
1993	1,369,185	80,815	828,566	459,804	531
1994	1,476,621	85,500	904,647	486,474	567
1995					
June 30	1,561,836	89,334	965,458	507,044	594
December 31	—	89,538	989,007	—	—
1996					
June 30	1,630,940	93,167	1,019,281	518,492	615
Percent change,					
6/30/95–6/30/96	4.4%	4.3%	5.6%	2.3%	
Annual average increase,					
12/31/85–6/30/96	7.8%	9.5%	8.1%	6.9%	
12/31/90–6/30/96	6.6%	8.7%	7.5%	4.6%	

Note: Jail counts are for midyear (June 30). Counts for 1994–96 exclude persons who were supervised outside of a jail facility. State and Federal prisoner counts for 1985 and 1990–94 are for December 31.
—Not available.

*Total of persons in custody per 100,000 residents on July 1 of each reference year.

TABLE 2
Prisoners under the Jurisdiction of State or Federal Correctional Authorities, by Region and Jurisdiction, June 30 and December 31, 1995, and June 30, 1996

Region and jurisdiction	Total			Percent change from —		Prison incarceration rate, 6/30/96[a]
	6/30/96	12/31/95	6/30/95	6/30/95 to 6/30/96	12/31/95 to 6/30/96	
U.S. total	1,164,356	1,126,073	1,105,551	5.3%	3.4%	420
Federal	103,722	100,250	99,466	4.3%	3.5%	33
State	1,060,634	1,025,823	1,006,085	5.4	3.4	388
Northeast	165,224	161,837	158,184	4.5%	2.1%	306
Connecticut[b]	14,975	14,801	15,005	(0.2)	1.2	319
Maine	1,468	1,396	1,459	0.6	5.2	112
Massachusetts	11,996	11,687	11,469	4.6	2.6	178
New Hampshire	2,050	2,014	2,065	(0.7)	1.8	177
New Jersey	27,753	27,066	25,626	8.3	2.5	347
New York	68,721	68,489	68,526	0.3	0.3	379
Pennsylvania	33,939	32,410	29,844	13.7	4.7	281
Rhode Island[b]	3,226	2,902	3,132	3.0	11.2	198
Vermont[b,c]	1,096	1,072	1,058	3.6	2.2	143
Midwest	199,414	193,220	190,573	4.6%	3.2%	318
Illinois[c,d]	38,373	37,658	37,790	1.5	1.9	322
Indiana	16,582	16,125	15,699	5.6	2.8	281
Iowa[c]	6,176	5,906	5,692	8.5	4.6	216
Kansas	7,462	7,054	6,927	7.7	5.8	289
Michigan[c]	41,884	41,112	41,377	1.2	1.9	436
Minnesota	5,040	4,846	4,764	5.8	4.0	108
Missouri	20,541	19,134	18,940	8.5	7.4	383
Nebraska	3,248	3,074	2,801	16.0	5.7	193
North Dakota	640	608	610	4.9	5.3	90
Ohio[d]	45,314	44,663	43,521	4.1	1.5	405
South Dakota	2,049	1,841	1,820	12.6	11.3	279
Wisconsin	12,105	11,199	10,632	13.9	8.1	209
South	467,900	454,182	446,755	4.7%	3.0%	487
Alabama	21,495	20,718	20,082	7.0	3.8	487
Arkansas	9,430	9,411	9,081	3.8	0.2	358
Delaware[b]	5,148	4,802	4,651	10.7	7.2	425
District of Col.[b]	9,763	9,800	10,484	(6.9)	(0.4)	1,444
Florida[c]	64,332	63,879	61,992	3.8	0.7	448
Georgia[c]	34,808	34,266	34,111	2.0	1.6	468
Kentucky	12,652	12,060	11,949	5.9	4.9	325
Louisiana	26,673	25,195	24,840	7.4	5.9	611
Maryland	22,118	21,453	21,441	3.2	3.1	413
Mississippi	13,785	12,684	12,446	10.8	8.7	486
North Carolina	30,671	29,253	26,818	14.4	4.8	397
Oklahoma[d]	19,134	18,151	17,605	8.7	5.4	580
South Carolina	20,814	19,611	19,482	6.8	6.1	540
Tennessee	15,634	15,206	14,933	4.7	2.8	293
Texas	129,937	127,766	127,092	2.2	1.7	659
Virginia	28,827	27,415	27,310	5.6	5.2	421
West Virginia	2,679	2,512	2,438	9.9	6.6	144
West	228,096	216,584	210,573	8.3%	5.3%	375
Alaska[b]	3,583	3,522	3,237	10.7	1.7	355
Arizona[c]	22,143	21,341	20,907	5.9	3.8	481
California	142,814	135,646	131,860	8.3	5.3	438
Colorado[d]	11,742	11,063	10,757	9.2	6.1	306
Hawaii[b]	3,693	3,560	3,583	3.1	3.7	225

TABLE 2 continued

Region and jurisdiction	Total			Percent change from —		Prison incarceration rate, 6/30/96[a]
	6/30/96	12/31/95	6/30/95	6/30/95 to 6/30/96	12/31/95 to 6/30/96	
Idaho	3,623	3,328	3,240	11.8	8.9	304
Montana	2,182	1,992	1,894	15.2	9.5	247
Nevada	8,064	7,713	7,487	7.7	4.6	493
New Mexico	4,528	4,078	4,121	9.9	11.0	253
Oregon	8,564	7,886	7,505	14.1	8.6	221
Utah	3,643	3,452	3,272	11.3	5.5	182
Washington	12,059	11,608	11,402	5.8	3.9	218
Wyoming	1,458	1,395	1,308	11.5	4.5	301

( ) *Indicates a negative percent change.*
[a]*The number of prisoners with a sentence of more than 1 year per 100,000 in the resident poulation.*
[b]*Prison and jails form one integrated system. Data include total jail and prison population.*
[c]*Population figures are based on custody counts.*
[d]*Population counts for inmates sentenced to "more than 1 year" include an undetermined number of inmates sentenced to "1 year or less."*

RATES OF PRISON INCARCERATION RISE

The incarceration rate of State and Federal prisoners sentenced to more than a year reached 420 per 100,000 U.S. residents on June 30, 1996. Texas had the highest rate of incarceration (659 sentenced prisoners per 100,000 State residents), followed by Louisiana (611 per 100,000), Oklahoma (580), and South Carolina (540). Three States—North Dakota (90), Minnesota (108), and Maine (112)—had rates that were less than a third of the national rate. The District of Columbia, a wholly urban jurisdiction, held 1,444 sentenced prisoners per 100,000 residents at midyear 1996.

Since 1990 the number of sentenced inmates per 100,000 residents has risen by more than 40%, increasing from 292 to 420. During this period prison incarceration rates rose the most in the South (from 316 to 487) and West (from 277 to 375). The rate in the Northeast rose from 232 to 306, and the rate in the Midwest from 239 to 318. The number of sentenced Federal prisoners per 100,000 U.S. residents increased from 20 to 33 over the same period.

FEMALE PRISONER POPULATION GREW AT FASTER PACE

During the 12 months ending June 30, 1996, the number of women under the jurisdiction of State and Federal prison authorities grew from 69,161 to 73,607, an increase of 6.4%. The number of men rose 5.2%, from 1,036,390 to 1,090,749. At midyear 1996 women accounted for 6.3% of all prisoners nationwide, up from 4.1% in 1980 and 5.7% in 1990.

Relative to the number of men and women in the U.S. resident population, the incarceration rate was more than 16 times higher for men than for women. On June 30, 1996, the rate for inmates serving a sentence of more than a year was 809 sentenced males per 100,000 U.S. male residents, compared to 50 females per 100,000 female residents.

AT MIDYEAR THE NATION'S JAILS SUPERVISED 591,469 OFFENDERS

On June 28, 1996, an estimated 591,469 offenders were held in or supervised by the Nation's local jails. Jail authorities supervised 12% of these offenders (72,977) in alternative programs outside the jail facilities. An estimated 518,492 offenders were housed in local jails.

As defined in this report, jails are locally-operated correctional facilities that confine persons before or after adjudication. Inmates sentenced to jail usually have a sentence of a year or less, but jails also incarcerate persons in a wide variety of other categories.

For the first time in 1995 the Annual Survey of Jails obtained counts of the number of offenders under community supervision. Respondents were asked if their jail jurisdiction operated any community-based programs and how many persons participated in them. Offenders under the supervision of a probation, parole, or other correctional agency were excluded from these counts. Because jail authorities reported offenders in treatment programs administered by the jail jurisdiction in 1996, it is difficult to compare totals with those in 1995.

Among persons under community supervision by jail staff in 1996, slightly less than half were required to perform community service (17,410) or to participate in an alternative work program (14,469). More than a fifth were in a weekend reporting program (16,336). An estimated 10,425 offenders under jail supervision were in a drug, alcohol, mental health, or other medical treatment program. Another 7,480 offenders were under home detention with electronic monitoring.

JAIL POPULATION GREW 2.3% DURING 12-MONTH PERIOD

Between July 1, 1995, and June 28, 1996, the number of persons held in local jail facilities grew 2.3%—from 507,044 to 518,492. The 12-month increase was much lower than the 4.2% increase in the previous 12-month period ending June 30, 1995, and about a third the annual average since 1985.

Since 1985 the Nation's jail population has nearly doubled on a per capita basis. During this period the number of jail inmates per 100,000 residents rose from 108 to 196. Including offenders under community supervision by jail authorities, the rate totaled 223 offenders per 100,000 U.S. residents at midyear 1996.

An estimated 8,100 persons under age 18 were housed in adult jails on June 28, 1996 (table 3). Over two-thirds of these young inmates had been convicted or were being held for trial as adults in criminal court.

The average daily population for the year ending June 30, 1996, was 515,432, an increase of 1.1% from 1995.

CHARACTERISTICS OF JAIL INMATES CHANGED LITTLE

Male inmates made up 89% of the local jail inmate population at midyear 1996, nearly 3 percentage points lower than at midyear 1985. On average, the female jail population has grown 10.2% annually since 1985, while the male inmate population has grown annually by 6.1%. On June 28, 1996, local jails held nearly 1 in every 207 adult men and 1 in 1,828 women.

At midyear 1996 a majority of local jail inmates were black or Hispanic. White non-Hispanics made up 41.6% of the jail population; black non-Hispanics, 41.1%; Hispanics, 15.6%; and other races (Asians, Pacific Islanders, American Indians, and Alaska Natives), 1.7%.

Relative to their number of U.S. residents, black non-Hispanics were 6 times more likely than white non-Hispanics, over twice as likely as Hispanics, and over 8 times more likely than persons of other races to have been held in a local jail on June 30, 1996.

TABLE 3
Average Daily Population and the Number of Men, Women, and Juveniles in Local Jails, Midyear 1985, 1990–96

	1985	1990	1991	1992	1993	1994	1995	1996
Average daily population[a]	265,010	408,075	422,609	441,889	466,155	479,757	509,828	515,432
Number of inmates, midyear[b]	256,615	405,320	426,479	444,584	459,804	486,474	507,044	518,492
Adults	254,986	403,019	424,129	441,780	455,500	479,800	499,300	510,400
Male	235,909	365,821	384,628	401,106	411,500	431,300	448,000	454,700
Female	19,077	37,198	39,501	40,674	44,100	48,500	51,300	55,700
Juveniles[c]	1,629	2,301	2,350	2,804	4,300	6,700	7,800	8,100
Held as adults[d]	—	—	—	—	3,300	5,100	5,900	5,700
Held as juveniles	1,629	2,301	2,350	2,804	1,000	1,600	1,800	2,400

Notes: Data are for June 30 in 1985 and 1992–95; for June 29, 1990; and for June 28, in 1991 and 1996.
Detailed data for 1993–96 were estimated and rounded to the nearest 100.
—Not available.
[a]The average daily population is the sum of the number of inmates in a jail each day for a year, divided by 365.
[b]Inmate counts for 1985 and 1990–93 include an unknown number of persons who were under jail supervision but not confined. Detailed counts for 1994–96 were estimated based on number of inmates held in jail facilities.
[c]Juveniles are persons defined by State statute as being under a certain age, usually 18, and subject initially to juvenile court authority even if tried as adults in criminal court. In 1994 the definition was changed to include all persons under age 18.
[d]Includes juveniles who were tried or awaiting trial as adults.

ABOUT HALF OF ALL ADULTS UNDER JAIL SUPERVISION WERE CONVICTED

On June 28, 1996, an estimated 48.8% of all adults under supervision by jail authorities had been convicted on their current charge. An estimated 284,200 of the 582,300 adults under jail supervision were serving a sentence in jail, awaiting sentencing, or serving a sentence in an alternative program outside a jail facility.

AT MIDYEAR 1996, 92% OF JAIL CAPACITY WAS OCCUPIED

At midyear 1996 the rated capacity of the Nation's local jails totaled an estimated 562,020, an increase of 16,257 in 12 months. Rated capacity is the maximum number of beds or inmates allocated by State or local rating officials to each jail facility. The growth in jail capacity during the 12-month period ending on June 30, 1996, was smaller than in any previous 12-month period since 1987.

As of June 30, 1996, 92% of the local jail capacity was occupied. As a ratio of all inmates housed in jail facilities to total capacity, the percentage occupied increased considerably after 1983, reaching a record 108% in 1989 and then falling to 92% in 1996. Since 1990 rated capacity has risen nearly 173,000 beds, while the number of inmates held in jail facilities has increased approximately 113,200.

The Jail

JOHN IRWIN

Social scientists, like the general public, have shown a great interest in the prison but have almost completely ignored the jail. Since John Howard's historic report on English jails, *The State of the Prisons in England and Wales* (1777), there have been perhaps a dozen other reports (most of which are listed in the bibliography), whereas there are hundreds of studies on the prison. The opposite focus is more appropriate for several reasons. First, many more people pass through the jail. The estimates range from 3 to 7 million a year in the United States, and this is at least thirty times the number handled by all state and federal prisons. Second, when persons are arrested, the most critical decisions about their future freedom are made while

Source: Excerpted from Irwin, John. *The Jail: Managing the Underclass in American Society*. Berkeley, CA: University of California Press, 1985.

they are either in jail or attached to it by a bail bond. These decisions, like the decision to arrest, are often highly discretionary and raise disturbing questions about the whole criminal justice system. Third, the experiences prisoners endure while passing through the jail often drastically influence their lives. Finally, the jail, not the prison, imposes the cruelest form of punishment in the United States.

In a legal sense, the jail is the point of entry into the criminal justice system. It is the place where arrested persons are booked and where they are held for their court appearances if they cannot arrange bail. It is also the city or county detention facility for persons serving misdemeanor sentences, which in most states cannot exceed one year. The prison, on the other hand, is a state or federal institution that holds persons serving felony sentences, which generally run to more than one year.

The public impression is that the jail holds a collection of dangerous criminals. But familiarity and close inspection reveal that the jail holds only a very few persons who fit the popular conception of a criminal—a predator who seriously threatens the lives and property of ordinary citizens. In fact, the great majority of the persons arrested and held in jail belong to a different social category. Some students of the jail have politely referred to them as the poor: "American jails operate primarily as catchall asylums for poor people."[1] Some have added other correlates of poverty: "With few exceptions, the prisoners are poor, undereducated, unemployed, and they belong to minority groups."[2] Some use more imaginative and sociologically suggestive labels, such as "social refuse" or "social junk."[3] Political radicals sometimes use "lumpen proletariat" and argue over whether its members are capable of participating in the class struggle.[4] Some citizens refer to persons in this category as "street people," implying an excessive and improper public presence. Others apply such labels as "riffraff," "social trash," or "dregs," which suggest lack of social worth and moral depravity. And many police officers, deputies, and other persons who are familiar with the jail population use more crudely derogatory labels, such as "assholes" and "dirt balls."

In my own research, I found that beyond poverty and its correlates—undereducation, unemployment, and minority status—jail prisoners share two essential characteristics: detachment and disrepute. They are detached because they are not well integrated into conventional society, they are not members of conventional social organizations, they have few ties to conventional social networks, and they are carriers of unconventional values and beliefs. They are disreputable because they are perceived as irksome, offensive, threatening, capable of arousal, even protorevolutionary. I shall refer to them as the *rabble*, meaning the "disorganized" and "disorderly," the "lowest class of people."[5]

I found that it is these two features—detachment and disrepute—that lead the police to watch and arrest the rabble so frequently, regardless of whether or not they are engaged in crime, or at least in serious crime. (Most of the rabble commit petty crimes, such as drinking on the street, and are usually vulnerable to arrest.)

These findings suggest that the basic purpose of the jail differs radically from the purpose ascribed to it by government officials and academicians. It is this: the jail was invented, and continues to be operated, in order to manage society's rabble. Society's impulse to manage the rabble has many sources, but the subjectively perceived "offensiveness" of the rabble is at least as important as any real threat it poses to society.

By arguing that arrest procedures and the jail are used mainly to manage the rabble, I do not mean to imply that crime is not an issue. Rather, I would like to emphasize that the culpability of those persons had what Egon Bittner has called "restricted relevance."[6] That is, they violated standards that are enforced with a great deal of discretion by the police and mainly in order to manage the rabble rather than to enforce the law.

Some of the more serious crimes, such as robbery and assault by one disreputable on another, usually come to the attention of the police because of the social setting and the status of the disreputables. Disreputables commit their crimes in a much more obvious fashion than reputable people, and the police, in performing their rabble management function, are keeping their eye on them and expecting them to commit crimes. Police do overlook a lot of criminal conduct by disreputables. However, disreputables commit an enormous amount of petty crime out in the open, and the police see a great deal of it.

Likewise, when disreputables are arrested for violating the private property rights of respectable citizens, it is because the police are at least as interested in managing the rabble as in enforcing the law. It is not simply the fact of theft that provokes arrest; it is who commits the theft and what type of theft it is. Our society—like its predecessors, chiefly England— has been quicker to criminalize covetous property accumulation by the rabble than by other classes. The police are always on the lookout for purse-snatching, theft from cars, and shoplifting, but they almost never patrol used-car lots or automobile repair shops to catch salesmen or repairmen breaking the law, and they never raid corporate board rooms to catch executives fixing prices. The difference between these crimes is not seriousness or prevalence; it is offensiveness, which is determined by social status and context.

The interviews and follow-up of the random samples of arrestees indicate that the persons who fill the jails in the big cities are largely members of the rabble class, that is, persons who are poorly integrated into the society and who are also seen as disreputable.

To understand fully the jail's purposes, we must keep in mind that it is intended to hold the rabble, not other persons. Reputable people commit crimes and occasionally are arrested; but it has never been social policy to keep them in jail while they await trial. Other provisions have always been made for them. As we have seen, when the jail first came into use in England, bail to assure a court appearance was used more often than jail. Today, in addition to setting bail, most jurisdictions systematically release many persons on their own recognizance (OR), and the decision to do so is directly related to reputability.* Recently, many cities have introduced "citation" programs in which police officers may treat some misdemeanor offenses as if they were traffic violations; they may simply issue a citation that requires the offender to pay a fine or appear in court. The decision to cite is usually discretionary, and like all discretionary judicial decisions, it is related to repute. Consequently, when reputable people are arrested, they are almost always cited, bailed out, or released on their own recognizance. The only significant exception is when they are arrested for drunk driving, for which most state laws require a short period of detention for sobering up.

All persons who build and manage jails assume that the jail is almost exclusively for the rabble. Certain significant physical characteristics and management processes of jails reflect the fact that they are intended to hold only the rabble. First, because many of the rabble are not trusted to appear at their court hearings or even to stay in jail, security has been the fundamental concern in the construction of jails. In the United States this concern almost invariably results in massive buildings, complicated locking systems, and elaborate surveillance techniques, which because the rabble are not expected to behave themselves in jail, they must be controlled. This is partly a concern for the safety of deputies, citizens, and prisoners; it is believed that some prisoners may harm others or destroy property. The concern for control, however, stretches far beyond protecting life and property. It extends to enforcing behavioral conformity for managerial convenience, and even beyond that.

The concern for control is also expressed in extensive measures to prevent immoral behavior by prisoners, such as drinking, gambling, taking drugs, and engaging in sex. Moreover, when officials plan jails, they go to great lengths to keep prisoners out of sight. For the last two centuries our society has been removing most problem populations (such as convicts and the insane) to remote asylums.[7] The jail, however, because of its relationship to the court, must be in or near the center of the city.* Therefore, prisoners are hidden deep within a massive building. In the last several decades, jail planners have successfully hidden even the jail itself, by placing it out of public view at the top of a building and disguising its special features (such as barred windows).

---

*In programs patterned after the original Vera Institute experiment, as most OR programs are, recommendations are made on the basis of ties to the community. Having continuously lived and worked in the city for a certain length of time and having local residents vouch for one earn a person a recommendation to be released on OR. See Daniel J. Freed and Patricia M. Wald, *Bail in the United States.*

*For sentenced prisoners, as opposed to pretrial detainees, many counties maintain additional facilities, often farms or camps. San Francisco, Los Angeles, and Yolo counties all maintain additional facilities outside the city.

Finally, officials and jail administrators have always assumed that the prisoners in jail are culpable and generally deserving of punishment. This has been true since jails first appeared in England.

The purpose of punishment not only manifests itself in the structure of the jail, which has less space and fewer physical resources and material amenities than other "total institutions," such as prisons and mental hospitals. It is also expressed in the general management style of the jailers, which is one of malign neglect. The jail's policies and informal custodial practices, and much of the interaction between jailers and the jailed, contain a thinly disguised element of intentional meanness. This is so because most persons who determine jail policy or manage the jail, as well as the general public, believe that jail prisoners are disreputables who deserve to be treated with malign neglect.

UNINTENDED CONSEQUENCES

One of the consequences of these structural features and processes is that a jail prisoner generally experiences more punishment per day than a convict in a state prison.* Furthermore, this punishment is intended.[8] But several processes that are unintended and socially undesirable also occur. Going to jail and being held there tends to maintain people in a rabble status or convert them to it. To maintain membership in conventional society and thereby avoid a rabble status, a person must sustain a conscious commitment to a conventional set of social arrangements. When persons are arrested and jailed, their ties and arrangements with people outside very often disintegrate. In addition, they are profoundly disoriented and subjected to a series of degrading experiences that corrode their general commitment to society. Finally, they are prepared for rabble life by their experiences in jail, which supply them with the identity and culture required to get by as a disreputable. These processes—disintegration, disorientation, degradation, and preparation—will be examined.

When persons are arrested and jailed, they suffer more than the obvious forms of discomfort and deprivation: sudden interruption of their affairs; instant and total loss of mobility; abrupt initiation into the jail; a subsequent restriction of activities to a very small area; virtual absence of all opportunities for recreation and expression; unavoidable and constant close contact with strangers, many of whom are threatening or repulsive; and a reduced

---

*This is generally acknowledged by persons who have experienced both forms of incarceration. For example, when I accompanied prisoners being transferred from the county jail to a state prison, we experienced initial elation over our drastically improved situation. Recently a friend told me that his brother had been sent to a state prison but did not want to enter an appeal because it might cause him to be returned to the county jail, which he would do anything to avoid.

health regimen that can lead to physical deterioration and occasionally to serious illness. These discomforts and deprivations are generally well recognized, tolerated, and often intended by jail administrators, other criminal justice decision makers, and most of the public. Officials and the public want prisoners to suffer and to be controlled. But prisoners are more than inconvenienced and deprived. They are extricated and held away from outside social positions and relationships. When these weaken or disappear, future participation and membership in society becomes difficult. I shall refer to these changes as "disintegration."

PICKING UP THE PIECES

Some prisoners are released immediately after going to a court hearing if the charges against them are dismissed—and they may hope for or expect such a release.[9] But the majority are released with no advance warning and abruptly thrown back into the outside society. They walk out of the jail into the city at all hours. There is no one to meet them. Most of them have no money, or very little. Their personal belongings, which were taken from them at the time of arrest, have been stored in a "property room." If they are released during the day when the room is open, they may retrieve their property immediately. Otherwise they must come back for it during the prescribed hours.

Unlike released convicts and mental patients, they have received no official preparation for their release.[10] And when they do get out, city, county, and private agencies rarely offer them any help in coping with the problems of reentering society.[11] In trying to pick up the pieces of their shattered lives, most of them will be working alone, with virtually no resources and many handicaps.

RABBLE, CRIME, AND THE JAIL

Over the years, scholars and critics have made many recommendations for diminishing the worst effects of the jail. They have suggested that a high percentage of the jail's intake population could be eliminated through decriminalization.

Critics have suggested that many more persons who are arrested could be "diverted" before trial. It has been suggested that by expanding programs for release on one's own recognizance, all but a very few of those not diverted could be released before trial, and it has even been suggested that money bail could be abolished.

Some critics have argued that pretrial detainees should be given speedy trials or should be held for trial under very different circumstances: "Persons detained awaiting trial should be entitled to the same rights as those persons admitted to bail or other form of pretrial release except where the nature of confinement requires modification."[12]

Finally, critics have suggested that most defendants who are convicted should not be subjected to the cruel and pernicious practices of our current jails but should be placed in programs designed to improve their life chances after release: "Ideally, jails as we have known them should be eliminated. They should be replaced by a network of newly designed, differently conceived [metropolitan and rural] detention centers."[13]

We cannot be certain that these recommendations would solve all the jail's problems or that they would not produce new ones we cannot foresee.* From a practical point of view, however, this lack of certainty seems almost irrelevant. Reform proposals like these have been made many times during the last twenty years, and yet with few exceptions (usually in small, rural jurisdictions) they have not been implemented, and jails have remained the same or become worse.[14] The reason for this is simple: the public and most criminal justice functionaries do not want to see the rabble treated any differently from the way they are now.

The public does not want the rabble confined in a hotel; it wants them to suffer in a jail. In our society, the jail will not change until we significantly reduce the size of the rabble class or significantly change our attitudes toward it. Unfortunately, the existence of both a rabble class and public hostility toward it seems to be firmly rooted in our society.

CONCLUSIONS

Reform of our jails requires either that we drastically reduce the size of the rabble class, a highly remote possibility, or that we abandon our self-serving fictions about crime and deviance. I believe that instead of arguing over which particular reform proposals might work, we should concentrate our efforts on the second task, that is, on developing and disseminating a more honest perspective on the nature and causes of crime and deviance and on the limits and consequences of various control policies.

Progress on this agenda, if it occurs at all, will necessarily be slow. Reforming sluggish processes and static structures, particularly in the economic realm, is the work of decades, generations, even centuries. But that should

---

*All these recommendations sidestep a central problem in criminal justice—the misuse of discretionary power. When some, but not all, persons are diverted, released on their own recognizance, or sentenced to "alternatives," the decisions are bound to be influenced by whim and prejudice. This problem was examined at length by the American Friends Service Committee, which produced *Struggle for Justice* (1971), a key document in the literature of modern criminal justice. As one who worked on the report, I am convinced that the misuse of discretionary power is a fundamental issue in jail reform. But to delve into its complexities here would divert attention from what I consider the primary obstacle to reform—the public and government posture toward the rabble.

not deter us, because no progress at all can be made on reforming the jail until we begin to reform our fundamental social arrangements. Until we do, the police will continue to sweep the streets of the rabble and dump them in the jails. By casting a broad net, they will snare a few disreputable persons whose crimes are serious, and these few will be punished severely. Crime rates will not be affected by these efforts; they will continue to rise and fall as they always have in response to changes in broader social arrangements. And the rabble will continue to suffer our harshest form of imprisonment, the jail—an experience that confirms their status and replenishes their ranks.

NOTES

1. Ronald Goldfarb, *Jails: The Ultimate Ghetto of the Criminal Justice System*, p. 29.

2. Edith Flynn, "Jails and Criminal Justice," in *Prisoners in America*, ed. Lloyd E. Ohlin, p. 57.

3. See Andrew Scull, *Decarceration*, p. 153.

4. See esp. Morton G. Wenger and Thomas A. Bonomo, "Crime, the Crisis of Capitalism, and Social Revolution," in *Crime and Capitalism*, ed. David Greenberg, pp. 420–34.

5. *Webster's Third New International Dictionary* (Springfield, MA: G. & C.).

6. Bittner makes this distinction in a convincing fashion in "Police on Skid-Row."

7. See David Rothman, *The Discovery of the Asylum*.

8. Ralph B. Pugh, *Imprisonment in Medieval England*, p. 3.

9. Malcolm Feeley has recently argued that the punishment that is intentionally delivered to most persons processed by the criminal justice system is not the sentence that is imposed after conviction but the process of being held in jail before trial and having to make court appearances; see *The Process Is the Punishment*.

10. Most of the prisoners in our misdemeanor sample had their charges dismissed or were cited and released before going to court. In our felony sample, 20 percent of the prisoners had their charges dismissed before going to court, 37 percent were released on bail or OR in the first few days, and 12 percent had their charges dismissed at the first hearing.

11. Preparing for release is a major activity in prisons and mental hospitals; see Irwin, *The Felon*, ch. 4.

12. In San Francisco I heard of a few prisoners who had managed to contact persons in prisoner services or in the Northern California Service League (NCSL), a private agency. Prisoner services occasionally help a prisoner who is approaching his release day to communicate with a San Francisco County social services department where he may receive "general assistance," and NCSL supplies some clothes to released prisoners. However, only a small minority receive even these scanty aids.

13. National Advisory Commission on Criminal Justice Standards and Goals, *Report on Corrections*, p. 133.

14. Besides the proposals by Mattick, Flynn, and Goldfarb quoted above, and others like them, sets of standards have been developed by many individuals and government bodies, notably Myrl E. Alexander, in *Jail Administration*, and the National Advisory Commission on Criminal Justice Standards and Goals, *Report on Corrections*. The most recent and perhaps the most complete set of standards is contained in *The Little Red Jail Book*, prepared for the American Friends Service Committee by its Criminal Justice Committee in 1983. In the 1970s intense interest in jail reform led to the establishment in Boulder, Colorado, of the Jail Center, a branch of the National Institute of Corrections, which has attempted to improve American jails through a variety of research and training programs. For examples of two successfully implemented reforms, see the descriptions of the Benton County jail in Oregon and the Hampton County jail in Massachusetts, in Mark Pogrebin, *Managing Scarce Resources for Jails: Information Package*. This report was produced by a grant processed through the Jail Center.

BIBLIOGRAPHY

Alexander, M. E. 1957. *Jail Administration*. Springfield, IL: C. Thomas.

American Friends Service Committee. 1971. *Struggle for Justice*. New York: Hill & Wang.

———. 1983. *The Little Red Jail Book*. San Francisco: Criminal Justice Committee, Northern California Regional Office.

Bittner, E. 1967. "The Police on Skid-Row: A Study of Peace Keeping." *American Sociological Review* 32 (October): 699–715.

Feeley, M. 1979. *The Process Is the Punishment*. New York: Russell Sage.

Flynn, E. 1973. "Jails and Criminal Justice." Pp. 49–85 in *Prisoners in America*, ed. L. E. Ohlin. Englewood Cliffs, NJ: Prentice-Hall.

Freed, D. J., and P. M. Wald. 1964. *Bail in the United States*. Washington, D.C.: U.S. Department of Justice; New York: Vera Foundation.

Goldfarb, R. 1975. *Jails: The Ultimate Ghetto of the Criminal Justice System*. New York: Doubleday.

Howard, J. 1780. *The State of the Prisons in England and Wales*. 2d ed. London: Cadell and Conant.

Irwin, J. 1970. *The Felon*. Englewood Cliffs, NJ: Prentice-Hall.

Mattick, H. 1974. "The Contemporary Jails of the United States: An Unknown and Neglected Area of Justice." Pp. 777–848 in *Handbook of Criminology*, ed. D. Glaser. Chicago: Rand-McNally.

National Advisory Commission on Criminal Justice Standards and Goals. 1973. *Report on Corrections*. Washington, DC.

Pogrebin, M. 1981. *Managing Scarce Resources for Jails: Information Package*. Unpublished report to the National Institute of Corrections, Washington, DC.

Pugh, R. B. 1968. *Imprisonment in Medieval England.* Cambridge, England: Cambridge University Press.

Rothman, D. 1971. *The Discovery of the Asylum.* Boston: Little, Brown.

Scull, A. 1977. *Decarceration.* Englewood Cliffs, NJ: Prentice-Hall.

Wenger, M. G., and T. A. Bonomo. 1981. "Crime, the Crisis of Capitalism, and Social Revolution." Pp. 420–34 in *Crime and Capitalism,* ed. D. Greenberg. Palo Alto, CA: Mayfield.

Who Is in Jail? An Examination of the Rabble Hypothesis

JOHN A. BACKSTRAND
DON C. GIBBONS
JOSEPH F. JONES

John Irwin's *The Jail* contends that jails are filled with petty offenders or persons who have committed no crime at all but who are socially offensive members of "the rabble." However, the research reported here indicates that a large number of persons charged with seemingly serious crimes were incarcerated in two Pacific Northwest jail systems. Although more research is in order, this article suggests that Irwin's thesis may well be overstated.

Curiously, in light of the importance of jails and lockups in the justice machinery, these places have received relatively little attention, particularly by criminologists. Houston, Gibbons, and Jones (1988) have sorted the relatively meager literature on jails into four general groupings, the first consisting of essays focusing on the deplorable physical and social features that have been characteristic of American jails. On this point, Mattick and Aikman (1969) have identified jails as "the cloacal region" of American corrections, that is, they have likened these places to sewers into which the social waste products of society are deposited.

The second group of materials on jails noted by Houston, Gibbons, and Jones (1988) consists of discussions of problems of jail management, and the third centers on commentaries about the legal rights, or lack thereof, of persons detained in jails. Finally, Houston et al. (1988) drew attention to a group of research studies having to do with the impact, if any, of variations in physical design features of jails on the inmates and/or staff members in these places. Houston, Gibbons, and Jones (1988) reported on a study of this latter kind, carried out in jail systems in three western states.

Source: Excerpted from Backstrand, John A., Gibbons, Don C., and Jones, Joseph F. "Who Is in Jail? An Examination of the Rabble Hypothesis." *Crime & Delinquency* 38(2): 219–229, April 1992.

A number of important and revealing sociological studies of American prisons have been conducted, particularly in the 1960s (for a review of these investigations, see Gibbons, 1992:501–20). However, parallel inquiries into the social role of jails, the internal social structure of these places, and kindred questions, have been rare indeed. For this reason alone, John Irwin's (1985) *The Jail* is an important work, for it is one of the relatively few contributions by sociologists to the understanding of the nature and functioning of jails in American society. At the same time, although it may be too extreme to argue that Irwin's thesis has the ring of implausibility, his argument strikes us as less than entirely convincing. The research reported in this article was designed to collect evidence bearing on the accuracy of Irwin's contentions.[1] But first, let us set out the broad outlines of his argument and the research procedures he employed.

MANAGING THE RABBLE

The thrust of Irwin's discussion can be stated in a few words. He contends that the majority of persons who end up in jails are drawn from that part of the population that some have termed the "underclass," and that others have been referred to by such terms as the alienated, detached, discredited, or marginal members of society. Irwin refers to this part of the population as "the rabble." An even more important claim is that the majority of the rabble residents of the jails are in those places, not because they have committed serious crimes, but because they are defined as offensive persons by the police and/or other members of the community. Like much criminological writing, Irwin's exposition is less than a model of clarity in that it contains some seemingly contradictory assertions.

It seems fair to say that Irwin's more radical assertions about jails that have been favorably received by others are at the heart of his book. What are these dramatic claims about jails? Consider the following examples from his book:

> My critical discovery was that instead of "criminals," the jail receives and confines mostly detached and disreputable persons who are arrested more because they are offensive than because they have committed crimes (p. xiii).

> The vast majority of the persons who are arrested, booked, and held in jail are not charged with serious crimes. They are charged with petty ones or with behavior that is no crime at all … the primary purpose is to receive and hold persons because they are "offensive" (p. 18).

How did Irwin arrive at these conclusions about jails and the persons who populate them? For the most part, they were derived from his research in San Francisco County. More specifically, he and a research assistant interviewed 100 newly booked felony arrestees who had been randomly selected over a 1-year period from the San Francisco City and County jails and also examined the jail and booking records on these 100 felony cases. They also scrutinized the booking records of 100 randomly selected, newly booked misdemeanor arrestees (these persons were not interviewed because they had been released within a few hours of arrest).

The seriousness of the alleged offenses of the 100 persons arrested for felonies was determined through judgments made by a collection of students in a university criminology class who were presented with accounts of the alleged crimes and who were asked to place them within the crime seriousness scale developed in the National Crime Survey (Bureau of Justice Statistics, 1984). It was on this basis that Irwin concluded that 75% of the persons arrested for felonies had been apprehended for petty offenses. The misdemeanor cases were not sorted into seriousness categories in that, by definition, these arrests were for relatively petty crimes.

Turning to offensiveness, Irwin (p. 23) suggests that "offensiveness is a definition that conventional witnesses or their agents (the police) impose upon events; it is a summation of the meanings they attach to the acts, the context, and above all, the character of the actors." The offensiveness of the acts of the 100 sample members arrested for felonies was apparently determined through "eye-balling" the interview data, resulting in 61 cases being identified as mild, 28 as moderate, and 10 as high on an offensiveness ranking (one person was judged not to have been offensive).

These data on offense seriousness and offensiveness are the major bases for Irwin's (p. 40) conclusion that "offensiveness, as much or more than crime seriousness, was what led to being arrested, held in jail until disposition, and then perhaps being sentenced to jail."

Perhaps Irwin's conclusion is correct, but there are a number of problems with his data that make them less than convincing. For one, the claim that offensiveness is a major determinant of getting arrested seems shaky in light of Irwin's report that nearly two-thirds of his felony sample were judged to be *mild* on offensiveness! Also, the seriousness judgments made by student "judges" are somewhat suspect, for criminology students might be expected to respond less negatively to the criminal acts in question than might a different set of citizens.

There is a third problem with Irwin's methodology as well, which is that findings drawn from samples of new bookings may not be representative of jail populations as a whole. . . . A sampling of jail bookings would most likely turn up a relatively large number of fairly petty offenders, whereas an examination of those held for longer pretrial periods or of sentenced prisoners would most probably reveal a larger proportion of more serious offenders.

This sampling issue would be relatively unimportant if sentence-servers were relatively uncommon in jails. However, the 1989 national jail survey indicated that of 393,000 persons in jail, 189,000 of them were convicted timeservers (Flanagan and Maguire, 1990:574). On this same point, Klofas (1990:78) has presented data from a 1983 national sample of jail inmates that suggest that a considerable number of persons who are in jail have been charged with or have been convicted of serious offenses. Accordingly, Irwin's contentions drawn solely from new bookings may understate the extent to which jails serve as places of confinement for relatively serious offenders. It is to this issue of the seriousness of jail prisoners that the research reported in this article was directed.

RESEARCH DESIGN

This study involved two working hypotheses. First, we hypothesized that larger numbers of both booked suspects and convicted time-servers who have been involved in relatively serious offenses are in jail than Irwin indicated, and second, relatively larger percentages of offenders charged with or convicted of serious offenses would be found in urban rather than rural jails. These working hypotheses were evaluated using data from two Pacific Northwest county jail systems, that of Multnomah County (Portland) in Oregon and Skamania County, Washington, located about 50 miles northeast of Portland. The Multnomah County jail system consists of five units: a modern high rise detention center located in Portland; a second, smaller jail; a correctional center for convicted offenders located outside of the city; a smaller treatment facility within Portland; and the Court House Jail. By contrast, the Skamania County Jail, located in Stevenson, Washington, is a relatively small one in a relatively rural area.

Jail population data for these six jail units were collected from the booking and jail population records of the two county systems. More specifically, information was gathered on all of the bookings into the Multnomah County jails of two randomly selected days in 1991 and all of the bookings in Skamania County during a 1-week period (in order to obtain a sufficient number of bookings for examination). Additionally, a one-day count of the entire jail population of the six jails on a randomly selected day was compiled from jail records. In this way, we were able to answer questions about the entire population of the jails as well as about newly booked persons.

Although it would have been desirable to have obtained "rap sheet" or arrest history data on all of the persons who were included in this study, these data were not available. Instead, we restricted our attention to the current charges for which persons had been arrested and/or incarcerated. In addition, information was obtained on the number of individuals with multiple charges, offense information for both males and females, the age and racial distributions of prisoners within the two systems, dispositions of booked persons, and time spent in detention.

As we have indicated, Irwin employed student judges to gauge the seriousness of the offenses that arrestees had allegedly committed. By contrast, we used the criminal codes of the two states for assessing offense seriousness. All crimes, including felonies, misdemeanors, and "violations" are classified in the Oregon Revised Statutes and the Revised Code of Washington in terms of the seriousness of the criminal act. Sixteen seriousness categories are involved in the criminal statutes of these two states, ranging from Class A felonies that carry maximum penalties of life imprisonment to the category of "no charge." The top 5 categories of this seriousness scale have to do with felonies, an additional 4 categories consist of misdemeanors of different grades of severity, and the remaining 7 groupings involve infractions or other minor illegal acts. These 16 categories were employed as a statutory seriousness scale.

Although no system of measuring offense seriousness is perfect, the strength of this statute-based scale is that it was drawn from the criminal codes of the two states. Although individual citizens might cavil with some of the ratings given to specific offenses, it is a scale agreed on by lawmakers and that is consistently applied to offenses. Moreover, it would be difficult to argue that seriousness judgments embodied in criminal codes are irrational or markedly out of sorts with public sentiments. These two sets of statutes are the result of lengthy efforts by state legislatures to review the penalty structure of the laws so as to insure that punishments are in tune with public views of crime severity.

FINDINGS

During the 2-day study period, there were 154 newly booked persons who entered the Multnomah County jail system, and during the 1-week period in Skamania County, 13 persons were booked, thus a total of 167 newly booked persons formed the new bookings sample. In addition, the total one-day count of persons who were in jail (additional to the newly booked persons who were still incarcerated at the time of the one-day count) was 1,139 persons.

There is a wide variety of specific circumstances and acts that result in persons being placed in jail. The data on primary charges lodged against individuals indicated that the 167 newly booked persons had been charged with 91 separate offenses (when individuals had been charged with multiple offenses, the statutorily most serious one was counted as the primary charge). The 1,306 persons included in this research had been charged with 153 different primary offenses, although many of these 153 separate charges are permutations of the same general crime, such as Robbery I and Attempted Robbery I or Promoting Prostitution and Compelling Prostitution.

OFFENSE SERIOUSNESS

However, the variability among jail prisoners in terms of offenses is not the issue here, rather, our concern is with the nature of these activities in terms of seriousness. Tables 1 and 2 shed light on that question. Table 1 indicates the number of booked persons whose primary charge fell into one or another general offense category, and Table 2 presents similar information on the persons who were in jail at the time of the one-day count.

An examination of the data in Tables 1 and 2 casts a good deal of doubt on Irwin's claims, particularly those which extend his findings from San Francisco to jails throughout the country.

Table 1 indicates that in this study, 46.7% of the newly booked persons in the jails were charged with felonies of one level or another of seriousness, and an additional 44.3% of the bookings were on charges of Class A misdemeanors, that is, the most serious category of such charges. In short, over 90% of the bookings were for charges of a seemingly serious nature. Even if one concedes that some of these charges are likely to be reduced at subsequent states of justice system processing, and even that some of the booked individuals may have been guilty of no offense whatever, it still seems

TABLE 1
Distribution of Newly Booked Persons, by Offense Seriousness

	Number	**Percentage**
Class A felony	11	6.6
Class B felony	11	6.6
Class C felony	48	28.7
Unspecified or unclassified felony	8	4.8
Class A misdemeanor	74	44.3
Class B misdemeanor	1	0.6
Class C misdemeanor	1	0.6
Unspecified misdemeanor	11	6.6
Other	2	1.2
Total	167	100.0

TABLE 2
Distribution of Jail Population, by Offense Seriousness

	Number	**Percentage**
Class A felony	262	23.0
Class B felony	199	17.5
Class C felony	381	33.5
Unspecified or unclassified felony	97	8.5
Class A misdemeanor	136	12.0
Class B misdemeanor	2	0.2
Class C misdemeanor	4	0.4
Unspecified misdemeanor	56	4.9
No charge	2	0.2
Total	1,139	100.0

difficult to conclude that these data principally describe a collection of offensive but relatively petty offenders.

One other indicator of the seriousness of the charges leveled against booked persons is that, of the 167 cases, 69.5% were placed in custody awaiting arraignment and further justice system processing, whereas only 22.8% were released on their own recognizance.

The data in Table 2 are even more damaging to Irwin's thesis, in that 82.5% of the persons who appeared in the one-day jail counts were either charged with or convicted of felony offenses. These data do not appear to support Irwin's claims about detached and disreputable persons whose real problem is offensiveness, not serious criminality.

Recall that one of our working hypotheses suggests that rural jails might differ somewhat from urban ones in terms of the kinds of persons held in them. Of the 13 Skamania County bookings included in the total of 167 bookings, 85% of them were on misdemeanor charges. Additionally, the one-day count information on prisoners in Skamania County, as well as conversations with jailers in that county, indicated that most jail prisoners in that county were in custody for game law violations, domestic violence charges, offenses having to do with drunkenness and public order disruption, and motor vehicle offenses. In short, these data paralleled those collected by Gibbons (1972) in two hinterland or rural jail systems in Oregon, which pointed to a large number of relatively petty "folk criminals" residing in rural jails.

We also noted earlier that the Multnomah County jail system involves five separate facilities, with the largest being the downtown detention center that is the initial destination for all newly arrested persons. In all five facilities, over two-thirds of the persons in them had been charged with felonies, but not surprisingly, the proportion of persons with felony charges was somewhat lower in the detention center.

CONCLUSIONS

We began by arguing that John Irvin's claim that American jails are filled with members of the rabble class who have been put there, not because of serious crimes they have committed but for being socially offensive, is overdrawn. This contention was based in considerable part on what we saw as flaws in Irwin's research and the fact that much of his data was relatively "soft." By contrast, our "harder" data suggest that offense seriousness, rather than offensiveness, is a major determinant of being booked into jail, and in particular, of being incarcerated there as a serious offender.

However, it would be well to acknowledge that although the data in our study were superior in some ways to those collected by Irwin, they are at the same time less than ideal. Put another way, a large-scale, complex, and costly study would be required in order to adequately probe Irwin's argument about the social functions of jails. Let us acknowledge some limitations of our research.

For one thing, our claim that fairly large numbers of persons are incarcerated in jails for serious offenses would be considerably strengthened if interview data had been collected from prisoners and had the accounts of those persons been consistent with the legal charges placed against them. Also, it would have been desirable to have had data on the actions taken against persons subsequent to their being booked. Conceivably, many of the persons who were in jail may have later had their cases disposed of through pleading guilty to lesser charges, and in some cases, the charges against them may have been dismissed. Then, too, our study casts no light on the extent of discriminatory law enforcement, in which members of the rabble are harassed on the street or sometimes arrested and taken into custody although they have not committed crimes. In short, although our data are "harder" than those of Irwin, they do not close the case on this argument between Irwin and ourselves.

We suspect that although our conclusions about offense severity as a major determinant of who gets jailed are essentially correct, Irwin's claim that members of the rabble *sometimes* get jailed even though they have not committed serious crimes is also correct. We probably need to spell out hypotheses about the kinds of rabble who are most likely to be dealt with by the police and the circumstances in which police intervention is most likely. We also need to deal with the kinds and extent of more serious forms of lawbreaking that exist in the community and that are likely to provoke an official response from the justice system, including arrest, booking, and incarceration in a jail. Further, research is needed to allow a separation of the "offensiveness" of the offender from the "offensiveness" of the law-violating behavior if the contentions of Irwin regarding the management of the rabble are to be more fully evaluated. Research scrutiny of a complex argument of this kind would probably require a variety of methodological procedures, both "hard" and "soft."

We come now to one final point. Although we have argued that Irwin may have overstated his case, claiming that jailed persons are less involved in serious criminality than is the case, we agree with him regarding the broader issues of public policy toward members of the rabble class who get caught up in lawbreaking, and in many cases, who get sent to jails. We find nothing in our data that argues for expanded use of jails in American society. We agree with Irwin (1985:101–18) that we ought to pursue policies of decriminalization, diversion, expansion of pretrial release, speedy trials, humane incarceration for pretrial detainees, sentencing alternatives, and a humane system of incarceration for persons serving jail sentences.

NOTES

1. A more detailed critique of Irwin's book, a fuller discussion of previous research on jails, and additional information on the research reported in this article can be found in Backstrand (1991).

2. Irwin identified as petty cases, those that received a score of 4.9 or lower on the National Crime Survey scale, whereas 21 cases that received scores of 5.0 to 9.9 were identified as medium cases. Only 4 cases received seriousness scores of 10 or higher and were designated by Irwin as serious cases. However, it ought to be noted that of the 204 crimes that were ranked in the National Crime Survey, only 35 received scores of 10 or higher, and 169 received scores of 9.9 or less. A number of the offenses in the 5–9.9 range appear to be matters that many citizens might regard as fairly serious, even though they do not rank as highly as relatively rare events such as bombing of a public building and killing 20 people, which was regarded as the most serious offense in the national survey. Also, a public official taking $1,000 of public money for his or her own use received a score of 9.4 in the national survey, and a person committing an illegal abortion received a score of 8.6. Again, these are acts that many citizens quite probably would regard as relatively serious crimes.

REFERENCES

Backstrand, J. A. 1991. "Who's in Jail? An Examination of Irwin's Rabble Hypothesis." Doctoral dissertation, Portland State University.

Bureau of Justice Statistics. 1984. *Bulletin: The Severity of Crime.* Washington, DC: U.S. Department of Justice.

Flanagan, T. J., and K. Maguire, eds. 1990. *Sourcebook of Criminal Justice Statistics, 1989.* Washington, DC: U.S. Department of Justice.

Gibbons, D. C. 1972. "Crime in the Hinterland." *Criminology* 10:177–90.

———. 1992. *Society, Crime, and Criminal Behavior,* 6th ed. Englewood Cliffs, NJ: Prentice-Hall.

Houston, J. G., D. C. Gibbons, and J. F. Jones. 1988. "Physical Environment and Jail Social Climate." *Crime & Delinquency* 34:449–66.

Irwin, J. 1985. *The Jail.* Berkeley: University of California Press.

Klofas, J. 1990. "The Jail and Community." *Justice Quarterly* 7:69–102.

Mattick, H. W., and A. Aikman. 1969. "The Cloacal Region of American Corrections." *Annals of the American Academy of Political and Social Science* 381:109–18.

The Jail and the Community

JOHN M. KLOFAS

Two themes pervade the literature on local jails. The first is their importance; paradoxically, the second is their neglect by social scientists. The case

Source: Excerpted from Klofas, John. "The Jail and the Community." *Justice Quarterly* 7 (1):70–102, 1990.

for the social significance of these institutions is convincing. With over 16 million admissions and releases each year, the jail touches more people's lives than does any other form of correctional service. Likewise, the important roles of these institutions are revealed in the heterogeneity of their populations. Jail inmates may be serious repeat offenders, novices in crime, or even naive traffic violators. They may ultimately be found guilty or they may be completely innocent. The jail holds inmates who are awaiting trial, undergoing criminal processing, and serving sentences. Viewed in another way, the jail serves a complex population of criminally as well as civilly committed inmates. From still another viewpoint, the jail houses inmates with a myriad of personal and social difficulties: mental health problems, alcoholism, homelessness, and even an offensiveness that may be so generic as to merit the label of "rabble" for the offender.

Jails are not only socially significant but also important to the lives of the people who pass through them. As Irwin points out, the most critical decisions about inmates' future freedom are made while they are in jail. Furthermore, the experiences that inmates endure while passing through the jail often influence their lives drastically. Finally, "the jail, and not the prison, imposes the cruelest form of punishment in the United States" (Irwin, 1985:xi).

Although most jail researchers have considered differences between prisons and jails, two bodies of work stand out for the consistency with which they have examined these differences: the sociological analyses of John Irwin and the social psychological analyses of John J. Gibbs. Although they take very different approaches, each scholar portrays the jail as an institution that has little in common with the prison and that is tied intimately to its local community. Both authors suggest that focusing on the functions of the jail in the community is valuable in offering some notion of a general context or lay of the land from which to interpret existing studies and to develop hypotheses for additional research.

John Irwin's (1985) book *The Jail: Managing the Underclass in American Society* provides the most comprehensive available analysis of the role of the jail in the community and of the resulting social structure within the jail. Irwin's study of the San Francisco city and county jails included interviews with newly admitted inmates. The major conclusion from those interviews is that the jail has little to do with serious crime. As Irwin notes, "The jail holds only a few persons who fit the popular conception of a criminal—a predator who seriously threatens the lives and property of ordinary citizens" (p. 1). Instead the jail is populated by "members of the rabble class, that is, persons who are poorly integrated into the society and who are also seen as disreputable" (pp. 39–40). This group includes petty hustlers, derelicts, junkies, and others who share not involvement in serious crime, but detachment from conventional society and disrepute in the community. It is not that the members of this group are not charged with some crime; rather, their crime is not particularly relevant. Their offensiveness rather than their offense is what matters, and offensiveness is defined in the context of community. There they are seen as "the lowest class of all," but as Goffman (1963:3) stated with regard to the concept of stigma, "A language of relationships, not attributes, is needed."

Irwin emphasizes the role of the jail in the community rather than in the criminal justice system. Whereas others have focused on the jail as a filter in the criminal justice process and have been concerned with the effects of passing through that filter, Irwin focuses on those remaining behind, caught by the filter. This approach leads him to portray the jail as deliberately less benign than is apparent in some of the other writing on the subject. According to Irwin, the jail was invented to control rabble and continues to operate for that purpose.

Irwin's sampling procedures certainly may have influenced his conclusions. Because he used jail admissions, his sample contained few of the most serious violators, who are received at jail in comparatively small numbers but who make up a larger proportion of a cross-sectional sample because they stay in jail longer. This fact, however, does not suggest that his conclusions can be regarded simply as methodological artifacts. In studying a complex institution that may fulfill several functions, Irwin explores the jail's most unique role, its role in the community, which distinguishes it completely from the prison.

John Gibbs's research also approaches local jail as an institution tied much more closely to the community than to the prison. In several studies (1975, 1982d, 1987) Gibbs distinguishes the social psychological consequences of confinement in jail from those of confinement in prison. Unlike the stresses of prison, which are linked to isolation and to distance from the street, the stresses associated with being in jail often are linked to the inmates' temporal, physical, and psychological proximity to the street. The pains of jail confinement are tied to four interrelated problem areas (Gibbs, 1982a:99): withstanding entry shock, maintaining outside links, securing stability in a situation of seeming chaos, and finding activities to fill otherwise empty time.

By entry shock, Gibbs refers to the sudden and dramatic change in status that accompanies going to jail. "From the perspective of some prisoners it is almost as if they were gamboling down the street one minute and pondering their fate in a jail cell the next" (1982a:100). For some inmates this experience has resulted in symptoms of serious psychological disturbance, which may include self-injury or suicide. By their nature and frequency, these problems reveal themselves to be different from those encountered in prison settings.

After entry shock, the jail inmate finds himself in limbo, struggling to maintain ties to the street in the wake of his unplanned departure. At the same time, he faces uncertainty over his fate and unpredictability in his environment; he does not know how long he may be in jail or whether he can make bail, and he wonders about the competence of his counsel, the intentions of prosecutors, and "the meaning of a hundred other factors related to his legal predicament" (Gibbs, 1982a:100). The turmoil and chaos of early confinement are accompanied by the intense boredom and physical inactivity that characterize program-impoverished holding facilities.

Gibbs and Irwin focus on very different aspects of jail confinement and approach them from very different perspectives. Significant similarities remain, however. Both scholars view jails as institutions that differ fundamentally from prisons. For Irwin, the prison, but not the jail, is responding to serious crime. For Gibbs, the experience of jail is unlike the experience of prison. Further, although neither author discusses differences across localities, the tie between the jail and the community is central to both analyses. In Gibbs's analysis, adjustment problems center around attachments to the street; according to Irwin, the jail reflects community definitions of reputation and rabble. Although ideas about the jail and the community are developed most clearly in these works, they are present to a greater or lesser degree in many other jail studies. These ideas suggest a broad context that can help to organize existing research and that may stimulate additional studies.

Jails have been recognized broadly as fulfilling a variety of roles. Like Irwin, some authors have described jail as inflicted primarily on people whose social status or circumstances, rather than any particular offense, make them offensive and thus excludable (Flynn, 1973; Spradley, 1970). Jails also have been described as performing a variety of social service tasks by temporarily accommodating homeless drunks and vagrants and by furnishing involuntary lodging for transients who never may be brought to trial but who are merely "assisted" in their travel to other jurisdictions (Flynn, 1983:918). On a less critical note, jails have been characterized as asylums (albeit neglected ones) for the indigent, the mentally ill, substance abusers, and other "pseudo-offenders" in need of a variety of services (Briar, 1983:387).

One exploration of the multiple roles of local jails is offered by Goldfarb (1975), who characterized jails as "the ultimate ghetto of the criminal justice system." By examining the jail population, Goldfarb argues that jail continues to serve as the poorhouse of the twentieth century by punishing the poor who cannot make bail and by confining a variety of inmates whose violations are civil and often are related to their inability to pay fines, alimony, or child support. Although jail confinement resulting from civil actions still is widely recognized, few recent investigations of this phenomenon have been made (for an exception see Lempert, 1981–82).

Goldfarb also states that the jail is used frequently to confine persons who have been defined as sick and, in particular, mentally ill. The mental health of inmates may be related to the causes of their confinement in two ways. Some are held in jail while they are screened or processed through the criminal justice and/or mental health system. They may be awaiting competency hearings or pursuing insanity defenses. In some jurisdictions the jail remains a primary avenue into the mental health system. Other inmates with mental health problems may be in jail as a result of the deinstitution-alization of the mentally ill that took place in the 1960s and 1970s and the subsequent reduction in admissions to mental hospitals (see Morrissey and Tessier, 1982). According to a popular argument, these changes have led to increases in the number of persons in the community who are suffering from mental illness. These people then are often arrested on misdemeanor charges when police recognize that jail and release are their only options. Some evidence supports this hypothesis and there is little disagreement that the rate of mental health problems among jail inmates is higher than in the population as a whole. Teplin (1983), however, argues that many of these studies suffer from methodological shortcomings and that there is no clear support for the argument regarding changes in mental health policy. It simply may be that the deinstitutionalization movement has heightened the awareness of this long-term problem in jails (Steadman, McCarty, and Morrissey, 1986).

The literature also suggests another approach to elaborating and explaining the roles of local jails. Warren (1978) described community organizations as existing in a network of relationships with other organizations in the community and with organizations outside the community. Attention to these links also may help to identify and explain differences in the roles of local jails. As Smith (1986) demonstrated in her historical study, jails and jail populations reflect changes in state and federal laws. They also may be influenced more directly in their relationships with organizations outside the community. They may house state inmates temporarily or may contract with the Federal Bureau of Prisons to hold some sentenced offenders or illegal immigrants. The particular role of the jail also is influenced by the pattern of interaction with other community agencies. The availability of mental health services or programs for the homeless or differences in judges' pretrial detention practices will help to define the role of the jail in the local community.

THE EXPERIENCE OF JAIL CONFINEMENT

Extensive research on the experience of confinement has been conducted in the prison setting. That work covers a broad range of topics: the description and explanation of a prisoner subculture, the study of institutional violence, and investigation of differences in inmates' prison experiences and environmental needs. Few comparable studies have been conducted in local jails. Possibly researchers have assumed that some aspects of the confinement experience are similar across prisons and jails or that many of the issues examined in the prison research are irrelevant to jails because of the brevity of most jail stays (for a review of these arguments see Stojkovic, 1986). One study of institutional subcultures provides some support for these arguments.

In a survey of inmates admitted to three New Jersey jails, Garofalo and

Clark (1985) investigated whether the distribution of subcultural values which has been described in prison studies also exists among jail inmates. They found little evidence of parallels between the prison and the jail experience. Among jail inmates, subcultural attachments did not differ by demographic variables, psychological stability, or current offense. The strongest subscription to subcultural norms was found among inmates with substantial prior confinement experience. The jail thus is described as a place that may elicit positive orientations toward subcultures among inmates who already possess those ideas. It is not regarded, however, as a place in which the subculture is learned by novices.

Rottman and Kimberly (1985) took a different approach to the study of jail social structure. The prison literature led them to hypothesize differences between prison and jail subcultures. They drew on prison research which found that the nature of external communications profoundly affects internal prison processes (Mathiesen, 1971). Rottman and Kimberly argue that this finding should be even more applicable to jails because "to an extent not paralleled in prisons or mental hospitals, jails are embedded in a web of intra-organizational and other involvements to a specific locality" (p. 126). Then they focused on the "social context" of jails and concluded that further research as well as action toward social change must focus on the connections between the jail and the larger society.

The most systematic research on the impact of jail confinement focuses on the legal consequences of pretrial detention. Early studies concluded that pretrial detention rather than pretrial release carried a significant prejudicial effect resulting in higher rates of conviction (see Rankin, 1964). Later research introduced controls for seriousness of current offense and for criminal history. In a controlled comparison of bailed and jailed defendants, Goldkamp (1979) concluded that a prejudicial effect remained. The effect, however, was not likely to be reflected in the chance of conviction but rather in the likelihood of diversion and in the severity of sentence.

Though commonly acknowledged, the impact of jail on other aspects of an inmate's life has received only limited study. An exception is found in Irwin's interview study, in which he describes a process of "disintegration" (1985:42) that begins the separation from the street and marks the initiation into rabble existence. He describes three categories of unintended consequences. First, almost immediately upon arrest and booking, the inmate begins to lose personal property. Automobiles are impounded, street clothes are taken, and in time apartments are lost because of unpaid rent. In addition, inmates experience a loss of social ties. Visits, correspondence, and telephone calls are frequently difficult and are not an adequate substitute for presence on the street. Finally, there is a "loss of capacity to take care of business"; inmates, for example, do not have the ability to clear up criminal cases in neighboring jurisdictions.

In another study of the impact of jail, Weisheit and Klofas (1989) used systematic interviews to assess the tangible consequences of going to jail.

Even when inmates were confined for only brief periods, the consequences could be quite severe. One-third of the inmates interviewed said that they lost their apartments or were evicted by family and friends as a result of incarceration. The same percentage reported that personal property was stolen or lost. In many cases apartments were burglarized when associates learned that someone had been jailed. Nearly two-thirds of the inmates who had jobs reported that being jailed would affect their work status; the same percentage said that jail strained their relationship with their families. The researchers also examined variables that might aggravate or mitigate the costs of going to jail. They found that resources, including financial resources, education, and emotional support, were unrelated to the tangible effects of jail but that those effects were aggravated by other difficulties such as alcohol, drug, or emotional problems. Finally, the authors examined the relationship between the costs of going to jail and a measure of adjustment in jail. The more jail disrupted one's life in the community, the greater were the adjustment problems in jail.

As noted earlier, some studies of adjustment have been useful in distinguishing the jail from the prison and in highlighting the importance of the community context. That research has focused on the transition from the street to the jail as a particularly traumatic experience. Gibbs (1982b:35) describes the early stages of confinement as

> . . . a discordant limbo. A man has just come from the street where he had some measure of control over his life, and he has not yet been immersed in the daily routine of doing time. He is between worlds, and master over neither. In this situation, feelings of anxiety, confusion, and helplessness surface. A man's sense of control may be destroyed. The need for some measure of predictability, certainty, and order may be very difficult to satisfy.

Such descriptions explain adjustment problems by emphasizing the stress of being plucked from one's life in the community and deposited in jail. An alternative hypothesis focuses on the instability of those entering the jail. Such "person-centered" explanations of jail mental health problems have received some support from research that finds a higher incidence of mental health problems among newly admitted jail inmates than in the population as a whole. A third explanation parallels perspectives on the prison by suggesting that the experience of confinement itself, rather than any predisposition or transitional experience, is a significant contributor to jail adjustment problems.

Using a standardized self-report measure of symptoms of psychopathology, Gibbs (1987) found some support for all of the explanations, but transitional factors appeared to be most important.

The importance of proximity to the street also is evident in research on the most severe problems of maladjustment in jail. Suicide is the leading cause of death in jail (Winfree, 1988) and differs substantially from suicide on the street or in prison (Beigel and Russell, 1973). Although suicide rates have been constructed in studies of individual jails or of samples of jails, the most reliable figures were presented by Winfree (1988), who calculated rates for comparable at-risk populations in and out of jails. Using 1982 national data, he reported a jail suicide rate of 112.1 per 100,000, compared with an equivalent general population rate of 21.7 per 100,000.

Several variables have been associated with suicide in jails. Self-destructive behavior occurs most often among inmates in detention (Heilig, 1973) and usually occurs relatively soon after arrest and booking (Esparza, 1973; Heilig, 1973). The findings regarding the type of offense charges and the presence of a history of mental health problems are less consistent. Although suicide profiles are not likely to be robust enough to be useful in developing suicide prevention policies (Kennedy and Homant, 1988), they illustrate some of the unique qualities of the problem in the jail setting.

There are many topics related to the experience of jail confinement on which little or no research has been conducted. Although studies show that homicide rates in jail are far below those in the general population (Winfree, 1988) and also are below prison homicide rates, we know very little about the nature and levels of violence within jails. It is likely that there is great diversity in violence across jails; we have reason to believe that in some jails, violence problems are more severe than in prisons. In a classic study of sexual assault in the Philadelphia jails, Davis (1968) found a rate of assault five times greater than that reported in most prison research (see Lockwood, 1980; Nacci and Kane, 1983). In addition, little research has been conducted on the formal and informal control systems operating in local jails. Even descriptions of disciplinary processes are not available, and the roles of corrections officers in jail are gaining attention only now.

Studies of prison incarceration would seem to offer only limited insight into the experience of jail. The research suggests significant differences in the social structure of these institutions and in their impact, including both the tangible and the emotional costs associated with confinement. Physical and psychological proximity to the street give form to jail incarceration; our knowledge may be advanced by studies of the effects of the permeability of the border between the jail and the community.

CHANGE AND REFORM IN THE JAIL

The literature has been consistent in its criticism of jail conditions. Over the years, jails have been described as "crucibles for crime" (Fishman, 1923), simply as "lousy" (Lewis, 1935), as correction's weakest link (President's Commission on Law Enforcement and the Administration of Justice, 1967), as "cloacal" (Mattick and Aikman, 1969), as "sick" (McGee, 1975), as "still cloacal" (Reixach and Weimer, 1983), and as "a millenarian albatross that has remained stubbornly immune to successive attempts toward reform" (Advisory Commission on Intergovernmental Relations, 1984).

With varying degrees of optimism, these descriptions have been accompanied by prescriptions for reform. Perhaps the most pessimistic account is found in a recent review on jails. Flynn (1983:919) concludes that "jails have tenaciously resisted change for more than eight centuries. If the past is prologue, the combined forces of history, system inertia, conflicting political interests, and outright resistance to reform do not portend any significant change in the foreseeable future."

One means of regulating the jail has been through lawsuits filed in the federal courts. As with other aspects of the criminal justice system, jails have not escaped liability under Section 1983 of the Civil Rights Act (42 U.S.C. 1983). Local governments, jail managers, and employees can be held liable for unconstitutional jail conditions or procedures. In 1986 a survey of local jails found that almost one-third of facilities had come under court order; more than half reported that they were party to a pending lawsuit (*Corrections Compendium* 1986). A study of Section 1983 filings revealed that over 20 percent of those suits came from local jails (Turner, 1979).

A review of court intervention in local jails highlights the limitations of this approach to change. Differences between prisons and jails require different analyses of legal issues. Because jail terms are often brief, courts have overlooked conditions in local jails which have not been tolerated in state prisons. The courts also have found that pretrial detainees, unlike prisoners, cannot be punished. The application of this principle, however, requires that jail inmates prove the intent of jail staff. Finally, in jail cases even more than in prison cases, courts have deferred to the expertise of corrections officials.

The research on court-ordered change in local jails is quite limited and permits only tentative conclusions. With regard to legal rights, jail inmates are disadvantaged when compared to their imprisoned counterparts. Differences between the status of prisoners and of jail inmates require separate analyses, but the case law has not evolved to the same degree in both areas. Jail inmates have not benefited to the same degree as prison inmates during the period of active court involvement in corrections. When sweeping changes have been ordered by the court, results have been mixed. Differences in outcomes may be related to the nature of the relationship between the jail and extracommunity organizations, including the degree to which the court becomes actively engaged in local politics and government and the degree to which the jail is linked to a professional network.

Another form of coercive relationship with outside organizations is seen in the movement toward state-mandated standards for local jails. Thompson and Mays (1988) report that these mandates often have been met by resistance from local jails because the intrusion of outsiders and the cost of implementation are resented. A similar response to federal initiatives to force the removal of juveniles from local jails also has been reported (Schwartz, Harris, and Levi, 1988). The most extreme form of state control is illustrated by six states in which a variety of approaches caused local jail functions to be integrated into the state corrections system.

The current wave of jail construction may appear regressive to those who argue that jail reform must involve transfer of inmates to community-based alternatives (see Flynn, 1983) or that reform requires a drastic reduction in the size of the rabble class (Irwin, 1985). With regard to the conditions of confinement within jails, however, construction also has been seen as an opportunity for reform (Nelson, 1986). That potential, though, has not always been realized. As Mattick (1974:836) warned, "For the most part, what has passed as jail reform has been periodic replacement of old structures by new ones." Most commentators regard new-generation jails, with their emphasis on podular, direct supervision, as a radical departure from earlier designs, which emphasized linear, intermittent supervision (see Nelson, 1986).

Researchers are only beginning to evaluate the impact of these changes. Their preliminary studies show mixed results. The research compares the attitudes of inmates and staff in new-generation and in traditional jails and uses pretest-posttest designs where new facilities have opened. One study of corrections officers found that direct supervision produced more enriched jobs, higher levels of job satisfaction, and an improved organizational climate than did traditional practices (Zupan and Menke, 1988). A related study found that inmates, too, rated the social climates of new-generation jails more highly (Zupan and Stohr-Gilmore, 1988). The results showed more positive evaluations of both the jail facilities and the staff and lower levels of symptoms of stress and anxiety.

One study, using a different measure of social climate, produced less positive findings. Houston, Gibbons, and Jones (1988) found only marginal improvements in staff perceptions of climate, and no change among inmates, after the transition to a new-generation jail. Their conclusion echoes earlier cautions: "The data seem to confirm a long-held suspicion in the criminal justice field, to wit, the attractiveness or unattractiveness of buildings and physical features of correctional facilities often have relatively little to do with the attitudes of staff or inmates toward the facility."

CROWDING AND THE FUTURE OF THE AMERICAN JAIL

No issue is more salient in today's jails and more important to their future than overcrowding. Jail crowding, like prison crowding, has been associated with a variety of harmful effects on inmates (see Wallenstein, 1981; Wright and Goodstein, 1989). It increases tensions between inmates and staff; it strains physical facilities and local budgets. Crowding may disrupt normal jail management to such a point that jail policy will come to be defined almost exclusively as controlling crowding.

The strategies employed to control crowding also may have important effects. Although discretionary decisions by the police may control the entry into the criminal justice system, that power may be rivaled by policies which emanate from the predicament at the jail. Court intervention, for example, has forced drastic policy responses, including construction, limiting admissions to jail, establishing corrections alternatives, and mandating population ceilings that force the early release of some inmates (Bell, 1981). In Cook County, Illinois, 1,200 inmates were released in a one-month period to avoid violation of a federal court order. Such responses to crowding may have still more significant implications. As Mancini (1988:10) points out, "Early release of offenders solely because of the shortage of space calls into question the integrity of the administration of justice and could pose a threat to public safety."

The problem of prison crowding has been described as "little short of maddening" (Conrad, 1989), but it may pale in comparison to jail crowding. In jails, crowding may reflect not only a combination of crime, available space, and decisions regarding sentencing and release but also a myriad of decisions made throughout the criminal justice system. Hall et al. (1985) described 15 separate decision points at which the size of the jail population is influenced. These include law enforcement decisions to use arrest or citation release for low-seriousness violations, station house release decisions, bail and recognizance release, the decision to release pending appeal, and ultimately parole or conditional release decisions. The influences also have been described as reflecting local as well as state-level factors (Bolduc, 1985). Police, prosecutors, public defenders, probation departments, and judges establish local policies that influence jail crowding. Other agencies affect jail populations from outside the locality. Appellate courts exert an influence through the promulgation and enforcement of rules requiring speedy trials. State legislatures exert their influence through such measures as statewide citation and release programs, preventive detention statutes, and mandated pretrial service agencies. State departments of corrections may mitigate or aggravate problems by the speed at which they accept sentenced inmates from the jail or by their use of the jail to control their own crowding.

Efforts to address jail crowding have taken into account these multiple influences. Two themes emerge from the literature on remedies. One is the need for analysis to be tailored to the specific jurisdiction. "Solutions," it is argued, "will lie in the unique needs and desires of individual communities" (Hall, et al., 1985:3). The second theme reflects the need for a system perspective which acknowledges that jail construction may not solve the problem and that more productive working relationships between the jail and other actors in the criminal justice system may be needed.

When the subject is viewed this way, two things become clear. First, the use of local jails is not likely to diminish independent of developments in other approaches to social control. Second, jails are likely to be immersed further in a network of alternative methods of control such as intensive probation supervision, home detention, and specialized treatment programs. As a result, the jail itself may be growing less useful as a unit of analysis for jail research. Steele and Jacobs (1975) made the argument that the social structure, the administration, and other aspects of a prison no longer can be understood without reference to other institutions in a state's corrections system. A similar argument can be made about jails. As alternatives emerge, they influence the population, structure, and functions of jails. The modern jail cannot be understood without reference to those influences.

REFERENCES

Advisory Commission on Intergovernmental Relations. 1984. *Jails: Intergovernmental Dimensions of a Local Problem.* Washington, DC: Advisory Commission on Intergovernmental Relations.

American Jail Association. 1987. "Mega-Jail Survey." *American Jail Association Newsletter* (Fall): 4.

Beigel, A., and H. Russell. 1973. "Suicidal Behavior in Jail: Prognostic Considerations." Pp. 107–18 in *Jail House Blues: Studies in Suicidal Behavior in Jail and Prison*, ed. B. L. Danto. Orchard Lake, MI: Epic Publications.

Bell, M. 1981. "Ceilings, Lids, Limits and Caps." *Prison Journal* 61:19–27.

Bolduc, A. 1985. "Jail Crowding." *Annals, American Academy of Political and Social Science* 478:47–57.

Briar, K. H. 1983. "Jails: Neglected Asylums." *Social Casework* 7:387–93.

Conrad, J. P. 1989. "Epilogue: The Researcher's Work Is Never Done." Pp. 273–86 in *The American Prison: Issues in Research and Policy*, ed. L. Goodstein and D. L. MacKenzie. New York: Plenum.

Davis, A. 1968. "Sexual Assaults in the Philadelphia Prison System and Sheriff's Vans." *Transaction* 6:8–16.

Fishman, J. F. 1923. *Crucibles of Crime, A Shocking Story of American Jails*. New York: Cosmopolic, reprinted by Patterson Smith in 1969.

Flynn, E. 1973. "Jails and Criminal Justice." Pp. 49–88 in *Prisoners in America*, ed. L. Ohlin. Englewood Cliffs, NJ: Prentice-Hall.

———. 1983. "Jails." Pp. 915–22 in *Encyclopedia of Crime and Justice*, ed. S. H. Kadish. New York: Free Press.

Garofalo, J., and R. Clark. 1985. "The Inmate Subculture in Jails." *Criminal Justice and Behavior* 12:415–34.

Gibbs, J. J. 1975. "Jailing and Stress." In *Men in Crisis: Human Breakdowns in Prison*, ed. H. Toch. Chicago: Aldine.

———. 1982d. "The First Cut Is the Deepest: Psychological Breakdown and Survival in the Detention Setting." Pp. 97–114 in *The Pains of Imprisonment*, ed. R. Johnson and H. Toch. Beverly Hills, CA: Sage.

———. 1982b. "Disruption and Distress: Going from Street to Jail." Pp. 29–44 in *Coping with Imprisonment*, ed. N. Parisi. Beverly Hills, CA: Sage.

———. 1987. "Symptoms of Psychopathology among Jail Prisoners: The Effects of Exposure to the Jail Environment." *Criminal Justice and Behavior* 14:288–310.

Goffman, E. 1963. *Stigma: Notes on the Management of Spoiled Identity*. Englewood Cliffs, NJ: Prentice-Hall.

Goldfarb, R. 1975. *Jails: The Ultimate Ghetto of the Criminal Justice System*. Garden City, NY: Anchor Books.

Goldkamp, J. S. 1979. *Two Classes of Accused: A Study of Bail and Detention in American Justice*. Cambridge, MA: Ballinger.

Hall, A., D. A. Henry, J. Perlstein, and W. F. Smith. 1985. *Alleviating Jail Crowding. A Systems Perspective*. Washington, DC: National Institute of Justice.

Heilig, S. 1973. "Suicide in Jails." Pp. 47–56 in *Jail House Blues: Studies of Suicidal Behavior in Jail and Prison*, ed. B. Danto. Orchard Lake, MI: Epic Publications.

Houston, J. G., D. C. Gibbons, and J. F. Jones. 1988. "Physical Environment and Jail Social Climate." *Crime and Delinquency* 34:449–66.

Irwin, J. 1985. *The Jail: Managing the Underclass in American Society*. Berkeley, CA: University of California Press.

Kennedy, D. B., and R. J. Homant. 1988. "Predicting Custodial Suicides: Problems with the Use of Profiles." *Justice Quarterly* 5:441–56.

Lempert, R. 1981–82. "Organizing for Deterrence: Lessons from a Study of Child Support." *Law and Society Review* 16:513–68.

Lewis, B. G. 1935. "Our Lousy Jails." *Proceedings of the 65th Annual Congress of the American Correctional Association*. Washington, DC: American Correctional Association.

Lockwood, D. 1980. *Prison Sexual Violence*. New York: Elsevier.

Mancini, N. 1988. *Our Crowded Jails: A National Plight*. Washington, DC: Bureau of Justice Statistics.

Mathiesen, T. 1971. *Across the Boundaries of Organizations: An Exploratory Study of Communication Patterns in Two Penal Institutions*. Berkeley, CA: Glendessary.

Mattick, H. 1974. "The Contemporary Jails of the United States: An Unknown and Neglected Area of Justice." Pp. 777–848 in *Handbook of Criminology*, ed. D. Glaser. Chicago: Rand McNally.

Mattick, H., and A. Aikman. 1969. "The Cloacal Region of American Corrections: Prospects for Jail Reform." *Annals of the American Academy of Political and Social Science* 381:109–18.

Mays, G. L., and J. A. Thompson. 1988. "Mayberry Revisited: The Characteristics and Operations of America's Small Jails." *Justice Quarterly* 5:421–40.

McGee, R. A. 1975. "Our Sick Jails." Pp. 8–16 in *Jails and Justice*, ed. P. Cromwell. Springfield, IL: Thomas.

Morrissey, J., and R. Tessler. 1982. "Selection Processes in State Mental Hospitalization: Policy Issues and Research Directions." In *Social Problems and Public Policy: A Research Annual*, Volume 2, ed. M. Lewis. Greenwich, CT: JAI.

Nacci, P., and T. Kane. 1983. "The Incidence of Sex and Sexual Aggression in Federal Prisons." *Federal Probation* 47:31–36.

Nelson, W. R. 1986. "Changing Concepts in Jail Design and Management." Pp. 167–80 in *Sneaking Inmates down the Alley: Problems and Prospects in Jail Management*, ed. D. Kalinich and J. Klofas. Springfield, IL: Thomas.

President's Commission on Law Enforcement and the Administration of Justice. 1967. *Task Force Report Corrections*. Washington, DC: U.S. Government Printing Office.

Rankin, A. 1964. "The Effects of Pretrial Detention." *New York University Law Review* 39:641.

Reixach, K., and D. Weimer. 1983. "American Jails: Still Cloacal after Ten Years." Pp. 95–108 in *Criminal Corrections: Ideals and Realities*, ed. J. Doig. Lexington, MA: Heath.

Rottman, D. B., and J. R. Kimberly. 1985. "The Social Context of Jails." Pp. 125–39 in *Correctional Institutions*, 3d edition, ed. R. Carter, D. Glaser, and L. Wilkins. New York: Harper and Row.

Schwartz, I., L. Harris, and L. Levi. 1988. "The Jailing of Juveniles in Minnesota: A Case Study." *Crime and Delinquency* 34:133–49.

Smith, B. 1986. "An Historical View of the Multiple Roles of Jails: The McLean County Jail between the World Wars." Pp. 7–22 in *Sneaking Inmates down the Alley: Problems and Prospects in Jail Management*, ed. D. Kalinich and J. Klofas. Springfield, IL: Thomas.

Spradley, J. P. 1970. *You Owe Yourself a Drunk*. Boston: Little, Brown.

Steadman, H., D. McCarty, and J. Morrissey. 1986. *Developing Jail Mental Health Services: Practice and Principles*. Rockville, MD: National Institute of Mental Health.

Steele, E. H. and J. B. Jacobs. 1975. "A Theory of Prison Systems." *Journal of Research in Crime and Delinquency* 21:68–83.

Stojkovic, S. 1986. "Jails versus Prisons: Comparisons, Problems and Prescriptions on Inmate Subcultures." Pp. 23–38 in *Sneaking Inmates down the Alley: Problems and Prospects in Jail Management*, ed. D. Kalinich and J. Klofas. Springfield, IL: Thomas.

Teplin, L. 1983. "The Criminalization of the Mentally III: Speculation in Search of Data." *Psychological Bulletin* 94:54–67.

Thompson, J. A. and G. L. Mays. 1988. "State-Local Relations and the American Jail Crisis: An Assessment of State Jail Mandates." *Policy Studies Review* 7:567–80.

Wallenstein, A. M. 1981. "A Jail Warden Looks at Overcrowding and Alternatives." *Prison Journal* 61:3–13.

Warren, R. 1978. *The Community in America*. Chicago: Rand McNally.

Weisheit, R., and J. Klofas. 1989. "The Impact of Jail: Collateral Costs and Affective Response." *Journal of Offender Counseling, Services and Rehabilitation* 14:51–65.

Winfree, L. T. 1987. "Rethinking American Jail Death Rates: A Comparison of National Mortality and Jail Mortality, 1978, 1983." *Policy Studies Review* 7:641–59.

Wright, K., and L. Goodstein. 1989. "Correctional Environments." Pp. 253–66 in *The American Prison: Issues in Research and Policy*, ed. L. Goodstein and D. L. MacKenzie.

Zupan, L., and B. A. Menke. 1988. "Implementing Organizational Change: From Traditional to New Generation Jail Operations." *Policy Studies Review* 7:615–25.

Zupan, L., and M. K. Stohr-Gilmore. 1988. "Doing Time in the New Generation Jail: Inmate Perceptions of Gains and Losses." *Policy Studies Review* 7:626–40.

CHAPTER 6

Future Issues and Trends

During the 1990s dramatic increases in the size of the prison population and the rate of incarceration in the United States have captured the attention of government policy makers, correctional administrators, prison observers, and the general public. Each year the Justice Department's announcement of the year-end state and federal prison population is accompanied by terms such as "historic," "burgeoning," and "unprecedented." Penologists and others have attempted to sort out the forces driving this phenomenon, to understand the implications of the population increases for prison management and state budgets, and to estimate the impact of mounting prison populations on the crime rate. This massive public investment in confinement of offenders threatens state fiscal policy, challenges notions of America as a developed and free nation, and raises considerable concern about the payoff in terms of public safety. Of course some argue that this approach to crime control is already reaping rewards, and point to declining crime rates during the 1990s as evidence. Others contend that declining crime rates are driven by demographic changes in the population, and that some funds currently spent on imprisonment would be better invested in prevention initiatives.

The chapters in this section address several of the most nettlesome issues concerning incarceration now and in the next century. Langan's article seeks to understand the social and legal forces that have driven up incarceration rates in recent years. His analysis suggests that stiffer sentencing practices—a higher percentage of cases resulting in conviction and an increasing proportion of convictions receiving prison sentences—are more potent explanatory factors than demographic changes or changes in arrest rates. Langan's study indicated that the increasing length of prison terms was not a key factor during the time period he examined, but as inmates are held longer than previous cohorts because of statutory changes, the predictable result will be that prison populations will increase well into the twenty-first century.

Logan's article is an effort to articulate performance measures that are appropriate and measurable for prisons. His "confinement model" stipulates that prisons should not be held accountable for criminogenic factors beyond their control, so the proper frame of reference from which to judge prisons is what has been called "humane containment." McDonald explores the expanding movement to privatize the prison business in the United States, England, and Australia. His chapter amply illustrates that prisons exist within a political and economic context that has direct implications for their operations and administration.

The selections by Tonry and Skolnick remind us that dramatic growth in prison populations produces a number of "side effects" that challenge social relations. Tonry examines the overwhelming racial imbalance in prisons in the United States and other countries. He argues that evidence of deliberate differential processing by the criminal justice system is insubstantial, but policy decisions such as declaration of a street-level "war" on drugs have differential consequences across racial groups. Skolnick extends the argument, and contends that when incarceration is the cornerstone of crime policy, the pursuit of crime reduction incurs social, economic, and human costs that are enormous. In the final essay, the editors offer some insights into where American incarceration policy is headed, the aftermath of these developments for prisons, and the impacts on persons who live and work within them.

Criminal Justice Performance Measures for Prisons

CHARLES H. LOGAN

This paper starts with a very brief and general definition of criminal justice from a retributive (or "just deserts") perspective.[1] Such a perspective is rights-based rather than utilitarian, which implies that evaluative indicators and measures of criminal justice should focus more on the satisfaction of certain standards, values, and constraints than on the production of particular consequences. In Herbert Packer's terms, they should focus more on the "Due Process Model" than on the "Crime Control Model" of criminal jus-

Source: Logan, Charles H. Criminal Justice Performance Measures for Prisons. In *Performance Measures for the Criminal Justice System*, US Department of Justice, Bureau of Justice Statistics 1993 (NCJ-14305), pp. 22–32.

tice.[2] The paper will then outline the "confinement model" of imprisonment, which rests on a normative statement of mission for a prison or prison system. Finally, the paper will offer a set of empirical indicators that can be used as performance measures for prisons and that concentrate on the competent, fair, and efficient administration of confinement as a form of deserved punishment. While based on the deserts theory of criminal justice, these measures will be seen to be at least somewhat sensitive also to such goal-based concerns as rehabilitation of inmates and protection of society, albeit for reasons independent of those utilitarian justifications of imprisonment.

WHAT IS CRIMINAL JUSTICE?

Justice is the quality of treating individuals according to their rights and in ways that they deserve to be treated by virtue of relevant conduct. Criminal justice is rights-respecting treatment that is deserved by virtue of criminal conduct.

This definition of justice is rights-based, rather than utilitarian or consequentialist. A rights-based theory of justice gives a central role to punishment as a morally necessary response to the violation of rights. To believe in rights is to believe in duties; those are alternative statements of the same concept. To believe in duties is to accept, implicitly but of logical necessity, the corollary of punishment. When we say that people have a duty to refrain from violating the rights of others, we are saying that there must be some sanction if they fail to meet that duty. Duties are given meaning by the consequences that attach to their nonfulfillment. Thus, the meaning of a duty, like that of any other norm, must be socially constructed through the attachment of sanctions to behavior. A norm (a rule, a law, a duty, a right) that had no sanction attached to its violation would be empty and without meaning.

Justice by this definition is backward-looking. It requires that we treat people according to what they have done, not what they (or others!) might do in the future as a result of how we treat them now. Justice requires that all persons, including offenders, be treated as autonomous and responsible actors and as ends in themselves, not as means to social ends.

Finally, a rights-based theory sees justice as a process, an ongoing property of criminal sanctioning as it occurs, not as an expected outcome. Criminal justice is thus a value in itself and not merely useful as a means to some other end. Sanctioning that is evaluated as to its justice or injustice may, *in addition*, be evaluated in terms of its consequences for other values, such as freedom, order, happiness, wealth, or welfare, but those are separate concerns. This means that questions about the effectiveness or efficiency of the criminal justice system in achieving various "goals" or "purposes" should be kept separate from, and secondary to, an evaluation of the performance of the justice system in its most basic mission: doing justice.[3]

THE NONUTILITARIAN CONCEPT OF PRISON PERFORMANCE

To date, most evaluation research on prisons has focused on utilitarian questions. What are the goals of imprisonment? To what extent and at what cost are they achieved? How does imprisonment compare to alternatives in these respects? If we want evaluations of prison performance that are based on a normative rather than a utilitarian view of criminal justice, we need to reframe our question. We might ask, for example, "To what values do prisons commit themselves in their mission statements, and how well do they live up to those values?"

Social scientists are not comfortable with the idea of applying the tools of measurement directly to questions of value. That's why criminologists are attracted to utilitarianism, because it allows them to treat evaluative research on prisons as if it were a purely objective, scientific enterprise. In contrast, a court-appointed special master, who is usually a lawyer rather than a social scientist, evaluates a prison mostly from a formalistic rather than a utilitarian perspective. That is, the prison and its activities are examined not as means to an end (rehabilitation or crime control) but in terms of standards and criteria of "proper" performance, or conduct in fulfillment of duty. Consider this statement by a prominent prison master:[4]

> In summary, the ideal prison provides basic human services in a decent and healthful physical environment. Such a prison abjures idleness and its consequent human deterioration by offering constructive employment, programming, and recreational activities to the greatest extent possible; it addresses the human needs of prisoners for self-expression, faith, and maintenance of ties of importance to all human beings; it ensures safety from random violence, rape, and exploitation of the weak by the strong; it insulates decisions affecting the lives of prisoners from arbitrary chaos by adhering to due process of law; and it infuses the institutional environment with constructive expectations through use of positive incentives for hard work and good behavior.

That is not a bad statement of the mission of a prison, and it is probably one with which most correctional officials could agree. The most important point to note here is that it does not focus on ultimate goals, such as treatment or punishment, but on a set of abstract values and normative criteria against which to evaluate the day-to-day operation of a prison.

A PRISON MISSION STATEMENT UNDER THE CONFINEMENT MODEL

We ask an awful lot of our prisons. We ask them to correct the incorrigible, rehabilitate the wretched, deter the determined, restrain the dangerous, and punish the wicked. We ask them to take over where other institutions of society have failed and to reinforce norms that have been violated and rejected.

We ask them to pursue so many different and often incompatible goals that they seem virtually doomed to fail. Moreover, when we lay upon prisons the utilitarian goals of rehabilitation, deterrence, and incapacitation, we ask them to achieve results primarily outside of prison, rather than inside.[5] By focusing on external measures, we set prisons up to be judged on matters well beyond their direct sphere of influence.

If we do not want to set them up for failure, we must assign to prisons a function and a mission that we might reasonably expect them to fulfill. This mission ought to be fairly narrow and consistent in scope, and it ought to be special to prisons, rather than conflated with the functions of other social institutions such as schools or welfare agencies. It also ought to be achievable and measurable mostly within the prison itself.[6] Finally, a prison's mission ought to have intrinsic, and not just instrumental, value. That is, it should identify activities that have value in themselves, when they meet certain standards and criteria of performance, not activities that have value only if, when, and because they are effective in achieving some further goal.

The prison mission statement proposed here is based on a "just deserts" theory of criminal justice, one that calls for a punitive and purely retributive (that is, a non-utilitarian) response to criminal conduct. Punishment under such a theory does not need to take the form of incarceration, but since this paper is about prison performance measures, I will narrow the theory down to what I call the "confinement model" of imprisonment.

Under the confinement model, *the essential purpose of imprisonment is to punish offenders—fairly and justly—through lengths of confinement proportionate to the gravity of their crimes*. Thus the term, "confinement model," may be thought of as a shortened version of a clumsier but more explicit label: the "doing justice through confinement as a form of punishment model."

The mission of a prison under the confinement model can be summarized quite succinctly:

> The mission of a prison is to keep prisoners—to keep them in, keep them safe, keep them in line, keep them healthy, and keep them busy—and to do it with fairness, without undue suffering, and as efficiently as possible.

The confinement mission of prisons is not as narrow as it may seem at first, nor is it necessarily harsh or insensitive to the welfare of prisoners. It should be noted that under the confinement model offenders are sent to prison *as* punishment, not *for* punishment. It is not within the legitimate mission of a prison to attempt to *add to* (any more than to avoid or to compensate for) the pain and suffering inherent in being forcibly separated from civil society. Stated more positively, coercive confinement carries with it an obligation to meet the basic needs of prisoners at a reasonable standard of decency. Thus, measures of health care, safety, sanitation, nutrition, and other aspects of basic living conditions are relevant. Furthermore, confinement must meet constitutional standards of fairness and due process, so it is not just the effectiveness and efficiency, but also the procedural justice with which confinement is imposed that is important. In addition, programmatic activities like education, recreation, and work can be seen as part of the conditions of confinement, regardless of their alleged effects on rehabilitation. In short, confinement is much more than just warehousing.

Under the confinement model, a prison does not have to justify itself as a tool of rehabilitation or crime control or any other instrumental purpose at which an army of critics will forever claim it to be a failure. It proclaims itself to be, first and foremost, an agent of justice, and not necessarily an agent of either individual or social change. It asks to be judged only on its performance in carrying out the sanction of confinement-as-punishment; the effectiveness of that sanction may be a valid and important question, but it is not relevant to the measurement of prison performance under the confinement model.

What, then, are the relevant criteria?

PRISON PERFORMANCE CRITERIA UNDER THE CONFINEMENT MODEL

It might seem that measuring prison performance within a confinement model would be fairly simple—and indeed it is more straightforward than attempting to measure the success of rehabilitation, deterrence, or incapacitation (let alone the net effects of imprisonment on all three of these in combination)—but it is by no means easy. Still, the confinement model does facilitate performance measurement, because it focuses less on the achievement of ultimate and abstract goals and more on the fulfillment of delimited and immediate tasks. It shifts our attention away from hard-to-determine outcomes and toward more directly observable processes and adherence to measurable standards.

The confinement mission of a prison, as stated above, identifies eight distinct dimensions for prison performance measures: Security, Safety, Order, Care, Activity, Justice, Conditions, and Management. Each of these dimensions will be discussed briefly.

1. *Security* ("keep them in"). A secure facility is one that is impervious in either direction, outward or inward. Escapes are an obvious indicator of a lack of security, but inward penetration, of drugs or other contraband, also represents a breakdown of external security. Internal security would include control over movement of prisoners within the prison and control over internal movement of contraband, such as food or silverware from the dining hall, drugs from the infirmary, or tools from workshops.

2. *Safety* ("keep them safe"). Inmates and staff need to be kept safe, not only from each other but from various environmental hazards as well. Thus, measures of safety would include assault statistics, safety inspection results, and accidental injury reports.

3. *Order* ("keep them in line"). Prisons run on rules, and the ability of

prison administrators to enforce compliance is central to prison performance. Allowing for variation in the nature of their populations, it seems proper to evaluate prisons according to their ability to prevent disturbances, minimize inmate misconduct, and otherwise preserve order inside their walls.

4. *Care* ("keep them healthy"). I use the term "care" rather than "service" to cover the ministrations of such personnel as doctors, dentists, psychiatrists, psychologists, and dietitians. The distinction is primarily one of degree and entitlement. Convicts are entitled only to a very basic, minimal level of personal care consistent with the principle that it is not the purpose of imprisonment to *inflict* physical suffering. At a minimum, prisons have an obligation to try to prevent suicide, malnutrition, exposure to the elements, and the spread of contagious diseases. Beyond the level of very basic care, however, the simple fact of confinement does not entitle convicts to levels of service or to degrees of personal welfare that exceed what they are able to obtain with their own resources. Therefore, when rating prisons on this dimension an evaluator might choose not to make distinctions beyond a certain level.

5. *Activity* ("keep them busy"). When evaluating prisons under a rehabilitation model, heavy emphasis is usually given to inmate programs; under a confinement model, programs are still relevant, but on a different basis. Programs can be classified into five different types: work, training, education, recreation, and therapy. All five types are relevant under a confinement model but in each case any rehabilitative effect a program might have is not directly relevant to its evaluation. Therapeutic programs are so closely associated with the rehabilitative ideal that they are difficult to recast in terms of the confinement model. They can, however, be offered as a form of "care," and evaluated according to the principles discussed under that dimension. Programs of the other three types should be judged according to how much opportunity they provide inmates to engage in constructive activity or enterprise.

"Constructive" activity is not defined here as "contributing to the betterment of inmates" but as activity that is, on its face, consistent with the orderly, safe, secure, and humane operation of a prison. Idleness and boredom can be seen as wrong in themselves, from a work ethic standpoint, or as so fundamentally related to mischief as to be undesirable for that reason. Either way, prison programs of work, training, and education should be evaluated under the confinement model as forms of constructive activity and as antidotes to idleness, not as methods of rehabilitation.[7]

Under a rehabilitation model, work, education, and training are seen as benefits that are offered to prisoners, or even forced upon them, in the hope that this will make them better and more law-abiding citizens. Under the confinement model, work, education, and training are not benefits; they are opportunities, available to prisoners who are willing to make productive use of them. Ideally, prisons would have, or would fit into, an economy in which inmates could earn money by producing goods and performing services having real value. Inmates might then seek education and training, not to impress a parole board or a prison counselor, but to be able to perform a more valuable and higher paying job.

The availability of opportunities for education and employment should offset some of the austerity of a prison organized around a strict confinement model. However, amenities, privileges, and benefits that might be justified under a rehabilitation model as a worthwhile investment of taxpayers' money should not be provided free to prisoners under a confinement model. Any social benefits that are guaranteed to all citizens should be provided to prisoners as well (within limits imposed by security needs), but beyond that prisoners would have to earn or purchase them at their own expense. Examples would include higher education, entertainment, and medical, dental, or psychological services beyond the minimal levels entailed in the confinement model.

Some people believe that constructive activity should be more than just an opportunity available to inmates; it should be a prisoner's obligation as well. Offenders, in this view, should be held financially as well as morally responsible for their crimes and their imprisonment. Thus, prisoners should be required to work, to make restitution to their victims, to support their families, and to pay something toward the cost of their incarceration. Financial responsibility is not inconsistent with the confinement model, and could therefore be included under the dimension of activity. However, it is independent of, rather than integral to, a prison's primary mission of confinement-as-punishment.

6. *Justice* ("do it with fairness"). In measuring the performance of justice within prisons, the propriety of the sentence may be taken for granted; what remains to be judged is the fairness with which the sentence is administered. Stated more broadly, governing with justice requires adherence to the rule of law inside prisons just as it does on the outside. Rules ("laws") must be clear, sanctions for their violation must be specified in advance and applied consistently, enforcement and adjudication must follow due process, and there should be provisions for independent review of decisions. Relevant to this dimension would be procedures and practices in imposing discipline and allocating good time, grievance procedures, availability of and access to legal resources, and inmate perceptions of the fairness and legitimacy of rules and their enforcement.

7. *Conditions* ("without undue suffering"). A confinement model obviously requires some evaluation of the conditions of confinement. This broad term would include such things as population density, food, clothing, bedding, noise, light, air circulation and quality, temperature, sanitation, recreation, visitation, and communication with the outside. As with the dimension of "care," evaluation of living conditions and quality of life should not be completely linear (the more the better, without limits). In principle, this dimension is curved, so that differences imply improvements at the lower end but have declining or even negative merit ("too good for them") above

some higher point. Most prisons today, however, probably lie along the middle range of this dimension, where comparison can be linear.

8. *Management* ("as efficiently as possible"). Quality of management is probably the single most important source of variation in the first seven dimensions of quality of confinement. As such, there may be some redundancy in evaluating management as, itself, a separate component of prison performance. However, it is better to over-measure than to under-measure, and many management variables bear a strong enough presumptive relationship to overall quality of institutional operation that they can be used as indicators of otherwise hard to measure concepts.

For example, such management-related variables as staff morale, absenteeism, and turnover are visible reflections of institutional stress and tension. Training levels may be both a cause of quality (through increased staff competence) and a result of quality (as a product of institutional concern with proper procedure in treatment and discipline of inmates). Thus, various sorts of management information can be used as a measure as well as an explanation of confinement quality. Good management is also a legitimate end in itself. The public has an interest in seeing that the money it spends on imprisonment is not wasted, through over-staffing, high turnover, or other management-related problems.

These eight dimensions—security, safety, order, care, activity, justice, conditions, and management—are appropriate concerns of prison professionals under the confinement model of imprisonment, and therefore constitute relevant focal points when measuring prison performance. Moreover, they are relatively precise concepts susceptible to operationalization and empirical measurement. First, however, each dimension must be divided into its component parts, or subdimensions.

NOTES

1. John J. DiIulio, Jr., *Rethinking the Criminal Justice System: Toward a New Paradigm, BJS Discussion Paper.* NCJ-139670 (Washington, DC: Bureau of Justice Statistics, 1993).

2. Herbert L. Packer, *The Limits of the Criminal Sanction* (Stanford University Press, 1968).

3. Again, however, the measures of justice to be derived here from a normative and nonutilitarian model will be seen to overlap considerably with measures that might be derived independently from a utilitarian model.

4. Vincent M. Nathan, "Correctional Health Care: The Perspective of a Special Master," *The Prison Journal*, vol. 65, No. I (Spring–Summer, 1985), pp. 73–82, at p. 76.

5. For each of these three goals, the principal measure of its achievement is the number of crimes avoided in the general community. This is true even of incapacitation, because that refers not to maintaining order within prisons but to

avoiding the crimes that current prisoners might have continued to commit if they were not in custody. Incapacitation thus reflects much more the performance of the police, prosecutors, and judges who catch, select, and send offenders to prison than it does the performance of those who simply hold them there.

6. This last requirement pretty much rules out crime control and rehabilitation, at least as criteria for evaluating the performance of particular prisons, if not as goals of imprisonment generally.

7. While a confinement model may sometimes be in conflict with a rehabilitation model, it is not necessarily so. In the confinement model, it is desirable to keep inmates constructively busy, quite apart from the question of whether that does them any rehabilitative good. That does not mean, however, that it does not matter from some other perspective whether the programs have any rehabilitative effect. It would be very nice if prison programs had rehabilitative effects. However, when we say that the primary purpose of prison is to punish through confinement, we become more interested in the operation of these programs inside the prison gates and less concerned about their effects beyond.

Public Imprisonment By Private Means: The Re-emergence of Private Prisons and Jails in the United States, the United Kingdom, and Australia

DOUGLAS C. MCDONALD

Although privately operated imprisonment facilities were commonplace in previous centuries in England and the United States (Holdsworth, 1922–4:397; Crew, 1933:50; McKelvey, 1977:197–216; Feeley, 1991), by the twentieth century, governments had assumed responsibility for nearly all imprisonment and most other criminal justices functions. Indeed, the principle of public responsibility for the administration of justice—and especially for imprisonment—has become so well established that imprisonment is seen by many as an intrinsic function of government (American Bar Association, 1989:3; DiIulio, 1990:172–77; Robbins, 1988:44; Howard League for Penal Reform, 1990:3). Beginning in the mid-1980s, however, a debate emerged in the United States, Britain, and in some other English-speaking countries over the propriety of governments contracting with private firms to operate and even own prisons, jails, and other places of imprisonment. This has gone be-

Source: McDonald, Douglas C. Public Imprisonment by Private Means: The Re-emergence of private prisons and jails in the United States, the United Kingdom, and Australia. *British Journal of Criminology*, 34 (Special Issue), 1994, pp. 29–48.

yond talk, for governments in the United States, Britain, and Australia are now contracting with private, for-profit firms to operate penal facilities of various types, and a private imprisonment industry has emerged (or, taking a longer historical view, re-emerged).

This essay surveys developments in the United States, Britain, and Australia, the only countries that have so far moved to delegate operations of imprisonment facilities to private entities. Some of the principal issues raised by private imprisonment, including some of the important research questions, are identified and discussed briefly.

THE REDISCOVERY OF PRIVATE IMPRISONMENT IN THE UNITED STATES

The contemporary movement to expand private authority over the administration of penal and detention facilities owes its origins to independent developments on both sides of the Atlantic, although there has been considerable cross-fertilization. Whereas in Britain, the earliest proposals came from policy reformers—for example, the Adam Smith Institute (1984) and McConville and Williams (1985)—the stimulus in the United States came largely from business entrepreneurs who were promoting their own ventures. Policy reformers later developed a more elaborate rationale for opening government to business interests (e.g., President's Commission on Privatization, 1988; Stewart, 1986; Logan, 1990).

One of the principal seedbeds for the current wave of private imprisonment firms in the United States was the network of detention centres under the authority of the US Immigration and Nationalization Service (INS). Beginning in 1979, the INS began contracting with private firms to detain illegal immigrants pending hearings or deportation. By the end of 1988, the number of private detention facilities had grown to seven, and they held about 800 of the approximately 2,700 aliens in INS custody (McDonald, 1990a:92).

Government officials in the INS "went private" chiefly because contractors were able to create new detention facilities much more quickly than could the federal government. (Government procurement procedures required long lead times.) Indeed, Wackenhut was able to construct and open a 150-bed facility at breakneck speed: 90 days from the contract's signing. Conveniently, the cost of acquiring this new capacity could be paid for out of the government's operating funds—through per diem reimbursements—rather than requiring the allocation of capital funds for facility construction, which could be a bureaucratically cumbersome process (McDonald, 1990a).

In addition to the INS detention centres, the private imprisonment industry also established early sites with various low-security facilities, and in the less visible regions of the adult and juvenile penal systems. For example, the federal government's Bureau of Prisons had been contracting with private firms since the late 1960s to operate community treatment centres, halfway houses to which federal prisoners were transferred prior to being paroled (Bronick, 1989:12–14).

These developments provoked little controversy or even notice. That changed, however, in late 1985 and 1986. Private firms began taking over or building facilities that were closer to the core of the adult penal system, which had previously been the nearly exclusive preserve of government.

What brought the issue to public attention and ignited a public policy debate were two incidents. One was CCA's audacious offer to take over the entire state of Tennessee's troubled prison system, with a 99-year lease from the state, for which it would pay $250 million. CCA would then house the state's convicted prisoners at a negotiated per diem rate and would guarantee that the system would meet standards set by a federal court judge, who had earlier found the entire system to be in violation of the US Constitution because of inadequate conditions of confinement. The state ultimately turned down the offer after several months of consideration, but the matter became a national news story (Corrections Corporation of America, 1985; Tolchin, 1985a, 1985b; Press, 1990).

The second signal event was the opening of a small privately operated facility, called the 268 Center, by one Philip E. Tack, in rural Cowansville, Pennsylvania. Tack arranged with the District of Columbia authorities to transfer 55 inmates from the District's jails to relieve overcrowding there, but the townspeople were not pleased. Among other things, the inmates were all black, the townspeople all white. Local residents organized themselves and patrolled the streets with shotguns, fearing escapes. This caught the attention of a prison reform group that got the state legislature to declare a moratorium on privately-operated prisons (Joint State Government Commission, 1987; Press, 1990; Bivens, 1986).

In the train of these events, private imprisonment emerged as one of the most salient issues in correctional circles.

The issue remained in the public eye for a few years, prompting a spate of articles, books, and reports. By the turn of the decade, however, the debate had died down. There had neither been a rush to privatize correctional facilities, nor had the nascent industry been stopped dead in its tracks. Instead, the industry continued to grow slowly, and new facilities were opened, including major maximum security prisons (four in Texas, for example). The large firms have also broadened their reach into other markets—the United Kingdom and Australia.

Parallel to these developments was another form of privatization: the construction of privately owned facilities that were leased to governments for direct government operation. This first emerged in Colorado, where an investment banking firm put together a lease-purchase deal for a county government that wanted to build a new jail. A private corporation was formed to build the new jail, and investors bought "certificates of participation"—what amounted to corporate bonds. The jail was then leased to the county, and the lease payments were used to repay investors (McDonald, 1990c). Similar arrangements were developed for prison and jail construction in places (Chaiken and Mennemeier, 1987).

These emerged largely because of constraints on public officials' ability to authorize capital expenditures for new prisons, and have been used to finance other types of public purchases (Leonard, 1986, 1990). In the United States, most state governments build prisons by issuing bonds purchased by investors, but must first obtain the approval of voters to incur these debt obligations. Spurred by a tax revolt that spread across the United States in the late 1970s and early 1980s, citizens were voting down these bonding proposals, even though they were demanding at the same time that more criminals be imprisoned in the hopes of making their communities safer. Public officials saw the "creative financing" techniques such as lease-purchase arrangements as a convenient way out of this dilemma, as a rent payment could be paid out of government operating budgets. How many facilities were built through lease-purchase arrangements is difficult to determine, for lack of a central accounting system in the United States's fragmented federal system.

DEVELOPMENTS IN BRITAIN

Although proposals for privately operated prisons first surfaced in 1984 and 1985, advanced by the Adam Smith Institute (1984) and two academics, McConville and Williams (1985), the government had already been contracting for immigrant detention services for a decade and a half (Green, undated; Ruterford, 1990).

It appears that current developments to contract out for prisons resulted from separate initiatives. In 1986, when attention to private prisons was high in the United States, the Home Affairs Committee of the House of Commons, which exercises parliamentary oversight of the prison system, decided to examine private prisons and jails in the United States as part of its broader inquiry into the state of prisons and jails in England and Wales (Rutherford, 1990). On that trip, the chair of the committee, Sir Edward Gardiner, became an enthusiastic proponent of privatization, and the short report that resulted from this visit recommended that the Home Office should, as an experiment, permit private firms to tender for the construction and management of custodial institutions. The committee also recommended that priority be given to contracting out the remand centres "because it is there that the most overcrowding in the prison system is concentrated" (Home Affairs Committee, 1987).

This was followed by, two reports, one by Peter Young of the Adam Smith Institute who argued that the "monopolistic provision" of imprisonment services should be broken to encourage an increase in the supply of beds, improvements in quality, and cost reductions. In the same year,

Maxwell Taylor and Ken Pease (1987), two liberal academics, wrote a paper supporting privatization because it could serve as a "springboard for the development of a truly rehabilitative programme." This could be done by building incentives into the contracts. As *The Independent* declared, this support by the liberal wing of the penal reform lobby "gave crucial new authority to the campaign" (5 March 1987).

On 30 March 1988, the government announced that it intended to publish a discussion document (a "Green Paper") on private sector involvement in the remand system, and that private management consultants would be engaged to consider the details (Gill, 1992:1). The paper was published the following July (HMSO, 1988) and the consultants appointed. Their report, published in March of the following year (Deloitte, Haskins, and Sells, 1989), offered a number of specific recommendations. It recommended issuing contracts to private firms to design, construct, and operate remand centres, and to turn existing remand centres over to the private sector. It also recommended issuing between four and ten separate contracts for court and escort duties, each corresponding to geographical districts to be designated. (These tasks include escorting prisoners to and from court, guarding prisoners at court, and providing court security.) This separation between remand centre and escort duties was recommended as a means of increasing the efficiency of staff and managers that would result from concentrating specially trained employees on their principal missions, rather than requiring (or permitting) them to do both. This report was followed by the government, in July 1990, issuing another discussion paper that adopted most of the consultants' recommendations, inviting comment (Home Office, 1990).

In December 1991, the government announced its intentions to proceed with contracting out the court escort services, beginning with one newly defined district that would include East Midlands and Humberside. Tenders were received from six firms and a contract was signed in 1993 with Group 4. Service was planned to commence in April 1993 (Gill, 1992:9).

Although the consultants recommended contracting with private firms for the design, construction, and operation of new remand centres, the prison population took one of its inexplicable nosedives, such that the urgent need for new places to be built receded (Gill, 1992:3). The government decided instead to contract out a new prison that was under construction in the North East of England, the 320-bed Wolds remand prison, in North Humberside. Enabling legislation was needed for this, which was obtained in the Criminal Justice Act 1991. This Act provided the power to contract out the management of new prisons for unsentenced inmates, but was extended once in July 1992 to encompass sentenced prisoners and again in February 1993 to enable contracting out of *existing* prisons. A five-year contract for operating The Wolds remand prison was signed in November 1991, with the Group 4 Remand Services Ltd (Gill, 1992:5).

The second prison to be contracted out was a new one at Blakenhurst, a 650-bed local prison for sentenced and unsentenced prisoners. This contract was awarded in 1992 to UK Detention Services, a consortium of the Corrections Corporation of America and British construction firms John Mowlem and Sir Robert McAlpine (Ford, 1992; Corrections Corporation of America, 1992). Private operations were scheduled to commence in April 1993 (Clarke, 1992).

A frontier of sorts is being crossed in a more recent development: the "market testing" of the Prison Services' administration of the Manchester prison ("Strangeways"). In contrast to The Wolds and Blakenhurst competitions, the Prison Service was permitted to submit a bid for the Strangeways contract. In mid-July of 1993, Derek Lewis, the Director General of the Prison Service announced that the "in-house bid team"—the Prison Service itself—had won the competition to manage the prison. In the wake of this decision, in September 1993, the government announced that it would further stimulate the development of a private correctional industry by seeking contracts for a number of other prisons. "Our aim is to create a private sector able to provide sustained competition," said Michael Howard, the Home Secretary. "[The] private sector must be large enough to provide sustained competition and involve several private sector companies—a genuinely mixed economy" (HM Prison Service, 1993b).

It is possible that contracting out will advance further in Britain than in the United States, in large part because of the government's broader commitment to rolling back the public agencies' domain. Unlike the United States, a single national government has authority over prisons and jails, permitting a more rapid implementation of changed policy. In the United States, the growth of the private prison industry is slowed by the existence of separate governments (and, therefore, markets) in 3,400 counties, and 50 states, in addition to the federal government. Conversely, a change in administration in Britain might bring a rapid halt to developments there, whereas the march of the private prison industry in the United States is less likely to be affected by the defeat of a conservative administration at the federal level.

AUSTRALIA

A 1988 report to the Queensland Corrective Services Commission that provided a blueprint for correctional reform in Queensland called for the development of one prison operated and managed by the private sector under contract to the commission (Kennedy, 1988). This, the report argued, would create a competitive market for correctional institutions in Australia and Queensland, speeding reform of the prison system. The commission accepted the recommendation and invited tenders to manage and operate the Borallon Correctional Centre, a new 240-bed facility near Brisbane. The contract was awarded in November 1989 to the Corrections Corporation of Australia, a newly formed consortium made up of the Corrections Corporation of America, Wormald Security, and John Holland Constructions. Private operations began in January 1990, under a three-year contract that had an option for renewal for another two years. By the end of the first year, the prisoner population was predominantly a medium security one (Macionis, 1992:9).

A second privately operated prison resulted from the breakdown of negotiations between the commission and the labour union representing staff to be employed at the newly constructed 380-bed Remand and Reception (Arthur Gorrie) Centre at Brisbane. When no agreement could be reached regarding work rules and procedures, the commission informed the government in October 1991 that it intended to call for tenders for the private sector operation of this facility. This came to pass shortly, and in March 1992, a contract was awarded to Australasian Contract Management (ACM), a consortium of Wackenhut Security and ADT, an Australian-based security company, and the centre went operational in June 1992. This facility is a critical piece of the Queensland correctional system, as it is the main reception centre for the state's 11 facilities; all the initial assessment and classification of prisoners is conducted there (Macionis, 1992:3–4).

The Junee prison in New South Wales, scheduled for opening in March 1993, was the third facility to be contracted out. This 600-bed prison was designed and constructed by ACM, to be operated by that firm for an initial period of five years, with options for renewing a three-year term (Harding, 1992:1). Observing these developments, Harding wrote that "the momentum seems inexorably to be increasing. Indeed the Wacol contract [for the Queensland Remand and Reception Center] could mean that, for cash-strapped governments, the ideological walls will now come tumbling down. The question is thus not whether privatization will occur; but rather to what extent, in relation to what sorts of institutions and which types of prisoner ... and above all whether it will improve the overall imprisonment system" (Harding, 1992:1).

WHY CONTRACT FOR PRISON AND JAIL OPERATIONS?

It is interesting that the development of privately operated prisons has emerged in a few English-speaking countries. Part of this results from language barriers, making it difficult for American firms to penetrate markets where English is not spoken widely (such as France, where the Mitterand Government held discussions with officials of the Corrections Corporations of America in the 1980s).

ROLLING BACK THE STATE

A deeper explanation, however, is found in the ideological orientation of the governments in power at the time of the nascent industry's development.

In Britain, the United States, and Queensland, conservative governments held sway. In the former two countries, these governments launched a concerted attack on the institutional structures and ideology of the welfare state. Certainly the most aggressive programme of cutting back the public sector has been in Britain, following Thatcher's election in 1979, which has continued under John Major's administration. This movement of privatization and contracting out for operations in government-owned facilities has been extensive, cutting across a wide variety of services. In the United States, the movement has been less aggressive, largely because the federal government (which was under divided Republican and Democratic control) holds relatively few assets that can be privatized. Nonetheless, the public landscape was combed in the United States in search of targets for privatization of assets or contracting, and prisons were sighted by those advocating broader private sector involvement in the delivery of public services (e.g., President's Commission on Privatization, 1988).

RISING PRISONER POPULATIONS

Another contributing factor to these developments was the increasing demand for prison and jail beds, at least in the United States and in Britain. Between 1973 and 1990 in the United States, the numbers of prisoners under custody at any one time grew nearly fourfold (Bureau of Justice Statistics, 1991). At the same time, the federal courts were finding a large number of imprisonment facilities—and even entire state prison systems—to be in violation of the Constitution's prohibition of "cruel and unusual punishment," largely because of overcrowding and inadequate conditions of confinement. By mid-1991, 40 states were operating prisons found by the courts to have unconstitutional conditions (Bernat, 1991). The result of both was strong pressure on governments at all levels to acquire new imprisonment facilities, either by constructing new ones or converting buildings once dedicated to other uses.

Similar pressures were being felt in Britain. During the 1980s, prison populations were rising because of the increasing proportions of convicted persons receiving custodial sentences, the imposition of longer prison sentences, and some lengthening of delays in bringing people to trial. Between 1980 and 1987, the growth of the prisoner population was twice that of the increase in capacity, so that by the end of 1987, a capacity shortfall of about 5,800 beds existed. The government responded by increasing expenditures for prison services substantially: a 72 per cent increase between 1980 and 1987, and a prison building programme projected a 53 per cent increase in capacity between 1980 and 1995. Despite this higher level of expenditure, about 40 per cent of all prisoners in 1986–7 were being held in overcrowded facilities, mostly in remand facilities. Remand prisoners were also backed up into police cells; during 1987, police cells held an average of 530 such prisoners (Rutherford, 1990:44–46).

SPEEDY EXPANSION OF CAPACITY

In the United States, the private sector had a special advantage over government that was appealing to public managers: lengthy procurement procedures could be evaded by issuing contracts with private firms. Moreover, public managers did not have to risk having requests to increase public debt for prison construction turned down at the ballot box, because payments for contracted imprisonment facilities could be made with funds from accounts for operations rather than capital accounts. Because these constitutional constraints do not exist in Britain, the private firms were not so advantaged there.

LOWER COSTS

Certainly an important stimulus to contracting has been the belief or hope that contracting will be less costly than direct governmental provision. In the United States, leaders of the private firms have proclaimed this to be a fact. In Britain, this quest for more cost-effective (or, at least, less costly) imprisonment services appears to be a main reason for turning to the private sector (Clarke, 1992), although data on private firms' costs are not public because the government has agreed to consider this information proprietary and confidential. In Australia, one of the principal reasons that the Queensland Corrective Commission resorted to contracting was that it was unable to obtain agreements from the staff regarding work procedures and, therefore, costs (Macionis, 1992). Whether private contracting is, in fact, less costly and more cost-effective remains an open question, as discussed below.

INCREASED MANAGERIAL CONTROL

Although some have argued that contracting with independent private firms weakens the ability of government managers to control the provision of public services (e.g., DiIulio, 1990; AFSME, 1984), some government officials who have turned to contractors report that they have done so to *increase* control and better ensure performance. In the United States, the need to increase governmental control was a significant factor in some of the earliest contracts. For example, the Bay County (Florida) commissioners turned to contractors because they were unable to gain assurances from the jail administrator (the sheriff) that the conditions of confinement would be improved. They then contracted with CCA and obliged it to meet certain specified standards by a fixed date (McDonald, 1990c; Press, 1990). Santa Fe (New Mexico) county commissioners also turned to CCA because they were unable to control the costs of a newly constructed jail (Press, 1990). Jails in the United States pose a special case because they are typically under the authority of sheriffs, who are independently elected and do not serve at the pleasure of county commissioners or executives. However, even where political control of prisons is not so fragmented, as in the case of England, the need for gaining stronger managerial control over prisons and prison systems is given as a reason for contracting (Gill, 1993; Clarke, 1992).

The belief that privatization offers enhanced control over public services appears to be based on several different dynamics of contracting. First, the pressure to compete forces a reconsideration and change of work rules that have been built up in the public sector. Inefficient practices will be more difficult to support if one's employment is at risk. Secondly, contracting forces government agencies to establish specific and written performance standards and goals, something that is done less frequently in direct public provision of services. Thirdly, private firms are exposed to more risk for failing to meet these standards, at least compared to public employees who have expansive rights and protections against dismissal. Fourthly, some have argued (e.g., O'Hare *et al.*, 1990) that contracting permits managers to focus attention on the quality of output (including services), rather than on the myriad processes by which outputs are produced.

Finally, in instances where higher-level political or managerial authority is unable to control by command the performance of subordinates, turning to contractors may result in higher levels of compliance with policy and performance objectives. For example, in Massachusetts during the early 1970s, a reform-oriented manager was appointed to run the state's correctional services for youth, but failed to get the entrenched and tradition-bound employees of the agency to change their practices. Nearly overnight, he closed the large closed training schools and contracted with a number of smaller private organizations to care for the youths. Although this event has usually been understood as a crucial event in the "deinstitutionalization" movement, undertaken to supplant a custodial culture with one that gave higher priority to juvenile rehabilitation, contracting was the tool for accomplishing the reform objective (Coates *et al.*, 1978).

This finds an echo in Australia, where contracting has just begun. The Queensland Corrective Commission announced its aim of creating a "more rehabilitative" environment in its correctional centres. "In order to achieve this, custodial staff would need to adopt a much different approach to their work than that of the traditional stony face guard on a fixed post. . . . [It] has been difficult to bring about the type of cultural change required. Private sector involvement has provided an opportunity to establish centres where staff could be recruited with skills and attitudes commensurate with today's philosophy and direction" (Macionis, 1992:7).

THE MAIN ISSUES AND RESEARCH QUESTIONS

Contracting for imprisonment services raises a number of issues, both normative and empirical. Resolution of the normative questions, posed as either legal or policy issues, turns on choosing values and principles that are to govern practice. Other questions, empirical in nature, can be resolved by observation and, if needed, systematic research.

Is Contracting Proper?

Probably the central normative issue concerns the proper responsibility of government for imprisonment. In the United States, this has been framed in part as a question of constitutionality: Does government's contracting with private entities for imprisonment conform to the general principles established in the US Constitution? One committee of the American Bar Association has argued that it probably does not: "there can be no doubt that an attempt to delegate total operational responsibility for a prison or jail would raise grave questions of constitutionality under both the federal Constitution and the constitutions of the fifty states" (American Bar Association, 1989). No direct constitutional challenges to private prisons have been brought to the courts, however. Nor are there realistic hopes for such challenges. Since *Carter v. Carter Coal Company* (1936), the courts have upheld the federal government's delegation of broad powers to private actors. Delegation by state and local governments has also not been seen to pose federal constitutional issues since the 1920s (Lawrence, 1986). Private bail bondsmen's powers to arrest and detain those for whom they have posted bond have been consistently upheld *(Corpus Juris Secundum* undated), as have the detention powers of private security firms (Schearing and Stenning, 1981). To be sure, laws in some states regarding private delegation are inconsistent and confusing, so that several legislatures seeking to support privately operated correctional facilities have passed laws explicitly granting these powers.

That private prisons have not been declared unconstitutional does not resolve the question whether delegation of administrative authority over imprisonment is proper and desirable, however. Some have argued that imprisonment is "intrinsically governmental in nature" (Robbins, 1988), but this ignores the historical record. Others argue that governments should retain full and direct control over the administration of criminal justice because not to do so weakens the social compact in a pluralistic society (DiIulio, 1990). The contrary view is that what matters most is not the legal status of the service provider—whether public or private employee—but the quality of the service, and whether the service conforms to established standards and law (Logan, 1990; McDonald, 1990c).

What Are the Consequences of Contracting?

Beyond the question of propriety lie a number of empirical questions. What are the consequences of delegating imprisonment authority to private entities? Are privately operated facilities more efficient (by some measure to be specified) and less costly? If a cost difference is found, from what does it result? Is market provision of imprisonment services inherently more cost-efficient than direct government provision? If there is no inherent superiority, under what conditions are privately operated facilities more efficient or less costly? Are there inherent pressures or incentives for private firms to deliver higher or lower quality services? What are the consequences for inmates of delegating imprisonment administration to private firms? Are prisoners cared for and are their rights safeguarded better or worse than in public facilities? Will public policies be adversely affected by the existence of an organized private imprisonment industry?

Unfortunately, many of these questions have not been studied. Many developments are too recent to have been subjected to systematic evaluation. However, parallel experiences that could be studied profitably have been largely overlooked. For example, much could be learned by studying the private sector's involvement in holding delinquent juveniles and other children in trouble. In both Britain and the United States, the institutions for wayward youths were developed largely by the voluntary charitable organizations in the nineteenth century. Although governments in both countries assumed direct control over many parts of the system (more so in Britain than in the United States), there continue to this day two tracks: privately provided and publicly provided juvenile correctional services (McDonald, 1992; Lerman, 1982; Rutherford, 1990). In the United States, the private sector has grown substantially in recent years; by 1989, 67 per cent of all juvenile correctional facilities were privately operated, and held 42 per cent of all children in custody that year (McDonald, 1992). These institutions have been little studied, especially for the purpose of assessing the benefits and costs of public and private management. The same is apparently true in Britain. Rutherford writes that even though the British system for "youth in trouble" is publicly funded, it remains largely hidden from public view, little information about it is collected systematically, and the number of children being held in it is not even known (Rutherford, 1990: 55–56).

Is Private Imprisonment Less Costly?

On this important question, advocates and critics have advanced a number of claims. Proponents of contracting argue that government is inherently inefficient (or, in the less absolute version, tends toward inefficiency), relative to private firms (e.g., President's Commission on Privatization, 1988). Some see this as the result of government's "monopolistic" provision of services, devoid of competition, reinforced by the public manager giving higher value to the expanding power rather than controlling costs or delivering cost-effective services (Stewart, 1986; Young, 1987). Others argue that the costs are lower and efficiency greater because managers in private facilities have more freedom to manage effectively—that is, without countervailing labour organizations and constraints of negotiated work rules (Tolchin, 1985a). Critics argue that contracting is more expensive because the cost to government of contracting and monitoring contracts outweighs any savings that may result (e.g., Keating, undated). Donahue (1990) argues that the technical means of producing the service of imprisonment (consisting largely of people guarding other people) are not susceptible to significant improvements in productivity, so that there is little room for a private firm's cutting costs except by reducing services. The limited labour-saving technologies that do exist (e.g., greater use of electronic monitoring and communications systems) are available to government as well as to private correctional organizations.

Few systematic studies comparing the costs of public and private facilities have been done. In the United Kingdom, independent assessments of the relative costs and cost effectiveness of private imprisonment will be especially difficult because, as mentioned above, financial information is considered proprietary and is kept secret by the government and the firms.

As discussed more fully elsewhere (McDonald, 1990a, 1992), the findings of several of the published studies of costs are of questionable validity because of inconsistencies and shortcomings in the accounting methodologies employed. Public and private accounting systems are quite different, and the costs that these differing systems identify are not always comparable. Costs measured on a per inmate basis are also misleading if facilities differ in their utilization rates, suggesting that crowded facilities appear less costly to operate than less crowded ones which may affect the public/private comparison (McDonald, 1980, 1989; Wayson and Funke, 1989; Clear, Harris, and Record, 1982). Because so few of the studies have conducted a rigorous and comparable accounting of both public and private costs, it is premature to conclude that we know much about the relative cost advantages of privately operated facilities.

Further experience with private imprisonment services and systematic studies of those experiences will probably show that there is no inherent superiority of contracting, in terms of cost-effectiveness, but that certain privately operated facilities may be more cost-effective than the available public alternatives. The comparative advantage that a private firm will have probably depends upon the conditions found in the public agency that would operate the facility in the absence of contracting. For example, some jails run in the United States by incompetent and independently elected sheriffs may be operated more cost-effectively by contracted firms, but one cannot assume that this will be true for all jails. Where inefficient work rules or practices prevail in publicly operated facilities, and where the constraints on eliminating them are powerful, private firms may have a distinct advantage, especially if they employ unorganized labour. (This advantage may diminish if employees of private firms organize, however.)

Do Profit-seeking Firms Provide Poorer Services?

A frequent argument is that the principal incentives operating in profit-seeking private firms work to keep costs at a minimum, which is most readily accomplished by diminishing services or the quality of those services (American Bar Association 1986:4). However, at least in the early stages of contracting, there appear to be certain disincentives to diminish services: if performance falls below agreed-upon standards in those "showcase" facilities, firms risk losing contracts and clients. Some managers also argue that cutting services creates morale problems among both inmate and staffs and makes facilities more difficult to manage (Rees, 1987). For whatever reason, studies of facilities operated by private firms in recent years have generally reported finding good conditions and services, relative to the public facilities (Logan, 1991; Urban Institute, 1989; Green, undated).

Are Prisoners' Rights Diminished or Jeopardized?

One obvious worry is that prisoners' rights and welfare will be sacrificed if they conflict with the pursuit of private profit. Even if private firms agree to respect established rights, it is feared the exercise of these rights will be curtailed. Because prisons are so hidden from public view, the likelihood of detecting such violations is low, and prisoners are relatively powerless to bring attention to their grievances. (This is not unique to private prisons, however, for the actions or public officials managing prisons are kept from public view with nearly equal ease.)

Although these concerns are real, private imprisonment is not likely to be a reprise of the nineteenth century private prisons and jails, at least in the United States. The principle is well established that what matters with respect to supporting prisoners' various rights are the actions of the prison officials, and whether they conform to the existing law and standards, and not the name on the officials' shoulder patch. Moreover, the courts have stepped in and established prisoners' rights, have set standards for prisons and prison officials to meet, and in some instances have hired private individuals ("special masters") to monitor the prison administration's compliance with court orders. To increase further the monitoring of conditions and the operators' compliance with law and standards, several institutional arrangements recommend themselves. These include establishing independent ombudsmen in the private prisons, grievance procedures—including independent grievance and disciplinary boards—and putting full-time government monitors in the private facilities. Procedures for protecting prisoner's rights can also be written into the contract, so that failure to uphold them can be termed a violation of the contract.

Has a "Penal-industrial Complex" Captured Policy Making?

Some observers have argued that the emergence of private imprisonment firms is hastening the development of an unhealthy alliance of private/public interests resembling the military-industrial complex. Schoen (1985) warns that private operators, whose business opportunities derive from the shortfall of cell space relative to demand, may provide influential support for "get tough" sentencing policies that heighten the demand for prisons and jails. Lilly and Knepper (1992) note further that the real money in the corrections industry is being made not by private prison operators but by firms that supply goods and services to corrections agencies, and conclude that "the corrections-commercial complex operates without public scrutiny and exercises enormous influence over corrections policy." Moreover, observing that these firms are increasingly marketing their wares outside the United States, they see a "correctional policy imperialism" at work, whereby "First World nations" are finding "another means to increase their control over the future of punishment in Third World nations."

Using the terms "imperialism," "subgovernments," and "military-industrial complexes," Lilly and Knepper paint a picture in which public correctional and penal policy making is distorted—and even captured—by private interests. However, this is a misreading of public–private dynamics in the United States, at least—the only country I know well. There is no evidence that private firms have had any influence over the key decisions that have created the booming prisoner populations. Sentencing laws began to get tougher in the early 1970s for a number of reasons, including a turn away from civil commitment of drug abusers toward one that relied on tough criminal sanctions, growing public fears of crime, and the discovery by political leaders that being tough on crime was an effective strategy for getting elected. Moreover, a key strategy among Republican Party leaders seeking to attract conservative Democratic voters into the Republican tent was to focus attention on social and cultural issues rather than economic ones. Coming on the heels of widespread turmoil in the United States—with the civil rights and black power movements, student unrest, and a popular uprising against the government's war in Vietnam—calls for "law and order" became very effective political tools. Contemporary penal policy in the United States was thus forged in the course of a political and policy battle, in which self-interested private correctional interests have played no significant role.

To be sure, businesses have made money from this growing industry, as they have from all large-scale, capital-intensive government programmes. Governments themselves do not manufacture goods, and many businesses have emerged to provide needed services. There has also been a movement of personnel between private firms and public correctional policy making positions (e.g., Sir Edward Gardiner left Parliament to join a private imprisonment firm), but this does not in and of itself indicate that *sentencing* policy is being distorted by private interests. Where private firms are more likely to affect government decision making is in the choice of public or private provision of correctional services. Private firms have been aggressive in lobbying governments to convert at least some of their public operations to privately contracted ones. Where governments have to be careful is to avoid becoming too dependent upon private provision. Strategies to minimize the risks of this include government retaining ownership of existing correctional facilities, and contracting only for management of new ones—because firms that establish themselves with physical assets in a particular jurisdiction may develop an unbeatable edge over potential competitors in future contract competitions.

THE CHALLENGES TO PUBLIC ADMINISTRATION

The likely outcome of current developments is that correctional systems will probably not be wholly public or wholly private, and that public imprisonment responsibilities will be delivered by differing mixes of private firms and public agencies. At least in the United Kingdom and the United States, interest in introducing market mechanisms such as contracting into more command-oriented public administration will probably survive changes in governing parties. The issue of whether imprisonment operations should be delegated to private contractors will certainly remain controversial, however, because the intersection between state power and individual liberty is felt most sharply in prisons, jails, and other detention centres. Not surprisingly, views about private imprisonment services are most closely linked to deeper political values, which makes it difficult to resolve the public policy debate about contracting. However, knowing more about the actual experiences and consequences of contracting will go a long way toward identifying the most desirable combinations of public and private responsibilities and interests.

There are, I think, three principal challenges to public policy that are posed by private imprisonment firms, all of which deserve the attention of the research community. The first is to devise procedures to assure that prisoners' rights and welfare are protected (which is, of course, a challenge in publicly operated prisons and jails as well). This is not a difficult task, and there are well-developed models to follow. Learning about the effectiveness of these models in privately operated prisons should be a high priority for research.

The second challenge is to prevent governments' dependence upon private firms, and especially upon entrenched suppliers. Ideally, one might accomplish this by governments creating conditions that engender competition among firms rather than monopolistic dominance by a few giants. (Privatization does not necessarily create a competitive environment.) Precisely how this can be done is difficult to prescribe, as the future shape of a mature private imprisonment industry is not yet known. Current experience offers a relatively wide array of cases to learn from, which are characterized by varying combinations of large and small jurisdictions, centralized and decentralized (or fragmented) correctional systems, differences in scope of contracts (including whether facilities are owned or only operated by contractors), and different contracting arrangements.

The third challenge is to protect the integrity of government procurement processes—one that is faced in nearly all areas of public administration. To the extent that new knowledge needs to be developed here, looking beyond corrections to those other areas of administration is likely to be profitable.

REFERENCES

Adam Smith Institute. (1984). *The Omega Justice Report*. London: Adam Smith Institute.

American Bar Association. (1986). *Report to the House of Delegates*, unpublished document. Chicago: American Bar Association.

———. (1989). *Report to the House of Delegates*, unpublished document dated February 13. Chicago: American Bar Association.

Bernat, B. (1991). American Civil Liberties Union, National Prison Project. Personal communication with author, 27 September.

Bivens, T. (1986). "Can Prisons for Profit Work?," *Philadelphia Inquirer Magazine*, 3 August.

Bronick, M. J. (1989). "The Federal Bureau of Prisons' Experience with Privatization," unpublished paper. Washington, DC: US Bureau of Prisons.

Bureau of Justice Statistics. (1991). *Prisoners in 1990*. Washington, DC: US Department of Justice, Bureau of Justice Statistics.

Carter v. Carter Coal Company (1936), 298 US 238.

Chaiken, J., and Mennemeyer, S. (1987). *Lease-Purchase Financing of Prison and Jail Construction*. Washington, DC: National Institute of Justice.

Clarke, K. (1992). "Prisoners with Private Means," *The Independent*, 22 December.

Clear, T., Harris, P., and Record, A. (1982). "Managing the Cost of Corrections," *The Prison Journal*, 62.

Coates, R. B., Miller, A. D., and Ohlin, L. E. (1978), *Diversity in a Youth Correctional System. Handling Delinquents in Massachusetts*. Cambridge, MA: Ballinger Publishing Company.

Corpus Juris Secundum (undated), vol. 8, section 87. St. Paul, MN: West Publishing Company.

Corrections Corporation of America. (1985). *Proposal for State of Tennessee*. Nashville, TN: Corrections Corporation of America.

———. (1992). "CCA Wins First British Prison Contract," press release, 8 December. Nashville, TN: Corrections Corporation of America.

Crew, A. (1933). *London Prisons of Today and Yesterday*. London: I. Nicholson and Waston.

Deloitte, Haskins, and Sells (1989). "A Report to the Home Office on the Practicality of Private Sector Involvement in the Remand System," unpublished document.

DiIulio, J. J. (1990). "The Duty to Govern: A Critical Perspective on the Private Management of Prisons and Jails," in D. C. McDonald, ed., *Private Prisons and the Public Interest*. New Brunswick, NJ: Rutgers University Press.

Donahue, J. D. (1990). *The Privatization Decision*. New York: Basic Books.

Feeley, M. M. (1991). "Privatization of Prisons in Historical Perspective." In W. Gormley, ed., *Privatization and Its Alternatives*. Madison, WI: University of Wisconsin Press.

Ford, R. (1992). "Private Prison Firms Start Brain Drain from Public Sector," *The Times*, 24 December.

Gill, L. F. (1992). "Private Sector Involvement in the Prison System of England and Wales," unpublished paper delivered at Australian Institute of Criminology Conference, Wellington, New Zealand, 30 Nov.–2 Dec. 1992.

———. (1993). Home Office Remand Contracts Units. Private communication with author on 4 January.

Green, P. (undated). *Private Sector Involvement in the Immigrant Detention Centres*. London: The Howard League for Penal Reform.

Harding, R. (1992). "Private Prisons in Australia," *Trends and Issues in Crime and Criminology*. Canberra: Australian Institute of Criminology.

HM Prison Service. (1993*b*). "Michael Howard Unveils Plan for More Private Sector Involvement in the Prison Service," News release, 2 September.

HMSO. (1988). *Private Sector Involvement in the Remand System*, Cm. 434.

Holdsworth, W. S. (1992–4). *A History of English Law*, vol. 4, 3rd ed. London: Cambridge University Press.

Home Affairs Committee. (1987). *Contract Provision of Prisons, Fourth Report of the Home Affairs Committee*. HC 291.

Home Office. (1990). "Court Escorts, Custody and Security: A Discussion Paper." London: Home Office.

Howard League for Penal Reform. (1990). "Private Sector Involvement in the Remand System: The Howard League Response to the Discussion Paper 'Court Escorts, Custody and Security'." London: The Howard League for Penal Reform.

Joint State Government Commission. (1987). "Report of the Private Prison Task Force." Harrisburg, PA: General Assembly of the Commonwealth of Pennsylvania.

Keating, M. J. (undated). *Seeking Profit in Punishment: The Private Management of Correctional Institutions*. Washington, DC: American Federation of State, County and Municipal Employees.

Kennedy, J. J. (1988). *Final Report of the Commission of Review into Corrective Services in Queensland*. Brisbane: State Government Printer.

Lawrence, D. (1986). "Private Exercise of Governmental Power," *Indiana Law Journal*, 61: 649.

Leonard, H. B. (1986). *Checks Unbalanced: The Quiet Side of Public Spending*. New York: Basic Books.

Lerman, P. (1982). *Deinstitutionalization and the Welfare State*. New Brunswick, NJ: Rutgers University Press.

Lilly, J. R., and Knepper, P. (1992). "An International Perspective on the Privatisation of Corrections," *The Howard Journal*, 31/3: 174–91.

Logan, C. H. (1990). *Private Prisons: Cons and Pros*. New York: Oxford University Press.

———. (1991). *Well Kept: Comparing Quality of Confinement in a Public and a Private Prison*. Washington, DC: Report to the National Institute of Justice.

Macionis, S. (1992). "Contract Management in Corrections: The Queensland Experience," unpublished paper written for a conference, "The Private Sector and Community Involvement in the Criminal Justice System," in Wellington, New Zealand, 30 Nov.–2 Dec. 1992.

McConville, S., and Williams, J. E. H. (1985). *Crime and Punishment: A Radical Rethink*. London: Tawney Society.

McDonald, D. C. (1980). *The Price of Punishment: Public Spending for Corrections in New York*. Boulder, CO: Westview Press.

———. (1989). *The Cost of Corrections: In Search of the Bottom Line*. Washington, DC: US Department of Justice, National Institute of Corrections.

———. (1990a), "The Costs of Operating Public and Private Correctional Facilities," in D. C. McDonald, ed., *Private Prisons and the Public Interest*. New Brunswick, NJ: Rutgers University Press.

———. (1990c). "When Government Fails: Going Private as a Last Resort," in D. C. McDonald, ed., *Private Prisons and the Public Interest*. New Brunswick, NJ: Rutgers University Press.

———. (1992). "Private Penal Institutions: Moving the Boundary of Government Authority in Corrections," in M. Tonrey, ed., *Crime and Justice: An Annual Review of Research*. Chicago: University of Chicago Press.

McDonald, D. ed. (1996). *Private Prisons and the Public Interest*. New Brunswick, NJ: Rutgers University Press.

McKelvey, B. (1977). *American Prisons: A History of Good Intentions*. Montclair, NJ: Patterson Smith.

Miller, A. D., Ohlin, L. E., and Coates, R. B. (1977). *A Theory of Social Reform: Correctional Change Processes in Two States*. Cambridge: Ballinger Publishing Company.

National Institute of Justice. (1987). *Contracting for the Operation of Prisons and Jails*. Washington, DC: US Department of Justice.

O'Hare, M., Leone, R., and Zeagans, M. (1990). "The Privatization of Imprisonment: A Managerial Perspective," in D. C. McDonald, ed., *Private Prisons and the Public Interest*. New Brunswick, NJ: Rutgers University Press.

President's Commission on Privatization. (1988). *Privatization: Toward More Effective Government*. Washington, DC: The White House.

Press, A. (1990). "The Good, the Bad, and the Ugly: Private Prisons in the 1980s," in D. C. McDonald, ed., *Private Prisons and the Public Interest*. New Brunswick, NJ: Rutgers University Press.

Rees, J. (1987). Private communication with author. (Mr. Rees was the chief manager of the Correctional Corporation of America's staff at the Santa Fe County jail.)

Robbins, I. P. (1988). *The Legal Dimensions of Private Incarceration*. Washington, DC: American Bar Association.

Rutherford, A. (1990). "British Penal Policy and the Idea of Prison Privatization," in D. C. McDonald, ed., *Private Prisons and the Public Interest*. New Brunswick, NJ: Rutgers University Press.

Schearing, C. D., and Stenning, P. C. (1981). "Modern Private Security: Its Growth and Implications." *Crime and Justice: An Annual Review*. Chicago: University of Chicago Press.

Schoen, K. (1985). "Private Prison Operators," *The New York Times*, 28 March.

Stewart, J. K. (1986). "Costly Prisons: Should the Public Monopoly Be Ended?," in P. B. McGuigan and J. S. Pascale, eds, *Crime and Punishment in Modern America*. Washington, DC: The Institute for Government and Politics of the Free Congress Research and Education Foundation, pp. 365–88.

Taylor, M., and Pease, K. (1987). Unpublished document, later published in R. Matthews, *Privatization Criminal Justice*. London: Sage.

Tolchin, M. (1985*a*). "Prisons for Profit: Nashville's CCA Claims Operations Aid Government." *The Tennessean*, 24 Feb.

Urban Institute. (1989). *Comparison of Privately and Publicly Operated Corrections Facility in Kentucky and Massachusetts*. Washington, DC: Report to the National Institute of Justice.

Wayson, B. L., and Funke, G. S. (1989). *What Price Justice? A Handbook for the Analysis of Criminal Justice Costs*. Washington, DC: US Department of Justice, National Institute of Justice.

Young, P. (1987). *The Prison Cell*. London: The Adam Smith Institute.

Racial Disproportion in U.S. Prisons

Michael Tonry

Outside the United States, probably the best known characteristics of America's correctional system are that capital punishment continues in use and that American incarceration rates are four to 15 times higher than those in other developed countries. Within the United States, the most notable characteristics are the absolute numbers in confinement and that they are disproportionately black. Blacks in 1991 made up 12 per cent of America's population but 48 per cent of both prison and jail inmates.[1] Forty per cent of the occupants of "death row" on 31 December 1991 were black. In public juvenile facilities in 1989, 48 per cent were black. Americans of Hispanic origin, by contrast, America's second largest minority group, in 1991 constituted 9 per cent of the general population, 13 per cent of the prison

Excerpted from: Tonry, Michael. Racial Disproportion in US Prisons. *British Journal of Criminology*, 34 (Special Issue), 1994, pp. 97–115.

population, 14 per cent of the jail population, and 8 per cent of the death row population.

America's incarceration rates[2] are seen by many as evidence of draconian criminal justice policies. The overrepresentation of black offenders is seen by many as evidence of racial bias. Both critiques have merit; the latter rests, however, in part on a misconception that racial disproportion in prisons is markedly worse in the United States than elsewhere. This appears not to be the case.

Four findings stand out when incarceration rates are disaggregated by race in Australia, Canada, England and Wales, and the United States. First, the white American incarceration rate, compared with those in other English-speaking countries, is not as much higher as is generally believed. Secondly, patterns of differential incarceration by race in England and Wales (white and black), Australia (non Aboriginal and Aboriginal), and Canada (white and native) resemble American patterns. In all these countries, members of disadvantaged visible minority groups are seven to 16 times likelier than whites to be confined in correctional institutions.

Thirdly, when the different racial compositions of national prison populations are taken into account, apparent differences in national rates of incarceration diminish. If, for example, America's 1990 general population were, like England and Wales's in 1991, 94.1 per cent white and 1.8 per cent black, America's jails and prisons in 1990 would have housed 759,632 black and white inmates (the actual black and white total was 1,133,820). This assumes that incarceration rates by race would be the same as in 1990. The national incarceration rate (assuming the 1990 rate of 241 per 100,000 for the residual 4.1 per cent "other") would fall from 474 per 100,000 to 315.

When the opposite exercise is carried out, if England and Wales's black/white general population percentages were America's, the results would be more striking. In 1990, combining remand and sentenced prisoners, England and Wales incarcerated 77 whites per 100,000 whites and 547 blacks per 100,000 blacks. If the general population were 80 per cent white, 12 per cent black, there would be 30,732 white and 32,748 black prisoners and an overall incarceration rate (attributing the current 164 per 100,000 rate to the remaining 8 per cent of prisoners) of 140 per 100,000. England and Wales would have more black than white prisoners and its national incarceration rate would be more than 50 per cent higher (140 versus 89). This assumes that a sixfold increase in the black population would not be accompanied by heightened racial tensions that would exacerbate existing racial disproportions in confinement decisions and patterns (e.g., Hood, 1992).

Fourth, racial disproportion in prisons within countries is distributed in ways not commonly recognized. In 1988, for example, black-white incarceration rate differentials in some southern American states were relatively low (4 to 1 in Mississippi, South Carolina, and Tennessee). In some states traditionally considered politically liberal and governmentally progressive, like Wisconsin (12 to 1), Iowa (16 to 1), Connecticut (17 to 1), and Minnesota (19 to 1), the differentials were much higher. Similar patterns exist in Australia where Aboriginal–non-Aboriginal differentials ranged from 3.4 to 1 in Tasmania to 19.7 to 1 in Western Australia in January 1993.

This essay examines racial differences in incarceration, mostly in the United States but with occasional mention of other English-speaking countries. To anticipate the conclusion, a large part (but by no means all) of the long-term incarceration rate differential by race in the United States results from racial differences in participation in the kinds of crime, like homicide, robbery, and aggravated assault, that typically result in prison sentences; a recent short-term worsening of racial incarceration differences results from foreseeable discriminatory effects of conscious policy decisions of the Reagan and Bush administrations in launching and conducting the federal "War on Drugs." More generally, rough comparability in majority and minority group incarceration patterns in Australia, Canada, England and Wales, and the United States exposes the failure of social policies aimed at assuring full participation by members of minority groups in the rewards and satisfactions of life in industrialized democratic countries.

One caveat concerning data reliability needs mention. Analyses such as this one that depend on unadjusted general population census data share the limits of the data. In the United States, for example, the decennial population survey conducted by the US Bureau of the Census undercounts members of minority groups. With a complete general population census, the black population count would be higher, which would make black denominators in incarceration rates larger and the resulting black rates lower. Similarly, after blacks, whites, Native-Americans, and Asians are counted, the 1990 census reports nearly 10,000,000 respondents as "others," which distorts denominators, and rates, in unknown ways. Likewise, the prison and jail censuses report residual "other, not known, or not reported" categories which necessarily lend imprecision to these data. In this essay, I rely on official black and white counts and generally do not adjust for estimates of the racial composition of "other" groups, except in long-term trends where Hispanics are included within black and white counts.

Here is how this essay is organized. Part 1 (Long-term Trends) describes long-term patterns of racial differences in incarceration rates in the United States. Part 2 (Cross-national Comparisons) examines American and other countries' comparative reliance on incarceration. Part 3 (Sub-national Comparisons) shows American state-by-state comparisons. Part 4 (Explanation of Minority Over-representation) examines the underlying causes of both long-term patterns and recent worsening of racial differentials in incarceration rates. Part 5 (Redressing Racial Imbalance) suggests lessons for criminal justice and social welfare policies that derive from those differences.

LONG-TERM TRENDS

That members of ethnic and racial minority groups are disproportionately involved in common law crimes and disproportionately ensnared in the American criminal justice system, by itself, is neither unprecedented nor especially worrisome. These patterns typically characterize low-income immigrant groups and typically abate as subsequent generations are assimilated into American economic and social life.

America's first national crime commission, the US National Commission on Law Observance and Enforcement (1931), concentrated on two subjects—prohibition and "crime among the foreign-born." The commission's final report examined patterns of criminality among the foreign-born in general and Mexican immigrants in particular. The fundamental findings were that crime was less common among the foreign-born than among either non-immigrants or the immigrants' children and grandchildren. The relatively low involvement by immigrants in crime should come as no surprise. Most chose the uncertainties and dislocations of immigration and were determined to work hard and succeed. For many, material conditions of life in America as immigrants compared favorably, with conditions in the natal homeland.

The problem of immigrant crime was preponderantly among the second and third generations to whom English was a native tongue, to whom worse conditions in the old country, were mere words, and on whom relative deprivation could have a corrosive effect. Victims too often of ethnic stereotyping and discrimination, enjoying fewer legitimate opportunities than did assimilated middle-class and working-class youth, second and third generation immigrants were especially susceptible to the allure of juvenile gangs and especially likely to exploit illicit opportunities when legitimate opportunities were few, unattractive, or blocked (Glazer and Moynihan, 1963).

Mass immigration declined after the 1930s. From 1900 to 1930, the United States received nearly 19 million people, thereafter falling to 1.5 million from 1930 to 1950 and 2.5 million during the 1950s (Bureau of the Census 1992, table 5). By the 1950s, the phrase "crime and the foreign-born" had an archaic if not xenophobic ring, and had disappeared as a major symbol of crime problems.

In retrospect, "crime and the foreign-born" as a prominent public policy problem in the 1920s and 1930s was a foreseeable, and foreseeably temporary, product of the transition of newly arrived immigrants into what was once called a "melting pot." Similar patterns appeared among southern black farm labourers and tenant farmers, made technologically obsolete by the mechanization of agriculture, who migrated to northern cities in the 1950s and 1960s. Employment rates were higher, and welfare dependency was lower among southern-born black migrants in the 1960s and 1970s than among northern-born blacks (despite the higher average education among the northern-born) (Wilson, 1987:55–6; Katz, 1989:203). Participation in crime by adult migrants was less extensive than was that of their children. Recent reports of developing Asian youth gangs look like a variation on a familiar story, as the children of Asian immigrants of the 1970s and 1980s face the problems confronted by children of eastern and southern European immigrants early in the twentieth century.

Unfortunately, the migration-is-comparable-to-immigration hypothesis is at best a partial explanation of modern patterns of crimes and punishments of American blacks. If the immigration analogy were apt, crime among Northern American blacks should be little more salient today, 45 years after the beginning and 25 years after the end of the major South-to-North migration, than was crime among Southern and Eastern Europeans in the 1950s.

The American pattern of social and economic progress by blacks is much more complicated. Something akin to Disraeli's two nations is appearing within the American black community. A large portion of the black population is becoming much more fully assimilated into American economic and social life; black/white gaps in education, household income, residence patterns, and various public health measures are closing. By some measures—e.g., personal and household incomes of college-educated younger blacks, especially females—some groups of blacks are doing as well or better than their white peers (Jaynes and Williams, 1989; Hacker, 1992; Jencks, 1992).

However, a minority of blacks, disproportionately located in "Rust belt" and "Snow belt" cities, are not making progress and by many measures—welfare dependence, labour force participation, illegitimacy, single-parent households, crime victimization, criminality—are doing worse. It is from this group, sometimes (and sometimes controversially) called the black urban underclass, that black offenders and prisoners grossly, disproportionately come.

For the urban black underclass, at least, the immigration hypothesis does not appear to explain social conditions or criminality. Explanations abound and range from conservative "culture of poverty" and "welfare dependence" (Murray, 1984) arguments to centrist social and structural accounts that emphasize the flight of unskilled jobs and the black middle class from the inner city and general economic conditions (Wilson, 1987) to liberal "legacy of racism" (Lemann, 1991) and radical "contemporary racial discrimination" explanations. Whatever the ultimate reasons, and those mentioned here are but a few among many that have been offered, American blacks' involvement in crime and their presence in jails and prisons remain high.

Most people are instinctively uneasy about black rates of incarceration that appear to be three to four times higher than white rates. The uneasiness is warranted but the disproportion is far greater than three or four to one. The initial tendency to compare American blacks' proportion of the general population, 12 per cent, to their presence in the prison and jail populations, 48 per cent, is understandable, but wrong, and it greatly underestimates the scale of the problem. The better comparison is between racially disaggregated incarceration rates measured as the number of confined persons of a racial group per 100,000 population of that group. By that measure, black incarceration rates are six to seven times higher than white incarceration rates.

CROSS-NATIONAL COMPARISONS

Racial disproportions in the United States among jail, prison, and juvenile inmates, awful as they are, are not radically different from those in Australia, Canada, and England and Wales.

The conventional cross-national comparisons of incarceration rates, limited and methodologically flawed as they are, show gross American incarceration rates to be much higher than those for other countries.

Cross-national comparisons are best seen as crude order-of-magnitude indicators and not as anything more precise. Different countries handle and report pre-trial detainees and short- and long-term prisoners in different ways. In Canada, for example, sentences of two years or longer are served under the authority of the national prison system; sentences under two years are administered by the provinces. In the United States, pre-trial detainees and convicted offenders are distributed among federal, state, and local authorities. The US Bureau of Prisons handles all federal confinement, including pre-trial. In most states, the state prison system houses offenders sentenced to terms of one year or longer and county institutions house pre-trial detainees and under one year sentenced offenders. There are, however, exceptions. Some states, like Connecticut and Delaware, have unified state departments of corrections that house detainees and all convicted offenders. In other states, local jails house offenders serving longer sentences; Pennsylvania's county facilities, in which terms up to five years can be served locally, are the extreme case.

The organization of corrections in the United States presents problems for counting offenders. If, for example, a count of all confined convicted offenders is wanted, data must be obtained from the Federal Bureau of Prisons, 50 state departments of corrections, the District of Columbia, and upwards of 3,312 county jails.

The most accessible source of population data is a series entitled "Prisoners in America," which is compiled and reported semi-annually and reports all confined offenders under the jurisdiction of the Federal Bureau of Prisons and the departments of corrections of the 50 states and the District of Columbia. Counts are provided for total populations on a census date (including detainees and short-term prisoners in unified systems) and prisoners serving sentences of one year or longer. Jail populations are less reliably known. There have been a number of special censuses (in 1972, 1978, 1983, and 1989) and since the early 1980s, an annual "Jail Inmates" report, based partly on estimates, has been published.

The only feasible way to calculate national incarceration rates is to combine the census-date population data reported for a given year in "Prisoners in America" and "Jail Inmates." So calculated, both aggregate and racially disaggregated incarceration rates climbed steadily between 1972 and 1991.

It appears that patterns of differential incarceration by race in Australia, Canada, England and Wales, and the United States are much more similar than differences in their gross incarceration rates suggest. As noted earlier, the ratio of black to white incarceration rates in England and Wales in 1990 was 7.10:1, slightly higher than America's 6.44:1. Differential incarceration of Aboriginal people in Australia makes these patterns appear modest. The Royal Commission into Aboriginal Deaths in Custody (1990) found that "for Australia as a whole, adult Aboriginal people are 15.1 times more likely than adult non-Aboriginal people to be in prison, but they are only 8.3 times more likely to be serving non-custodial correctional orders." Biles (1993*b*) shows that, among persons 17 years and older, Aboriginals were 18.2 times likelier than non-Aboriginals to have been incarcerated on 30 June 1991. Comparisons with Canada are especially difficult because most Canadian jurisdictions, including Ontario, have prohibited the collection and dissemination of racially disaggregated statistics, except concerning the native population. Data obtained privately, excluding Quebec, from the Canadian Centre for Justice Statistics, a division of Statistics Canada, indicate that in 1986–7 natives were admitted to correctional institutions at a rate of 2,662 per 100,000 native population, compared with 315 non-native admissions per 100,000 non-native population (Birkenmayer, 1992). Although these are admissions rather than population data as for the other countries, the admission ratio of 8.45:1 native to non-native is not unlike the population ratios of the other countries.

There seems to be general agreement that violent crime rates are higher in the United States than in other developed countries and that property crime rates are among, but not invariably, the highest. World Health Organization and Interpol comparisons of officially recorded crimes show American crime rates that are much higher than other countries' (Kalish, 1988). Cross-national comparisons of official crime records are, however, subject to even more measurement problems than are incarceration comparisons. Just as national governments increasingly look to victimization surveys for an independent measure of crime that is less subject than police records to variability in reporting and recording, efforts have been made to obtain cross-national victimization data. The most ambitious effort to date concluded that victim-reported crime in the United States was higher than in most developed countries but that, for some offences, American rates were lower than elsewhere, and that the differences between American and other countries' rates were much lower than is revealed by official-rate comparisons (Van Dijk, Mayhew, and Killias, 1990; Van Dijk and Mayhew, 1993).

When America's higher crime rates are taken into account, three findings stand out. First, relative to crime rates, America's incarceration rates are closer to other countries' rates than might otherwise be expected. Secondly, relative to white incarceration rates, or absolutely, America's black incarceration rate is shockingly high. Thirdly, relative to white incarceration rates, Australia, Canada, and England and Wales handle their most prominent visible minority groups no less differentially harshly than does the United States.

The overriding problem turns out not to be a unique American problem of overreliance on incarceration but a general problem in English-speaking white-dominant countries that minority citizens are locked up grossly out of proportion to their numbers in the population.

EXPLANATIONS OF MINORITY OVER-REPRESENTATION

Among numerous questions presented by the preceding data on incarceration of members of minority groups, three stand out. What causes the broad long-term patterns of overincarceration of blacks? Why do some not conspicuously punitive jurisdictions have racial incarceration ratios that are especially unfavourable to blacks? Why has racial disproportionality in American prisons worsened in recent years? Although these same questions appear to apply equally to Australia, Canada, England and Wales, and the United States, my comments here concern the United States; appropriately adapted they may also apply to other countries.

Long-term Racial Disproportion

Much, not all, black over-representation in American prisons over the past 20 years appears to be associated with disproportionate participation by blacks in the kinds of crimes—"imprisonable crimes" like homicide, robbery, aggravated assault, rape—that commonly result in prison sentences. Alfred Blumstein some years ago (1982) analysed black and white incarceration patterns in relation to arrest patterns (and, from victim surveys, victims' identifications of assailants' races, when known) and concluded that 80 per cent of the disproportion appeared to result from blacks' participation in imprisonable crimes. The remaining 20 per cent, he speculated, included some mixture of racially discriminatory discretionary decisions and other, arguably legitimate, sentencing considerations like prior criminal record. Hood (1992) in his study of Crown Courts in the English Midlands similarly concluded that 80 per cent of black-white incarceration differences "can be accounted for by the greater number of black offenders who appeared for sentence . . . and by the nature and circumstances of the crimes they were convicted of" (p. 205).

Blumstein's conclusion that involvement in crime, not racial bias, explains much of the black disproportion among prisoners in the early 1980s is consistent with most recent reviews of empirical research on discrimination in sentencing (Wilbanks, 1987). Most analyses of the past 15 years using multivariate techniques do not reveal racial bias as a major predictor of sentencing outcomes.

Most likely, however, if Blumstein's study were redone today, his imprisonable crimes analyses would be less powerful (e.g., Hawkins, 1986). As noted below, drug offenders make up a steadily increasing proportion of prisoners, and they are even more disproportionately black than are other felony offenders.[3] Although I see no reason to believe that court processing is more racially biased than in recent years, both the national policy decision to launch a War on Drugs and local police decisions to focus on street trafficking foreseeably increased black arrests, prosecutions, convictions, and incarcerations.

The absence of research evidence of invidious discrimination is not evidence of its absence. Bias no doubt remains common—sometimes as a matter of conscious ill-will, more commonly as a result of unconscious stereotyping and attribution by middle-class and white officials of special dangerousness to underclass minority offenders. Moreover, all but the most sophisticated studies can be confounded by cross-cutting biases that result in harsher treatment of some black offenders and less harsh treatment of offenders (generally black) whose victims are black. Another complication is that many of the arguably legitimate bases for distinguishing among offenders, such as the nature of a criminal record, systematically adversely affect blacks (whose average first arrest is at a younger age than the average first arrest for whites and who, controlling for age and offence, are likely to have accrued more prior arrests and convictions, which may themselves result from earlier conscious and unconscious discrimination against blacks). Nonetheless, at day's end, there is relatively little empirical basis for concluding that all or a large portion of the long-term disproportion in prison numbers results from invidious racial discrimination in processing of cases once arrests have been made.

Variations in Racial Ratios

That Minnesota and Wisconsin, generally considered among America's most socially and politically progressive states, and leaders in setting enlightened sentencing and corrections policies, have the most racially disproportionate incarceration rates in the country may strike many as surprising. They achieved that dishonour not only in the data reported here but in earlier analyses using 1979 (Hawkins, 1985) and 1982 (Blumstein, 1988) data.

At least three considerations partly explain the seeming anomaly. First, in jurisdictions in which blacks constitute a small percentage of the population, like Minnesota and Wisconsin (and England), the minority population is typically concentrated in urban areas. Crime rates are higher in urban than in suburban and rural areas; that a preponderantly urban black population experiences higher rates of criminality and incarceration than do groups that are more widely dispersed geographically is to be expected. In states like Georgia, Mississippi, and South Carolina, blacks live throughout the state and thus come from low, moderate, and high crime areas.

Secondly, black Americans are likelier than whites to be unemployed, ill educated, and to have been raised in single-parent households and impoverished circumstances (Jaynes and Williams, 1989). All of these things are associated with increased participation in crime and, not unnaturally, are also associated with heightened arrest and incarceration probabilities (Blumstein et al., 1986).

Thirdly, in states like Minnesota, Iowa, and Wisconsin that have relatively low incarceration rates, prison spaces are principally used for persons convicted of violent and otherwise especially serious crimes. If the black populations of such states are small in number, concentrated in urban areas, and socially disadvantaged, they are disproportionately likely to be involved in serious crimes. By contrast, in states like Georgia, Alabama, California, and Texas, in which imprisonment rates are high, reflecting incarceration of many persons convicted of less serious crimes, larger proportions of white offenders are imprisoned and racial disproportions are less.

No doubt racial discrimination, especially in unconscious forms related to stereotyping and attribution of threatening characteristics to minority offenders, also plays a role in the extreme racial incarceration ratios in states like Minnesota. Nonetheless, much of the variation appears explicable in terms of crimes committed and previous criminal records.

The Short-term Worsening of Racial Ratios

Racial disproportion has worsened markedly in recent years, as shown by a series of recent analyses showing that one in four black American males aged 20 to 29 is in jail or prison, on probation or parole (Mauer, 1990) and that in the District of Columbia (Miller, 1992a) and Baltimore (Miller, 1992b), 42 and 56 per cent, respectively, of black males aged 18 to 35 were under the control of the criminal justice system.

The recent worsening is the result of deliberate policy choices of federal and state officials to "toughen" sentencing, in an era of failing and stable crime rates, and to launch a "War on Drugs" during a period when all general population surveys showed declining levels of drug use, beginning in the early 1980s (e.g., National Institute on Drug Abuse, 1991).

At every level of the criminal justice system empirical analyses demonstrate that increasing black disproportion has resulted from the War on Drugs—in juvenile institutions (Snyder, 1990), in jails (Flanagan and Maguire, 1992, table 6.49), and in state (Flanagan and Maguire, 1992, table 6.81; Perkins, 1992, tables 1–5) and federal (US Sentencing Commission, 1991) prisons. The experience in several state prison systems is illustrative.

One example is black and white admissions per 100,000 same-race population to North Carolina prisons from 1970 to 1990. White rates held steady during the entire period. Black rates doubled between 1980 and 1990 from a higher starting point, increasing most rapidly after 1987. According to Stevens Clarke, the foremost scholar of North Carolina sentencing and corrections trends, the War on Drugs has increasingly targeted blacks: "in 1984 about twice as many whites (10,269) as blacks (5,021) were arrested for drug offenses. . . . By 1989, annual drug arrests of blacks had grown by 183 per cent, reaching 14,192; drug arrests of whites increased only by 36 per cent (to 14,007)" (Clarke 1992:12).

In Pennsylvania, drug commitments of black males increased by 1,613 per cent during the decade; white males by 477 per cent. The pattern for females was similar, though the differences were less dramatic. In 1990, 11 per cent of Pennsylvanians were black; 58 per cent of state prisoners were black (Clark, 1992).

In Virginia, 62 per cent of drug offenders committed in 1983 were white, 38 per cent were non-white. By 1989, those percentages had more than reversed; 65 per cent of drug commitments were non-white, 35 per cent were white. Drug commitments have continued to rise since 1989; current data would show worse racial disproportion.

Phrased most charitably to the officials who launched and conducted America's latest War on Drugs, worsening of racial incarceration patterns was a foreseen but not intended consequence. Less charitably, the recent blackening of America's prison population is the product of malign neglect.

REDRESSING RACIAL IMBALANCE

Problems of race and punishment in America are both more severe than is generally recognized and yet, controlling for crime rates, not all that much worse than in other English-speaking countries. Although increasing numbers of American blacks are moving into the middle-class, for a sizable minority the traditional pattern of assimilation of in-migrants is not working. In any case, the immigration analogy patently does not hold for black residents of southern states. In the black urban underclass, rates of unemployment, illegitimacy, single-parent households, delinquency, and other correlates of social disorganization are far higher than in other population groups.

These patterns pose formidable—if obvious—policy problems. Concern for victims' rights to live their lives free from fear, assaults, and property loss obliges the state to respond to predatory crime and criminals. Because much crime is intra-racial, concern for minority victims necessarily occasions criminal justice system intervention in the lives of minority offenders. Insofar as predatory crime is concentrated in the inner cities and predatory criminals disproportionately come from groups that lack opportunities, resources, and social supports, blacks are likely to continue to be disproportionately present among arrestees and defendants.

Nonetheless, there are things that could be done to diminish racial disproportion. First, although the criminal law cannot acknowledge extreme social adversity as an affirmative defence, at all stages from prosecution to sentencing and parole, adversity can be recognized as an informal mitigating circumstance to justify diversion from prosecution and avoidance of prison in all possible cases and to justify, provision of drug and alcohol treatment, remedial education, vocational training and placement, and supportive social services to minority and other disadvantaged offenders.

Secondly, designers of law enforcement policies should take account of foreseeable racial effects of alternative policy choices. Although American constitutional law sometimes distinguishes between actions taken with the purpose of discriminating against blacks, and actions taken for other purposes but with knowledge that they will systematically disadvantage blacks, policymakers should generally treat purpose and knowledge as moral equivalents (as they are in criminal law *mens rea* doctrines). The decision heavily to favour law enforcement over prevention and treatment strategies in the American War on Drugs, for example, was pre-ordained to affect young black males especially severely and for that reason alone (there are others) the "War" should never have been launched.

Thirdly, policymakers generally should begin to look to delinquency and criminality as diagnostic markers of group social distress. Among recent immigrant groups, those in which offending is conspicuously more common than in other contemporaneous immigrant groups should be targeted for social services and supports. South-east Asian tribal immigrants in the United States like the Meo and the Hmong, for example, were less well-situated than the Vietnamese, many of whom were educated urban dwellers, to succeed in America's capitalist economy. If second and third generation, Meo and Hmong people demonstrate unusually high levels of criminality (it is too soon to tell), that will be powerful evidence that, as a group, they are having particular difficulty adjusting to life in a new country, and, accordingly, that the state should allocate resources to help them overcome barriers to assimilation.

American blacks are the paradigm case of an identifiable subgroup that needs special aid in entry, into full participation in American life. Fewer than 30 years have passed since discrimination against blacks in many settings ceased to be legal and full legal rights have only slowly, and as yet imperfectly, been institutionalized in day-to-day life. All American blacks suffer from the legacy of slavery and legal racism and many, especially southern agricultural migrants and their children and residents of inner city underclass areas, have suffered from inadequacies in education, employment opportunities, and health care. American social policy since the 1970s has not provided adequate educational programmes, housing, and income support to disadvantaged blacks, and their disproportionate participation in crime is in part the result. The War on Drugs has worsened the prospects for disadvantaged blacks by giving a majority of young urban black males criminal records, thereby diminishing prospects for jobs, marriage, and law-abiding material success. Conversely, the deteriorating life chances of underclass black males have made them less promising prospects as life partners of black women and are contributing to declining marriage rates and accelerating illegitimacy and single-parent households among black women.

Americans have a remarkable ability to endure suffering by others. Racially disaggregated incarceration patterns show that black Americans are suffering severely. Whether the recent presidential election will produce a more caring government and a more compassionate climate, prepared to deal seriously with the problems of disadvantaged American blacks, remains to be seen. If not, the intolerable racial disproportion in America's prisons and jails is likely long to continue.

NOTES

1. With some exceptions, prisons hold convicted offenders serving terms of one year or longer; jails hold pre-trial detainees and convicted offenders serving terms up to one year.

2. "Incarceration rate," as used in this essay, refers to the numbers confined on a census date, or the average daily confined population, per 100,000 residents.

3. More recently Blumstein (1993) analysed 1991 data and concluded that 76 per cent of the variance could be explained on the basis of arrests (the decline resulted from black over-representation among the greatly increased numbers of those arrested for drug offences).

REFERENCES

Allen-Hagen, B. (1991). *Public Juvenile Facilities, Children in Custody 1989*. Washington, DC: US Department of Justice, Office of Juvenile Justice and Delinquency Prevention.

Austin, J., and McVey, A. D. (1989). *The Impact of the War on Drugs*. San Francisco: National Council on Crime and Delinquency.

Biles, D. (1993a). Personal correspondence with the author, 23 March.

———. (1993b). "Imprisonment in Australia," *Overcrowded Times*, 4(3): 4–6.

Birkenmayer, A. (1992). Communication from the Chief, Corrections Program. Canadian Centre for Justice Statistics, Statistics Canada.

Blumstein, A. (1982). "On the Racial Disproportionality of United States' Prison Populations," *Journal of Criminal Law and Criminology*, 73: 1259–81.

———. (1988). "Prison Populations: A System Out of Control?" in M. Tonry and N. Morris, eds, *Crime and Justice*, vol. 10. Chicago: University of Chicago Press.

———. (1993). "Racial Disproportion of U.S. Prison Populations Revisited," *University of Colorado Law Review*, 64: 743–60.

Blumstein, A., Cohen, J., Roth, J., and Visher, C., eds. (1986). *Criminal Careers and "Career Criminals."* Washington, DC: National Academy Press.

Bureau of Justice Statistics. (1984). *The 1983 Jail Census.* Washington, DC: US Department of Justice.

———. (1985). *Jail Inmates, 1983.* Washington, DC: US Department of Justice.

———. (1987). *Correctional Populations in the United States, 1985.* Washington, DC: US Department of Justice.

———. (1989*a*). *Correctional Populations in the United States, 1987.* Washington, DC: US Department of Justice.

———. (1989*b*). *Correctional Populations in the United States, 1986.* Washington, DC: US Department of Justice.

———. (1991*a*). *Correctional Populations in the United States, 1989.* Washington, DC: US Department of Justice.

———. (1991*b*). *Correctional Populations in the United States, 1988.* Washington, DC: US Department of Justice.

———. (1991*c*). *Census of Local Jails, 1988.* Washington, DC: US Department of Justice.

Bureau of Justice Statistics. (1992). *Jail Inmates, 1991.* Washington, DC: US Department of Justice.

———. (1992). *Statistical Abstract of the United States—1992.* Washington, DC: US Government Printing Office. Washington, DC: US Department of Justice, Bureau of Justice Statistics.

Glazer, N., and Moynihan, D. (1963). *Beyond the Melting Pot.* Cambridge, MA: MIT Press.

Hacker, A. (1992). *Two Nations: Black and White, Separate, Hostile, Unequal.* New York: Scribner.

Hawkins, D. F. (1985). "Trends in Black–White Imprisonment: Changing Conceptions of Race or Changing Conceptions of Social Control?," *Crime and Social Justice*, 24: 187–209.

———. (1986). "Race, Crime Type, and Imprisonment," *Justice Quarterly*, 3: 251–69.

Home Office. (1991). *The Prison Population in 1990.* London: Home Office, Statistical Department.

Hood, R. (1992). *Race and Sentencing.* Oxford: Oxford University Press.

Jankowski, L. W. (1992). *Correctional Populations in the United States, 1990.* Washington, DC: US Department of Justice, Bureau of Justice Statistics.

Jaynes, D. G., and Williams, R. M., Jr., eds. (1989). *A Common Destiny: Blacks and American Society.* Report of the Committee on the Status of Black Americans, National Academy of Sciences. Washington, DC: National Academy Press.

Jencks, C. (1992). *Rethinking Social Policy.* Cambridge, MA: Harvard University Press.

Kalish, C. (1988). *International Crime Rates.* Washington, DC: US Department of Justice, Bureau of Justice Statistics.

Katz, M. (1989). *The Undeserving Poor.* New York: Pantheon.

Krisberg, B., and DeComo, R. (1992). *National Juvenile Custody Trends 1978–89.* Washington, DC: US Department of Justice, Office of Juvenile Justice and Delinquency Prevention.

Langan, P. A. (1991). *Race of Persons Admitted to State and Federal Institutions, 1926–86.* Washington, DC: US Department of Justice, Bureau of Justice Statistics.

Lemann, N. (1991). *The Promised Land—The Great Black Migration and How It Changed America.* New York: Alfred Knopf.

Mauer, M. (1990). "Young Black Men and the Criminal Justice System," Washington, DC: The Sentencing Project.

Miller, J. G. (1992a). "42% of Black D.C. Males, 18 to 35, Under Criminal Justice System Control," *Overcrowded Times*, 3(3): 1, 11.

———. (1992b). "56 Percent of Young Black Males in Baltimore Under Justice System Control," *Overcrowded Times*, 3(6): 1, 10, 16.

Murray, C. (1984). *Losing Ground—American Social Policy, 1950–1980.* New York: Basic.

National Institute on Drug Abuse. (1991). *National Household Survey on Drug Abuse: Population Estimates 1990.* Washington, DC: US Government Printing Office.

Perkins, C. (1992). *National Corrections Reporting Program, 1989.* Washington, DC: US Department of Justice, Bureau of Justice Statistics.

Perkins, C., and Gilliard, D. K. (1992). *National Corrections Reporting Program, 1988.* Washington, DC: US Department of Justice, Bureau of Justice Statistics.

Proband, S. C. (1991). "Black, White Incarceration Rates," *Overcrowded Times*, 2(3): 6–7.

Royal Commission into Aboriginal Deaths In Custody. (1990). *Report.* Canberra.

Snyder, H. N. (1990). *Growth in Minority Detentions Attributed to Drug Law Violators.* Washington, DC: US Department of Justice, Office of Juvenile Justice and Delinquency Prevention.

US National Commission on Law Observance and Enforcement. (1931). *Report on Crime and the Foreign Born.* Washington, DC: US Government Printing Office.

US Sentencing Commission. (1991). *The Federal Sentencing Guidelines: A Report on the Operation of the Guidelines System and Short-term Impacts on Disparity in Sentencing. Use of Incarceration, and Prosecutorial Discretion and Plea Bargaining.* Washington, DC: US Sentencing Commission.

Van Dijk, J., and Mayhew, P. (1993). *Criminal Victimisation in the Industrialised World: Key Findings of the 1989 and 1992 International Crime Surveys.* The Hague: Ministry of Justice.

Van Dijk, J., Mayhew, P., and Killias, M. (1990). *Experiences of Crime Across the World: Key Findings from the 1989 International Crime Survey.* Boston: Kluwer.

Wilbanks, W. (1987). *The Myth of a Racist Criminal Justice System.* Monterey, CA: Brooks/Cole.

Wilson, W. J. (1987). *The Truly Disadvantaged: The Inner City, the Underclass, and Public Policy.* Chicago: University of Chicago Press.

What Not to Do about Crime—
The American Society of Criminology
1994 Presidential Address

JEROME H. SKOLNICK

The 1960s drew to an end exactly a quarter of a century ago and have already been catalogued into history as the decade of protest and civil disorder. Some of us can recall vividly the bitter and divisive race riots that shook dozens of American cities from Los Angeles to Detroit to Newark. Protest against American involvement in Vietnam had become so familiar that it had almost acquired the status of an institution.

I was asked in the summer of 1968 to direct a so-called "task force" on "Violent Aspects of Protest and Confrontation" for the National Commission on the Causes and Prevention of Violence. The task force report, published in June 1969 under the title *The Politics of Protest* (Skolnick, 1969), did not interpret protest as merely irrational and unseemly behavior committed by immoral miscreants. On the contrary, my young colleagues and I tried to understand the reasons motivating protest and confrontation. We were not alone in our approach and research. Perhaps the most famous and disturbing conclusion about the urban riots was from the Kerner Commission report:

> What white Americans have never fully understood—but what the Negro can never forget—is that white society is deeply implicated in the ghetto. White institutions created it, white institutions maintain it, and white society condones it (Kerner Commission, 1968:2).

Our report concluded with a reference to garrison cities (a concept introduced by political theorist Harold Lasswell), where order is achieved by force rather than by consent. And we wrote:

> If American society concentrates on the development of more sophisticated control techniques, it will move itself into a destructive and self defeating position. A democratic society cannot depend upon force as its recurrent answer to longstanding and legitimate grievances (Skolnick, 1969:326).

The Kerner report found that a large proportion of riot participants were young, between 15 and 24 years of age, and that, in the African American community, this age group experienced extraordinarily high unemployment rates, often around 50% (Skolnick, 1969). Is it merely a coincidence that this high-unemployment age group is responsible for a disproportionately high crime rate? I do not believe so.

Source: Skolnick, Jerome. What Not to Do about Crime—The American Society of Criminology 1994 Presidential Address. *Criminology* 33 (1): 1–16, 1995.

Although the causal relationship between crime and employment is complex, it cannot be dismissed. It is not only that people who have reasonably well-paying jobs are less likely to commit crimes than those who don't. It is rather that work is a fundamental aspect of social control. Work disciplines one's daily rounds. Work brings responsibility. Work supports the family life and moral values that conservatives complain we have lost. In the distinction Joan McCord drew in her Sutherland Award lecture (McCord, 1994), unemployment is a risk factor for crime. Patterned unemployment, through time and across racial and ethnic divisions, is a cause. Youth is also a risk factor. Jobless youth, who tend to be impetuous, to engage in male bonding activities that we call gangs—are likely to be free from ordinary social constraints. Nor are they likely to be deterred by the threat of imprisonment, partly because they are not rational, long-range cost-benefit calculators, partly because the threat of apprehension is not entirely credible, but mostly because they have few alternatives.

The threat of imprisonment can be attenuated by even a rational risk assessor who has little to lose and much to gain by a life of crime, especially the crime of drug marketing. We do need jobs programs, but not necessarily costly governmental ones. When employment rises, the Federal Reserve Board typically raises interest rates to mollify the bond market's fears of inflation, likely without even considering the link between employment opportunity and crime.

It is important that we develop a broader understanding of the social, economic, and historical causes of crime. Based on social science research and analysis, the commissions of the 1960s—the Crime Commission, the Kerner Civil Disorders Commission, and the Eisenhower Violence Commission—cautioned the nation about underlying social needs and problems. If the lessons of history and research had been absorbed, and their conclusions followed, contemporary crime policy could have been set on a positive course. Instead, crime has emerged as a "hot button" political issue, driven by the anxieties of the moment, the politics of resentment, and the shadow of race. Legislators are passing such measures as expansion of the death penalty; habitual offender laws; increased mandatory and minimum sentencing provisions; the removal of athletic facilities, television sets, and radios from jails and prisons; and even, as in Mississippi, requiring prisoners to wear striped uniforms with the word "convict" emblazoned across the back (Nossiter, 1994). Such measures are scarcely an effective response to the crime problem. But they are a satisfying symbolic response to public fears.

Sociologists familiar with the work of Emile Durkheim will appreciate the genesis of such punitive impulses. Thus, David Garland (1990:32) writes that for Durkheim, "The essence of punishment is irrational, unthinking emotion fixed by a sense of the sacred and its violation. Passion lies at the heart of punishment."

Yet Durkheim also comprehended that durable social control arises not from the pain and suffering punishment imposes, but by binding the individual to the social group, "by making his society an integral part of him, so that he can no more separate himself from it than from himself" (Durkheim, 1961:277). In consequence, he writes in his lectures on moral education, "To punish is not to make others suffer in body or soul; it is to affirm, in the face of an offense, the rule that the offense would deny" (Durkheim, 1961:176). Tragically, this deeper comprehension of the nature, purpose, and limitations of punishment is rarely evident among aspirants for public office.

While this is a discouraging period, it is not a time to despair. There is much to be said critically and constructively about laws and policies that divert tax dollars from vital purposes, solidify the entrenchment of an already powerful enforcement-correctional complex, and leave the public as insecure and unsafe as ever. What NOT to do about crime is as commanding a topic for criminologists as what to do about it, and that is what I propose to discuss.

THE LIMITS OF INTUITION

Everyone I suggest, is motivated by two responses to serious crime—the urge to retaliate and the wish for public and private safety. Intuitively, most people, and lately most legislators, presume that lengthy imprisonment, determinate sentencing, mandatory minimum sentencing, and severe habitual offender laws offer safety along with retribution. But as criminologists and other social scientists have often shown, intuition alone isn't a sound basis for judging what will or won't work, at what cost, and with what side effects.

The most compelling evidence against the lock 'em up impulse is found in recent history. As a nation, we have not been hesitant to imprison offenders. Imprisonment rates doubled in the 1970s, tripled in the 1980s, and threaten to go ballistic by the turn of the century. United Nations data show the United States to have the highest rate of imprisonment of any country in the world. In 1991 we had 426 prisoners per 100,000 compared to South Africa's 333 and the former Soviet Union's 268 (Mauer, 1991).

However imprecise international statistics may be when comparing democratic countries with totalitarian states, one fact is clear—especially during the 1980s—we have not been, as is often alleged in the political arena, "soft on crime." The Bureau of Justice Statistics (1994a) reported on October 27 that the number of men and women in American prisons on June 30, 1994, was 1,012,851, topping one million for the first time. The prison population grew by 1,500 a week in 1994 (Holmes, 1994). (This does not include the jail population, which, when last counted in 1992, amounted to 445,000.) But we may have been incarcerating the wrong people, the wrong way, and have failed to distinguish those who, on grounds of justice and prudence, merit lengthy incapacitation from those whose offenses are less serious and entrenched in character. Moreover, we have packed our prisons and erected a vast criminal and sometimes dangerously violent enterprise by addressing a public health problem—drug dependence and addiction—through the criminal law. More about that later.

The District of Columbia has the highest incarceration rate in the nation (1,578 per 100,000), followed by Texas (545) and Louisiana (514). My state, California, the nation's largest, is also the nation's biggest jailer, with one out of eight American prisoners occupying our cells (Bureau of Justice Statistics, 1994a). During the past 16 years, the California prison population has increased sixfold and at a huge cost to the taxpayer. The prison budget has increased 400% in the past decade, the corrections budget 500%, while violent crime has risen by 40%. In 1983–84, 14% of the California budget was allocated to higher education and 4% to prisons. Today, the education and prison budgets meet at 9% (Baum and Bedrick, 1994).

My emphasis on California should not be dismissed as merely parochial. In a special "Prisons" edition of *The British Journal of Criminology*, Franklin E. Zimring and Gordon Hawkins show that correctional growth in California has been "in a class by itself in the 1980's," constituting "a singular event in American correctional history" (Zimring and Hawkins, 1994a:83). The three other major American state prison systems, those of New York, Texas, and Florida, experienced half the growth of California, and western European systems about a quarter. Our high growth rate should have made our citizens feel far safer in the 1990s than they did in the 1980s. It would be hard to claim that they do.

And yet California is looking to a future of more unprecedented spending on imprisonment. The State Department of Corrections (DOC) released an analysis of the costs of California's "Three Strikes" law on February 28, 1994, estimating that 20 more prisons would be needed in addition to the current 28 and the 12 on the drawing board (California Department of Corrections, 1994). The DOC estimates that by the year 2027 the costs of housing extra inmates will peak at $5.7 billion. "Three Strikes" will force the state to incarcerate 275,621 more inmates over the next three decades—the equivalent of building an electrified fence around the population of Anaheim. The Rand Corporation released a study in October 1994 predicting that in only eight years (from FY92) Three Strikes will consume 18% of California's budget. Consequently, when Three Strikes is actually implemented, scarcely 1% of state funds will be available for higher education in California in the 21st century (Rydell et al., 1994).

Our recently passed Three Strikes bill is complicated, but it unquestionably casts the widest offender net, even wider than those of the states of Washington and New York, and the new federal bill. California's law defines the first two strikes as violent and "serious" felonies. The third strike is any felony. In some California counties more than half of the "third strike" cases filed have involved such nonviolent offenses as shoplifting, auto burglary, theft of cigarettes and—in one Los Angeles case—theft of a pizza. A juvenile can be involved in two auto thefts. Years later, if convicted of passing a bad check, he can be sent to prison for life. District attorneys across the state have assailed the law, arguing that it will clog courts, result in costly litigation, require an enormous expansion of courts and prison facilities, and result in disproportionate punishment for nonviolent offenders.

On September 13, 1994, Los Angeles officials gave testimony to the Board of Supervisors that seemed perfectly to illustrate Robert K. Merton's celebrated "unanticipated consequences of purposive social action" concept. Sheriff Sherman Block testified that during the first six months since the Three Strikes law's enactment 1,700 inmates were added to county jails that were already under court order to limit crowding. Block, District Attorney Gil Garcetti, and a panel of trial judges warned that although the law was meant to clear the streets of career criminals, the gridlock it is causing could force officials to release thousands of petty criminals "as the wheels of justice grind to a halt." The only solution, the law enforcement officials warned, will be cutbacks in public services or higher taxes (Muir, 1994).

However irrational as a crime control measure, "Three Strikes and You're Out" appears to have mesmerized the public and politicians from one coast to the other and across party lines. It may be the most potent conjoining of crime and politics in the history of the Republic.

Why has crime become America's number one problem in the polls? Crime statistics are ambiguous. Reported crime rates have in the past several years been stabilizing or declining. Thus, the Federal Bureau of Investigation's (1993) Uniform Crime Report (released on October 3, 1993) states that its "Crime Index" showed a decline of 4% from 1991 to 1992. In California, a report released by Attorney General Dan Lundgren, based on 1993 numbers from the 63 law enforcement jurisdictions that serve populations of 100,000 or more, showed a decline in robbery (3.7%), forcible rape (8.1%), aggravated assault (4%), and burglary (5.2%). Only homicide was up, by 5% (California Department of Justice, 1994).

Yet on the other coast, New York City reported a slight decline in homicides, 1,960 in 1993, as compared to 1,995 in 1992. And these homicides were clustered in 12 of the city's 75 police districts, places like East New York (which is in Brooklyn) and the South Bronx. "On the east side of Manhattan," Matthew Purdy wrote in *The New York Times*, "in the quiet streets of exclusive apartments, the gunfire might as well be in a distant city" (Purdy, 1994:B5). However, an October 30, 1994, press release summarizing the National Crime Victimization Survey—which obviously excludes victims of homicide—offers a complex picture. Overall, the crime rate was essentially unchanged, yet violent crime rose by 4.6% in 1993. At the same time, rape and sexual assault declined by nearly 21%. Attempted assaults without a weapon were up 11%. However, other petty crime, such as theft of cash or property under $50, fell 7%. According to the Bureau of Justice Statistics summary:

> The data reflect a recent pattern in which the levels of certain completed
> violent crimes, such as simple assault completed with injury, have been de-

clining or holding steady while the levels of attempted victimizations, such as attempted simple assault without a weapon, have generally been on the increase (Bureau of Justice Statistics, 1994b).

The complexity of these figures aside, what we know is most disturbing to victims and potential victims alike is random street violence.

Franklin Zimring and Gordon Hawkins recently reviewed the crime statistics of Los Angeles and Sydney, Australia (Zimring and Hawkins, 1994b). The cities are comparably populated and multicultural, although Sydney is less so. Sydney's burglary rate is actually 10% higher than that of Los Angeles and its theft rate is 73% of LA's. But its robbery and homicide rates are strikingly lower—only 12.5% of LA's robbery rate and only 7.3% of LA's homicide rate. And so my wife and I, like other tourists, walked the streets of Sydney in 1993 confident that we would not be assaulted.

Whatever the real level of random violence, fear of crime tends to be higher and rises with publicity. Crime reportage has long been the staple story of the evening news; and the volume of television news has exploded in the past 30 years.[1] Moreover, in the post-modern world of satellite technology, a crime committed in Petaluma, California, frightens viewers in Poughkeepsie, New York. Another contribution to fear of crime may, paradoxically, be the response of politicians. Does a Willy Horton advertisement respond to fear of crime or cause it? It is probably both, consequence and cause—and an opportunity for political exploitation. In any case, a combination of shocking crimes—Polly Klaas's abduction and murder in such a serene place as Petaluma, California, the venue for Ronald Reagan's "Morning in America" commercial, the killing of tourists in south Florida, the roadside murder of basketball star Michael Jordan's father, televised reportage of grisly murders in a variety of workplaces, and the killing of commuters on a Long Island Railroad train, as well as an outbreak of political advertisements focusing on fear of crime—sent a scary message of social breakdown to the majority of Americans who do not reside in the inner cities. The message? You are not longer immune from random violence anywhere—not in your suburban home, commuter train, office building, or automobile—and the police and courts cannot or will not protect your. Three words—"soft on crime"—have become the crowning curse of political discourse. And sharply rising incapacitation measures have been its consequence.

The cost-effectiveness of incapacitation has recently formed part of the debate in California, as it has elsewhere. Philip Romero, chief economist and chief deputy director of the Governor's Office of Planning and Research, issued a report on March 31, 1994, arguing that despite the high costs of incapacitation, we save because the costs of crime are so high (Romero, 1994). This analysis makes a number of highly questionable assumptions. Romero estimates that each incarcerated offender saves—he says conservatively—around $200,000 annually in victim and social costs. Thus, in 1995, the addition of 3,580 inmates will save $716 million. By such estimates, the 140,000 we now imprison saved us $28 billion.

There are at least four flaws in this analysis: (1) It assumes a finite group of criminals, without considering youngsters who will become criminals while incarcerated convicts age into sharply lower crime-committing years. (2) It assumes an average criminal, although in California we will be locking up more auto thieves than the seriously violent. (3) It assumes hypothetical benefits, while prison costs are real and will grow as the prison population ages. Although it currently costs about $21,000 annually to keep one 30-year-old inmate in a California state prison for one year, the costs rise to $60,000 when that inmate reaches 50. For those 60 and over, the annual cost is projected to be $69,000 in this lowest recidivating cohort (Zimbardo, 1994). (4) It ignores opportunity costs. Thus, a new prison costs more than $333 million (including interest on construction bonds). That money could put more than 8,000 teachers into school classrooms or support nearly 90,000 children in Head Start programs (Zimbardo, 1994).

Crime statistics are complex, but data strongly suggest that locking people up has scarcely led to a reduction in crime. As James Austin and John Irwin point out in their 1993 National Council on Crime and Delinquency pamphlet *Does Imprisonment Reduce Crime?*, the states with the highest crime rates also have the highest imprisonment rates. "If the imprisonment/crime reduction hypothesis were valid," they write, "the safest jurisdiction in the country would be Washington D.C. which has by far the highest imprisonment rate in the world (1,168 per 100,000 residents)" (National Council on Crime and Delinquency, 1993:16–17). And from 1960 to 1991, although there have been fluctuations in crime rates, "the fact remains that in the face of a 165 percent increase in imprisonment rates, the overall UCR crime rate has increased by over 200 percent, property crimes by nearly 200 percent, and violent crime by over 370 percent" (pp. 16–17).

The intuitive reply is that we haven't locked up enough criminals. American Enterprise Institute Fellow Ben Wattenberg began a December 17, 1993, article in the *Wall Street Journal* by saying that, "Thanks to angry American voters, the 'crime issue' is prominent again, as it ought to be. It is our biggest problem" (Wattenberg, 1993:14). Criminologists and crime policy wonks, Wattenberg added, don't know what works. What works, he wrote, is what everyone intuitively knows. It is this: "A thug in prison cannot shoot your sister." Of course. But in reality, imprisoning a thug will not save a sister from an abusive spouse or boyfriend, or from offenders who are entering the age cohort in which crime begins, and in which crime control faces its greatest challenge.

THE COMPLEXITY OF CRIME CONTROL

The major increase in serious violent offending has been among teenagers and young men in their twenties. The ages of 15 to 24 are generally recognized as the high crime-risk years. The National Youth Survey (a longitudinal study of a probability sample of 1,725 American youth conducted by Delbert S. Elliott and reported on in last year's Presidential Address) found that serious violent offending (aggravated assault, rape, or robbery involving some injury or weapon) peaks at age 17. At 24, it's half as much as it was at 17 (Elliott, 1994:5).

Serious violent offending declines significantly as offenders mature into their thirties, but teenage male involvement in serious violent offending is astonishing and frightening. "At the peak age (17)" Elliott reported, "36% of African American (black) males and 25% of non-Hispanic (white) males report one or more serious violent offenses" (p.5). As if to confirm Elliott's self-report data, the Centers for Disease Control and Prevention released a report on October 13, 1994, showing that from 1985 to 1992, the annual rate at which young men 15 to 19 years old were being killed jumped 154%, far surpassing the rate changes in any other group. Practically all of the increase was attributable to the use of guns, which a director of the study, Dr. Mark Rosenberg, called "an epidemic of firearms death among young men" (Butterfield, 1994:AlO).

If we imprison youthful violent offenders for life, rather than into their thirties, we will do so in the twilight of their criminal careers, while other young offenders take their place. If we are primarily interested in preventing crime, rather than in punishing offenders, we need to address crime prevention by youngsters who are growing into the high-crime cohort. "Three Strikes for Life" laws will eventually fill our prisons with geriatric offenders, whose care will be increasingly expensive when their propensities to commit crime are at the lowest.

THE RISE IN IMPRISONMENT

Two trends are responsible for confinement's rise. First, longer sentences are being imposed for such nonviolent felonies as larceny, theft, and motor vehicle theft. In 1992, these crimes accounted (according to the Uniform Crime Report) for 66% of crime in America. As James Q. Wilson, who has not in the past been averse to imprisonment, recently wrote: "very large increases in the prison population can produce only very modest reductions in crime rates." "Judges," he observes, "already send the most serious offenders with the longest records to prison," and "the most serious offenders typically get the longest sentences" (Wilson, 1994:38).

Second, everyone who works in the criminal justice system recognizes that drugs have become its driving force. According to the Bureau of Justice Statistics (1992) more than half of all violent offenders in state prisons said they were under the influence of alcohol or drugs at the time of their offense.

There has been an explosion of arrests and convictions and increasingly longer sentences for possessing and selling drugs. A Justice Department study, completed last summer, but not released until February, found that of the 90,000 federal prison inmates, one fifth are low-level drug offenders with no current or prior violence or previous prison time (Fagan, 1994b). They are jamming the prisons. The federal prison population, through mandated and determinate sentences, has tripled in the past decade. It will rise by 50% by the century's turn, with drug offenders accounting for 60% of the federal prison population. Yet as Jeffrey Fagan concluded, following his own field research and a review of the literature on the effect of criminal sanctions on drug selling:

> As long as demand for drugs remains high, and the likelihood of marginal gains from drug selling are sufficient to neutralize motivations to avoid crime or participate in illicit work, offenders in socially and economically marginal neighborhoods may continue to perceive strong economic benefits from participation in the drug economy (Fagan, 1994a:206).

Nevertheless, our primary antidrug policy has been to threaten sizable dealers, particularly so-called drug kingpins, with long prison terms or death to punish them, to incapacitate them, and most of all, to deter others from following in their felonious paths. Unfortunately, this policy results in the Felix Mitchell paradox, which I named in honor of the West Coast's once most notorious drug kingpin. In the 1980s, dogged Oakland, California, detectives provided evidence to the federal government to send Mr. Mitchell to a federal prison for the rest of his life. Mitchell was killed in prison, so his life was short. Were potential drug sellers in the Bay Area deterred by Mr. Mitchell's life sentence, indeed his death sentence? On the contrary, drug sales continued and, with Mitchell's monopolistic pricing eliminated, competition reduced the price of crack-cocaine. The main effect of Mitchell's imprisonment was to destabilize the market, lowering drug prices and increasing violence as rival gang members challenged each other for market share. The aftermath saw a rise in drive-by shootings, street homicides, and felonious assaults. By indirection, effective law enforcement, followed by incapacitation, had stimulated serious random violence.

On January 3, 1994, the *San Francisco Chronicle* reported the successful arrest and prosecution of some of Mr. Mitchell's successors, Timothy Bluitt and Marvin Johnson. The *Chronicle* also reported that other gangsters are already vying for control of the Bay Area drug market. "When a guy like Bluitt goes down, someone takes his place and gets an even bigger slice of the pie," the *Chronicle* reported an anonymous federal agent as having said, "The whole process is about consolidating turf and power." It didn't take long for that to happen. Eight months later, the Drug Enforcement Administration and local police carried out the largest roundup of drug dealers ever conducted in Northern California. Authorities arrested 25 suspected gang members, seized 20 kilograms of cocaine, and confiscated 43 weapons and $200,000 in cash. Bob Bender, the special agent in charge with the Drug Enforcement Administration entertained no illusions about the impact of the raid on drug marketing. "We certainly have not stopped the flow of cocaine coming from South America," he said, "and probably won't in the foreseeable future as long as we have a demand" (Lee, 1994:A21). Crime, drugs, and violence make up the contemporary American dilemma, one that has been growing since the 1960s. (Readers of *Justice Without Trial* may recall that this author participated in what was then the largest drug bust in the history of Northern California. The drug was, of course, heroin. See Skolnick, 1993.) Youngsters who sell drugs in Oakland, Detroit, Los Angeles, Kansas City, Atlanta, and New York are part of generations who have learned to see drug marketing and associated crime as economic opportunity. Whether because of criminal records or lack of education or technical skills, a formidable economic wall separates young inner-city youths from the world of legal work (Fagan, 1994b). This does not excuse their criminal behavior, but it does intensify our need to change it, to break the cycle of poverty, abuse, and violence that dominates their lives and moves them in criminal directions. Prisons do not deter partly because the Mitchells and Bluitts and the Johnsons do not rationally calculate with the same evaluative standards that legislators have, and partly because they live in a world already more foreboding than any prison, one which continually threatens street-imposed death penalties. The soaring homicide rates of the late 1980s and early 1990s are largely the consequence of an underground drug economy, where legal remedies for breach of contract are unavailable, but where efficient and hazardous assault weapons are increasingly accessible.

So we need to move in two directions. First, as Alfred Blumstein (1993) suggested in his Presidential Address two years ago, our criminogenic, and thus expensive, failing and violence-producing drug prohibition policies need to be reconsidered and recast. We need to move from policies that precipitate illegal markets to the maximization of public health through regulation, education, and treatment. Second, the crime commission mandated by the 1994 Crime Bill should focus on crime prevention, not merely on punishment. As economist Robert Eisner (1994:A27) recently wrote, such a program would "include measures to bring up a new generation of educated citizens who would be productive in a technologically advanced economy." Ultimately, crime reduction depends on economic growth, opportunity, and productivity. Unless we achieve those goals, we will intensify economic inequality. We are already projecting its correlate—an American archipelago of imprisonment, which cannot be in the interest of a free society.

CONCLUSION: POLITICS AND CRIMINOLOGY

Criminologists have long faced a troubling dilemma. How do we address crime and social problems with our research results and analytical strategies in the face of public and political demands for emotionally generated punitive measures that many of us regard as shortsighted, ineffectual, and as in the case of drug policy, counterproductive? First, we must consider and appreciate our lineage. The discipline of criminology was initiated by such Enlightenment philosophers as Beccaria and Bentham. The contemporary legal philosopher H.L.A. Hart (1982:45) wrote that the Enlightenment philosophers made the form and severity of punishment "a matter to be *thought* about, to be *reasoned* about, and *argued*, and not merely a matter to be left to feelings and sentiment." Our contemporary research and thinking must remain true to this heritage.

Second, public opinion can be changed, possibly even in this controversial sphere. Daniel Yankelovich (1994), the public opinion and social trends researcher, distinguishes between "raw opinion," the early stages of public debate on an issue, and responsible public judgment, when the public has the opportunity to consider alternatives and payoffs. Our task as criminologists is to bring evidence and reasoned discussion to the debate over crime control, to inform the public about these "alternatives and payoffs," and to move the discussion from "raw opinion" to "responsible public judgment." As descendants of the philosophers of the Enlightenment, we should do no less. But my message is not elitist. We should try to influence public policy through the opinion pages of newspapers, magazine articles, television, and radio. It is a time to stand up and be counted as well as to count. The alternative, which is inaction and despair, should be unacceptable.

NOTE

1. The explosion of news and bad news is a point made in a special report on "Antipolitics: Anger and Divisiveness in the '94 Campaign" in the *New York Times* on October 16, 1994. Candace McCoy and I made a similar observation a few years earlier in "Police Accountability and the Media" (Skolnick and McCoy, 1993).

REFERENCES

Baum, N. and B. Bedrick. 1994. *Trading Books for Bars: The Lopsided Funding Battle Between Prisons and Universities.* San Francisco: Center on Juvenile and Criminal Justice.

Blumstein, Alfred. 1993. *Making Rationality Relevant.* Criminology 31:1–16.

Bureau of Justice Statistics. 1992. *Drugs, Crime and the Justice System: A National Report from the Bureau of Justice Statistics.* Washington, DC: Government Printing Office.

———. 1994a. *State and Federal Prison Population Tops One Million—State and Federal Prisoners at Midyear 1994.* Pre-publication press release, October 27, 1994. Washington, DC: Bureau of Justice Statistics.

———. 1994b. *Crime Rate Essentially Unchanged Last Year.* Pre-publication press release, October 30, 1994. Washington, DC: Bureau of Justice Statistics.

Butterfield, F. 1994. "Teen-age Homicide Rate Has Soared." *New York Times*, October 14, 1994:A10.

California Department of Corrections. 1994. *Population and Fiscal Estimate of the "Three Strikes" Initiative.* Sacramento: California Department of Corrections, Offender Information Services Branch, Legislative Estimates Unit.

California Department of Justice. 1994. *Crime and Delinquency in California, 1993.* Sacramento: California Department of Justice, Office of Management, Evaluation and Training, Division of Law Enforcement.

Cronin, T. E., M. Horowitz, C. Burr. 1994. "Special Report—Antipolitics: Anger and Divisiveness in the '94 Campaign." *New York Times*, October 16, 1994:37ff.

Durkheim, E. 1961. *Moral Education: A Study in the Theory and Application of the Sociology of Education.* New York: Free Press.

Eisner, R. 1994. "A Choice and an Echo." *New York Times*, October 26, 1994:A27.

Elliott, D. S. 1994. *Serious Violent Offenders: Onset, Developmental Course, and Termination.* Criminology 32:1–21.

Fagan, J. A. 1994a. "Do Criminal Sanctions Deter Drug Crimes?" In Doris L. McKenzie and Craig Uchida (eds.), *Drugs and Crime.* Thousand Oaks, CA: Sage.

———. 1994b. *Legal and Illegal Work: Crime, Work and Unemployment.* Paper prepared for the Center for Urban Affairs and Policy Research, Northwestern University.

Federal Bureau of Investigation. 1993. *Crime in the United States, 1992.* Washington, DC: Government Printing Office.

Garland, D. 1990. *Punishment and Modern Society: A Study in Social Theory.* Chicago: University of Chicago Press.

Hart, H. L. A. 1982. *Essays on Bentham: Jurisprudence and Political Theory.* New York: Oxford University Press.

Holmes, S. A. 1994. "Ranks of Inmates Reach One Million in a Two-Decade Rise." *New York Times*, October 28, 1994:A1.

Lee, H. K. 1994. Drug Gang Power Shift Expected. *San Francisco Chronicle*, September 2, 1994:A21.

Kerner Commission. 1968. *Report of the National Advisory Commission on Civil Disorders.* New York: Bantam Books.

Mauer, M. 1991. *America Behind Bars: A Comparison of International Rates of Incarceration.* Washington, DC: The Sentencing Project.

McCord, J. 1994. *Three Issues Regarding a Search for Causes. Edwin H. Sutherland Award Address.* Annual Meeting of the American Society of Criminology. November 10, Miami, FL.

Muir, F. M. 1994. "Supervisors Warned on Three Strikes." *Los Angeles Times*, September 14, 1994:Bl.

National Council on Crime and Delinquency. 1993. *Reducing Crime in America: A Pragmatic Approach.* San Francisco: National Council on Crime and Delinquency.

Nossiter, A. 1994. "Making Hard Time Harder: States Cut Jail TV and Sports." *New York Times*, September 17, 1994:Al.

Purdy, M. 1994. "1993 Homicides Fewer but More Clustered Around New York City." *New York Times*, January 10, 1994:B5.

Romero, P. J. 1994. *How Incarcerating More Felons Will Benefit California's Economy*. Sacramento, CA: Governor's Office of Planning and Research.

Rydell, C. P., A. F. Abrahamse, J. P. Caulkins. 1994. *Modeling the Costs and Benefits of Three Strikes Laws*. Santa Monica, CA: Rand Corporation.

Skolnick, J. H. 1993. *Justice Without Trial: Law Enforcement in Democratic Society*. 3d ed. New York: Macmillan.

──────. 1969. *The Politics of Protest*. A Task Force Report submitted to the National Commission on the Causes and Prevention of Violence. New York: Simon and Schuster.

Skolnick, J. H. and C. McCoy. 1984. "Police Accountability and the Media." *American Bar Foundation Research Journal* 3:521–558.

Wattenberg, B. J. 1993. "Crime Solution—Lock'em Up." *Wall Street Journal*, December 17, 1993:14.

Wilson, J. Q. 1994. "Prisons in a Free Society." *Public Interest* 117:37–40.

Yankelovich, Daniel. 1994. "What Polls Say—And What They Mean." *New York Times*, September 17.

Zimbardo, P. G. 1994. *Transforming California's Prisons in Expensive Old Age Homes for Felons: Enormous Hidden Costs and Consequences for California's Taxpayers*. San Francisco: Center on Juvenile and Criminal Justice.

Zimring, F. E. and G. Hawkins. 1994a. "The Growth of Imprisonment in California." *The British Journal of Criminology* 34:83–96.

──────. 1994b. *Crime Is Not the Problem*. Unpublished paper (chapter in a forthcoming book) presented to the Berkeley Roundtable on Crime Policy, California Policy Seminar, Center for the Study of Law and Society, University of California at Berkeley.

The Bull Market in Corrections

Kenneth Adams

With a resounding chant that echoes loudly across the nation, America's solution for the crime problem can be heard—"Lock 'em up, lock 'em up, lock 'em all up." When it comes to correctional systems, the nation has stolen the motto of the Empire state—Excelsior! Bigger is definitely better.

Source: *The Prison Journal*, Volume 76, Number 4, December 1996, pp. 461–467, Sage Periodicals Press, Thousand Oaks, CA.

America has experienced a tremendous bull market in corrections, with unprecedented growth in offender populations and astonishing increases in expenditures. The statistics are indeed impressive. The average annual rate of expansion in corrections over the past 15 years has been 7.6%. Currently, more than 5 million men and women, representing 2.7% of the adult population, are under correctional supervision. According to some estimates, as many as one out of twenty-two adult males were in correctional custody on any given day in 1993. Of those under supervision, some one and a half million offenders were incarcerated in prisons and jails. In 1995, the prison population set another record increase: 90,000 new inmates were sentenced to prisons translating into 1,725 new prison beds a week. Forecasts indicate that by the year 2000, the prison population will increase again by half, putting the total population in the neighborhood of two and a quarter million inmates. For 1996, corrections again leads the way in state appropriations, outpacing every other category of spending with an average 13.3% increase. As savvy investors have known for some time, there's profit to be made in corrections. Now, they are asking themselves, How much higher can this market go? Will the bubble burst? What does the future hold for corrections?

The fundamentals of the prison industry are very solid. The estimated costs of incarcerating 1.3 million inmates is $26.8 billion annually, and at least six states have a prison budget greater than $1 billion. Consumer demand has been strongly trending upward for well over a decade and shows no signs of abating. Demand is driven by sophisticated marketing strategies, and key market makers, legislators, judges, and policy wonks are trying to outdo each other vying for the public's admiration. Bill Bennett, former secretary of education, has been riding around the nation with his lock 'em up gang trying to stir up support for more record breaking increases in prison construction. (Schools and prisons must have more in common than we think!) His chief gunslinger, John DiIulio, who prefers pen to pistol, stands ready to shoot it out with anyone who challenges the desirability of massive increases in prison spending. In what may be the greatest advertising gimmick of the decade, second perhaps only to Joe Camel, DiIulio has been promoting the "super-predator"—a fatherless, godless, jobless, armed to the teeth, gang-involved urban teenager—as the compelling reason for more prisons. Having raised the art of fear-mongering to an all-time high, the beauty of this promotional strategy is that it comes at a time when crime rates are going down, thereby fending off the possibility that other competitors for the taxpayers' money, such as education, commerce, and health, may divert the revenue stream. Never mind that the "super-predator" is about as elusive as the Loch Ness monster. The image is so terrifying that even otherwise sensible Nebraska farmers are willing to pay for more prison construction. Look for a CLIO award next year.

With demand at an all-time high, consumers stand ready to buy any and all prison construction schemes with little concern for value or quality. Take

Pennsylvania, for example. Prison expansion has cost about $760 million. Eight new prisons have been built in the last five years. Yet, the inmate population stands at 41% over capacity. [Pennsylvania] Auditor General Barbara Hafer, stated "We simply cannot build prisons fast enough to alleviate the chronic problem of prison overcrowding." Or take Massachusetts. The state sent 299 inmates halfway across the country to Texas to ease overcrowding at a cost of $4.5 to $5 million. Bean towners go to the rodeo. There's a curious picture.

The supply-demand picture is likely to remain out of balance for some time. States pretty much have a monopoly in the prison industry. There is little competition because the product is unique and because financial barriers to market entry are high in the form of capital investment. Although private companies, backed by venture capital firms, have been trying to cash in on the prison boom, so far they have only made progress through niche marketing. Furthermore, knowledgeable investors are aware that in the prison industry the supply demand function often works in reverse. More supply brings increased demand. Industry insiders know that there are more than enough inmates to go around.

The industry has received a substantial injection of new capital from government sources, which are notorious for profligate spending. Raw materials, in form of inmates, are relatively cheap and in constant supply. According to some experts, formal education is a real liability in prison work, so prison workers are plentiful and wages are accordingly low. With only a few weeks training, a new hire can be walking the galleys supervising inmates. The basic technology of the industry is very simple and not subject to obsolescence. The product has been around for more than two centuries, essentially in its original form. Although new products, such as intensive probation, electronic monitoring, and drug treatment centers, are being developed, they pose little threat to prisons. In the industry, these products are called "intermediate sanctions," yet no one really knows where they fit in. At best, intermediate sanctions might capture the low end of the market by providing more sanctions at lower price points.

There are, however, a few dark spots in this otherwise bright picture. These should be considered as growing pains rather than serious illnesses. Turnover of personnel is high, which decreases returns on investments in human capital and puts pressure on recruitment and training budgets. In Florida, dangerously high turnover rates have led most prisons to be staffed at minimum levels, despite a budget of almost one and a half billion dollars. To aggravate the situation, prison administrators use antiquated management techniques dating back to the inception of the industry. This shortcoming is most obvious in the area of personnel, where concepts such as participatory management and quality work circles are rarely recognized or understood. Contemporary management practices could be used productively to offset the liabilities of working for low wages in potentially dangerous environments. However, as long as work tasks are kept simple the supply of semi-skilled laborers should be adequate. Furthermore, prison systems are notoriously loyal to employees when it comes to job security. When was the last time a prison worker was laid off? The promise of lifetime job tenure can reduce staff turnover among experienced employees. One has only to look at college professors to realize this is the case.

On occasion, inmates will show signs of instability in form of riots and disturbances. When the U.S. House of Representatives voted to keep the enhanced penalties for crack cocaine, inmates at FCI Talladega in Alabama rioted and set fire to part of the facility. Disturbances also occurred at five other federal prisons, leading the Department of Justice to order a lock down of all medium and maximum security facilities. North Carolina inmates housed in Tennessee prisons have rioted to protest being incarcerated away from home. These incidents are rare and are properly seen by the industry as local aberrations.

Workplace safety gets raised as an issue, and excessive workman's comp expenditures can negatively impact the balance sheet. The rate of inmate attacks in Florida prisons has increased 62% from 1990 to 1994. Similarly, assaults at high-security prisons in the federal prison system increased by 18% in FY '94. The industry, however, is taking aggressive steps to deal with this problem. A new product line is being introduced, the ultra high-security prison, which test marketing indicates will be very popular with consumers. Code named the "maxi-maxi," this prison uses state-of-the-art technology that virtually eliminates management problems. Imagine a prison in which inmates almost never come into contact with another person! This dream is now made possible through the miracle of modern electronics. While the product sells at a premium, the promised savings in operational costs makes the product popular even among cost-conscious buyers. Once this new product penetrates the market, industry revenues are expected to grow tremendously.

Pessimists will point out that the maxi-maxi may be subject to regulation because it involves human rights violations. However, there is little threat that regulatory interference will undermine the success of this product. An unwritten code of etiquette keeps one government agency from interfering with the business of another. Even the most august of governmental bodies, the Supreme Court, gives virtually free reign to prison managers citing the exigencies of dealing with offenders. Prison is an industry with mystique—a mystique based on security concerns that pays off in terms of a loosely regulated managerial environment.

Some analysts will point out that the quality of prison output is difficult to measure and that raw materials are not always of highest quality, often requiring considerable processing in the form of educational and health services. They also observe that cash flow is starting to be squeezed by governments that are starting to show some reluctance to huge increases in prison expenditures. They fail to realize, however, that aggressive steps are being taken to bring prison costs under control. The traditional private or semi-private room for inmates is lost to nostalgia. Double bunking, dormitories, barracks, and pup tents are now the norm.

Costs in some areas, such as health care, are escalating rapidly, and the issue is particularly serious with respect to elderly inmates. The size of the elderly inmate population is doubling every four years as a result of longer sentences and restrictions on parole, and it costs $69,000 a year to incarcerate an inmate over 60 years of age compared to a national average of $18,333. The industry is effectively meeting these challenges through a variety of cost-containment measures. Medical care is being outsourced, and the age-old prison concept of "just in time" medical care is being revitalized to minimize even further the inventory of medical personnel and supplies. Ideas also are being adapted from industries in other sectors of the economy. Co-payments for inmate medical services are being required in some prison systems to discourage unnecessary requests for treatment.

Another important development designed to reduce costs is the concept of "no frills" prisons. In these institutions, non-essential items such as televisions, telephones, hot plates, and weightlifting equipment are eliminated. Because these are not "big ticket" items they do not impact the balance sheet in a major way. However, the "no-frills" message is transforming prisons into "lean and mean" organizations in which everyone, including inmates, assumes responsibility for controlling costs. Between maxi-maxi and no frills institutions, prisons are revamping their product line from top to bottom to meet the needs of a changing market.

Within the next year, Texas may become the world leader in the no frills market. Proposals are on the table to eliminate all prison programs that do not reduce recidivism. Staff that do not contribute to the bottom line will be eliminated. This sort of radical downsizing epitomizes the commitment of industry leaders to meeting the challenges of the future. Just wait until the idea catches on and the same kind of hard-nosed cost-benefit analysis is applied to every aspect of prison operations. If it doesn't prevent crime, eliminate it. The savings will really start to roll in! Such ruthlessly tough management strategies will undoubtedly keep America at the forefront of the prison industry.

Industry watchers are especially excited by this development given Texas's record for innovative thinking. Its "vita-pro" campaign took the industry by surprise. The concept is so simple that it is hard to understand why another prison system did not think of it first. By using vita-pro—an inexpensive, soybean-based meat extender—in prison meals the cost of food service can be reduced dramatically. What is most amazing about the vita-pro campaign are the unanticipated benefits. The taste of food became so offensive that inmates refused to eat and guards were no longer tempted to pilfer from the prison pantry. Food service costs plummeted! With a keen eye towards the future, the Texas prison system jockeyed to become the exclusive national distributor of vita-pro. Now, the state stands to make enormous profits as the third largest prison system throws its clout behind this innovative product.

Looking back over the course of the bull market in corrections, one can see that the market has been very generous to investors. Yet, the rising tide has not affected all ships equally, the gains having been spread unevenly. Professional traders, in the form of lobbyists and executives of prison-related industries, have made a killing, the likes of which have not been seen since the last great bull market in the defense sector. Small cap companies in private corrections have done exceedingly well, and can be expected to outperform in the future. Among the better known companies, Wackenhut Corrections Corporation reported an 86% increase and Corrections Corporation of America an 85% increase in third quarter net income from 1994 to 1995. Based on the first three quarters of 1995, combined annual revenues for these two companies should be close to $300 million. Finally, one IPO, boot camps, has captured the imagination of investors, moving in a short time from an unknown, fledgling industry to a serious contender for the light-weight correctional championship.

In contrast, returns for the average citizen have been decidedly mixed, especially for stakeholders in big-cap states, such as California, New York, and Texas, who have watched state balance sheets erode in a turbulent economic environment. Between 1980 and 1992, non-violent offenses accounted for 84% of the increase in court commitments. The true return on this investment remains to be determined. Although crime rates are coming down, much of the decline can be attributed to the changing demographics of the country and the aging of the baby boom generation. Small investors also have been blind to attractive investment opportunities in other sectors, such as education, health, and other social services, and thus may suffer from lost opportunity costs. For the first time in California's history, the corrections budget ($3.8 billion) equals that for higher education, and it is predicted that three strikes legislation will cause the corrections budget to double as a percent of total state spending by 2002, wiping out expenditures in higher education unless taxes are raised.

Professional sentiment on the future of the corrections bull market is mixed. Liberals are extremely bearish, calling for a severe correction and perhaps even a market collapse. However, their pessimistic prognostications have failed to materialize for many years now, leaving them to cry "chicken little" with each prison bond issue. Law and order conservatives, in contrast, are bullish, cheering on each record high in prison populations. In support of their enthusiasm, one of the most respected houses on the street, the U.S. Department of Justice, recently has entered the prison market in a big way. This white shoe firm has set up a $10.5 billion margin account via the Violent Crime Control and Law Enforcement Act of 1994. The account is intended to encourage prison expansion by allowing states to invest in prison construction at a discount to market price.

With each new market high, there are signs of behavior which suggest that the market may have reached its top. Some actions are mildly silly. Inmates in Georgia are required to wear uniforms with large bold type declaring the wearer a state prisoner. Mississippi inmates are required to wear color-coded, zebra striped uniforms. North Carolina has a toll-free hot-line so that citizens can phone in work assignments for prison inmates. Other actions are a bit more serious. Florida recently became the third state, along with Alabama and Arizona, to initiate forced inmate labor or chain gangs. The Mississippi House of Representatives approved a measure that allows hard labor or corporal punishment to be imposed on inmates. In Tennessee, there was a proposal to cane offenders on courthouse steps. These developments are to be expected as a natural by-product of a frothy market. Only when the enthusiasm for punishment reaches the extreme should we worry about such developments.

Some analysts point out that when judged by traditional valuation ratios the market may be oversold. They do not understand that the dynamics of the market have changed. The average citizen is willing to bet the proverbial farm on incarceration, hoping for impressive long-term returns. Although historical evidence indicates that these expectations are unrealistic, emotion has its way of driving prison populations still higher. Fear and greed are the dominant market forces, and fear is rarely in short supply when it comes to dealing with crime. Those who portend disaster only provide the wall of worry that the market needs to climb in order to go higher. For those who are concerned about the continuation of the bull market in corrections, there is only one piece of advice to be offered: Consider investing in tulips.

REFERENCE

Hafer, B. (Auditor General). P.A. Auditor General reveals financial impact of prison overcrowding. Corrections Alert, 2(18),6.

The Future of the Penitentiary

KENNETH ADAMS
TIMOTHY J. FLANAGAN
JAMES W. MARQUART

Predicting the future is risky business. The safest course is to assume that in the short run the future will be very similar to the recent past. In the longer term, however, there are very few time series describing social, economic, and political trends that do not show wide swings in *both* directions. As of mid-1997, the Dow Jones Industrial Average hovers at 8,000, following meteoric increases between 1987 and 1997. The giddiness associated with this economic trend may portend its own reversal. Unabashed confidence in the future leads to foolish behavior such as failing to hedge bets and neglect of fundamental principals, such as not putting all of your eggs in one basket.

For those without a sense of history, it is tempting to predict that the massive increases we have seen in American prison and jail populations since 1980 are a trend that will characterize the United States "in the long run." During the twentieth century, however, prisoner populations have both risen and fallen; there have been extended periods of growth punctuated by periods in which the inmate count has actually declined.

Just 30 years ago a blue-ribbon President's Commission on Law Enforcement and Administration of Justice, appointed by Lyndon B. Johnson, spoke authoritatively and forcefully about such concepts as a "moratorium on prison construction" in the United States and referred to community-based alternatives to imprisonment as "the last best hope for corrections." The 1960s were characterized by declining incarceration rates in the United States, and by optimism about the possibility of rehabilitation and reform of criminals through the developing science of penology. Since 1980, however, there have been important changes in the forces that affect incarceration rates. Unless the policy-relevant forces that drive incarceration rates shift, our historically high contemporary rates may continue to grow well into the twenty-first century.

First, the faith and optimism that surrounded "the rehabilitative ideal" in corrections is virtually extinguished. Nearly all subgroups of the American public—from university freshmen to inner city residents—report pessimistic views about the prospect of rehabilitating criminals. The pursuit of correctional rehabilitation has been replaced by the twin ideologies of punishment and incapacitation. Prisons and jails are increasingly seen not as instruments of public safety because of activities and programs that occur within them to change lawbreakers, but as institutions that secure public safety simply by keeping offenders away from the rest of us. This view of the prison is compatible with changing public sentiment about the causes and motivations of criminal behavior. Where crime was once viewed as a "social problem" facilitated by the failure of society to provide for its members, today society is blameless and the individual offender is seen as a wholly volitional creature who makes "rational choices" to engage in crime. Such people cannot be changed, accordingly to the contemporary view, but they *can* assuredly be confined to protect others from the effects of their choices. For many, declining crime rates in the early 1990s concomitant with increasing incarceration rates is powerful evidence of the wisdom of this strategy. The annual announcement of crime rate reductions is therefore coupled with calls for more prisons, longer sentences, and harder time.

The last quarter-century has also been characterized by declining confidence in government, academia, and other social institutions, and a consonant increase in the demand for accountability for public funds. In this context, expenditures for correctional treatment programs are questioned, especially in the face of three-year reincarceration rates that exceed 40 percent. Public officials and citizens wonder why they must invest in teachers, psychologists, and other treatment personnel in prisons when so much of the work of these expensive professionals appears to be inconsequential in terms of recidivism. These funds could be redirected to bricks and mortar, to construct additional prisons that would enable us to lock up more offenders for longer periods of time. And, regardless of what happens to the criminal behind bars, we assure ourselves of the popular truism that "a thug in jail can't shoot your sister." As a result, spending public funds to enlarge prison capacity is transformed into an "investment" in public safety, while treatment and rehabilitation efforts are viewed as "luxuries" that already-burdened taxpayers can ill afford.

Numerous scholars and commentators have observed that the "public mind" in relation to crime and criminal justice has changed in recent decades. Attitudes of the public toward crime and criminals have hardened; survey after survey shows strong support for incarcerating more criminals and for longer periods of time. Similarly, support for capital punishment has risen among all segments of the population. In this context, imprisonment has become the public's "punishment of choice" for dealing with criminals, and community alternatives to prison have lost support. Despite scholars' plans for sliding scales of "intermediate sanctions," the evidence suggests that the public views prison as the only penalty (other than the death penalty) that really matters.

Elected public officials have read these trends (some argue that politicians have *led* these trends) and operationalized them in an astonishing array of statutory changes. The litany of "get tough" laws began in earnest with mandatory imprisonment statutes for certain high-profile offenses (e.g., drug offenses, weapons offenses). These were followed by the ambitious determinate sentencing laws that simultaneously appealed to liberals (because they curtailed unwanted discretionary authority of judges and other criminal justice officials) and to conservatives (who applauded restoration of sentencing authority to legislatures and prosecutors). More recently, legislators have found life-without-parole provisions and the enormously popular "three strikes and you're out" laws to be potent weapons in the "get tough" movement. Even more recently, legislation designed to make life *within* prisons more punitive has been embraced with fervor, as efforts are undertaken to strip prisons of education, recreation, and other programs toward the goal of more, and more populated "no-frills" prisons. The reemergence of the concept of "last resort" prisons for inmates who require "maxi-maxi" security is another illustration of this trend.

CONSEQUENCES

What have been the consequences of this movement to make prisons the principal weapon in the war against crime and drug use? First, and predictably, the number of correctional facilities, the number of persons confined within prisons and jails, and the rate of incarceration in America have increased to historic levels. The rapid expansion of the correctional apparatus in most states has made corrections the fastest growing segment of state government employment and expenditures during the last decade, outstripping growth in Medicaid, welfare, education, and other services. In terms of the percentage of the population who are confined, the percentage of public dollars spent to support corrections, and the percentage of government funds spent on criminal justice activities, corrections has been America's premier "growth industry" since 1980.

Along with the gigantic growth in prisoners and budgets, there have been other effects of the explosion of incarceration. Racial disproportionality of the nation's prisons has worsened during this period. Numerous observers have noted that the captives of the national "War on Drugs" have been disproportionately African-Americans, and that the largest increases in recent years have been among Hispanic inmates. In addition to growing racial disproportionality, regional differences in the use of prisons have become more apparent during the great prison build-up. Southern states remain the undisputed national leaders in terms of the percentage of citizens jailed and imprisoned, and the variance between southern incarceration rates and those of other parts of the country have been accentuated.

The last decade also has witnessed a revitalization of the private prison industry in the U.S. and other nations. As governments struggle to keep pace with the ever-increasing demand for more incarceration and the associated strain on state and local budgets, the appeal of private firms that promise to build prisons more quickly, with less bureaucratic red-tape, and for less money is evident. When coupled with creative financing packages and contractual per-diem operating charges, the allure of privatization—the increased capacity to deliver a valuable public service more economically to citizens who clamor for it—is considerable.

According to some forecasts, if the current rate of growth continues, the U.S. prison population will exceed five million by the end of the first decade of the twenty-first century, and total spending on corrections will equal all current government spending today. These dire forecasts most likely will not come to pass. More temperate extrapolations indicate that the present rate of growth in corrections probably is not sustainable. Crime rates appear to be coming down across the nation, and already people are starting to question the need for additional prison space. If the declining trend in crime rates continues, the need for more prison space will appear less compelling, especially in light of increasing competition for government spending from other sectors. Correctional populations will continue to grow, however, albeit at a much more modest rate.

In the balance of this essay, we explore several likely developments in prison operations, administration, policy, and programs as America's great "prison experiment" continues into the twenty-first century.

PRISON OPERATIONS

Several aspects of the expansion will influence future prison operations. Most of the new prison cells that were built during the expansion boom were medium or minimum security beds. Consequently, the overall security profile of prison systems has been shifted downward. Since inmate classification systems were modified to accommodate this change, this shift in system-wide security profiles should be relatively permanent. As a result, prison administrators should have added flexibility in assigning inmates to facilities and programs in the future.

The rapid expansion of prison systems also has meant that many relatively young employees could rise to positions of responsibility very quickly. Additionally, as a matter of economy, many new correctional facilities have been built in close proximity to pre-existing facilities, creating "institutional clusters" or "local correctional complexes" that make it possible to advance or change jobs without having to relocate. Thus, a major drawback of career advancement has been reduced at the same time that more opportunities for advancement have been created. These developments may make corrections a more attractive option for those contemplating criminal justice careers. However, this rapid rate of career development may set unrealistic expectations for the future. As the pace of career advancement slows, as it probably will if growth in prison construction slows, dissatisfaction may set in among middle and upper management. Many correctional executives may "jump ship" when the retirement clock tolls an attractive tune, perhaps taking positions in private corrections or in other human service fields.

Another aspect of rapid prison growth is the need to hire large numbers of entry-level employees. Recruitment in corrections has always been a difficult sell, given the salaries and working conditions. In order to be successful, large scale recruiting measures either have to be very aggressive or have to tap groups that historically have not entered prison work. Whether these new employees have the skills and commitment to work successfully in prison environments remains to be seen. Job satisfaction and performance are tied to training, which unfortunately has been given short shrift in many prison systems during the construction frenzy of the late 1990s.

At various junctures, we will likely find that prison expansion has been overdone and that institutional capacity has been overbuilt. This situation presents two options. Older prison facilities can be "mothballed," thereby improving overall prison conditions. Alternatively, surplus prison facilities can be adapted to other purposes where security issues are important. For example, in Texas, thousands of prison beds initially built for adult offenders are being converted for use by juveniles. Such developments will bring a blurring of the line between prisons and other institutions that have to deal with recalcitrant clients, most clearly with regard to the physical plant and probably also in terms of the institutional climate and staff roles.

INCREASED ACCOUNTABILITY

Across all areas of government, there have been calls for more accountability. The trend has not left corrections unaffected. Correctional decisions now have to be justified at all levels, from governors and legislators down to wardens and prison guards. With accountability comes oversight and scrutiny, something that in the past has not always endeared itself to prison administrators. Gone are the days when the warden was king of his own private correctional island where decisions went unquestioned unless a crisis developed. Today, there are many bureaucrats employed by central corrections agencies who are dedicated to scrutinizing, circumscribing, and even dictating the day-to-day aspects of facility operations.

In carrying out the mandate for greater accountability, the common standard for scrutiny will be economy and public safety. These themes are most clearly seen in some aspects of prison operations such as health care, where spiraling costs scream out from the ledger sheet for control, while courts and medical professionals stand ready to pass judgment on the adequacy of inmate medical care.

In some cases, demands for accountability will pose new challenges, especially in the area of prison programming. For example, inmate education programs in Texas have been criticized for not *demonstrating* their contribution to reducing recidivism. More generally, legislators periodically argue that all prison programs should justify their existence through demonstrable reductions in postrelease crime rate—the traditional "bottom-line" outcome measure for corrections.

Another consequence of increased accountability is that information systems and the persons who manipulate the data in these systems will become increasingly important. Information is the cornerstone of accountability. Again, these issues can be seen clearly in the area of health care. Prison systems are implementing computerized health care information systems in order to document service delivery for legislators, courts, and treatment providers.

EMPHASIS ON PUBLIC SAFETY

A concern for public safety has permeated all aspects of the criminal justice system. As discussed above, a major reason underlying the tremendous growth in prison populations is the perception that more severe punishment will bring down the crime rate. In corrections, this emphasis has influenced not only the *number* of persons sent to prison, but the *types* of persons who are incarcerated, the length of prison *terms*, and the types of *activities* that are carried out in prisons.

Changes brought about by the emphasis on public safety can be radical. The goal conflict between treatment and custody that has saddled prisons since their inception is a relic, an historical curiosity of interest mainly to scholars who write correctional textbooks. The major rationale for prison programming is no longer treatment but "dynamic security." Thus a program's impact on an offender's criminality is subjugated to the more immediate concerns of keeping inmates busy and out of trouble. Nowadays, prison programs are seen more as a means of riot prevention than crime prevention.

Concerns over public safety clearly have affected who comes to prison and how long they stay. While these matters are not directly under control of prison administrators, being largely under the purview of prosecutors and judges, they have greatly influenced correctional work. Prison populations increasingly consist of young offenders and violent offenders. As a result of changes in waiver statutes, many young violent offenders who previously would have been dealt with as juveniles are being prosecuted as adults and sentenced to the adult prison system. Mandatory sentences for violent offenses, repeat violent offender enhancements, and "three strikes" legislation also have fueled an influx of violent offenders. At the back end of the prison system, changes in good time programs and in early release programs have contributed further to extended prison stays for violent offenders.

These developments have impacted prison operations in many ways from classification procedures, facility and cell block assignments, and program assignments, disciplinary and good time procedures to parole release decisions. In the case of violent offenders, the problems are at least familiar to prison officials, even if their magnitudes have increased, and familiar strategies typically are deployed on an ad hoc basis. However, given that the time line for inmates has lengthened, a systematic perspective seems warranted over a "tried and true" piecemeal approach. In many cases, it makes sense to think about inmates in terms of prison careers, meaning the changes in an inmate's actions, activities, attitudes and associations that take place over the course of a prison term. The career perspective accommodates change and development by placing cross-sectional situational elements in the larger context of an inmate's prison term. An advantage of the career approach is that it does not reify an inmate's status as violent, disruptive, noncooperative, dangerous, or recalcitrant. Also, the approach emphasizes the prison system's impact on the inmate along with the inmate's impact on the system.

Another consequence of the influx of violent offenders is that prison work has become more dangerous. The "professional thief" is a *rara avis* in today's prisons. Contemporary inmates are rooted in a synergistic nexus of drugs, guns, and gangs, an unholy trinity that in many cases implicates serious violence. Also, as many experienced wardens report, the inmate "code of honor" is a vestige of days gone by. Old taboos about how inmates are to interact among themselves or with prison staff have been cast aside, in the process increasing levels of apprehension and uncertainty across the board. Consequently, the social climate of many prisons has changed. Relations among inmates have become more predatory, and inmate-staff relations have become more hostile and unpredictable. In many prison systems, the number of assaults against prison staff has increased dramatically. Whether the increase can be attributed to changes in inmate populations, prison staff or both is not clear. However, this development poses security challenges in terms of operations and training and brings increased costs in the form of injuries to prison guards.

When it comes to dealing with violence in prisons, "doing more of what we have been doing" can be a reasonable response, although the strategy overlooks the fact that quantitatively different problems are sometimes best approached in qualitatively different ways. We are seeing a rise in popularity of the ultra-high security facilities or "maxi-maxi" prisons. These facilities represent the *ne plus ultra* of modern security, combining salty dog correctional wisdom with technological glitz. It remains to be seen whether these concrete and steel edifices of external restraint are as safe, efficient, cost-effective, and humane in the long run as they are said to be. In the short run, however, we can expect a continuation of this trend. More "maxi-maxi" prisons, the granddaddy of high security institutions, will be built, while its lesser cousin, the administrative segregation unit will continue to proliferate. Increases in the number of inmates placed in administrative segregation within regular prison units may be more consequential, given the volume of inmates involved and the decentralized, ubiquitous nature of these units.

While violent adult offenders present a familiar, albeit somewhat intractable problem, young offenders, particularly juveniles, present new and unfamiliar challenges. Just as junior high school students differ from high school students who differ from college students, so too do juvenile offenders differ from young offenders who differ from adult offenders. The differences, which often are captured under the heading of maturity, involve not only the range of life experiences, such as educational accomplishments and work histories, but also related aspects of cognitive, physical, intellectual, and emotional development. Adolescents need to be dealt with as such, even if they have committed the same crimes as adults. This reality poses new challenges for correctional staff, who not only must learn to deal with a new type of client but must do so while dealing with a wide range of other clients in an unattractive and, at times, hostile environment.

CONTAINING COSTS

Since at least the 1994 congressional elections, the movement toward smaller and more effective government has quickened. Today, elected officials at all levels of government readily pronounce the era of "big government" as finished. The driving force behind this movement has been the perception that government is far too costly. In many respects, corrections has escaped this trend because pressures for rapid and large expansion of prison capacity have obviated debates over cost-efficiency. However, as prison construction begins to slow down, we can expect that the expense of incarceration will be subject to greater scrutiny. When average citizens are told that a year in prison is as costly as a year at Harvard University, the response is not to ask "why do we incarcerate so many when the expense is so great?" Rather, the rejoinder seems to be "why is prison so expensive?" and the solution advanced is to make incarceration cheaper. "No-frills" prison and recent anti-amenity campaigns that call for drastic reductions in prison services are as much a call for cheaper prisons as they are a call for harsher punishment.

As discussed earlier, information management systems will play a greater role in prison administration in the next century. Reactively, information systems are needed to respond to oversight inquiries from elected officials who decide budget allocations. Proactively, information systems can be a major weapon in cost-containment, particularly in areas that heretofore have not been subject to scrutiny. Inmate health care again is a good example of this development. As in the private sector, prisons are implementing highly specialized information systems to manage the delivery of medical services.

A major development in the area of cost-containment has been the growth of private corrections. In fact, the expansion of private corrections has been so phenomenal that some might argue that it is a major trend in and of itself. In many essential respects, however, private corrections is an offshoot of concerns over government spending. By and large, private corrections has flourished because it is perceived to be more efficient than government corrections, in terms of total cost or flexibility and speed of operation or ability to achieve specific operational goals. Support for private corrections is pragmatic rather than philosophical. Of all the activities that governments engage in, the punishment of offenders ranks among the most highly defensible and appropriate from a symbolic and legal point of view. Private corrections has flourished because it promises to protect society for less money, and the day that private corrections fails to keep this promise will be the beginning of its demise.

Many observers predict a rosy future for private corrections based on past and current trends. While private corrections will continue to grow, there are serious challenges to be faced. Private corrections has flourished for two reasons. First, it has targeted the cream of the offender crop—low-risk offenders who can be placed in low-security settings. Having made considerable inroads with the low risk inmate population, future growth depends in large measure on dealing with medium- and high-risk inmate populations. However, as the difficulty of the client increases, costs increase because more services are required. Second, private corrections has not been subject to the same operational constraints as governmental corrections. For example, private corrections is free to pay its employees less, can withhold employee benefits such as retirement pensions, and can purchase nonpersonnel goods and services more efficiently than government-run prisons. The competitive landscape will change radically if government-run prisons are eventually freed from such restrictions or if private prisons are subject to more restrictions. Whether private corrections can keep its competitive edge in the long run, as it begins to deal with less attractive and potentially less profitable inmate populations, remains to be seen.

Another theme that arises when attention focuses on correctional costs is the role of inmate labor and prison industry in making incarceration cheaper. Prison labor can affect the cost of incarceration in two ways: by having prisoners perform work that the prison would otherwise have to pay for, and thus reducing expenditures, and by having inmates produce goods and services that are sold outside of the prison, thus "recovering" some costs of confinement through the profits of prison labor.

Americans have strongly supported prison labor for decades. Today, there is nearly universal support for the notion that prisoners should work hard at tasks that reduce the cost of confinement, instill productive work skills and inculcate a healthy work ethic, and produce products or services that benefit the state. While support for the prison industry is strong, the implementation of prison labor policies leaves much to be desired. In fact, fewer than 10 percent of state prison inmates are employed in industry positions that taxpayers would recognize as "full-time jobs," and prison employment has failed to keep pace with the rapidly expanding inmate population.

Why is such wholesale underemployment tolerated within these extraordinarily costly institutions? First, the capital investment needed to construct "factories with fences" around them, in the words of the late Chief Justice Burger, has not been forthcoming. As states have struggled to fund capacity growth, expansion of prison industrial operations has not kept pace. Second, given the educational and employment deficits that inmates bring to prison, a substantial investment in literacy development, job training, and skills development is needed before many prisoners can be prepared to work productively in industrial settings. Third, there remains substantial and vitriolic controversy about the role of inmate employment in job displacement in the civilian economy, so political and labor leaders continue to seek to limit prison labor at every turn. If the cost of incarceration is to be controlled in any meaningful fashion in the twenty-first century, Americans and their political and correctional leaders will have to commit the nation to a policy of full employment in prisons.

Discussion of the growing cost of imprisonment often turns to the cost of providing health care services to inmates. At the center of prison health care lies the challenge of dealing with HIV/AIDS in the prison context. The number of diagnosed cases of HIV infection and AIDS in prison has increased dramatically during the 1990s. The incidence of AIDS among prisoners is many times higher than among noninstitutionalized persons. The explosion of HIV/AIDS in U.S. prisons can be traced directly to the incarceration of individuals for drug-related offenses. Many of these offenders have engaged in very high-risk behavior such as intravenous drug use, sharing needles, and trading sex for drugs or money.

The policy issue that faces correctional systems most squarely regarding AIDS is whether to test all inmates or specific at-risk groups upon admission or at intervals during confinement. Because an HIV/AIDS diagnosis establishes a constitutional duty to provide necessary health care services, most state correctional systems do not carry out universal testing. The financial consequences of HIV/AIDS in prisons are astronomical when one considers the extremely high cost of AIDS treatment *added* to the already burdensome cost of incarceration. Of course, additional dilemmas also are involved, such as the privacy rights of infected inmates and the health and safety concerns of staff who must work in close and sometimes violent physical contact with prisoners.

Similar cost considerations are presented by the specter of a burgeoning population of elderly inmates, held well into their senior years as a result of life without parole and similar statutes. In this case, states face the costs of geriatric care *added to* the cost of correctional confinement. Already, health services is the fastest growing portion of state correctional budgets, and this cost pressure has provoked policy and programmatic changes. These include co-payment systems, reorganization of correctional health care into HMO-type arrangements with publicly funded medical schools, privatization, development of telemedicine technology to permit remote examination, and diagnosis that reduces health care transportation costs, and reconsideration of the concept of "mercy parole," the conditional release of terminal or aged offenders back into community settings.

RELIANCE ON TECHNOLOGY

Throughout society, there is an increasing reliance on technology to improve both the quality and efficiency of work. Increasing competition from the private sector in combination with political pressures for fiscal economy has led corrections to embrace technology as a method of cost reduction.

A substantial portion of correctional work is not amenable to replacement or enhancement by technology, especially work that involves highly sophisticated interpersonal skills (e.g., dealing with suicidal inmates). Yet, there are ways in which technology can make correctional work safer, more efficient, and perhaps even more effective. One has only to view the displays at a national conference of correctional administrators to realize that prisons are a major consumer of both low-tech and high-tech products. Razor wire, indestructible toilets, prefabricated living units, tamper-proof identification cards, automated gate opening systems, satellite television instruction, video recorders, computerized inventory systems, and drug testing kits, among other items, all find a major market in corrections.

At the managerial level, computerized information systems have become increasingly important. However, the implementation of these systems has been uneven across domains of correctional work. Even where implemented, information systems rarely have been used to full potential. For example, most correctional agencies have computerized systems for maintaining basic information on inmates, but these systems hold only a small fraction of the information contained in an inmate's file. Nearly every prison system starts an inmate's file completely anew at intake, regardless of whether the inmate is on the first or fifth prison sentence. Not only are such tasks duplicative in terms of work effort, correctional workers have little opportunity to learn about inmates based on past prison experiences. Likewise, correctional systems have computerized inmate disciplinary records only sporadically. In places where information systems are reliable and complete, little analysis is done to discover correlates of prison misbehavior that are relevant to management practices (i.e., rules violations in relation to housing and work assignments, type of facility, stage of prison sentence).

Computers and computer-related technologies can be expected to have a large impact on prison education programs. Distance-learning and computer-aided instruction are gaining support at all levels of educational programming, and prison education programs will be affected by this trend. These developments may increase the quality of instruction, and they may also improve the flexibility of educational programming. However, staff will have to deal with new security risks as inmates are given access to computers that can link to other computers throughout the world.

New advances in medical technologies may lead to improvements in alcohol and drug treatment programs. Already, urine analysis is being used to gauge the extent of illegal drug use in prison among inmates and, in some cases, staff. New drugs are being developed that may neutralize the euphoric benefits of addiction, thereby removing the major attraction of drug use. Other pharmacological developments hold potential for reducing violent behavior. These new drug therapies, if effective, will find applications in prison settings.

BETTER LIVING THROUGH INCARCERATION?

We've observed that the penitentiary is the most visible, most tangible, and most important component of Americans' response to crime. Capital punishment will likely continue to play an important *symbolic* role in American sanctioning policy, but unless there is a sea change in the law and practice of the death penalty, capital punishment is unlikely to return to practical prominence in the years ahead. Community-based correctional programs play a vast *supporting* role in the drama of American crime and justice. Despite the fact that more and more felons are receiving probationary sentences in America's courts, these alternatives to prison do not now enjoy the public support and confidence needed to develop into a meaningful array of intermediate sanctions within our system of justice. Too much of the public contends that community-based alternatives to prison represent leniency in the justice system, the so-called "slap on the wrist."

In the public's mind, prison—especially the fortress-like maximum security prison—represents the definitive, punitive mechanism through which we remove "them" from our midst. In the last quarter century, the definition of "them" has broadened, as fear of victimization and exasperation with the perceived failures of the justice system provoke incessant clamor to lock 'em up for longer and longer periods of time. In addition, concern and interest about what happens to "them" behind the walls has also dissipated. The contemporary "no-frills" prisons movement unites the themes of prison as a social institution where we send lawbreakers *as* punishment and *for* punishment.

The most likely rheostat to control endless expansion of the correctional apparatus is not satiation of our desire to punish but recognition of the extraordinary costs of doing so. As states spend an increasing proportion of their budgets to build and operate prisons, the trade-offs that will be required in terms of reduced support for schools, transportation, health care and other state services will drive us to a new view of prisons as institutions of social risk management. As we come to realize that there are real financial limits on our ability to incarcerate all those whom we wish to imprison, and to hold every prisoner for the rest of his/her life, we will face several critical decisions. First, we will have to learn much more about how to use incarceration *strategically*, which means deciding criminal sentences on the basis of crime prevention rather than retributive goals. Second, we will have to turn our attention once again to consideration of life *in* prisons, and the appropriate admixture of rules, policies, programs, services, amenities, and staff that interact in a way that reduces the social toxicity of criminals during confinement. We will be driven to the latter analysis by the frank recognition that except for a small percentage of inmates who die in prison, most will return to our neighborhoods and communities after their sentence expires. If the penitentiary is to achieve its objective of improving public safety and reducing criminal victimization, serious deliberation, study, and debate must focus on whom we send to prisons, for how long, and under what conditions. The role of the modern prison in contributing to social order depends on the resolution of these debates.